The Daily Telegraph
CRICKET
YEAR BOOK 89

The Daily Telegraph

CRICKET
YEAR BOOK 89

Michael Melford
Wendy Wimbush
Foreword by Dr Ali Bacher

Consultant Editor Michael Melford
Statistics Wendy Wimbush
Special articles E.W. Swanton, Trevor Bailey
Other contributors
Mike Beddow, Edward Bevan, Peter Deeley, Tony Cozier
(West Indies), Rachael Flint, John Fogg, David Green,
Neil Hallam, Doug Ibbotson, David Leggat (New Zealand),
R. Mohan (India), Michael Owen-Smith (South Africa),
Qamar Ahmed (Pakistan), Charles Randall, D.J. Rutnagur,
Alan Shiell (Australia), Sa'adi Thawfeeq (Sri Lanka)

Editor Norman Barrett

Acknowledgements Thanks are due to David Armstrong for
supplying the data for the Minor Counties and to Tim Lamb
and the TCCB for making the first-class fixtures available.
The Deloitte Ratings are published by kind permission of
Deloitte Haskins and Sells.

The photographs appearing in this book are reproduced by
kind permission of Patrick Eagar, All-Sport, Bill Smith,
Bob Thomas, and Popperfoto. The cover illustration is by
Major Splash Ltd.

The editors particularly wish to thank Radford Barrett,
Sports Editor of The Daily Telegraph, for his generous help.

Published by Telegraph Publications
Peterborough Court, At South Quay,
181 Marsh Wall, London E14 9SR

7th edition
© The Daily Telegraph 1988

Typeset by Michael Weintroub Graphics Ltd,
Kenton, Middx.
Printed and bound in Great Britain by
Biddles Ltd, Guildford and King's Lynn

British Library Cataloguing in Publication Data

The Daily Telegraph cricket year book: a complete
    account of the . . . season.
    —89–
    1. Cricket—Periodicals
    796.35'8'05   GV911

ISBN 0-86367-269-8

Contents

CRICKET TITLES
From
⊠ HEINEMANN KINGSWOOD

THE PLAYERS

A Social History of the Professional Cricketer

RIC SISSONS

This book should be compulsory reading for every cricketing authority.
Peter Roebuck

A landmark in cricket literature.
John Arlott

Price: £14.95

LEN HUTTON

A Biography

GERALD HOWAT

The first, comprehensive biography of Leonard Hutton, by leading cricket writer Gerald Howat, published to coincide with the 50th anniversary of his great "364" at the Oval.

Price: £12.95

ULTIMATE ONE-DAY CRICKET MATCH

VIC MARKS & ROBIN DRAKE

The first cricket adventure game. Your chance to captain England against the rest of the world.

Price: £3.95

Foreword

I have been asked to write about the vexing and complex issues of sports boycotts, isolation, rebel tours, normal sport in an abnormal society, apartheid, post apartheid and all that these mean as they pertain to cricket in South Africa.

Firstly, I would like to say that I was both lucky and unlucky regarding the sports boycott of South Africa. I was the last person to captain a South African XI in a Test match and this made me lucky, for the great captains that South Africa has produced since then have not had that extraordinary feeling of captaining in an international.

But where my luck ran out was in 1970, when I was about to realize every cricket captain's dream – to tour Britain. I had with me possibly the best team ever assembled in South Africa. So when the blow came – that we were banned, that we had become the pariahs of world cricket – then my disappointment was as acute as anything I have felt before or since.

Our banning was organized by a remarkable young South African who had been at school at Pretoria Boys High, Peter Hain. Almost single-handed, he had marshalled the anti-apartheid movement in Britain against us so successfully that he had even conquered the bastions of the British old-boy network that had loved and protected South African cricket for so long.

I would like to say at the outset that Hain was right and we were wrong. We had only too comfortably been going along our own merry cricketing way, with occasional frowns at the National Party Government, but without any real thought about the plight of Black South Africans. Certainly, from a cricketing point of view, we needed a jolt and we got one.

But even then we did not go far enough. When we went non-racial in 1977, it was a constitutional move more than anything. On paper, we were non-racial, but in practice we did not have a system that enabled Black people to have equal opportunity in the cricket system. It was fine to say that anybody could make the Springbok team regardless of race, colour, or creed. But where was the infrastructure to enable everybody to get there? It took us exactly 10 years to begin to do this, and I would like to come back to this shortly.

Isolation

After our isolation in 1970, our cricket went into a state of internal development, where the high standards of our players provided wonderful fare for the thousands of spectators who came to see the best in the world – because, with the West Indies, we were the best in the late 60s and 70s.

And then here we learnt our next lesson – we began to get tired of playing against each other, and the fans got tired of watching the same teams playing each other. This is a most important lesson of isolation – you cannot go it alone. Standards drop and, ultimately, the game must die.

By this time I was an administrator, and as such I had a duty to perform to my sport. We realized that we needed outside stimuli, outside competition, outside input, new ideas. We did not need these things because we were inferior, far from it. We, like all mankind, needed basic contact with others to survive.

And so we went out to get that contact, and the only way we could do it was through 'rebel' tours. We could not travel abroad because of visa and other restrictions, so we had to bring teams and individuals here to play against us. And it was then that we learnt our third important lesson – this contact costs lots and lots of money.

The sports boycott movement is such that players coming to South Africa face stiff penalties, including life bans. To get them to come, one has to pay vast sums of money – far out of proportion to their actual playing value.

Justifiably this has led to criticism that major sports have been letting large amounts of money out of the country into the hands of a few individuals when most of our people are very poor. This is an issue that has worried me a great deal. I am sensitive to the needs of our people, but I also owe a responsibility to the sport I represent. I do not believe that those who organize indiscriminate sports boycotts realize that their actions force this inflated money drain, nor do they show the kind of sensitivity that one learns from being and living here.

This lack of sensitivity (brought about by their own isolation overseas) was clearly shown recently when the sports boycott movement turned against Jomo Sono for playing for Pelé's World Celebrity XI, organized to raise funds to combat AIDS amongst youngsters. Here was one of South Africa's great sportsmen, coming from a Black-dominated democratic sport that has become the envy of all sports administrators in South Africa through its prowess over the past few years, being honoured by one of soccer's living legends – and somebody in his wisdom sitting in London says it is a crime punishable by death in sports terms. This is clearly ludicrous.

Soccer, although in a very healthy state, cannot operate in isolation either, as witnessed by the fact that most of the top teams have foreign players and coaches.

My Fourth Lesson

I learnt my fourth important lesson from a man of great wisdom in these matters – Legau Mathabathe, a former headmaster, a former detainee, a found member of the Soweto Committee of 10 with Dr Motlana, a soccer administrator, a community leader, a businessman and one who had been an avid follower of sports such as cricket and rugby in his youth.

It was two years ago and I felt desolate when I looked at life in the townships. There were flames everywhere. South Africa was divided as never before, and we looked at a situation that was heading for even worse times than 1976.

'What can cricket do to help?' I asked myself. It was a quixotic question because cricket was perceived to be a White elitist sport, bearing the brunt of perhaps the biggest anti-apartheid sports boycott.

I asked the question of two old friends, Joe Pamensky and business-man and cricket lover Mervyn King. We all agreed that cricket had given us all different things – all of them good. Cricket built friendships, cricket broke barriers. King said he would approach his business colleagues to raise 10 million rand over the next 10 years to take cricket to the people; Pamensky said he would give all the administrative and moral support needed.

I went to see Mathabathe and asked his advice. His fundamental message was: go into the townships yourself with cricket, be up front, learn about township life at first hand, don't have tours in isolation of any other developments in cricket, learn to be sensitive to the needs of the Black communities. We took his advice and began a grass-roots development programme that in scale and quality has not had its equal in any other sport.

In just two years, we have introduced about 60,000 children under the age of 14 to cricket – most of them Black. We have taught more than 1,000 Black teachers to be cricket coaches. We hold year-long clinics in all the major townships – Soweto, Mamelodi, Alexandra, Kagiso, Atteridgeville, Kwamashu, Tembisa, Rocklands in Bloemfontein, Kroonstad, Bethlehem, Galeshewe, Langa, Kayaletisha, Mondistane, Bisho.

Destroying Apartheid

Dismantle apartheid? We are destroying it. We are now truly non-racial, our programme is generating a warmth and feeling among all races that is absolutely astounding.

Looking back on my life in cricket, I can say without hesitation that the experiences I have had in the townships over the past two years have been more rewarding than anything else – including leading South Africa to a whitewash of the Australians.

We held a national convention recently to discuss development cricket and it looked like a meeting of the United Nations. At the end of it, the women delegates led us from the seminar room in dance and song.

We have revolutionized cricket in South Africa. In the Black communities, we have unearthed extraordinary talent among the children as players and extraordinary talent among the men and women teachers as coaches and administrators.

We are slowly mending those broken links between pupil and teacher through cricket. We are bringing pupils, teachers, and parents of all races together through cricket. We are providing new avenues for the kids to get out of the ghettos through cricket. We are becoming a cultural activity like Sticks Morewa's Soccer Association of South Africa by providing fulfilment for the whole family and the whole community. We are breaking down racial and cultural barriers that are harmful to all of us, and I believe that through cricket we will achieve what happened in the West Indies, where cricket was used to take the underprivileged to the top and to eradicate much of the discrimination imposed by old British colonial rule.

We will continue to have tours, rebel or otherwise, because cricket needs them. But we will not have them in isolation. Instead of them merely being a channel for money to leave South Africa, we will use them to further the development programme, because it is here where our cricket heart lies.

If we do not get an arena from the international community, we will not be deterred. But for them to continue to deny us is short-term and even churlish, because I believe that the days of indiscriminate sports boycotts should be over. Sport in South Africa is a powerful medium, as Hain showed us only too dramatically. Now is the time to use it in a more positive way. Nobody can say what will happen here over the next 15 years, but what I can guarantee is that if South Africa should then field a cricket team in the World Cup it will certainly not be a team like Zimbabwe has now, without Black players.

I would like to thank *The Daily Telegraph* for giving me this chance to bring honour and appreciation to those people working on the development programme. I have not named them, not because of fear of reprisals (although, heaven knows, there are too many life and death issues in the townships), but because there are too many of them to name individually. But they know who they are – and one day so will all the world.

Ali Bacher

Dr Ali Bacher,
Managing Director,
South African Cricket Union

Not so much a game . . .
by Michael Melford

Cricket was ill served by the long-drawn-out exchanges between the TCCB and the Indian Board as to whether England's tour of India should take place. As both sides were saying that the ball was in the other's court and sending each other ultimatums that were ignored, there were even signs that the TCCB would like the proposed ICC meeting in January brought forward, in order presumably that the decision might be taken for them. But tours have always been a matter for the two countries concerned, not the ICC. Thus English cricket was still further depicted to the general public as not only being unsuccessful on the field but weak and vacillating off it.

When the Indian government said it would refuse visas to eight of the England party with South African connections, it was incomprehensible to many that the TCCB did not simply cancel the tour with dignity. They had nothing of which to be ashamed. Moreover, the Indian Board were in contravention of the agreement reached unanimously at the ICC 'that team selection must be a matter solely for the governing body concerned'.

English cricketers have been coaching and playing in South Africa for most of the century. It is an opportunity arising from the fact that the English close season coincides with the playing season of all the other Test-playing countries. It is a help in boosting the fairly modest incomes of most English cricketers between September and April. It is also a help to those whom they coach.

An Honourable Job

As will be seen from Dr Ali Bacher's Foreword to this Year Book, South Africa are engaged in a huge effort to bring cricket to the under-privileged. English coaches have always been respected in South Africa and they coach players of all races. It is an honourable job and one can well understand their indignation at being barred in other countries that are doing vastly less, if anything, to help the non-Whites of South Africa or the underprivileged in their own country. It is a strange upside-down world in which the alleged 'baddies' are those who help the needy and the 'goodies' are those who will have nothing to do with them.

Indians may have seen the appointment of Graham Gooch as captain as provocative. For a notably unpolitical figure, he has somehow become an *homme fatal*, and the fuss about his presence in the team before the last tour to West Indies is still fresh in the mind. Selectors in England, however, are not dictated to by their board, except occasionally for disciplinary reasons. However baffling the choice of a reluctant Gooch, who had even found the captaincy of Essex too much for him, instead of the spirited Christopher Cowdrey, the Board would have been going against the intention of the ICC agreement if it had blocked the selectors' nomination.

It is understandable that the TCCB should be concerned about compensation for financial losses incurred through the cancellation of the tour. But principles cannot be measured in cash, and a disenchantment with cricket such as one heard in the autumn of 1988 could be more costly in the long run.

A bad year for pitches

There seemed to be fairly general agreement that the pitches in English domestic cricket in 1988 were unusually poor. The criticism was being levelled at grounds all over the country, which is just as well. Nothing irks the cricket committee of a winning county more than to be told that their success has come through rigging their pitches to suit themselves.

Their vigorous counter-attack to such blasphemy will usually start with figures showing that they have won more away matches than at home. They will be able to argue with some force that what they have been providing was a pitch giving an equal chance to both sides and on which one side or the other was likely to win. If they happen to be stronger than most of their opponents, it will follow that they win more matches than they lose. It may be, too, that their bowlers and batsmen will come to know what is needed on such pitches.

The other argument put out in favour of under-prepared pitches is that they provide more entertaining cricket than those which become ever easier so that on the last day nobody can get anybody out. This is perfectly true and is often reflected in larger gates and increased membership.

But this is where a county's local and national interests clash. A large part of their annual income is derived from Test matches, and England are more likely to have a successful Test team if they are used to good pitches. Otherwise batsmen lose, or anyhow do not gain, confidence. Bowlers do not need any great subtlety to take wickets. Things happen too easily for them. Thus when batsmen and bowlers play on a well-made five-day pitch they, like their county's pitches, are under-prepared.

The difficulties of groundsmanship in an uncertain climate are many, and some bad pitches are inevitable. But for the rest, the official instruction has to go on plugging the ideal of true pitches with pace and bounce – and that can lead to both entertainment and better players.

Ninety overs and four days

Of the experiments made in the 1988 season, the one requiring 90 overs a day in Test matches suffered from not having a penalty attached to a failure to comply. On days when both sides have contributed to a failure to bowl 90 overs in six hours the blame may be difficult to apportion. But, as applied in 1988, with play going on into the evening, it merely helps the stronger side by allowing them more time in which to finish off their opponents. The sinners, in fact, may be the ones to profit.

The inclusion of four-day matches in the Britannic Assurance Championship is hard to judge on one season's trial. The main requirements were good pitches and, as these were in even shorter supply than usual, there were plenty of four-day matches that finished in three days, even two.

How much the spinner benefited from the extra day is also uncertain. Each county played two fewer matches. The pitches may have taken more, or less, spin than in 1987. The bowler may have been more or less fit than then. But, for what they are worth, here are the number of overs bowled by nine spinners selected at random, with the 1987 number in brackets: Phil Carrick 593 (575); John Childs 656 (480); Nick Cook 770 (705); John Emburey 672 (570); David Graveney 613 (356); Geoff Miller 433 (379); Richard Illingworth 597 (478); Jack Simmons 629 (640); Richard Williams 331 (242).

These figures certainly suggest that spinners played a slightly bigger part, and there were several other advantages that come with a four-day match: a greater likelihood of avoiding a draw, thus lending the match extra importance; a better chance of making up time lost to the weather; a greater opportunity provided for often young, middle-order batsmen who are given more time in which to settle in and build an innings; and higher scoring. Without the fourth day Graeme Hick would not have made his 405 not out, which caught the public fancy.

Substitutes

The TCCB's timely move to halt the marked increase in the comings and goings of substitute fielders seemed to achieve its purpose, though not without some unfairness. The ruling that no substitute may take the field for five overs after a player leaves it, no matter what the reason for the latter's departure, did not distinguish between a player who had obviously suffered a crippling injury or illness and a player who wandered off the field to change his boots or refresh himself after bowling.

It will certainly curb sharp practices in limited-overs matches. I treasure the memory of a one-day match a decade or two ago when a senior, comfortably-built player of the fielding side developed a limp. He hobbled off the field, to be instantly replaced by the 12th man, a lightning-fast youth. Within a few minutes the young man had run out one batsman, sprinted along the boundary to catch another, and changed the course of the match.

The Cost of Brilliant Fielding

One cricketing topic on which there seems to be total agreement is that the standard of fielding is higher than it has ever been. Usually the limited-overs game is credited with this, which may be so. But the improvement would not have been possible if the players nowadays were not younger and therefore more agile.

Somehow the mind will not conjure up a picture of the dignified figures of Sir Jack Hobbs and Frank Woolley rushing along the boundary and hurling themselves full length to save one run. In their late 40s they would also have found that sprinting between the wickets had lost its charm. Yet they were still among the great players of the day.

Generally, English cricketers have not been at their best until they were approaching 30. Fifty years ago, in a different society, good players waited patiently in their county second XI for their chance. By the time it came, they were experienced batsmen or bowlers but had lost some of their fleetness of foot.

In one other respect the lowering of the average age has probably not been for the good of the game. Fast bowlers now come on the scene at an age when the human frame is not fully developed. Hence the high percentage who break down. By contrast, Alec Bedser, who seldom missed a match, attributed his fitness during his playing career to the fact that during the war, when he was in his 20s, he had three years or more without cricket.

Trouble in Pakistan

A lot of water has flowed down the Indus since England's ill-starred tour of Pakistan in late 1987, but there seem to be two points worth reiterating. One is the importance of sending a team in the right frame of mind. Boring as it is to hear the visiting captain on arrival going through the ritual of expressing high confidence in the performance of his talented team, it is better than hearing that they have played too much cricket and are faced with a most oppressive tour. However true that may be, if they also give the impression that they expect to be cheated, that is a classic recipe for a low morale.

In the circumstances, it did also seem that an opportunity was lost in not sending Chris Broad home after he had refused to leave the crease when given out to a catch at the wicket. That would have been almost unprecedented, but so was the offence, and the team's management would have been seen to be taking strong disciplinary action to stamp out what is tantamount to anarchy.

The Blight of Bad Light
by Trevor Bailey

Ever since giving one batsman out lbw who had hit the ball, another out caught who had not, and having miscounted the length of an over, all in the space of half an hour, I have held the gentlemen in white coats in high esteem. Umpiring is a hard, exhausting and often thankless job, which seldom receives the praise it deserves. The standard on our county circuit is outstanding, and, in the opinion of the majority of players, both home and overseas, is the best in the world. There are two reasons for this. First, they have far more practice and, secondly, most are former first-class cricketers, which provides them with a deep understanding and a love for the game that are so essential.

Although it is necessary to know and be able to interpret the Laws, it has always seemed to me that it is even more important to be able to judge correctly the difficult decisions, like the catch down the leg-side which flicks the glove, not the sleeve. These are frequently the result of a combination of instinct and personal experience. Towards the end of his career, the eyesight of the late and lovable Alec Skelding might have been said to have been on the wane, but he seldom made a mistake. He could smell an lbw with uncanny accuracy. At close of play, after he had removed the bails and before returning to the pavilion for a well-deserved pint, Alec would make the following announcement: 'And that, gentlemen, concludes the entertainment for the day.' His choice of the word 'entertainment' was not only correct, but was in no small way due to the way he had controlled the proceedings and made sure that nothing unsavoury occurred.

Pressure on Umpires

With big money at stake, especially in the Tests and limited-overs finals, the pressure on the umpires has increased. In addition, their decisions can be queried by action replays in slow motion on television.

Sitting comfortably in the BBC commentary box or at home, we are able to pontificate cheerfully and confidently on a difficult lbw, without any responsibility and with the benefit of five replays and plenty of time. In contrast, the umpire has to make quickly a decision that could affect the whole course of the match. What continues to amaze and delight me is that our umpires do not err more frequently, and I therefore am strongly in favour of anything that could be done to make their life more pleasant.

Just imagine an evenly balanced Test at Lords. The batsmen are playing some fine strokes, and despite an overcast sky a capacity crowd is revelling in the atmosphere, until the whole occasion is soured by what is surely the most depressing sight in cricket, umpires surreptitiously inspecting light meters. After several consultations the light is eventually offered to the batsmen, who decide, not because they cannot see, as they have been belting the ball all over the ground, to return to the pavilion. Play is suspended.

Not surprisingly, the spectators, who have paid a great deal of money, are frustrated, especially as they know that all the club games in the vicinity are continuing, and that limited-overs matches are frequently completed in far gloomier conditions. Rather unfairly they vent their anger on the umpires, who after all are only carrying out the instructions laid down for them. The blame lies with these instructions, not with the likes of Messrs Bird and Constant.

Never once throughout my cricketing career was I unable to see the ball from the bowler's hand when batting, though it was obviously easier in bright sunshine. I also used the tactical appeal against the light, whenever it was to my side's advantage. The only time I experienced real difficulty in picking up the flight of the ball in bad light was when fielding in the deep. Ironically, the fielding side are not given the opportunity to come off – although there was an exception once in a knock-out club match in Chalkwell Park. For various reasons I found myself on the boundary at 8.50 p.m. in late summer. By that time one fielded entirely by instinct, sound, and the shouted information from a colleague nearer to the action, though it should be stressed that neither the batsman nor the keeper seemed especially troubled. The game was eventually abandoned when I appealed for an lbw and the umpire confessed he was unable to make a decision, because he could not see that far.

A Simple Solution

Few things incense a crowd more and are a worse advertisement for the game than suspension of play because of bad light, especially when it occurs in the morning session. However, there is a very simple solution. All that is required is to treat bad light as a natural hazard, like a bad pitch, an outfield that has been slowed by rain, or a cloud cover that has encouraged swing. It is unquestionably far- harder, and considerably more dangerous, batting on a very poor wicket – of which there was no shortage last summer – than it is in the gloom.

However, nobody wants batsmen to be hurt. If the light should deteriorate to such an extent that the umpires believe fast bowling constituted a physical danger, then, as the arbiters of unfair play, they should be allowed to take the following action: Having informed the captain of the fielding side and the batsmen of their opinion, they would simply treat every ball that rose above shoulder height as a no-ball – simple, safe, and surely good for the game?

The Daily Telegraph Schools Cricket Awards
by D.J. Rutnagur

One consolation for Essex in a season that brought them no trophies was that three youngsters, either linked with the club already or under its close eye, figured in *The Daily Telegraph* Schools Cricket Awards, each worth £1,000 in cricket equipment to the winner's school and a trophy to the boy as a memento of his achievement.

It was fitting that Essex were so prominent in the roll of honour, for the club not only works very closely with nurseries of the game within its own area of jurisdiction and in neighbouring non-first-class counties, but also diverts part of its profits into schools cricket.

The Under-19 batting award went to **Nicholas Knight**, and for bowling to **Nadim Shahid**, for an unprecedented second time. Knight's home is in Cambridgeshire, but he has Essex affiliations by way of his school, Felsted (also the alma mater of Derek Pringle and John Stephenson). Shahid hails from Ipswich, but is a contracted Essex player. So will Knight be, in 1989.

Knight is something of a schoolboy C.B. Fry, described as he is by his cricket master, Mark Surridge, as Felsted's best all-round sportsman of all time. Son of a hockey international, Nicholas is a skilful centre-half and a quick fly-half at rugby. Since a very young age, however, he had his heart set on a career in cricket. Versatility also applies to Knight's cricket. He is a left-handed opening batsman, strong off the back foot. He topped the 1,000 runs mark for the school alone, with five centuries, and his aggregate of 1,523 was well out of the reach of any of his rivals for the award. He bowls in two styles – quick, from a slinging action, and leg-breaks. What is more, he is a quick-witted and inspiring captain and was an automatic choice to lead MCC Schools at Lord's.

Other leading run-getters in the category were Nicholson (Eastbourne), Nick Hunt (Nottingham HS), Nadim Shahid (Ipswich), 14-year-old Matthew Walker (King's School, Rochester), and Simon Eccleston (Bryanston).

Shahid, champion bowler for a second year, took 103 wickets, bowling his wrist spin with increased control and guile. His batting too showed such marked improvement that he has come to be rated as a genuine all-rounder. Not far behind Shahid, with 90 wickets, was another leg-spinner, James Gleasure (Lancaster Royal GS). An outstanding single performance was of Wellingborough's Robert Cousins in taking 9 for 11.

The third award winner from Essex, the Under-15 batsman, was **Darren Robinson**, an opener. His achievement was the greater for the fact that no organized cricket is played at his school, Tabor, in Braintree. His advance is owed to the Essex Schools CA and the Braintree CC. Robinson aggregated 805 runs, including 473 for the county and 332 in the Under-15 Beckenham Festival and in internationals.

Not many bowlers in this age group made an impact, but **Philip Weston** (Durham) was very prominent. A left-arm bowler, brisk for his years, Weston took 20 wickets for his county, seven for the North of England, and 13 in internationals.

The Daily Telegraph Cricketers of the Year
by E.W. Swanton

It says something about the incessant procession of Test matches and the consequent regular turn-around of players that only one of the eight cricketers named as their countries' chosen twelve months ago, Martin Crowe, has earned selection again. It is likewise significant surely that only two or three of the new heroes are assured at this stage of their careers of a secure place in history, say in the year 2000: Vivian Richards certainly, Miandad and Crowe maybe, others possibly.

The joint nomination by Michael Melford and me of **Graham Hick** as English cricket's player of the year needs an explanatory note, admitting that this remarkable young man is by birth a Zimbabwean who, having played in the World Cup for his native country in 1983, will not be qualified to wear England's colours until 1991. His record last summer speaks for itself – 37 innings, twice not out, 2,713 runs, highest score 405*, average 77.51, 9 hundreds. He is physically strong, technically sound, and at present hungry for runs. There is much talent in Hick. One hopes the long wait (inevitable, according to the rules) will not blunt his appetite. Meanwhile, a conclusive estimation must await the ultimate judgement dependent on performance at Test level.

David Boon had 'no challenger', writes Alan Shiell, as Australia's nomination. He bounced back, after being dropped, with conclusive figures in all versions of cricket, and an average of 71 in five Tests, including 184 not out against England in the Bicentennial Test; 75 against England in the final of the World Cup; 2,254 runs in all 33 matches, average 56. Boon finished 711 runs up on Allan Border, and is described, naturally enough, as 'Tasmania's sporting hero'. He is a bank man from Launceston.

Tony Cozier, the most experienced and respected of overseas correspondents, declares that **Vivian Richards,** after two critical years, won widespread acceptance as successor to Clive Lloyd as the West Indies' natural leader. The brilliant individualist had moulded himself into the job.

His young team, deprived of five of the older stalwarts, emerged with honour from their Indian tour (having been eclipsed at the last gasp by both England and Pakistan in the World Cup). The importance of his presence was underlined in the exciting, brief visit of Pakistan, and then came yet another comprehensive success in England.

The repeat of **Martin Crowe's** nomination for New Zealand was decided 'by a whisker', according to David Leggat, from Richard Hadlee, Ewen Chatfield, and Andrew Jones. Leggat credits Crowe with 4,000 first-class runs in a year, including his 9th Test hundred during England's tour down under. Those who deplore the excessive demands which the game now makes on the top cricketers can fairly cite the case of Crowe, who broke down while playing for Somerset early in the English summer of 1988.

It is tempting fate with a vengeance to acclaim a young cricketer on a single performance, and, even more so, a leg-spinner at that. Their art is an elusive one, as the promise and swift eclipse of another young Indian, L. Sivaramakrishnan has recently shown. Nevertheless, let the Indian nomination for 1987/88 be the 19-year-old **Narendra Hirwani** on the strength of taking 16 wickets – yes, 16 – in his first Test match, against the West Indies at Madras in January last.

The pitch, of course, took spin generously. Conditions were wholly favourable. Even so, the success of this bespectacled teenager – who, according to R. Mohan in *The Cricketer*, is reputed to have moved 'from the cricketing wilderness of Uttar Pradesh to Indore in order to pursue his dream of playing for India' – almost defies belief. His figures of 16 for 136 in 33.5 overs have only ever been bettered in Tests by Jim Laker and Sydney Barnes. Oddly, the only newcomer to Tests who has an almost identical record is R.A.L. Massie, who took 16 for 137 for Australia at Lord's. Incidentally, Hirwani enabled K.S. More to establish Test records by stumping five in an innings, six in a match.

Controversies apart, Qamar Ahmed's nomination of **Javed Miandad** is almost irresistible. He won the blighted Pakistan-England series at home, and on the Caribbean tour that followed made four hundreds, including two in the Tests at Georgetown and Port-of-Spain. He has joined the select list of three Pakistanis, Hanif, Mushtaq, and Asif Iqbal, who had previously made hundreds against every Test-playing country against whom they played. If Javed is to make an acceptable successor to Imran Khan he will need to subdue the fiery temperament that has got him into frequent trouble in the past.

The political upsets of recent months have come up at a cruel time for the newcomers to the World Test scene, Sri Lanka. Their performance at Lord's in 1984 won their cricketers much esteem, and seemed likely to be the prelude to a creditable immediate Test future in a junior role. The internal situation, however, is now depriving them of the chance of displaying their natural skills on their own pitches, and in doing so gaining the experience for which there is no substitute. In the circumstances, Sa'adi Thawfeeq has no doubt made a sound choice in **Ravi Ratnayake**, the all-rounder, right-arm medium-pace bowler, left-hand bat, who is the first man to have reached 500 runs and 50 wickets for his country in Tests and one-day Internationals.

Michael Owen-Smith, son of the legendary Tuppy (maker of a Test hundred for South Africa at 20 and captain of England at Rugby football), makes what he considers an 'obvious choice' in **Clive Rice**, who returned home after his last triumphal summer with Notts to lead Transvaal to yet another victory in the Currie Cup. Third in the batting averages, fifth in the bowling, he showed himself, at 38, still in the top bracket as an all-rounder as well as a captain under whom men were glad and happy to play.

The Reliance World Cup

The fourth World Cup, and the first to be played outside England, was successfully staged in October and November 1987, the hazards of joint organisation by India and Pakistan being far fewer than widely expected. Its public appeal was helped by the fact that, at the start of it, the clear favourites were Pakistan and India. Both indeed reached the semi-finals, but lost there to Australia and England, of whom Australia, who had had little recent success, emerged the winners.

The ambitious distribution of 27 matches to 21 centres dotted around a huge sub-continent meant travelling difficulties and an extension of the World Cup's overall length from the 17 days of 1983 to 32 days. However only one match, in Indore, was affected by rain, and even there Australia and New Zealand fitted in 30 overs aside. There was no provision for a second day if the first was interrupted or washed out. This was a change from the playing conditions of previous World Cups, as was the length of matches, only 50 overs against 60 in England. One improvement, however, was the fact that pitches generally helped spin bowlers and many more of them were seen in action than in England.

In Group A, played in India, Australia began with a victory over India, the holders, in Madras by one run. India had needed only 15 runs from the last four overs with four wickets in hand. Next day, in Hyderabad, New Zealand won by only three runs against Zimbabwe, though this proved to be far superior to other performances by Zimbabwe, whose main strength was athletic fielding. India improved as the group matches progressed and there was never much doubt that they and Australia would be the two qualifiers from this group. New Zealand, without Richard Hadlee, were never a force.

Group B, which except for two matches was played in Pakistan, was more closely fought. In the first match, in Hyderabad, Sind, Sri Lanka lost by only 15 runs to Pakistan, but they were disappointing thereafter, whereas Pakistan surged ahead, losing only to West Indies after having already qualified for the semi-final.

All, therefore, depended on whether England could twice beat West Indies, who were undoubtedly weakened by the absence of Malcolm Marshall. Through Lamb's 67 not out they somehow scraped home by two wickets with three balls to spare in the first match at Gujranwala, having needed 91 from the last 10 overs with only four wickets left. They then missed a clear chance of beating Pakistan in Rawalpindi, but eventually won the vital second match with West Indies in Jaipur by virtue, for once, of more effective middle batting.

At this stage, India and Pakistan still seemed on course to be finalists and the sub-continent was in a ferment of excitement.

In the first semi-final, at Lahore, however, Australia always looked just too good for Pakistan. Imran Khan brought his tally of wickets up to 17, but in Craig McDermott Australia had an equally successful fast bowler with stronger support. In one more match McDermott was to take 18 wickets in the tournament. At Lahore, his five for 44 was decisive. Australia batted solidly to make 267 for eight, Imran three for 36, and soon had Pakistan 38 for three, Ramiz Raja having been run out in the first over. Miandad and Imran added 112 in 26 overs, but 118 were needed from 15 overs and against McDermott this proved to be beyond the later batsmen.

In Bombay next day, England were put in, but Graham Gooch's 115 and Mike Gatting's 56 in 62 balls gave them a useful if not conclusive score of 254 for six. India's batting lacked Vengsarkar, absent with a stomach disorder, and suffered a severe blow when Gavaskar was soon bowled by DeFreitas. Though Kapil Dev made 30 quickly, England never quite lost their grip and the later Indian batsmen, forced to hurry, succumbed to the spin of Hemmings on a slow turning pitch.

Both Australia and England could approach the final with the buoyant feeling of sides who had exceeded expectations. However, it was Australia who controlled their destiny the better in front of the 70,000 crowd in Calcutta. They had batted first throughout the tournament, except in the one match which they had lost against India. In the final their early batsmen were again successful, Boon and Marsh making 52 in the first 10 overs off some wayward bowling by DeFreitas and Small. Foster and the spinners won back the initiative for England for a time, but Border, Veletta, and Waugh scored 65 invaluable runs off the last six overs.

A total of 253 for five on this pitch looked far from invincible, but when Robinson was out first ball to McDermott, Australia were given a moral advantage which they never really lost. Gooch, Athey, and Gatting restored the innings, and at 135 for two it was quite possible that England could win if Gatting continued in the same vein. At this point, however, in a worthily intentioned but utterly misplaced effort to dictate to the bowlers, he played a disastrous reverse sweep to Border's first ball, which was not on the right line for such a dangerous excess. The ball lobbed up to the wicket-keeper off the top edge.

The later batsmen could not keep up to the required rate against Waugh and O'Donnell and, though the final margin was only seven runs, the match was clearly safe in Australia's hands long before the end. England needed 17 off the final over and McDermott made sure that this was beyond them. The gold Reliance Cup went to Allan Border and his well-knit team, of whom David Boon won the Man of the Match award for the final.

Group Matches

8 October at Niaz Stadium, Hyderabad (P). PAKISTAN beat SRI LANKA by 15 runs. Toss: Pakistan. Pakistan 267-6 (50 overs) (Javed Miandad 103, Ramiz Raja 76). Sri Lanka 252 (49.2 overs) (R.S. Mahanama 89, P.A. De Silva 42). Award: Javed Miandad (103 and 1 ct).

9 October at M.A. Chidambaram Stadium, Chepauk, Madras. AUSTRALIA beat INDIA by 1 run. Toss: India. Australia 270-6 (50 overs) (G.R. Marsh 110, D.C. Boon 49). India 269 (49.5 overs) (N.S. Sidhu 73, K. Srikkanth 70; C.J. McDermott 100-564). Award: G.R. Marsh (110).

9 October at Municipal Stadium, Gujranwala. ENGLAND beat WEST INDIES by 2 wickets. Toss: England. West Indies 243-7 (50 overs) (R.B. Richardson 53, A.L. Logie 49, P.J.L. Dujon 46). England 246-8 (49.3 overs) (A.J. Lamb 67*, G.A. Gooch 47). Award: A.J. Lamb (67*).

10 October at Lal Bahadur Shastri Stadium, Hyderabad (I). NEW ZEALAND beat ZIMBABWE by 3 runs. Toss: Zimbabwe. New Zealand 242-7 (50 overs) (M.D. Crowe 72, M.C. Snedden 64). Zimbabwe 239 (49.4 overs) (D.L. Houghton 141, I.P. Butchart 54). Award: D.L. Houghton (141 and 1 ct).

12 October (no play), 13 October at Pindi Club Ground, Rawalpindi. PAKISTAN beat ENGLAND by 18 runs. Toss: England. Pakistan 239-7 (50 overs) (Salim Malik 65, Ijaz Ahmed 59). England 221 (48.4 overs) (M.W. Gatting 43; Abdul Qadir 100-314). Award: Abdul Qadir (12*, 100-314).

13 October at National Stadium, Karachi. WEST INDIES beat SRI LANKA by 191 runs. Toss: Sri Lanka. West Indies 360-4 (50 overs) (I.V.A. Richards 181, D.L. Haynes 105). Sri Lanka 169-4 (50 overs) (A. Ranatunga 52*). Award: I.V.A. Richards (181 and 8-0-22-0).

13 October at M.A. Chidambaram Stadium, Chepauk, Madras. AUSTRALIA beat ZIMBABWE by 96 runs. Toss: Zimbabwe. Australia 235-9 (50 overs) (A.R. Border 67, G.R. Marsh 62, S.R. Waugh 45). Zimbabwe 139 (42.4 overs) (S.P. O'Donnell 9.4-1-39-4). Award: S.R. Waugh (45 and 6-3-7-0).

14 October at Chinnaswamy Stadium, Bangalore. INDIA beat NEW ZEALAND by 16 runs. Toss: New Zealand. India 252-7 (50 overs) (N.S. Sidhu 75, Kapil Dev 72*, K.S. More 42*). New Zealand 236-8 (50 overs) (K.R. Rutherford 75, A.H. Jones 64). Award: Kapil Dev (72* and 10-1-54-0).

16 October at Gadaffi Stadium, Lahore. PAKISTAN beat WEST INDIES by 1 wicket. Toss: West Indies. West Indies 216 (49.3 overs) (I.V.A. Richards 51, P.V. Simmons 50; Imran Khan 8.3-2-37-4). Pakistan 217-9 (50 overs) (Salim Yousuf 56, Ramiz Raja 42; C.A. Walsh 10-1-40-4). Award: Salim Yousuf (56).

17 October at Shahi Bagh Stadium, Peshawar. ENGLAND beat SRI LANKA on faster run rate. Toss: England. England 296-4 (50 overs) (G.A. Gooch 84, A.J. Lamb 76, M.W. Gatting 58). Sri Lanka 158-8 (45 overs) (A. Ranatunga 40). (Sri Lanka target 267 off 45 overs). Award: A.J. Lamb (76).

17 October at Wankhede Stadium, Bombay. INDIA beat ZIMBABWE by 8 wickets. Toss: Zimbabwe. Zimbabwe 135 (44.2 overs) (A.J. Pycroft 61; M. Prabhakar 8-1-19-4). India 136-2 (27.5 overs) (D.B. Vengsarkar 46*, S.M. Gavaskar 43). Award: M. Prabhakar (8-1-19-4).

18 October (no play), 19 October at Nehru Stadium, Indore. AUSTRALIA beat NEW ZEALAND by 3 runs in a match reduced by rain to 30 overs. Toss: New Zealand. Australia 199-4 (30 overs) (D.C. Boon 87, D.M. Jones 52). New Zealand 196-9 (30 overs) (M.D. Crowe 58, J.G. Wright 47). Award: D.C. Boon (87).

20 October at National Stadium, Karachi. PAKISTAN beat ENGLAND by 7 wickets. Toss: Pakistan. England 244-9 (50 overs) (C.W.J. Athey 86, M.W. Gatting 60; Imran Khan 9-0-37-4). Pakistan 247-3 (49 overs) (Ramiz Raja 113, Salim Malik 88). Award: Imran Khan (9-0-37-4).

21 October at Green Park, Kanpur. WEST INDIES beat SRI LANKA by 25 runs. Toss: Sri Lanka. West Indies 236-8 (50 overs) (P.V. Simmons 89, A.L. Logie 65*). Sri Lanka 211-8 (50 overs) (A. Ranatunga 86*). Award- P.V. Simmons (89).

22 October at Feroz Shah Kotla, New Delhi. INDIA beat AUSTRALIA by 56 runs. Toss: Australia. India 289-6 (50 overs) (D.B. Vengsarkar 63, S.M. Gavaskar 61, M. Azharuddin 54*, N.S. Sidhu 51). Australia 233 (49 overs) (D.C. Boon 62, S.R. Waugh 42). Award: M. Azharuddin (54*, 3.5-0-19-3, and 1 ct).

23 October at Eden Gardens, Calcutta. NEW ZEALAND beat ZIMBABWE by 4 wickets. Toss: New Zealand. Zimbabwe 227-5 (50 overs) (A.J. Pycroft 52*, K.J. Arnott 51, D.L. Houghton 50, Ali Shah 41). New Zealand 228-6 (47.4 overs) (J.J. Crowe 88*, M.D. Crowe 58). Award: J.J. Crowe (88*).

25 October at Iqbal Stadium, Faisalabad. PAKISTAN beat SRI LANKA by 113 runs. Toss: Pakistan. Pakistan 297-7 (50 overs) (Salim Malik 100). Sri Lanka 184-8 (50 overs) (L.R.D. Mendis 58, A. Ranatunga 50). Award: Salim Malik (100 and 7-1-29-0).

26 October at Sawai Man Singh Stadium, Jaipur. ENGLAND beat WEST INDIES by 34 runs. Toss: West Indies. England 269-5 (50 overs) (G.A. Gooch 92, A.J. Lamb 40). West Indies 235 (48.1 overs) (R.B. Richardson 93, I.V.A. Richards 51). Award: G.A. Gooch (92).

26 October at Gujarat Stadium, Ahmedabad. INDIA beat ZIMBABWE by 7 wickets. Toss: India. Zimbabwe 191-7 (50 overs) (K.J. Arnott 60). India 194-3 (42 overs) (N.S. Sidhu 55, S.M. Gavaskar 50, Kapil Dev 41*). Award: Kapil Dev (10-2-44-2, 1 ct, and 41*).

27 October at Section 16 Stadium, Chandigarh. AUSTRALIA beat NEW ZEALAND by 17 runs. Toss: Australia. Australia 251-8 (50 overs) (G.R. Marsh 126*, D.M. Jones 56). New Zealand 234 (48.4 overs) (J.G. Wright 61, K.R. Rutherford 44). Award: G.R. Marsh (126*).

30 October at Nehru Stadium, Pune. ENGLAND beat SRI LANKA by 8 wickets. Toss: Sri Lanka. Sri Lanka 218-7 (50 overs) (R.L. Dias 80). England 219-2 (41.2 overs) (G.A. Gooch 61, R.T. Robinson 55, M.W. Gatting 46*, C.W.J. Athey 40*). Award: G.A. Gooch (61).

30 October at Barabati Stadium, Cuttack. AUSTRALIA beat ZIMBABWE by 70 runs. Toss: Zimbabwe. Australia 266-5 (50 overs) (D.C. Boon 93, D.M. Jones 58*, M.R.J. Veletta 43). Zimbabwe 196-6 (50 overs). Award: D.C. Boon (93).

30 October at National Stadium, Karachi. WEST INDIES beat PAKISTAN by 28 runs. Toss: West Indies. West Indies 258-7 (50 overs) (R.B. Richardson 110, I.V.A. Richards 67). Pakistan 230-9 (50 overs) (Ramiz Raja 70, Mudassar Nazar 40). Award: R.B. Richardson (110).

31 October at Vidarbha CA Ground, Nagpur. INDIA beat NEW ZEALAND by 9 wickets. Toss: New Zealand. New Zealand 221-9 (50 overs) (D.N. Patel 40). India 224-1 (32.1 overs) (S.M. Gavaskar 103*, K. Srikkanth 75, M. Azharuddin 41*). Award: S.M. Gavaskar (103*) and C. Sharma (10-2-51-3 – including the hat-trick).

Final Group Tables

Group A	P	W	L	Run-rate	Pts	Group B	P	W	L	Run-rate	Pts
INDIA	6	5	1	5.39	20	PAKISTAN	6	5	1	5.01	20
AUSTRALIA	6	5	1	5.19	20	ENGLAND	6	4	2	5.12	16
New Zealand	6	2	4	4.88	8	West Indies	6	3	3	51.6	12
Zimbabwe	6	0	6	3.76	0	Sri Lanka	6	0	6	4.04	0

Semi-Finals

4 November at Gaddafi Stadium, Lahore. AUSTRALIA beat PAKISTAN by 18 runs. Toss: Australia. Australia 267-8 (50 overs) (D.C. Boon 65, M.R.J. Veletta 48). Pakistan 249 (49 overs) (Javed Miandad 70, Imran Khan 58; C.J. McDermott 10-0-44-5). Award: C.J. McDermott (10-0-44-5 and 1ct).

5 November at Wankhede Stadium, Bombay. ENGLAND beat INDIA by 35 runs. Toss: India. England 254-6 (50 overs) (G.A. Gooch 115, M.W. Gatting 56). India 219 (45.3 overs) (M. Azharuddin 64; E.E. Hemmings 9.3-1-52-4). Award: G.A. Gooch (115 and 3-0-16-0).

England v Australia
Reliance World Cup Final

Australia won by 7 runs
Played at Eden Gardens, Calcutta, 8 November 1987
Toss: Australia. Umpires: R.B. Gupta and Mahboob Shah
Man of the Match: D.C. Boon

Australia		Runs	Mins	Balls	6	4
D.C. Boon	c Downton b Hemmings	75	158	125	–	7
G.R. Marsh	b Foster	24	71	49	–	3
D.M. Jones	c Athey b Hemmings	33	75	57	1	1
C.J. McDermott	b Gooch	14	7	8	–	2
A.R. Border*	run out (Robinson)	31	48	33	–	3
M.R.J. Veletta	not out	45	51	31	–	6
S.R. Waugh	not out	5	5	4	–	–
G.C. Dyer†	did not bat					
S.P. O'Donnell	,,					
T.B.A. May	,,					
B.R. Reid	,,					
Extras	(B1, LB13, W5, NB7)	26				
	(50 overs; 210 minutes)	253-5				

England		Runs	Mins	Balls	6	4
G.A. Gooch	lbw b O'Donnell	35	71	57	–	4
R.T. Robinson	lbw b McDermott	0	2	1	–	–
C.W.J. Athey	run out (Waugh)	58	156	104	–	2
M.W. Gatting*	c Dyer b Border	41	54	45	1	3‡
A.J. Lamb	b Waugh	45	65	65	–	4
P.R. Downton†	c O'Donnell b Border	9	10	8	–	1
J.E. Emburey	run out (Boon)	10	27	16	–	–
P.A.J. DeFreitas	c Reid b Waugh	17	10	10	1	2
N.A. Foster	not out	7	13	6	–	–
G.C. Small	not out	3	7	3	–	–
E.E. Hemmings	did not bat					
Extras	(B1, LB14, W2, NB4)	21				
	(50 overs; 214 minutes)	246-8				

‡ plus 1 five

England	O	M	R	W
DeFreitas	6	1	34	0
Small	6	0	33	0
Foster	10	0	38	1
Hemmings	10	1	48	2
Emburey	10	0	44	0
Gooch	8	1	42	1

Australia	O	M	R	W
McDermott	10	1	51	1
Reid	10	0	43	0
Waugh	9	0	37	2
O'Donnell	10	1	35	1
May	4	0	27	0
Border	7	0	38	2

Fall of Wickets

Wkt	A	E
1st	75	1
2nd	151	66
3rd	166	135
4th	168	170
5th	241	188
6th	–	218
7th	–	220
8th	–	235
9th	–	–
10th	–	–

England in Pakistan

Having exceeded expectations by reaching the final of the World Cup and losing only narrowly in it to Australia, England moved on in November 1987 to a tour of Pakistan. At first all went deceptively well for them, for they won all three one-day matches with increasing comfort. The public, already greatly disappointed by Pakistan's failure to reach the final of the World Cup, stayed away, and the aggregate attendance for the three games in Lahore, Karachi, and Peshawar was only 20,000.

This was certainly an encouraging start for England, but one had only to look at their record over the last year to realize that they had a stiff task ahead. In the summer they had lost at home to Pakistan and, though Imran Khan had now retired, they themselves were now without experienced Test players in Gower, Lamb, and Botham. The series in England had not been without incident, and the continued presence of Hasib Ahsan as manager of Pakistan made one fearful of what might lie ahead. The TCCB had not helped by refusing the Pakistan request during the tour of England to replace one of the Test umpires, David Constant. Even if the Pakistan complaint about him was unjustified, it was making it hard for the England management to get a sympathetic hearing if they wished to have a Pakistani umpire changed.

It was recognized, too, that Pakistan's batting in the one-day series had lacked the prolific Javed Miandad, who was now fit again; and one had only to watch Abdul Qadir, the great leg-spinner, bowling in the one-day internationals to realize how much more effective he would be when not restricted in the number of overs he could bowl. Only Gatting played him with certainty, and Qadir was obviously going to be a handful for the younger and less experienced batsmen on the sort of pitch he might expect.

One was also uneasy about what effect the preparation of pitches and especially the umpiring might have on the England party. The senior players who had been to Pakistan before knew the problems that might crop up, and a cloud of apprehension hovered over them. It was much in everybody's mind that as mild a man as Jeremy Coney had threatened to take his New Zealand side off the field in Karachi three years before, after Miandad had been given not out to a catch at the wicket.

Almost from the moment that Mike Gatting won the toss in Lahore – he won the other two tosses as well – England were in trouble. Predictably their tormentor was Qadir. Equally predictably there were numerous umpiring errors and, when Pakistan batted, Miandad was one of the batsmen who steered them into a big lead.

Early in England's second innings came Chris Broad's refusal to leave the wicket on being given out to a catch by the wicket-keeper. Failure to obey an umpire's decision is an act that strikes at the very heart of cricket, as he doubtless realized later. A large fine was envisaged, but he received only a reprimand, and on the same day the manager, Peter Lush, entered the lists with a statement to the Press that was unusually critical of the umpiring.

It must be hard for the public at home in England, who are accustomed to harmonious relations between players and umpires, to understand how these things can happen. But it is certainly a different world in Pakistan, and one in which a feeling of victimization may build up with unhappy results. This became still more apparent in the second Test, when Mike Gatting had his much publicized confrontation with Shakoor Rana, one of the umpires to whom the New Zealanders had taken exception in 1984.

The sinister new habit of siting a microphone by the pitch was always likely to publicize incidents that might normally have passed unnoticed. Now it added to the deplorable scene on the second evening. England had taken five wickets and were on top for once. They were trying to fit in another over when Shakoor Rana intervened from square-leg, misinterpreting a gesture made by Gatting just after he had had the courtesy to draw the attention of the batsman Sakim Malik to a change he had made in the field. As Hemmings bowled, Shakoor took it on himself to call 'dead ball'. When Gatting asked the reason for this, he was met by a shower of abuse and called a cheat. He blew up. One's heart sank as the arms waved furiously on both sides and the television cameras captured the dreadful sight for all time.

Apologies are not freely given on the sub-continent, and the third day's play was lost while Shakoor Rana waited for one from Gatting. Gatting, having been falsely accused of being a cheat, was not inclined to make one unless Shakoor did too. Eventually Gatting was ordered to make one by the TCCB, and, after the normal rest day, the match resumed.

The England players had turned up on time on the third day to find that there was nothing doing, and it seemed possible that they might go home without playing the third and last Test in Karachi. But the chairman of the TCCB, Raman Subba Row, and chief executive Alan Smith flew out to Karachi to repair the damage. In the course of their visit they caused some astonishment by Mr Subba Row's decision to give a sort of hardship bonus of £1,000 to each member of the side. They had certainly had a tough tour and had much to be aggrieved about, but they had allowed themselves to be drawn into reactions that were totally against the best interests of the game and, whatever the provocation, were inexcusable. Even in the quite well-umpired third Test, some England batsmen were showing signs of dissent when given out.

The atmosphere of the tour was such that none of the young players could be expected to show much improvement. Gooch batted well, but it was a tour that any one present will wish to forget.

First Test: Lahore, 25, 26, 27, 28 November.
Pakistan won by an innings and 87 runs.

England's recent success came to an abrupt halt on the first day when, having won the toss, they were bowled out for 175, of which the last two wickets made 81. Abdul Qadir took nine for 56 in 37 overs. He bowled superbly on a bare, cracked pitch and with strong support from the umpiring, which gave him four lbws. Whereas Pakistan had included their three spinners, England had left out Hemmings. Emburey and Cook never looked like being as effective as Qadir had been, and Mudassar and Miandad took Pakistan into the lead with only two wickets down during their stand of 142. Pakistan eventually led by 217. In England's second innings only three overs out of 82 were not bowled by Qadir, Qasim, and Tausif. Qadir took four more wickets and Pakistan won easily on the fourth day.

Second Test: Faisalabad, 7, 8, 9, 11, 12 December.
Match Drawn.

In spite of suffering one of the worst decisions of all when Gooch was given out to a catch, the ball having never been near the bat, England made a good start to the second Test. Broad dug in for seven hours for 116, Gatting made 79 with ferocious brilliance, and at one time the score was 241 for two. But the three spinners, who again took all the wickets, were too much for the later batsmen and the innings ended at 292. By the second evening, however, Emburey and Foster had taken the first five wickets for 106, and England were pressing for a win. It was at this point that Gatting and Shakoor Rana had their confrontation, and the third day's play was lost while the flames simmered. This made all the difference. When they resumed after Gatting had been ordered to apologize, Pakistan's innings ended with them 101 behind. But too much time had been lost, England had lost their momentum, and a match that could have been a splendid contest drifted to a draw.

Third Test: Karachi, 16, 17, 18, 20, 21 December.
Match Drawn.

Nothing much was expected of the final Test but, after the Pakistan Board had agreed to a change of umpire, a peaceful match ensued. England made 294 after being 85 for six, owing their respectability to a seventh-wicket stand between Capel, 98, and the remarkably consistent Emburey. Pakistan led on first innings by 59 after being 146 for six. Salim Malik, not for the first time in the series, looked a high-class player, and Aamir Malik in his second Test was unlucky to lose his last partner when 98. Batting again, England had to work hard for a draw, and at one time were 61 for four. But Gooch batted with massive patience for over six hours before Mudassar bowled him off his pads. Capel gave useful support and Emburey completed the defiant resistance against Qadir by batting almost as long as Gooch for 74 not out. Once again the most dangerous enemy was Qadir, who bowled 104.5 overs in the match for 186 runs and 10 wickets.

Pakistan v England 1987-88 1st Test

Pakistan won by an innings and 87 runs
Played at Gadaffi Stadium, Lahore, 25, 26, 27, 28 November
Toss: England. Umpires: Amnullah Khan & Shakeel Khan
Debuts: nil

England

G.A. Gooch	b Qadir	12		c Ashraf b Qasim	15
B.C. Broad	c Mujtaba b Qadir	41		c Ashraf b Qasim	13
R.T. Robinson	c Ashraf b Qadir	6		b Qadir	1
M.W. Gatting*	lbw b Qadir	0		lbw b Qadir	23
C.W.J. Athey	lbw b Qadir	5		c Ashraf b Tausif	2
D.J. Capel	c Mujtaba b Tausif	0	(7)	c Miandad b Qadir	0
P.A.J. DeFreitas	lbw b Qadir	5	(8)	c Tausif b Qasim	15
J.E. Emburey	b Qadir	0	(9)	not out	38
N.A. Foster	lbw b Qadir	39	(10)	c sub (Akram Raza) b Tausif	5
B.N. French†	not out	38	(6)	lbw b Qadir	9
N.G.B. Cook	c Miandad b Qadir	10		b Tausif	5
Extras	(B4, LB14, NB1)	19		(B4, LB4)	8
		175			**130**

Pakistan

Mudassar Nazar	lbw b Foster	120
Rameez Raja	b Emburey	35
Salim Malik	b Emburey	0
Javed Miandad*	c Gooch b Cook	65
Ijaz Ahmed	b DeFreitas	44
Asif Mujtaba	b Foster	7
Ashraf Ali†	b Emburey	7
Wasim Akram	c Broad b Cook	40
Abdul Qadir	st French b Cook	38
Iqbal Qasim	run out (Athey)	1
Tausif Ahmed	not out	5
Extras	(B18, LB8, NB4)	30
		392

Pakistan	O	M	R	W	O	M	R	W
Akram	14	4	32	0	2	0	6	0
Mudassar	5	3	9	0	1	0	4	0
Qadir	37	13	56	9	36	14	45	4
Tausif	23	9	38	1	20	7	28	3
Qasim	4	0	22	0	20.2	10	39	3

England	O	M	R	W
DeFreitas	29	7	84	1
Foster	23	6	58	2
Emburey	48	16	109	3
Cook	31	10	87	3
Capel	3	0	28	0

Fall of Wickets

	E	P	E
Wkt	1st	1st	2nd
1st	22	71	23
2nd	36	71	24
3rd	36	213	38
4th	44	272	43
5th	55	290	66
6th	70	301	70
7th	80	328	73
8th	90	360	105
9th	150	370	116
10th	175	392	130

Pakistan v England 1987-88 2nd Test

Match Drawn
Played at Iqbal Stadium, Faisalabad, 7, 8, 9, 11 (np), 12 December
Toss: England. Umpires: Khizer Hayat & Shakoor Rana
Debuts: Pakistan – Aamir Malik

England

G.A. Gooch	c Aamir Malik b Qasim	28	lbw b Qadir	65
B.C. Broad	b Tausif	116	st Ashraf b Qadir	14
C.W.J. Athey	c Aamir Malik b Qadir	27	b Mudassar Nazar	20
M.W. Gatting*	b Qadir	79	c Qadir b Qasim	8
R.T. Robinson	c Ashraf b Qadir	2	(8) not out	7
N.G.B. Cook	c Ashraf b Qasim	2		
D.J. Capel	c Aamir Malik b Qadir	1	lbw b Qasim	2
J.E. Emburey	st Ashraf b Qasim	15	(5) not out	10
N.A. Foster	c Aamir Malik b Qasim	0	(6) c Miandad b Qadir	0
B.N. French†	st Ashraf b Qasim	2		
E.E. Hemmings	not out	1		
Extras	(B10, LB5, W1, NB3)	19	(B1, LB9, NB1)	11
		292	(6 wkts dec)	137

Pakistan

Mudassar Nazar	c French b Foster	1	b Cook	4
Rameez Raja	c Gooch b Foster	12	not out	13
Salim Malik	b Cook	60	not out	28
Javed Miandad*	b Emburey	19		
Ijaz Ahmed	c Robinson b Emburey	11		
Shoaib Mohammad	b Emburey	0		
Aamir Malik	c French b Foster	5		
Ashraf Ali†	c French b Foster	4		
Abdul Qadir	c Gooch b Cook	38		
Iqbal Qasim	lbw b Hemmings	24		
Tausif Ahmed	not out	5		
Extras	(LB5, NB7)	12	(B4, LB1, NB1)	6
		191	(1 wkt)	51

Pakistan	O	M	R	W	O	M	R	W
Aamir Malik	5	0	19	0	3	0	20	0
Mudassar	3	0	8	0	12	1	33	1
Qadir	42	7	105	4	15	3	45	3
Tausif	28	9	62	1				
Qasim	35.2	7	83	5	10	2	29	2
Shoaib	1	1	0	0				

England	O	M	R	W	O	M	R	W
Foster	18	4	42	4	3	0	4	0
Capel	7	1	23	0				
Hemmings	18	5	35	1	7	3	16	0
Emburey	21	8	49	3	2	0	3	0
Cook	20.3	10	37	2	9	3	15	1
Gooch					2	1	4	0
Broad					1	0	4	0

Fall of Wickets

Wkt	E 1st	P 1st	E 2nd	P 2nd
1st	73	11	47	15
2nd	124	22	102	–
3rd	241	58	107	–
4th	249	77	115	–
5th	258	77	115	–
6th	259	115	120	–
7th	288	122	–	–
8th	288	123	–	–
9th	288	175	–	–
10th	292	191	–	–

Pakistan v England 1987-88 3rd Test

Match Drawn
Played at National Stadium, Karachi, 16, 17, 18, 20, 21 December
Toss: England. Umpires: Khizer Hayat & Mahboob Shah
Debuts: nil

England

G.A. Gooch	c Ashraf b Akram	12	b Mudassar		93
B.C. Broad	lbw b Akram	7	lbw b Qadir		13
C.W.J. Athey	b Qadir	26	c Ashraf b Jaffer		12
M.W. Gatting*	b Qadir	18	lbw b Jaffer		0
N.H. Fairbrother	c sub (Mujtaba) b Jaffer	3	c sub (Mujtaba) b Qadir		1
D.J. Capel	b Qadir	98	c Miandad b Qadir		24
P.A.J. DeFreitas	b Qadir	12	lbw b Qadir	(9)	6
J.E. Emburey	c Qadir b Jaffer	70	not out	(7)	74
B.N. French†	c Miandad b Salim Malik	31	lbw b Jaffer	(8)	0
N.G.B. Cook	lbw b Qadir	2	b Qadir		14
G.R. Dilley	not out	0	not out		0
Extras	(LB8, W1, NB6)	15	(B9, LB5, W1, NB6)		21
		294	(9 wkts)		**258**

Pakistan

Mudassar Nazar	lbw b DeFreitas	6
Rameez Raja	c French b Cook	50
Salem Malik	c Gatting b DeFreitas	55
Javed Miandad*	lbw b Emburey	4
Ijaz Ahmed	run out (Broad/French)	0
Aamir Malik	not out	98
Ashraf Ali†	c French b Dilley	12
Wasim Akram	c French b DeFreitas	37
Abdul Qadir	b Capel	61
Iqbal Qasim	c French b DeFreitas	11
Salim Jaffer	lbw b DeFreitas	0
Extras	(LB11, NB8)	19
		353

Pakistan	O	M	R	W	O	M	R	W
Akram	24.1	3	64	2				
Jaffer	23.5	6	74	2	42	9	79	3
Qadir	49.4	15	88	5	55	16	98	5
Qasim	18	4	51	0	27	10	44	0
Mudassar	1	1	0	0	4	3	2	1
Salim Malik	5	2	9	1	7	2	14	0
Aamir Malik					2	0	7	0

England	O	M	R	W
Dilley	21	2	102	1
De Freitas	23.5	3	86	5
Emburey	53	24	90	1
Cook	33	12	56	1
Capel	3	0	8	1

Fall of Wickets

Wkt	E 1st	P 1st	E 2nd
1st	20	18	34
2nd	41	105	54
3rd	55	110	54
4th	72	110	61
5th	72	122	115
6th	85	146	175
7th	199	222	176
8th	274	316	187
9th	291	349	246
10th	294	353	–

Test Match Averages: Pakistan v England 1987-88

Pakistan

Batting and Fielding	M	I	NO	HS	R	Avge	100	50	Ct/St
Salim Malik	3	4	1	60	143	47.66	–	2	–
Abdul Qadir	3	3	0	61	137	45.66	–	1	2
Ramiz Raja	3	4	1	50	110	36.66	–	1	–
Mudassar Nazar	3	4	0	120	131	32.75	1	–	–
Javed Miandad	3	3	0	65	88	29.33	–	1	5
Ijaz Ahmed	3	3	0	44	55	18.33	–	–	–
Iqbal Qasim	3	3	0	24	36	12.00	–	–	–
Ashraf Ali	3	3	0	12	23	7.66	–	–	8/3

Also batted: Amir Malik (2 matches) 5, 98*, 4ct; Asif Mujtaba (1 match) 7, 2ct; Salim Jaffer (1 match) 0; Shoaib Mohammad (1 match) 0; Tausif Ahmed (2 matches) 5*, 5*, 1ct; Wasim Akram (2 matches) 40, 37.

Bowling	O	M	R	W	Avge	Best	5wI	10wM
Abdul Qadir	234.4	68	437	30	14.56	9-56	3	2
Tausif Ahmed	71.2	25	128	5	25.60	3-28	–	–
Iqbal Qasim	114.2	33	268	10	26.80	5-83	1	–
Salim Jaffer	65.5	15	153	5	30.60	3-79	–	–

Also bowled: Aamir Malik 10-0-46-0; Mudassar Nazar 26-8-56-2; Salim Malik 12-4-23-1; Shoaib Mohammad 1-1-0-0; Wasim Akram 40.1-7-102-2.

England

Batting and Fielding	M	I	NO	HS	R	Avge	100	50	Ct/St
J.E. Emburey	3	6	3	74*	207	69.00	–	2	–
G.A. Gooch	3	6	0	93	225	37.50	–	2	3
B.C. Broad	3	6	0	116	204	34.00	1	–	1
M.W. Gatting	3	6	0	79	128	21.33	–	1	1
D.J. Capel	3	6	0	98	125	20.83	–	1	–
B.N. French	3	5	1	38*	80	20.00	–	–	7/1
C.W.J. Athey	3	6	0	27	92	15.33	–	–	–
N.A. Foster	2	4	0	39	40	10.00	–	–	–
P.A.J. DeFreitas	2	4	0	15	38	9.50	–	–	–
N.G.B. Cook	3	5	0	14	33	6.60	–	–	–
R.T. Robinson	2	4	1	7	16	5.33	–	–	–

Also batted: G.R. Dilley (1 match) 0*, 0*; N.H. Fairbrother (1 match) 3/1; E.E. Hemmings (1 match) 1*.

Bowling	O	M	R	W	Avge	Best	5wI	10wM
N.A. Foster	44	10	104	6	17.33	4-42	–	–
N.G.B. Cook	93.3	35	195	7	27.85	3-87	–	–
P.A.J. DeFreitas	52.5	10	170	6	28.33	5-86	1	–
J.E. Emburey	124	48	251	7	35.85	3-49	–	–

Also bowled: B.C. Broad 1-0-4-0; D.J. Capel 13-1-59-1; G.R. Dilley 21-2-102-1; G.A. Gooch 2-1-4-0; E.E. Hemmings 25-8-51-1.

Statistical Highlights of the Tests

1st Test, Lahore. Abdul Qadir returned the best figures for Pakistan in Test history and the best against England. It was the best in an innings at Lahore and the 5th best in all Tests. His match figures (13-101) are a record for Pakistan/England Tests, and his peronal best. England's 2nd innings total equals their lowest against Pakistan, set at The Oval in 1954. Mudassar Nazar scored his 10th Test hundred, his 3rd against England, in his 100th innings. Iqbal Qasim took his 150th Test wicket when he dismissed Broad in the 2nd innings. He became the 5th Pakistan bowler with 150 wickets. Javed Miandad reached 50 or more for the 50th time in his 50th Test. Broad passed 1,000 Test runs at 39 in the 1st innings of his 15th Test.

2nd Test, Faisalabad. Pakistan recorded their lowest total against England in Pakistan. Broad scored his 4th Test hundred, his 1st against Pakistan. Iqbal Qasim took five wickets for the 7th time, his 1st against England. Abdul Qadir played his 50th Test.

3rd Test, Karachi. Pakistan won their 3rd successive series against England and remain unbeaten in 26 Tests at Karachi. There have now been 11 wins and 15 draws. Abdul Qadir took 30 wickets in the series, a record for Pakistan/England Tests. He took five wickets for the 13th and 14th times and 10 wickets in a match for the 5th time. Dilley became the 29th England bowler to take 100 Test wickets when he dismissed Ashraf Ali. Gatting played his 50th Test catch. DeFreitas took five wickets for the first time. Gooch made his highest score against Pakistan. Emburey scored his 6th and 7th Test fifties and finished top of the England batting averages.

One-Day Internationals

18 November at Gadaffi Stadium, Lahore. ENGLAND beat PAKISTAN by 2 wickets. Toss Pakistan. Pakistan 166 (41.3 overs). England 167-8 (44.3 overs) (G.A. Gooch 43). Award: J.E. Emburey (8.3-2-17-3).

20 November at National Stadium, Karachi. ENGLAND beat PAKISTAN by 23 runs. Toss: England. England 263-6 (44 overs) (G.A. Gooch 142, D.J. Capel 50*). Pakistan 240-8 (44 overs) (Ramiz Raja 99 – obstructed the field). Award: G.A. Gooch (142).

22 November at Shahi Bagh Stadium, Peshawar. ENGLAND beat PAKISTAN by 98 runs. Toss: England. England 236-8 (45 overs) (B.C. Broad 66, G.A. Gooch 57, M.W. Gatting 53). Pakistan 138 (31.5 overs) (Salim Malik 52). Award: N.A. Foster (6.5-0-20-3).

England Tour of Pakistan 1987-88

First-Class Matches: Played 5; Lost 1, Drawn 4
All Matches: Played 8; Won 3, Lost 1, Drawn 4

First-Class Averages

Batting and Fielding	M	I	NO	HS	R	Avge	100	50	Ct/St
J.E. Emburey	4	7	3	74*	216	54.00	–	2	–
R.T. Robinson	4	7	1	118	261	43.50	1	2	1
G.A. Gooch	3	6	0	93	225	37.50	–	2	3
C.W.J. Athey	5	9	1	101	256	32.00	1	–	–
B.N. French	4	7	2	45	147	29.40	–	–	10/1
B.C. Broad	5	9	0	116	251	27.88	1	–	1
D.J. Capel	5	8	0	98	207	25.87	–	2	–
M.W. Gatting	4	7	0	79	141	20.14	–	1	1
E.E. Hemmings	3	3	1	34	35	17.50	–	–	–
N.H. Fairbrother	3	5	0	66	76	15.20	–	1	2
P.A.J. DeFreitas	3	6	0	25	79	13.16	–	–	–
N.G.B. Cook	5	7	1	32	72	12.00	–	–	–
N.A. Foster	2	4	0	39	40	10.00	–	–	–
G.R. Dilley	3	4	3	4*	6	6.00	–	–	–

Also batted: P.W. Jarvis (1 match) 8, 1ct; R.C. Russell (1 match) 4.

Bowling	O	M	R	W	Avge	Best	5wI	10wM
N.A. Foster	44	10	104	6	17.33	4-42	–	–
P.A.J. DeFreitas	64.1	14	195	9	21.66	5-86	1	–
N.G.B. Cook	129.2	46	277	10	27.70	3-37	–	–
E.E. Hemmings	61.3	17	170	6	28.33	4-70	–	–
J.E. Emburey	134	50	278	8	34.75	3-49	–	–

Also bowled: B.C. Broad 1-0-4-0; D.J. Capel 45-7-172-4; G.R. Dilley 50-7-206-4; M.W. Gatting 7-2-21-0; G.A. Gooch 2-1-4-0; P.W. Jarvis 17-2-51-1.

England in Australasia

Less than a year after the euphoria which marked England's retention of the Ashes in Australia, Mike Gatting and his side returned to that part of the world in a more sombre mood, which was to suit well the drawn three-match Test series with New Zealand. Even the Bicentenary Test in Sydney to mark the 200th anniversary of the arrival of the first white settlers did not fully meet the high expectations held out for it after the success of MCC's own bicentennial a few months earlier.

By the time the party first arrived in New Zealand, events had served to take much of the gloss off the high point of the Ashes victory. The loss of the summer series at home to Pakistan had been unexpected, and this disappointment had been many times magnified after the umpiring troubles and player dissent in Pakistan itself before Christmas.

Gatting continued to feel strongly about his confrontation with umpire Shakoor Rana and the apology forced from him by the TCCB. In the brief break at home between the two sets of tours he was publicly telling the Board that it could take him or leave him as captain even when the party was on the brink of departing for New Zealand.

Equally damaging to morale was the degree of exhaustion – both physical and mental – senior members felt from having played too much cricket. By the time they returned from New Zealand at the end of March, 1988, with only three weeks before the start of another domestic campaign, some had been 'on the go' in terms of travelling and playing for 17 months with only the barest of breaks.

To this modern 'evil' of saturation cricket could be added another side, equally destructive from the point of view of team success. Players were now opting out of winter tours because they needed the rest and to spend time with their families.

So for Australasia, England were without two of their best batsmen, Gower and Gooch, while Botham, having already stated he would not be going on any more England tours, had signed a three-year winter contract with Queensland (later abruptly terminated by that state).

In addition to these absences there was the damaging loss for England's prospects of Neil Foster with a knee injury, which necessitated his returning home for an exploratory operation. It was doubly unfortunate as Foster and Dilley were beginning to look a formidable new-ball partnership, particularly on the harder Australian wickets.

In order to accommodate the Bicentenary Test, England broke their tour of New Zealand after ten days and also played a one-day international in Melbourne, which they lost by 22 runs, before re-crossing the Tasman Sea. With the difference in firmness of pitches and Australia's much drier summer, it was perhaps not the best preparation.

If there was one word which ran as a theme through the tour of Australasia and which had found its echo earlier in Pakistan it was 'dissent'. (Later, the TCCB were to explain that there was a distinct difference between dissent and 'understandable disappointment'.)

First, there was Broad's stump-smashing exhibition of petulance in Sydney for which he was fined £500 by the Board. Then, in the first Test against New Zealand at Christchurch Dilley was fined £250 for uttering obscenities when the umpires refused to uphold a series of appeals.

Following Broad's stubborn refusal to accept a decision against him in the first Pakistan Test and Gatting's row with umpire Rana, there had been a feeling that discipline in the England camp was in danger of breaking down and tour manager Peter Lush was under instructions to stamp on any threats of a repetition.

What had particularly offended in Dilley's case was that his words had been picked up by microphone inside the Christchurch ground – just as Gatting's words at Faisalabad had been relayed round the world.

Though pitch microphones have never been considered necessary in England, the agreement by television to cover Tests in some countries, including Australia and New Zealand, includes permission for microphones buried in the base of the stumps, on the understanding they do not carry players' voices.

Mr Lush felt this agreement had been broken at Christchurch and that the pitch microphones had picked up Dilley's words – when in all probability it was the microphones around the boundary edge which were guilty. The stands were almost empty at the time, and Dilley's words had carried quite clearly to the naked ears of the spectators.

Mr Lush tried without success to get New Zealand television and the New Zealand Cricket Council to abandon the pitch microphones for the last two Tests. It was no more unreasonable a proposition than their contention that these were essential for television enjoyment of the game.

Before the announcement of Dilley's fine, there was a long dressing-room discussion between captain and vice-captain (Gatting and Emburey) and manager and team manager (Lush and Stewart) at which views as to the degree of blame to be visited on the bowler were sharply divided.

Ironically, Dilley and Broad were England's main successes on this tour, though Moxon enhanced his status as an alternative opener, while Jarvis and Capel did enough to keep their names in the selectors' minds for the coming series at home against West Indies.

But in truth, on what were almost all flat and slow wickets, this was poor Test match fare, with neither side, for reasons largely to do with absentees, rising much above the mediocre. For New Zealand, Richard Hadlee – on whom their attack inevitably centred – was injured in the first Test before he could take his record Test wicket (he and Botham were the joint leading wicket-takers with 373) and never returned.

England could have won the first Test if the weather had been kinder and the umpires more disposed to their appeals. But thereafter the dead nature of the pitches held out little hope of a breakthrough on either side. After the second Test, at Auckland, an out-of-form Jeff Crowe was relieved of the New Zealand captaincy and replaced by the Derbyshire batsman John Wright. Wright at least ensured that New Zealand did not lose their ten-year unbeaten home record. Later, after going 2-0 down in the four match one-day international series, he played a major part in guiding his country to victories in the last two games.

Bicentenary Test: Sydney, 29, 30, 31 January, 1, 2 February.
Drawn

Australia had not lost a Test at the SCG in the present decade and though England made them follow on here, the wicket had eased sufficiently over the final two days for the home side to save the game with ease.

Sixty years after being presented to MCC, the urn containing the Ashes was allowed to leave Lord's museum and take up temporary domicile in Sydney (where it was on show in a bank) for the duration of this game.

Gatting won the toss in very hot, dry conditions, and Broad and Moxon gave the tourists the best of starts with a 93-run opening partnership. With his Notts colleague Robinson joining in a stand of 99 for the second wicket, Broad had passed his century before the close of the first day, with England 221 for two, a total which benefited from a number of missed chances by the Australian fielders.

Broad had reach 139 the next morning when he tried to avoid a ball from Waugh which hit his forearm and fell onto the bails. In his annoyance with himself, Broad hit out at and flattened the leg stump with his bat. Within minutes of his return to the pavilion he had been fined £500 and later wrote a note of apology.

Every England batsman except Hemmings reached double figures in the total of 425, but having passed 300 for the loss of only four wickets they might have expected to do better had not off-spinner Peter Taylor, with four for 84, and Waugh, three for 23, exerted some control.

On a third day of great heat and very high humidity, it was Foster who made the first breakthrough and then Capel, first change, claimed two more quick wickets, including the vital one of the Australian captain Border, as the home side slumped to 34 for three. Nearly two hours were lost to bad light in the last session, with Australia in a poor way after the loss of Dean Jones for 56.

Australia's last four wickets went down in a little over an hour on a much cooler fourth morning and they followed on 211 behind. Foster, who had seemed to be bowling with great rhythm, got through 15 overs in the second innings before having to leave the field for treatment to the knee which had been troubling him all winter. Before the week was over, he had returned home, a considerable blow to England's hopes.

Dilley, too, had hurt himself, and it was left to Emburey and Hemmings to bear the burden of the attack with 90 overs between them. But the pitch had eased greatly and after Boon and Marsh had taken Australia's rearguard action on the last day to 162 for the first wicket, Boon batted on for more than eight hours for his sixth Test century, 184 not out, which won him the Man of the Match award.

A total of 103,831 people had watched the five days, a disappointing attendance considering the pre-match expectations and the country's general air of festivity. At the same time as the Bicentenary Test, the Sydney ground's computer had played its own visual 'Test' between the living 'greats' of the two nations. Australia eventually won by 37 runs.

Australia v England 1987-88 Bicentenary Test

Match Drawn
Played at Sydney Cricket Ground, 29, 30, 31 January, 1, 2 February
Toss: England. Umpires: A.R. Crafter and P.J. McConnell
Debuts: nil

England

B.C. Broad	b Waugh	139
M.D. Moxon	b Sleep	40
R.T. Robinson	c Veletta b Dodemaide	43
M.W. Gatting*	c Dyer b Waugh	13
C.W.J. Athey	c & b Taylor	37
D.J. Capel	c Sleep b Taylor	21
J.E. Emburey	st Dyer b Sleep	23
B.N. French†	st Dyer b Taylor	47
N.A. Foster	c Border b Taylor	19
E.E. Hemmings	not out	8
G.R. Dilley	b Waugh	13
Extras	(B4, LB9, W1, NB8)	22
		425

Australia

D.C. Boon	c French b Foster	12	(2) not out		184
G.R. Marsh	c French b Capel	5	(1) Athey b Emburey		56
D.M. Jones	c Emburey b Hemmings	56	c Moxon b Capel		24
A.R. Border*	c Broad b Capel	2	not out		48
M.R.J. Veletta	c Emburey b Hemmings	22			
S.R. Waugh	c French b Dilley	27			
P.R. Sleep	c Athey b Foster	41			
G.C. Dyer†	lbw b Dilley	0			
P.L. Taylor	c French b Hemmings	20			
A.I.C. Dodemaide	not out	12			
C.J. McDermott	c Foster b Dilley	1			
Extras	(LB10, W1, NB5)	16	(B3, LB7, NB6)		16
		214	(2 wkts)		**328**

Australia	O	M	R	W
McDermott	35	8	65	0
Dodemaide	36	10	98	1
Taylor	34	10	84	4
Waugh	22.5	5	51	3
Sleep	45	8	114	2

England	O	M	R	W	O	M	R	W
Dilley	19.1	4	54	3	13	1	48	0
Foster	19	6	27	2	15	6	27	0
Emburey	30	10	57	0	38	5	98	1
Capel	6	3	13	2	17	4	38	1
Hemmings	22	3	53	3	52	15	107	0

Fall of Wickets

Wkt	E 1st	A 1st	A 2nd
1st	93	18	162
2nd	192	25	218
3rd	245	34	–
4th	262	82	–
5th	313	116	–
6th	314	147	–
7th	346	153	–
8th	387	183	–
9th	410	209	–
10th	425	214	–

Statistical Highlights of the Test

Only Test, Sydney. Broad scored his 5th Test hundred, his 4th in six Tests in Australia. Boon scored his 6th Test hundred, his 2nd against England and his highest in Tests. He and Marsh recorded their 4th hundred opening partnership, a record for the 1st wicket for Australia v England at SCG. Border (43) passed Hammond (7,249) and moved into 6th place in Test history. At the end of the match he had 7,255 runs. Jones passed 1,000 Test runs when he scored his first run in the match. Emburey played his 50th Test. McDermott injured his left knee and was unable to bowl again in the innings. Dyer was injured at 4.54 on the 2nd day and required two stitches in his nose. Veletta took over the gloves.

One-Day International
4 February at Melbourne Cricket Ground (floodlit). AUSTRALIA beat ENGLAND by 22 runs. Toss: Australia. Australia 235-6 (48 overs) (G.R. Marsh 87). England 213-8 (48 overs). Award: G.R. Marsh (87). (England were fined for bowling fewer than 50 overs.)

1st Test: Lancaster Park, Christchurch, 12, 13, 14, 16, 17 February
Drawn

England decided not to send for a replacement for the injured Foster and called in Paul Jarvis for his Test debut. New Zealand won the toss and fielded, but lost the services of Hadlee after 18 overs for the rest of the series with a torn calf muscle. The Notts pair of Robinson and Broad put on 168 for the second wicket and Broad went on to his second century in successive Test innings. Dilley claimed the first five New Zealand batsmen and finished with a personal Test best of six for 38. England, 151 ahead, found equal trouble handling the seam attack of Snedden, four for 45, and Chatfield, four for 36. New Zealand began the last day needing 304 to win. Dilley dismissed the openers in the space of eleven balls but was then fined for dissent when umpire Aldridge twice refused to give bat-pad decisions against Martin Crowe.

2nd Test: Eden Park, Auckland, 25, 26, 27, 28, 29 February.
Drawn

On a slow, unhelpful wicket, Dilley was once again the most hostile bowler on view, with match figures of seven for 104. New Zealand this time blooded Mark Greatbatch, and he responded with a secondinnings century. Gatting, winning the toss, put New Zealand in, but poor slip catching – increasingly an adverse feature of England's fielding on this tour – enabled the home side to reach 301, built around Wright's sixhour innings of 103, Dilley claiming another five wickets. England took a first innings lead of 22, Moxon taking nearly six hours to score 99. It would have been a maiden Test century but for a leg glance for four in the 90s which was wrongly given as leg byes. Jeff Crowe was not prepared to gamble by setting England a target, and Greatbatch batted to the close, becoming the fourth New Zealander to make a century on his Test debut – all lefthanders.

It was announced after the game that the Test pitch was to be dug up, a task for which Gatting immediately volunteered his services.

3rd Test: Basin Reserve, Wellington, 3, 4, 5, 6, 7 March.
Drawn

New Zealand dropped their captain Jeff Crowe and appointed John Wright in his place for this game. The Derbyshire batsman responded by winning a toss which was to give New Zealand the upper hand for the only time in the series. England's troubles were compounded when Dilley broke down with a knee injury and bowled only eleven overs. Robert Vance, captain of Wellington and son of Bob Vance, chairman of the New Zealand Cricket Council, made his debut but was unluckily run out for 47. Martin Crowe and Greatbatch then put on 155, a record for New Zealand fourthwicket partnerships against England. Crowe went on to score 143 before falling to Gatting, who had claimed his wicket on the same ground four years before. Rutherford, missed when one, went on to a first Test hundred before New Zealand declared at 512 for six, their fifth highest Test score. England needed to bat for 17 hours to save the game, but in the end two days were washed out by torrential rains.

New Zealand v England 1987-88 1st Test

Match Drawn
Played at Lancaster Park, Christchurch, 12, 13, 14, 16, 17 February
Toss: New Zealand. Umpires: B.L. Aldridge and S.J. Woodward
Debuts: England – P.W. Jarvis

England

B.C. Broad	c Smith b Snedden	114	c sub (M.J. Greatbach) b Chatfield	20
M.D. Moxon	c Jones b Morrison	1	c Jones b Chatfield	27
R.T. Robinson	c Smith b Morrison	70	c Wright b Chatfield	2
M.W. Gatting*	c sub (M.J. Greatbach) b Morrison	8	b Snedden	23
C.W.J. Athey	c sub (M.J. Greatbach) b Morrison	22	c Smith b Snedden	19
D.J. Capel	c Bracewell b Chatfield	11	c M.D. Crowe b Chatfield	0
J.E. Emburey	c Jones b Morrison	42	run out (Morrison/Snedden)	19
B.N. French†	c Smith b Chatfield	7	c J.J. Crowe b Snedden	3
P.A.J. DeFreitas	c Morrison b Chatfield	4	lbw b Snedden	16
P.W. Jarvis	c Smith b Chatfield	14	not out	10
G.R. Dilley	not out	7	c Jones b Morrison	2
Extras	(LB11, W1, NB7)	19	(LB7, NB4)	11
		319		**152**

New Zealand

J.G. Wright	c Moxon b Dilley	10	lbw b Dilley	23
T.J. Franklin	c Athey b Dilley	10	lbw b Dilley	12
A.H. Jones	c French b Dilley	8	not out	54
M.D. Crowe	c Moxon b Dilley	5	c French b Jarvis	6
J.J. Crowe*	c French b DeFreitas	28	lbw b DeFreitas	0
J.G. Bracewell	c French b Dilley	31	not out	20
R.J. Hadlee	c French b Dilley	37		
I.D.S. Smith†	c Capel b Jarvis	13		
M.C. Snedden	lbw b DeFreitas	0		
D.K. Morrison	b Jarvis	0		
E.J. Chatfield	not out	0		
Extras	(B2, LB12, NB12)	26	(B6, LB4, NB5)	15
		168	(4 wkts)	**130**

New Zealand	O	M	R	W	O	M	R	W
Hadlee	18	3	50	0				
Morrison	21.1	3	69	5	21.1	4	64	1
Chatfield	42	13	87	4	30	13	36	4
Snedden	33	9	86	1	23	8	45	4
Bracewell	6	1	16	0				

England	O	M	R	W	O	M	R	W
DeFreitas	22	6	39	2	19	6	26	1
Dilley	24.5	10	86	6	18	5	32	2
Capel	10	2	32	0	13	5	16	0
Jarvis	21	8	43	2	17	7	30	1
Emburey	4	3	2	0	10	4	16	0

Fall of Wickets

	E	NZ	E	NZ
Wkt	1st	1st	2nd	2nd
1st	7	20	32	37
2nd	175	25	38	43
3rd	187	32	55	61
4th	219	40	95	78
5th	237	96	96	–
6th	241	131	99	–
7th	248	151	118	–
8th	260	155	125	–
9th	285	156	147	–
10th	319	168	152	–

New Zealand v England 1987-88 2nd Test

Match Drawn
Played at Eden Park, Auckland, 25, 26, 27, 28, 29 February
Toss: England. Umpires: F.R. Goodall and R.L. McHarg
Debuts: New Zealand – M.J. Greatbach

New Zealand

J.G. Wright	c French b Dilley	103	(2) c French b Radford		49
T.J. Franklin	b Jarvis	27	(1) b Dilley		62
J.J. Crowe*	c Capel b Dilley	11	lbw b Dilley		1
M.D. Crowe	c Capel b Emburey	36	lbw b Jarvis		26
M.J. Greatbach	c French b Dilley	11	not out		107
K.R. Rutherford	b Capel	29	b Emburey		2
J.G. Bracewell	c Moxon b Dilley	9	(8) lbw b Gatting		38
I.D.S. Smith†	c French b Jarvis	23	(9) not out		23
M.C. Snedden	c Moxon b Dilley	14	(7) c French b Capel		20
D.K. Morrison	not out	14			
E.J. Chatfield	c French b Capel	10			
Extras	(B1, LB2, W2, NB9)	14	(B8, LB8, NB6)		22
		301	(7 wkts)		**350**

England

B.C. Broad	c M.D. Crowe b Bracewell	9
M.D. Moxon	c J.J. Crowe b Chatfield	99
R.T. Robinson	c Morrison b Bracewell	54
M.W. Gatting*	c Smith b Morrison	42
N.H. Fairbrother	c Smith b Chatfield	1
D.J. Capel	c Bracewell b Morrison	5
J.E. Emburey	c Smith b Chatfield	45
B.N. French†	c Franklin b Bracewell	13
P.W. Jarvis	c Smith b Snedden	10
N.V. Radford	b Chatfield	8
G.R. Dilley	not out	8
Extras	(B12, LB12, NB5)	29
		323

England	O	M	R	W	O	M	R	W	Fall of Wickets			
										NZ	E	NZ
Dilley	28	9	60	5	23	9	44	2	Wkt	1st	1st	2nd
Jarvis	33	9	74	2	27	7	54	1				
Radford	30	4	79	0	20	4	53	1	1st	77	27	117
Capel	26.2	4	57	2	21	4	40	1	2nd	98	135	119
Emburey	17	7	28	1	57	24	91	1	3rd	169	211	119
Gatting					17	4	40	1	4th	191	220	150
Fairbrother					2	0	9	0	5th	207	222	153
Moxon					2	0	3	0	6th	219	234	232
									7th	254	267	296
New Zealand	O	M	R	W					8th	262	282	–
Morrison	32	7	95	2					9th	279	308	–
Chatfield	31.1	15	37	4					10th	301	323	–
Bracewell	39	8	88	3								
Snedden	33	14	71	1								
Rutherford	5	1	8	0								

New Zealand v England 1987-88 3rd Test

Match Drawn
Played at Basin Reserve, Wellington, 3, 4, 5, 6 (np), 7 (np) March
Toss: New Zealand. Umpires: B.L. Aldridge and S.J. Woodward
Debuts: New Zealand – R.H. Vance

New Zealand

J.G. Wright*	c Fairbrother b Capel	36
T.J. Franklin	lbw b DeFreitas	14
R.H. Vance	run out (Broad/ Emburey/French)	47
M.D. Crowe	lbw b Gatting	143
M.J. Greatbach	c DeFreitas b Emburey	68
K.R. Rutherford	not out	107
J.G. Bracewell	c Fairbrother b Capel	54
I.D.S. Smith†	not out	33
D.K. Morrison	did not bat	
S.L. Boock	,,	
E.J. Chatfield	,,	
Extras	(LB10)	10
	(6 wkts dec)	**512**

England

B.C. Broad	b Boock	61
M.D. Moxon	not out	81
R.T. Robinson	c Smith b Chatfield	0
M.W. Gatting*	not out	33
N.H. Fairbrother	did not bat	
D.J. Capel	,,	
J.E. Emburey	,,	
B.N. French†	,,	
P.A.J. DeFreitas	,,	
E.E. Hemmings	,,	
G.R. Dilley	,,	
Extras	(LB6, NB2)	8
	(2 wkts)	**183**

England	O	M	R	W
Dilley	11	1	36	0
DeFreitas	50.2	21	110	1
Capel	39	7	129	2
Emburey	45.5	10	99	1
Hemmings	45	15	107	0
Gatting	6	1	21	1

New Zealand	O	M	R	W
Morrison	6	0	41	0
Chatfield	23	10	38	1
Bracewell	23	9	44	0
Boock	26	9	53	1
Rutherford	1	0	1	0

Fall of Wickets

	NZ	E	
Wkt	1st	1st	2nd
1st	33	129	
2nd	79	132	
3rd	132	–	
4th	287	–	
5th	336	–	
6th	470	–	
7th	–	–	
8th	–	–	
9th	–	–	
10th	–	–	

Test Match Averages:
New Zealand v England 1987-88

New Zealand

Batting and Fielding	M	I	NO	HS	R	Avge	100s	50s	Ct/St
M.J. Greatbach	2	3	1	107*	286	93.00	1	1	–
K.R. Rutherford	2	3	1	107*	138	69.00	1	–	–
I.D.S. Smith	3	4	2	33*	92	46.00	–	–	10/–
J.G. Wright	3	5	0	103	221	44.20	1	–	1
M.D. Crowe	3	5	0	143	216	43.20	1	–	1
J.G. Bracewell	3	5	1	54	152	38.00	–	1	2
T.J. Franklin	3	5	0	62	125	25.00	–	1	1
M.C. Snedden	2	3	0	20	34	11.33	–	–	–
J.J. Crowe	2	4	0	28	40	10.00	–	–	2

Also batted: E.J. Chatfield (3 matches) 0*, 10; R.J. Hadlee (1 match) 37; A.H. Jones (1 match) 8,
54*, 4ct; D.K. Morrison (3 matches) 0, 14*, 2ct; R.H. Vance (1 match) 47.
S.L. Boock played in one match but did not bat.

Bowling	O	M	R	W	Avge	Best	5wI	10wM
E.J. Chatfield	126.1	51	198	13	15.23	4-36	–	–
D.K. Morrison	80.2	14	269	8	33.62	5-69	1	–
M.C. Snedden	89	31	202	6	33.66	4-45	–	–

Also bowled: S.L Boock 26-9-53-1; J.G. Bracewell 68-18-148-3; R.J. Hadlee 18-3-50-0;
J.R. Rutherford 6-1-9-0.

England

Batting and Fielding	M	I	NO	HS	R	Avge	100s	50s	Ct/St
M.D. Moxon	3	4	1	99	208	69.33	–	2	4
B.C. Broad	3	4	0	110	204	51.00	1	1	–
M.W. Gatting	3	4	1	42	106	35.33	–	–	–
J.E. Emburey	3	3	0	45	106	35.33	–	–	–
R.T. Robinson	3	4	0	70	126	31.50	–	2	–
P.W. Jarvis	2	5	1	14	34	17.00	–	–	–
G.R. Dilley	3	3	2	8*	17	17.00	–	–	–
B.N. French	3	3	0	13	23	7.66	–	–	11/–
D.J. Capel	3	3	0	11	16	5.33	–	–	3

Also batted: C.W.J. Athey (1 match) 22, 19, 1ct; P.A.J. DeFreitas (2 matches) 4, 16, 1ct;
N.H. Fairbrother (2 matches) 1, 2ct; N.V. Radford (1 match) 8.
E.E. Hemmings played in one match but did not bat.

Bowling	O	M	R	W	Avge	Best	5wI	10wM
G.R. Dilley	104.5	34	210	15	14.00	6-38	2	–
P.W. Jarvis	98	31	201	6	33.50	2-43	–	–
D.J. Capel	109.2	22	274	5	54.80	2-57	–	–

Also bowled: P.A.J. DeFreitas 91.1-33-175-4; J.E. Emburey 133.5-48-236-3;
N.H. Fairbrother 2-0-9-0; M.W. Gatting 23-5-61-2; E.E. Hemmings 45-15-107-0;
M.D. Moxon 2-0-3-0; N.V. Radford 50-8-132-1.

Statistical Highlights of the Tests

1st Test, Christchurch. An hour lost to bad light helped New Zealand bat all the final day to save the match. Hadlee, hoping to take the record 374th Test wicket, bowled 18 overs and had to leave the field with a calf injury, which prevented him from bowling again in the series. He thus remains equal with Botham on the all-time list. Morrison took five wickets for the 1st time and Dilley for the 4th, both returning their best Test match figures. Wright batted in a Test for the 100th time in the 2nd innings. Broad scored his 6th Test hundred, his first against New Zealand. Dilley was fined £250 for dissent when an appeal for a catch was turned down by Umpire Aldridge.

2nd Test, Auckland. Greatbach became the fourth New Zealand batsman to score a hundred on his debut. The others – J.E. Mills, B.R. Taylor, and R.E. Redmond – were also left-handed batsmen. Wright scored his 7th Test hundred, his 3rd against England. In the 2nd innings, he reached 1,000 runs against England when he scored 2, becoming the 3rd to do this for New Zealand (B.E. Congdon and B. Sutcliffe). Dilley took five wickets for the 5th time. Moxon became the 9th England batsman to be dismissed for 99 in a Test. He was the 3rd batsman in a Test against New Zealand, but the 1st England player. Smith completed the wicket-keeper double of 1,000 runs and 100 dismissals when he reached 19 in the 2nd innings.

3rd Test, Wellington. Cyclone Bola washed out the last two days to lengthen New Zealand's unbroken home series record to nine years. England registered their 6th consecutive draw, and had now been 13 Tests without a win. Wright captained New Zealand for the 1st time. Crowe extended his record of eight Test hundreds to nine, with his highest score and 3rd hundred against England. Crowe ended the series with 2,774 runs, having moved into 5th place for New Zealand when he passed Sutcliffe (2,727) on 97. Rutherford scored his 1st Test hundred, having scored only 224 runs in his previous 13 Tests. There were two record partnerships for New Zealand against England – 155 for the 4th between Crowe and Greatbach and 134 for the 6th between Radford and Bracewell.

One-Day Internationals
9 March at Carisbrook Park, Dunedin. ENGLAND beat NEW ZEALAND by 5 wickets. Toss: New Zealand. New Zealand 204 (49.4 overs) (J.G. Wright 70; J.E. Emburey 9.4-0-39-4). England 207-5 (49.2 overs) (N.H. Fairbrother 50, D.J. Capel 48, M.W. Gatting 42). Award: J.G. Wright (70).

12 March at Lancaster Park, Christchurch. ENGLAND beat NEW ZEALAND by 6 wickets. Toss: England. New Zealand 186-8 (45 overs) (J.G. Bracewell 43, J.G. Wright 43, C.M. Kuggeleijn 40). England 188-4 (42.5 overs) (B.C. Broad 56, R.T. Robinson 44). Award: B.C. Broad (56, 1ct).

16 March at McLean Park, Napier. NEW ZEALAND beat ENGLAND by 7 wickets. Toss: New Zealand. England 219 (47.3 overs) (B.C. Broad 106; M.C. Snedden 8.3-0-34-4). New Zealand 223-3 (46.3 overs) (J.G. Wright 101, M.J. Greatbach 64*). Award: J.G. Wright (101).

19 March at Eden Park, Auckland. NEW ZEALAND beat ENGLAND by 4 wickets. Toss: New Zealand. England 208 (50 overs) (N.H. Fairbrother 54, M.W. Gatting 48). New Zealand 211-6 (49.2 overs) (A.H. Jones 90, J.G. Wright 47; P.W. Jarvis 9.2-1-33-4). Award: A.H. Jones (90).

England Tour of New Zealand and Australia 1987-88

First-Class Matches: Played 8; Won 2, Lost 1, Drawn 5
All Matches: Played 13; Won 4, Lost 4, Drawn 5

First-Class Averages

Batting and Fielding	M	I	NO	HS	R	Avge	100	50	Ct/St
B.C. Broad	7	9	1	139	537	67.12	3	2	1
M.W. Gatting	7	9	3	97*	364	60.66	–	3	1
M.D. Moxon	8	10	2	117*	482	60.25	1	3	7
R.T. Robinson	7	11	1	166	489	48.90	1	3	2
P.W. Jarvis	5	5	3	36*	85	42.50	–	–	–
J.E. Emburey	6	6	1	45	193	38.60	–	–	5
N.H. Fairbrother	5	6	2	46	126	31.50	–	–	3
C.W.J. Athey	6	9	0	60	200	22.22	–	1	6
B.N. French	6	5	1	47	88	22.00	–	–	16/–
G.R. Dilley	7	5	3	13	30	15.00	–	–	1
C.J. Richards	2	3	1	20*	30	15.00	–	–	4/–
D.J. Capel	7	7	1	21	88	14.66	–	–	4
P.A.J. DeFreitas	4	5	0	41	64	12.80	–	–	2

Also batted: N.A. Foster (3 matches) 27*, 19, 3ct; E.E. Hemmings (4 matches) 8*;
N.V. Radford (4 matches) 23, 8, 3ct.

Bowling	O	M	R	W	Avge	Best	5wI	10wM
G.R. Dilley	201.1	49	506	23	22.00	6-38	2	–
D.J. Capel	196.2	45	476	15	31.73	3-50	–	–
N.V. Radford	134	32	351	11	31.90	4-24	–	–
P.W. Jarvis	159	43	410	12	34.16	4-24	–	–
N.A. Foster	86	23	226	6	37.66	2-23	–	–
P.A.J. DeFreitas	150.1	40	383	8	47.87	2-27	–	–
J.E. Emburey	239.2	73	505	7	72.14	1-10	–	–
E.E. Hemmings	164.4	43	409	5	81.90	3-53	–	–

Also bowled: C.W.J. Athey 4-0-25-0; N.H. Fairbrother 2-0-9-0; M.W. Gatting 29.2-6-78-3;
M.D. Moxon 4-0-8-0.

India v West Indies

The four-match series was the third in succession that the West Indies, so irresistibly dominant for most of the 1980s, could do no more than draw. West Indies comfortably held their lead, gained in the opening Test, until they were trapped on a hopelessly underprepared pitch in the last, in which they were put to rout by India's new legspinning discovery Narendra Hirwani, a teenager who plays in glasses.

The absence from the West Indies attack of Marshall and Garner, who both declined the tour, proved no hardship during the first two Tests, in which the pitches, at least for some duration, offered encouragement to the pace bowlers. Patterson, Walsh, and Davis were remarkable for the accuracy of their aim on or around the offstump.

Patterson was a major force in the first two Tests, taking 14 wickets, including two sets of five. Davis, swinging the ball, assisted in India's destruction in the first innings at Delhi, and when conditions were less favourable in the second, Walsh took five wickets. Although never explosively dangerous, Walsh was the outstanding bowler of the series and for courage and perseverance deserved his aggregate of 26 wickets. Making his debut, Winston Benjamin looked hostile in the first Test and could have left a bigger mark on the series. But for the remainder of the Tests, West Indies restricted their pace attack to three bowlers.

The West Indies batting did not look as impressive as in the past. Because of limited opportunities to make adjustments after the World Cup competition, their batsmen took time to come to terms with the demands of Test match batsmanship, as indeed did their opponents.

The first Test could have gone either way but for a sound, responsible hundred in the second innings by Richards. Greenidge was often unlucky, but made 141 in the third Test, in which Logie and Hooper also got centuries. Hooper, playing in only his second Test, looked an outstanding batsman in the making. Richardson was seldom brilliant, but always dogged and determined.

India, in their first series of the post-Gavaskar era, were heavily reliant on their new captain, Vengsarkar. Ironically, though, the Test India won was the one in which Vengsarkar, the leading run-getter on both sides, did not play, having fractured his hand in the third. Arun Lal worked diligently at opening the innings and a raucous century by Kapil Dev made victory more easily attainable in the final Test.

After Delhi, where the pitch was amenable and the West Indies batting at its most suspect, India looked thoroughly incapable of bowling them out. Even on the dreadful turner at Madras, Ayub, the new off-spinner, was nothing more than a run-saver. However, Hirwani, in taking 16 wickets on debut, fully exploited the West Indians' misgivings about the pitch and their traditional vulnerability against leg spin.

West Indies were runaway winners in the tediously lengthy one-day series, India managing to beat them only once in seven encounters. In fact, the gap between the sides widened with each succeeding match.

India v West Indies 1987-88 1st Test

West Indies won by 5 wickets
Played at Feroz Shah Kotla, New Delhi, 25, 26, 28, 29 November
Toss: India. Umpires: D.N. Dotiwala & V.K. Ramaswamy
Debuts: India – Arshad Ayub, S.V. Manjrekar. West Indies – W.K.M. Benjamin, W.W. Davis

India

K. Srikkanth	c Dujon b Patterson	0	c Harper b Patterson		5
Arun Lal	c Greenidge b Davis	20	c Benjamin b Walsh		40
R. Lamba	b Davis	1	b Patterson		0
D.B. Vengsarkar*	c Harper b Davis	10	c Greenidge b Walsh		102
R.J. Shastri	c Richardson b Benjamin	6	c Harper b Patterson		4
S.V. Manjrekar	c Harper b Patterson	5	retired hurt		10
Kapil Dev	c Dujon b Walsh	7	lbw b Benjamin		44
K.S. More†	not out	12	c Dujon b Walsh		49
Arshad Ayub	c Harper b Patterson	7	lbw b Walsh		17
C. Sharma	c Richardson b Patterson	0	b Walsh		24
Maninder Singh	b Patterson	0	not out		2
Extras	(LB1, W3, NB3)	7	(B17, LB7, W5, NB1)		30
		75			**327**

West Indies

C.G. Greenidge	lbw b Kapil Dev	0	lbw b Ayub	33
D.L. Haynes	c Lamba b Sharma	45	hit wicket b Ayub	27
R.B. Richardson	lbw b Kapil Dev	4	c Lamba b Kapil Dev	31
I.V.A. Richards*	c More b Sharma	9	(5) not out	109
A.L. Logie	lbw b Sharma	4	(6) lbw b Ayub	46
P.J.L. Dujon†	c Lamba b Kapil Dev	5	(7) not out	12
R.A. Harper	run out	4		
W.W. Davis	c & b Sharma	6		
W.K.M. Benjamin	b Ayub	19	(4) c sub (C.S. Pandit) b Ayub	1
C.A. Walsh	c Lamba b Sharma	16		
B.P. Patterson	not out	5		
Extras	(B3, LB1, W1, NB5)	10	(B1, LB9, NB7)	17
		127	(5 wkts)	**276**

In India's 2nd innings S.V. Manjrekar retired hurt at 105-4.

West Indies	O	M	R	W	O	M	R	W	Fall of Wickets				
										I	WI	I	WI
Patterson	8.5	1	24	5	29	6	100	3	Wkt	1st	1st	2nd	2nd
Davis	11	2	20	3	20	3	60	0	1st	0	0	6	62
Benjamin	7	0	17	1	23	3	76	1	2nd	7	4	6	69
Walsh	4	0	13	1	29.3	9	54	5	3rd	32	13	66	91
Harper					12	3	13	0	4th	42	17	82	111
									5th	42	25	178	203
India	O	M	R	W	O	M	R	W	6th	52	29	274	–
Kapil Dev	18	8	41	3	20	8	44	1	7th	58	49	277	–
Sharma	13.1	2	55	5	11	1	44	0	8th	75	102	318	–
Maninder	7	3	13	0	20	4	75	4	9th	75	122	327	–
Ayub	9	4	14	1	25	4	72	4	10th	75	127	–	–
Shastri					9	2	30	0					
Arun Lal					0.3	0	1	0					

India v West Indies 1987-88 2nd Test

Match Drawn
Played at Wankhede Stadium, Bombay, 11, 12 (np), 13, 15, 16 December
Toss: India. Umpires: R.B. Gupta and P.D. Reporter
Debuts: West Indies – C.L. Hooper

India

K. Srikkanth	b Walsh	71	b Patterson	65
Arun Lal	c Richardson b Walsh	3	c Greenidge b Patterson	1
M. Amarnath	c Butts b Walsh	1	c Richards b Walsh	8
D.B. Vengsarkar*	st Dujon b Butts	51	not out	40
M. Azharuddin	run out	34	c Davis b Patterson	5
R.J. Shastri	c Richards b Davis	0	c Butts b Davis	5
Kapil Dev	c Greenidge b Butts	47	c Dujon b Patterson	5
K.S. More†	c Dujon b Patterson	9	c Richards b Patterson	0
Arshad Ayub	c Richards b Walsh	8	b Walsh	18
C. Sharma	not out	22	b Walsh	0
Maninder Singh	c Richardson b Walsh	0	c Richardson b Walsh	0
Extras	(B4, LB15, NB16)	35	(B1, LB5, W8, NB12)	26
		281		**173**

West Indies

C.G. Greenidge	c Arun Lal b Shastri	15	c Kapil Dev b Sharma	2
D.L. Haynes	c sub (C.S. Pandit) b Shastri	58	not out	0
R.B. Richardson	lbw b Sharma	89	not out	0
I.V.A. Richards*	b Maninder	37		
A.L. Logie	run out (Shastri)	0		
C.L. Hooper	lbw b Kapil Dev	37		
P.J.L. Dujon†	c & b Shastri	14		
C.G. Butts	c More b Shastri	18		
W.W. Davis	c & b Sharma	30		
C.A. Walsh	c Srikkanth b Sharma	5		
B.P. Patterson	not out	21		
Extras	(LB8, W1, NB4)	13	(LB1, NB1)	2
		337	(1 wkt)	**4**

West Indies	O	M	R	W	O	M	R	W
Patterson	17	3	78	1	16	1	68	5
Davis	15	0	71	1	15	1	59	1
Walsh	17.4	2	54	5	14	2	40	4
Butts	18	5	59	2	1	1	0	0
India	O	M	R	W	O	M	R	W
Kapil Dev	25	8	72	1	1	0	2	0
Sharma	13	1	64	3	1	0	1	1
Ayub	20	1	54	0				
Maninder	17	5	68	1				
Shastri	28.3	9	71	4				

Fall of Wickets

	I	WI	I	WI
Wkt	1st	1st	2nd	2nd
1st	60	55	16	3
2nd	74	99	58	–
3rd	85	146	105	–
4th	157	146	112	–
5th	162	210	126	–
6th	222	258	132	–
7th	241	258	132	–
8th	247	300	173	–
9th	271	308	173	–
10th	281	337	173	–

India v West Indies 1987-88 3rd Test

Match Drawn
Played at Eden Gardens, Calcutta, 26, 27, 28, 30, 31 December
Toss: West Indies. Umpires: R.B. Gupta and P.D. Reporter
Debuts: nil

West Indies

C.G. Greenidge	c More b Kapil Dev	141	c sub (Sanjeev Sharma) b Shastri	69
D.L. Haynes	c Srikkanth b Kapil Dev	5	c and b Shastri	47
R.B. Richardson	c Azharuddin b Shastri	51	not out	8
I.V.A. Richards*	c Kapil Dev b Sharma	68		
A.L. Logie	c and b Maninder	101	(4) not out	20
C.L. Hooper	not out	100		
P.J.L. Dujon†	not out	40		
C.G. Butts	did not bat			
W.W. Davis	”			
C.A. Walsh	”			
B.P. Patterson	”			
Extras	(B2, LB12, NB10)	24	(B4, LB2, NB7)	13
	(5 wkts dec)	530	(2 wkts)	157

India

K. Srikkanth	c Dujon b Walsh	23
Arun Lal	lbw b Walsh	93
M. Amarnath	b Davis	43
D.B. Vengsarkar*	retired hurt	102
M. Azharuddin	c Logie b Walsh	60
R.J. Shastri	b Davis	47
Kapil Dev	lbw b Davis	4
K.S. More†	c Richardson b Richards	44
Arshad Ayub	c Richardson b Patterson	57
C. Sharma	b Walsh	27
Maninder Singh	not out	1
Extras	(B12, LB25, NB27)	64
		565

India	O	M	R	W	O	M	R	W
Kapil Dev	28	6	103	2	10	2	19	0
Sharma	15.1	0	80	1	4	0	24	0
Maninder Singh	36.5	5	111	1	16	2	43	0
Arshad Ayub	46	5	146	0	14	5	34	0
Shastri	22	4	60	1	10	3	13	2
Amarnath	3.5	0	16	0	4	0	11	0
Srikkanth					3	0	7	0
Arun Lal					1	1	0	0

West Indies	O	M	R	W
Patterson	22.2	0	107	1
Walsh	29	3	136	4
Davis	27	3	84	3
Butts	50	13	122	0
Richards	24	6	39	1
Hooper	20	5	40	0

Fall of Wickets

	WI	I	WI
Wkt	1st	1st	2nd
1st	13	56	114
2nd	160	152	129
3rd	284	201	–
4th	288	305	–
5th	457	403	–
6th	–	410	–
7th	–	505	–
8th	–	553	–
9th	–	565	–
10th	–	–	–

India v West Indies 1987-88 4th Test

India won by 255 runs
Played at Chidambaram Stadium, Chepauk, Madras, 11, 12, 14, 15 January
Toss: India. Umpires: R.B. Gupta and P.D. Reporter
Debuts: India – N. Hirwani, W.V. Raman, and A. Sharma. West Indies – P.V. Simmons

India

K. Srikkanth	c Davis b Walsh	23	lbw b Davis	17
Arun Lal	c Logie b Hooper	69	lbw b Walsh	1
M. Amarnath	c Dujon b Walsh	3	(4) c Richardson b Walsh	1
W.V. Raman	c Dujon b Davis	9	(3) c Dujon b Walsh	83
M. Azharuddin	c Haynes b Hooper	47	c Davis b Richards	39
A. Sharma	lbw b Richards	30	lbw b Patterson	23
Kapil Dev	c Richards b Walsh	109	lbw b Patterson	5
R.J. Shastri*	b Davis	23	not out	20
K.S. More†	b Davis	17	c Dujon b Walsh	0
Arshad Ayub	not out	23	not out	3
N. Hirwani	c Richardson b Davis	1		
Extras	(B15, LB4, NB9)	28	(B8, LB7, NB10)	25
		382	(8 wkts dec)	**217**

West Indies

D.L. Haynes	c Kapil Dev b Shastri	13	lbw b Hirwani	6
P.V. Simmons	c and b Kapil Dev	8	c Amarnath b Hirwani	14
R.B. Richardson	c Azharuddin b Hirwani	36	c Amarnath b Ayub	7
I.V.A. Richards*	b Hirwani	68	c Kapil Dev b Hirwani	4
A.L. Logie	c Azharuddin b Hirwani	12	st More b Hirwani	67
C.L. Hooper	lbw b Hirwani	2	st More b Hirwani	8
P.J.L. Dujon†	st More b Hirwani	24	st More b Hirwani	2
C.G. Butts	c Raman b Hirwani	0	c Sharma b Hirwani	38
W.W. Davis	lbw b Hirwani	1	st More b Hirwani	7
C.A. Walsh	c More b Hirwani	8	st More b Raman	0
B.P. Patterson	not out	0	not out	0
Extras	(B8, LB2, NB2)	12	(B4, LB1, NB2)	7
		184		**160**

West Indies	O	M	R	W	O	M	R	W
Patterson	15	1	62	0	9	2	17	2
Walsh	27	3	85	3	16	5	55	4
Davis	18.1	0	76	4	6	0	20	1
Butts	24	4	62	0	21	1	62	0
Richards	8	1	36	1	18	4	28	1
Hooper	12	3	42	2	6	1	20	0

India	O	M	R	W	O	M	R	W
Kapil Dev	7	0	20	1	4	3	8	0
Amarnath	3	0	8	0	2	0	7	0
Shastri	13	6	29	1	5	0	25	0
Arshad Ayub	28	10	47	0	14	5	33	1
Hirwani	18.3	3	61	8	15.2	3	75	8
Sharma	4	0	9	0				
Raman					1	0	7	1

Fall of Wickets

	I	WI	I	WI
Wkt	1st	1st	2nd	2nd
1st	30	17	3	22
2nd	38	47	36	24
3rd	64	98	37	33
4th	153	128	124	41
5th	156	132	185	61
6th	269	163	185	79
7th	313	175	190	138
8th	342	175	194	153
9th	369	183	–	160
10th	382	184	–	160

Test Match Averages:
India v West Indies 1987-88

India

Batting and Fielding

	M	I	NO	HS	R	Avge	100s	50s	Ct/St
D.B. Vengsarkar	3	5	2	102*	305	101.66	2	1	–
M. Azharuddin	3	5	0	60	185	37.00	–	1	3
Arun Lal	4	7	0	93	227	32.42	–	2	1
Kapil Dev	4	7	0	109	221	31.57	1	–	5
K. Srikkanth	4	7	0	71	204	29.14	–	2	2
Arshad Ayub	4	7	2	57	133	26.60	–	1	–
K.S. More	4	7	1	49	131	21.83	–	–	4/6
C. Sharma	3	5	1	27	73	18.25	–	–	2
R.J. Shastri	4	7	1	47	105	17.50	–	–	2
M. Amarnath	3	5	0	43	56	11.20	–	–	2
Maninder Singh	3	5	2	2*	3	1.00	–	–	1

Also batted: N. Hirwani (1 match) 1; R. Lamba (1 match) 1, 0, 4ct; S.V. Manjrekar (1 match) 5, 10 retired hurt; W.V. Raman (1 match) 9, 83, 1ct; A. Sharma (1 match) 30, 23, 1ct.

Bowling

	O	M	R	W	Avge	Best	5wI	10wM
N. Hirwani	33.5	6	136	16	8.50	8-61	2	1
C. Sharma	57.2	4	268	10	26.80	5-55	1	–
R.J. Shastri	87.3	24	228	8	28.50	4-71	–	–
Kapil Dev	113	34	309	8	38.62	3-41	–	–
Arshad Ayub	156	34	400	6	66.66	4-72	–	–

Also bowled: M. Amarnath 12.5-0-42-0; Arun Lal 1.3-1-1-0; Maninder Singh 96.5-19-310-2; W.V. Raman 1-0-7-1; A. Sharma 4-0-9-0; K. Srikkanth 3-0-7-0.

West Indies

Batting and Fielding

	M	I	NO	HS	R	Avge	100s	50s	Ct/St
I.V.A. Richards	4	6	1	109*	295	59.00	1	2	5
C.L. Hooper	3	4	1	100*	147	49.00	1	–	–
C.G. Greenidge	3	6	0	141	260	43.33	1	1	4
A.L. Logie	4	7	1	101	250	41.66	1	1	2
R.B. Richardson	4	8	2	89	226	37.66	–	2	9
D.L. Haynes	4	8	1	58	201	28.71	–	1	1
P.J.L. Dujon	4	6	2	40*	97	24.25	–	–	10/1
C.G. Butts	3	3	0	38	56	18.66	–	–	2
W.W. Davis	4	5	0	30	45	9.00	–	–	3
C.A. Walsh	4	4	0	16	29	7.25	–	–	–

Also batted: W.K.M. Benjamin (1 match) 19, 1ct; R.A. Harper (1 match) 4, 5ct; B.P. Patterson (4 matches) 5*, 21*, 0*, 0*; P.V. Simmons (1 match) 8, 14.

Bowling

	O	M	R	W	Avge	Best	5wI	10wM
C.A. Walsh	137.1	24	437	26	16.80	5-54	2	–
B.P. Patterson	117.1	14	456	17	26.82	5-24	2	–
W.W. Davis	112.1	9	390	13	30.00	4-76	–	–

Also bowled: W.K.M. Benjamin 30-3-93-2; C.G. Butts 114-24-305-2; R.A. Harper 12-3-13-0; C.L. Hooper 38-9-102-2; I.V.A. Richards 50-11-103-3.

Statistical Highlights of the Tests

1st Test, Delhi. Vengsarkar captained India in his 96th Test. In the 2nd innings he scored his 16th Test hundred, his 5th against West Indies. At 39 he reached 6,000 Test runs, the 18th player and 3rd Indian to do so. India's 1st innings total was their lowest in a home Test and their lowest in any Test against West Indies. West Indies' 1st innings total was their lowest against India. Richards scored his 21st Test hundred, his 7th against India. The innings lasted only 114 balls, with 13 fours. Patterson took five wickets for the 1st time and Walsh for the 2nd time, during which he passed 50 Test wickets in only his 14th Test. Chetan Sharma took five wickets for the 4th time. The match was completed on the fourth day, 18 wickets having fallen on the first.

2nd Test, Bombay. Nine hours' play was lost in all on the first two days, including the entire first day. It was the first time a complete day has been lost at Bombay. The Indian 2nd innings did not start until the fifth morning, and West Indies had only 11 overs in which to score the 118 required for a win. Walsh took five wickets for the 3rd time, his best Test bowling, and Patterson for the 2nd time.

3rd Test, Calcutta. Greenidge and Haynes opened the innings for the 100th time in Tests in the 2nd innings. Greenidge scored his 14th Test hundred, his 4th against India. Logie scored his 2nd Test hundred, and Hooper, in his 2nd Test, became the third youngest West Indies player to score a Test hundred. Vengsarkar scored his 17th Test hundred, his 6th against West Indies, before his left hand was broken by Davis. The captaincy was taken over by Shastri. 64 extras in the Indian innings was four short of the record set by West Indies against Pakistan at Bridgetown in 1976-77.

4th Test, Madras. Hirwani had the most successful debut in Test history – 16-136 – eclipsing Massie's 16-137 against England at Lord's in 1972. He is only the 4th player to take 8 wickets in an innings on a Test debut. More set a new record with five stumpings in an innings and six for the match. Kapil Dev scored his 6th Test hundred, his 3rd against West Indies, from only 105 balls. Shastri, captaining India for the first time, recorded the second best win in Indian Test history.

One-Day Internationals

8 December at Vidharba CA Ground, Nagpur. WEST INDIES beat INDIA by 10 runs. Toss: West Indies. West Indies 203-8 (50 overs) (C.L. Hooper 57*). India 193 (44.4 overs) (Kapil Dev 87); B.P. Patterson 9.4-0-29-6). Award: B.P. Patterson (9.4-0-29-6).

23 December at Nehru Stadium, Gauhati. WEST INDIES beat INDIA by 52 runs. Toss: India. West Indies 187-7 (45 overs) (I.V.A. Richards 41). India 135 (41.3 overs) (C.A. Walsh 7.3-2-16-4). Award: I.V.A. Richards (41, 8-0-37-1, and 1ct).

2 January at Eden Gardens, Calcutta. INDIA beat WEST INDIES by 55 runs. Toss: India. India 222-7 (45 overs) (M. Amarnath 70, Arun Lal 51, M. Azharuddin 44). West Indies 166 (41.5 overs) (C.G. Greenidge 44). Award: M. Amarnath (70, 9-0-46-1, and 1ct).

5 January at Rajkot. WEST INDIES beat INDIA by 6 wickets. Toss: India. India 221-7 (43 overs) (W.V. Raman 95). West Indies 225-4 (40.1 overs) (I.V.A. Richards 110*, D.L. Haynes 49). Award: I.V.A. Richards (110*, 8-0-42-3, and 1ct).

19 January at Mayur Stadium, Faridabad. WEST INDIES beat INDIA by 4 wickets. Toss: West Indies. India 230-6 (50 overs) (M. Amarnath 100*, Kapil Dev 45). West Indies 231-6 (49.1 overs) (P.V. Simmons 67, R.B. Richardson 49). Award: M. Amarnath (100* and 6-0-14-0).

West Indies Tour of India 1987-88

First-Class Matches: Played 7; Won 2, Lost 1, Drawn 3, No Play 1
All Matches: Played 14; Won 8, Lost 2, Drawn 3, No Play 1

First-Class Averages

Batting and Fielding	M	I	NO	HS	R	Avge	100	50	Ct/St
I.V.A. Richards	6	8	1	138	439	62.71	2	2	5
C.G. Greenidge	5	9	0	174	529	58.77	2	2	4
R.B. Richardson	7	12	2	147	456	45.60	1	2	10
P.J.L. Dujon	6	9	3	123	269	44.83	1	–	12/1
A.L. Logie	6	10	1	101	375	41.66	1	3	3
C.L. Hooper	5	6	1	100*	189	37.80	1	–	6
D.L. Haynes	5	9	1	70	271	33.87	–	2	1
R.A. Harper	3	4	0	82	112	28.00	–	1	8
P.V. Simmons	4	6	0	72	151	25.16	–	1	4
C.G. Butts	6	6	0	47	121	20.16	–	–	3
C.A. Walsh	5	5	0	50	79	15.80	–	1	–
W.W. Davis	7	8	1	30	89	12.71	–	–	4

Also batted: E.A.E. Baptiste (2 matches) 75*, 22; W.K.M. Benjamin (3 matches) 19
7*, 37*, 2ct; B.P. Patterson (5 matches) 11*, 5*, 21*, 0*, 0*;
D. Williams (2 matches) 33, 10, 2ct.

Bowling	O	M	R	W	Avge	Best	5wI	10wM
E.A.E. Baptiste	60.2	13	172	12	14.33	7-70	1	1
C.A. Walsh	147.1	24	472	29	16.27	5-54	2	–
I.V.A. Richards	59	16	131	5	26.20	1-8	–	–
B.P. Patterson	135.1	21	505	19	26.57	5-24	2	–
W.W. Davis	161.1	17	563	18	31.27	4-76	–	–
W.K.M. Benjamin	75	14	223	6	37.16	2-29	–	–

Also bowled: C.G. Butts 174.1-27-528-4; R.A. Harper 44-11-124-4; C.L. Hooper 58-12-175-3.

22nd January at Roop Singh Stadium, Gwalior. WEST INDIES beat INDIA by 73 runs. Toss: India.
West Indies 278-6 (50 overs) (C.L. Hooper 113*, A.L. Logie 54). India 205 (41 overs) (R.L. Shastri 73*,
Kapil Dev 52; B.P. Patterson 8-0-29-4). Award: C.L. Hooper (113*).

25 January at Trivandrum. WEST INDIES beat INDIA by 9 wickets. Toss: West Indies. India 239-8
(45 overs) (K. Srikkanth 101, M. Amarnath 56). West Indies 241-1 (42.5 overs) (P.V. Simmons 104*,
C.G. Greenidge 84). Award: P.V. Simmons (104*).

Man of the Series: I.V.A Richards.

Note: The match at Ahmedabad on 7th January was not an official one-day international as part of the
series.

Australia v New Zealand

Australia followed their unexpected triumph in the World Cup with their first Test-series win in four years – a pulsating 1-0 victory in a three-match home series against New Zealand. Australia had not won a series since their 2-0 defeat of Pakistan in Australia in 1983-84, the last summer of Greg Chappell, Dennis Lillee, and Rod Marsh.

This time, Australia strode to a nine-wicket win inside four days at Brisbane, had slightly the better of a batsman-dominated draw at Adelaide, and somehow managed to scramble a draw from the jaws of victory, then seemingly certain defeat, at Melbourne. Winning the toss at Brisbane and ordering New Zealand to bat first on a cloudy, breezy morning and on a bouncy pitch proved to be the most crucial stroke of the keenly fought series.

Richard Hadlee, 36, took 18 wickets at 19.61 off 156 overs to equal Ian Botham's Test record of 373 wickets, and, of course, was named Player of the Series. Hadlee's heroic 10-wicket haul in the third Test threatened to inspire New Zealand to the win they needed to retain the Trans-Tasman Trophy, until Australia's last-wicket pair, Craig McDermott and Michael Whitney, survived the last 30 balls to force a draw, with Australia just 17 runs short of their target of 247.

Hadlee was easily *the* personality of the Australian summer. Respecting his supreme bowling skills almost as much as the Australian batsmen, spectators reacted noisily and at times distastefully to his on-field swagger and vigorous appeals – and to his forthright, sometimes provocative, comments in a regular, ghosted newspaper column.

New Zealand's other superstar, batsman Martin Crowe, made 396 runs at 66 and, as always, was a joy to watch. Sadly, his older brother, Jeff, a competent captain and a fine ambassador, endured a wretched personal tour, managing only 78 runs (avg 13) in the Tests.

Rebuilding a team after the retirements of Bruce Edgar, John Reid, Jeremy Coney, Lance Cairns, and Stephen Boock, New Zealand were heartened by the batting impact of Andrew Jones, who proved a surprisingly effective number three after he had revealed some awkward, unorthodox methods against short-pitched bowling in the first Test. Bustling Danny Morrison showed potential as an opening bowler and left-hand opening batsman John Wright and off-spinning all-rounder John Bracewell were as determined and as competitive as ever.

The Australians were encouraged most by the successful return to Test ranks of opening batsman David Boon, who made a marvellous match winning century at Brisbane, the mature, energetic fast bowling of young Craig McDermott, the consistent batting contributions of leg-spin bowler Peter Sleep, and the startling debut at Melbourne of exciting Victorian all-rounder Tony Dodemaide.

Allan Border, the Australian captain, made a 10-hour double-century at Adelaide, his first in 159 Test innings. Border's 205 lifted his aggregate to 7,131 (avg 53.27) in 91 Tests and pushed him ahead of Greg Chappell and Sir Donald Bradman as Australia's most prolific run-getter.

Australia v New Zealand 1987-88 1st Test

Australia won by 9 wickets
Played at Woolloongabba, Brisbane, 4, 5, 6, 7 December
Toss: Australia. Umpires: A.R. Crafter and M.W. Johnson
Debuts: Australia – M.R.J. Veletta; New Zealand – D.K. Morrison

New Zealand

K.R. Rutherford	c Valetta b Reid	0	(2) c Dyer b McDermott	2
J.G. Wright	c Dyer b Hughes	38	(1) lbw b Reid	15
A.H. Jones	b McDermott	4	c Border b Reid	45
M.D. Crowe	c Waugh b Hughes	67	c Jones b Hughes	23
J.J. Crowe*	lbw b Waugh	16	lbw b Reid	12
D.N. Patel	c Dyer b McDermott	17	c Dyer b Hughes	62
R.J. Hadlee	c Boon b Hughes	8	c Marsh b McDermott	24
J.G. Bracewell	c Valetta b McDermott	11	c Dyer b McDermott	0
I.D.S. Smith†	lbw b Reid	2	c Veletta b Reid	9
D.K. Morrison	c Waugh b McDermott	0	c Dyer b Waugh	2
E.J. Chatfield	not out	0	not out	1
Extras	(B1, LB7, W4, NB11)	23	(B6, LB1, W1, NB9)	17
		186		**212**

Australia

G.R. Marsh	c Bracewell b Hadlee	25	(2) not out	31
D.C. Boon	run out (M. Crowe/Smith)	143	(1) lbw b Bracewell	24
D.M. Jones	b Hadlee	2	not out	38
A.R. Border*	lbw b Morrison	9		
M.R.J. Veletta	c Rutherford b Bracewell	4		
S.R. Waugh	c Jones b Morrison	21		
P.R. Sleep	c & b Bracewell	39		
G.J. Dyer†	lbw b Hadlee	8		
C.J. McDermott	c Wright b Morrison	22		
M.G. Hughes	c Smith b Morrison	5		
B.A. Reid	not out	8		
Extras	(B3, LB5, W2, NB9)	19	(LB1, W1, NB2)	4
		305	(1 wkt)	**97**

Australia	O	M	R	W	O	M	R	W
Reid	25	10	40	2	25	6	53	4
McDermott	22.2	6	43	4	21	2	79	3
Hughes	18	5	40	3	17	7	57	2
Waugh	22	9	35	1	2	1	2	1
Sleep	6	1	20	0	14	5	14	0

New Zealand	O	M	R	W	O	M	R	W
Hadlee	31	5	95	3	8	3	14	0
Morrison	28	7	86	4	8	0	32	0
Chatfield	34	11	58	0				
Bracewell	24.5	3	58	2	13	3	32	1
Patel					3.1	0	18	0

Fall of Wickets

Wkt	NZ 1st	A 1st	NZ 2nd	A 2nd
1st	0	65	18	37
2nd	28	72	20	–
3rd	80	110	66	–
4th	133	131	103	–
5th	143	219	104	–
6th	153	219	142	–
7th	175	250	142	–
8th	180	286	152	–
9th	181	291	204	–
10th	186	305	212	–

Australia v New Zealand 1987-88 2nd Test

Match Drawn
Played at Adelaide Oval, 11, 12, 13, 14, 15 December
Toss: New Zealand. Umpires: R.C. Bailhache and S.G. Randell
Debuts: Australia – T.B.A. May

New Zealand

J.J. Crowe*	c Veletta b Reid	0	c Boon b May	19
J.G. Wright	c Waugh b May	45	b McDermott	8
A.H. Jones	run out (McDermott)	150	c Border b Sleep	64
M.D. Crowe	c sub (M.G. Hughes) b Sleep	137	c Border b Sleep	8
D.N. Patel	c Marsh b McDermott	35	c Boon b May	40
E.J. Gray	c Boon b McDermott	23	c Border b May	14
R.J. Hadlee	c and b Jones	36	(9) not out	3
J.G. Bracewell	c Sleep b McDermott	32		
I.D.S. Smith†	not out	8	(8) c Dyer b Sleep	5
M.C. Snedden	c Veletta b McDermott	0	(7) not out	8
D.K. Morrison	did not bat			
Extras	(B3, LB7, W1, NB8)	19	(B2, LB4, NB7)	13
	(9 wkts dec)	**485**	(7 wkts)	**182**

Australia

G.R. Marsh	c Gray b Hadlee	30
D.C. Boon	b Hadlee	6
D.M. Jones	c Smith b Hadlee	0
A.R. Border*	st Smith b Bracewell	205
S.R. Waugh	lbw b Snedden	61
P.R. Sleep	c Smith b Morrison	62
M.R.J. Veletta	c sub (K.R. Rutherford) b Bracewell	10
G.J. Dyer†	run out (Jones/Hadlee)	60
C.J. McDermott	lbw b Hadlee	18
T.B.A. May	not out	14
B.R. Reid	c Smith b Hadlee	5
Extras	(B2, LB13, W1, NB9)	25
		496

Australia	O	M	R	W	O	M	R	W
Reid	7	0	21	1				
McDermott	45.5	10	135	4	10	3	29	1
Waugh	31	11	71	0	10	4	17	0
May	54	13	134	1	30	10	68	3
Sleep	34	5	109	1	32	14	61	3
Jones	3	1	5	1	3	2	1	0

New Zealand	O	M	R	W
Hadlee	42	16	68	5
Morrison	22	0	89	1
Bracewell	48	8	122	2
Snedden	32	6	89	1
Gray	44	10	102	0
Patel	7	3	11	0

Fall of Wickets

Wkt	NZ 1st	A 1st	NZ 2nd
1st	0	29	16
2nd	128	29	57
3rd	341	85	77
4th	346	201	139
5th	398	355	153
6th	405	380	170
7th	473	417	179
8th	481	451	–
9th	485	489	–
10th	–	496	–

Australia v New Zealand 1987-88 3rd Test

Match Drawn
Played at Melbourne Cricket Ground, 26, 27, 28, 29, 30 December
Toss: Australia. Umpires: A.R. Crafter and R.A. French
Debuts: Australia – A.I.C. Dodemaide

New Zealand

P.A.Horne	c Dyer b Dodemaide	7	c Boon b Dodemaide		27
J.G. Wright	c Dyer b McDermott	99	b Sleep		43
A.H. Jones	c Dyer b McDermott	40	run out (Sleep/Dodemaide/ Jones)		20
M.D. Crowe	c Veletta b McDermott	82	c Border b Dodemaide		79
J.J. Crowe*	lbw b McDermott	6	c Boon b Sleep		25
D.N. Patel	b McDermott	0	c Dyer b Dodemaide		38
J.G. Bracewell	c Dyer b Whitney	9	(8) c Veletta b Dodemaide		1
R.J. Hadlee	c Dodemaide b Whitney	11	(7) lbw b Sleep		29
I.D.S. Smith†	c Jones b Whitney	44	c Dyer b Dodemaide		12
D.K. Morrison	c Border b Whitney	0	b Dodemaide		0
E.J. Chatfield	not out	6	not out		1
Extras	(B1, LB4, NB8)	13	(B2, LB8, NB1)		11
		317			**286**

Australia

D.C. Boon	lbw b Hadlee	10	(2) c M.D. Crowe b Morrison		54
G.R. Marsh	c sub (K.R. Rutherford) b Hadlee	13	(1) c Bracewell b Hadlee		23
D.M. Jones	c Smith b Hadlee	4	c M.D. Crowe b Chatfield		8
A.R. Border*	c J.J. Crowe b Bracewell	31	lbw b Hadlee		43
M.R.J. Veletta	lbw b Hadlee	31	c Patel b Bracewell		39
S.R. Waugh	c Jones b Bracewell	55	c Patel b Chatfield		10
P.R. Sleep	lbw b Hadlee	90	lbw b Hadlee		20
G.C. Dyer†	run out (Bracewell/Smith)	21	c Smith b Hadlee		4
A.I.C. Dodemaide	c Smith b Morrison	50	lbw b Hadlee		3
C.J. McDermott	b Morrison	33	not out		10
M.R. Whitney	not out	0	not out		2
Extras	(LB8, NB11)	19	(B1, LB9, NB4)		14
		357	(9 wkts)		**230**

Bowling

Australia	O	M	R	W	O	M	R	W
McDermott	35	8	97	5	10	3	43	0
Whitney	33.3	6	92	4	20	5	45	0
Dodemaide	20	4	48	1	28.3	10	58	6
Waugh	10	1	44	0				
Sleep	12	1	31	0	26	5	107	3
Jones					8	3	23	0

New Zealand	O	M	R	W	O	M	R	W
Hadlee	44	11	109	5	31	9	67	5
Morrison	27.4	5	93	2	16	2	54	1
Chatfield	30	10	55	0	21	6	41	2
Bracewell	32	8	69	2	24	5	58	1
Patel	12	6	23	0				

Fall of Wickets

Wkt	NZ 1st	A 1st	NZ 2nd	A 2nd
1st	32	24	73	45
2nd	119	30	76	59
3rd	187	31	158	103
4th	221	78	178	147
5th	223	121	220	176
6th	254	170	272	209
7th	254	213	272	209
8th	280	293	281	216
9th	294	354	285	227
10th	317	357	286	–

Test Match Averages:
Australia v New Zealand 1987-88

Australia

Batting and Fielding	M	I	NO	HS	R	Avge	100s	50s	Ct/St
A.R. Border	3	4	0	205	288	72.00	1	–	6
P.R. Sleep	3	4	0	90	211	52.75	–	2	1
D.C. Boon	3	5	0	143	237	47.40	1	1	6
S.R. Waugh	3	4	0	61	147	36.75	–	2	3
G.R. Marsh	3	5	1	31*	122	30.50	–	–	2
C.J. McDermott	3	4	1	33	83	27.66	–	–	–
G.C. Dyer	3	4	0	60	93	23.25	–	1	13/–
M.R.J. Veletta	3	4	0	39	84	21.00	–	–	7
D.M. Jones	3	5	1	38*	52	.13.00	–	–	3

Also batted: A.I.C. Dodemaide (1 match) 50, 3, 1ct; M.G. Hughes (1 match) 5; T.B.A. May (1 match) 14*; B.A. Reid (2 matches) 8*, 5; M.R. Whitney (1 match) 0*, 2*.

Bowling	O	M	R	W	Avge	Best	5wI	10wM
A.I.C. Dodemaide	48.3	14	106	7	15.14	6-58	1	–
B.A. Reid	57	16	114	7	16.28	4-53	–	–
M.G. Hughes	35	12	97	5	19.40	3-40	–	–
C.J. McDermott	144.1	32	426	17	25.05	5-97	1	–
P.R. Sleep	124	21	342	7	48.85	3-61	–	–

Also bowled: D.M. Jones 14-6-29-1; T.B.A. May 84-23-202-4; S.R. Waugh 75-26-169-2; M.R. Whitney 53.3-11-137-4.

New Zealand

Batting and Fielding	M	I	NO	HS	R	Avge	100s	50s	Ct/St
M.D. Crowe	3	6	0	137	396	66.00	1	3	2
A.H. Jones	3	6	0	150	323	53.83	1	1	2
J.G. Wright	3	6	0	99	248	41.33	–	1	1
D.N. Patel	3	6	0	62	192	32.00	–	1	2
R.J. Hadlee	3	6	1	36	111	22.20	–	–	–
I.D.S. Smith	3	6	1	44	80	16.00	–	–	7/1
J.J. Crowe	3	6	0	25	78	13.00	–	–	1
J.G. Bracewell	3	5	0	32	53	10.60	–	–	1
D.K. Morrison	3	4	0	2	2	0.50	–	–	–

Also batted: E.J. Chatfield (2 matches) 0*, 1*, 6*, 1*; E.J. Gray (1 match) 23, 14, 1ct; P.A. Horne (1 match) 7, 27; K.R. Rutherford (1 match) 0, 2; M.C. Sneddon (1 match) 0, 8*.

Bowling	O	M	R	W	Avge	Best	5wI	10wM
R.J. Hadlee	156	44	353	18	19.61	5-67	3	1
J.G. Bracewell	141.5	27	339	8	42.37	2-58	–	–
D.K. Morrison	101.4	14	354	8	44.25	4-86	–	–

Also bowled: E.J. Chatfield 85-27-154-2; E.J. Gray 44-10-102-0; D.N. Patel 22.1-9-52-0; M.C. Snedden 32-6-89-1.

Statistical Highlights of the Tests

1st Test, Brisbane. Hadlee, in his 71st Test, passed Lillee (355 wickets) when he dismissed Marsh. Boon scored his 5th Test hundred, his 1st against New Zealand. Marsh reached 1,000 Test runs at 1 in the 2nd innings of his 15th Test. Waugh reached 500 Test runs at 18 in his 14th Test.

2nd Test, Adelaide. Border made his highest score in his 91st Test. It was his 22nd Test hundred and his 1st double hundred. The following milestones were reached during the innings: 46 (6,972) passed Hutton; 71 (6,997) passed Bradman; 74 (7,000) 2nd Australian, 8th world with 7,000 runs; 100, 22nd Test 100, 4th at Adelaide (22 = Boycott, Hammond, Cowdrey); 150, 7th score 150 in Tests; 153, highest score for Australia v New Zealand in Australia; 185 (7,111) passed G.S. Chappell, most Test runs for Australia; 197, his highest score in Test cricket; 200, his 1st 200 in Tests, the 10th 200 in Adelaide Tests; 205, 3rd highest score for Australia v New Zealand in any Test. Crowe scored his 8th Test hundred, a record for New Zealand. It was his 3rd against Australia. There were two record partnerships for New Zealand against Australia – 128, Wright and Jones (2nd), and 213, Jones and Crowe (3rd). Jones scored his 1st Test hundred in his 3rd Test. Hadlee took five wickets for the 30th time, 11th against Australia. Border and Waugh set a new 4th-wicket partnership of 116 for Australia against New Zealand. Bruce Reid injured his back after bowling his seven overs and was unable to field again during the match.

3rd Test, Melbourne. Australia, set 247 to win in almost a full day's play, were ensured a draw by their 10th-wicket pair facing the last 29 balls of the match. This produced the first series win for Australia since beating Pakistan in 1983-84. Crowe reached 310, a series record for New Zealand against Australia in Australia (later extended to 396), when he reached 75 in the 1st innings. Wright, captaining New Zealand for the first time, became the third New Zealand batsmen to score 3,000 Test runs when he reached 20 in the 2nd innings. His 99 in the 1st innings was the highest score for New Zealand at the MCG. McDermott took five wickets for the 3rd time and Dodemaide, in his 1st Test, became only the second Australian to score 50 and take five wickets on debut. He and McDermott put on a record 61 for the 9th wicket. Border became the 9th player with 100 Test catches when he dismissed Crowe in the 2nd innings. However, Crowe had by this time become the 7th player to score 4,000 runs in a calendar year. Hadlee took five wickets for the 31st and 32nd times (12th/13th against Australia), and 18 for the series, leaving him with 373 wickets, equalling Botham.

New Zealand Tour of Australia 1987-88

First-Class Matches: Played 6; Won 1, Lost 2, Drawn 3
All Matches: Played 16; Won 5, Lost 8, Drawn 3

First-Class Averages

Batting and Fielding	M	I	NO	HS	R	Avge	100	50	Ct/St
M.D. Crowe	5	9	1	144	715	89.37	3	4	4
P.A. Horne	3	5	0	125	218	43.60	1	–	2
A.H. Jones	6	11	0	150	439	39.90	1	2	5
J.G. Wright	5	10	0	99	383	38.30	–	1	3
D.N. Patel	6	11	0	105	374	34.00	1	1	3
R.J. Hadlee	5	8	3	36	151	30.20	–	–	1
E.J. Gray	3	5	1	26	89	22.25	–	–	4
I.D.S. Smith	6	11	2	62	193	21.44	–	1	13/1
K.R. Rutherford	4	7	0	36	133	19.00	–	–	4
J.G. Bracewell	4	7	1	41*	106	17.66	–	–	4
J.J. Crowe	6	11	0	36	158	14.36	–	–	6
W. Watson	2	3	1	27*	27	13.50	–	–	–
D.K. Morrison	5	6	1	5*	8	1.60	–	–	1

Also batted: E.J. Chatfield (4 matches) 0*, 1*, 4*, 6*, 1*, 1ct; M.C. Snedden (2 matches) 0, 8*.

Bowling	O	M	R	W	Avge	Best	5wI	10wM
R.J. Hadlee	237.4	63	564	29	19.44	5-30	5	2
W. Watson	69.2	13	201	8	25.12	4-42	–	–
J.G. Bracewell	207.5	39	553	18	30.72	7-98	1	1
D.K. Morrison	158.3	25	555	16	34.68	4-86	–	–
E.J. Gray	83	21	193	5	38.60	3-60	–	–
E.J. Chatfield	180	55	352	8	44.00	3-52	–	–

Also bowled: D.N. Patel 72.4-16-212-3; M.C. Snedden 64-10-171-3.

Benson & Hedges World Series Cup

Australia emphasized their improved, more mature appreciation of limited overs cricket by adding the Benson & Hedges World Series Cup to the Reliance World Cup they had won in India 11 weeks earlier. Successive, surprisingly easy, wins against New Zealand – by eight wickets at Melbourne and six wickets at Sydney – in the best-of-three final series gave Australia the WSC Trophy and a whopping $A84,000 in prize money and awards. New Zealand had to be content With $A36,000 consolation, and Sri Lanka, the third team in the triangular tournament, received $A14,000 – not bad considering they won only one of their eight qualifying games, by four wickets against New Zealand at Hobart. Australia won seven of their eight qualifying games (their only loss was to New Zealand by one run at Perth in the second match of the series) and New Zealand won four of their eight before the finals.

The competition, of 14 matches in 23 days, was sandwiched between the end of the third Test between Australia and New Zealand at Melbourne (December 30) and the start of the Bicentennial Test between Australia and England at Sydney (January 29). Big, sometimes full-house, crowds again provided another financial bonanza for the Australian Cricket Board and erased local administrators' concern about the wisdom of hosting a summer occupied mostly by New Zealand, traditionally poor crowd-pullers in Australia, and Sri Lanka, whose new-look side was virtually unknown, as well as being inexperienced and, as it proved, deficient.

Inevitably, there were the usual complaints about the volume and timing of the 'one-dayers'. New Zealand team manager Alby Duckmanton was one of the most vocal critics. He feared his players' one-day international commitments in Australia would leave them jaded for the pending home series against England. Duckmanton said the Kiwis had been exhausted after the last day of the third Test at Melbourne. 'We had 40 degrees (Celsius) of heat that day and from there we played in a series of one-day games with the temperatures in the high 30s and low 40s,' he said. 'After several tense games in that type of heat, the players never really recovered. In future, teams should return home for a couple of weeks' rest. It would allow the selectors to name new players.'

Australians filled three of the first four places on the combined batting and bowling averages. Dean Jones, Mike Veletta, and David Boon were their most consistent batsmen, and Tony Dodemaide, Craig McDermott, and Steve Waugh the most successful bowlers. Jones made a welcome return to form after a depressing time against Richard Hadlee in the three Tests. All-rounder Waugh won the Player of the Series award in the 12 qualifying matches, and Jones won the Player of the Finals award for his innings of 58 not out and 53 not out. Boon was voted the International Cricketer of the Year – and received a $A25,000 Nissan car. Boon beat Sri Lankan Aravinda de Silva by just 0.374 of a point.

Qualifying Rounds

2 January at WACA Ground, Perth. AUSTRALIA beat SRI LANKA by 81 runs. Toss: Sri Lanka. Australia 249-7 (50 overs) (D.C. Boon 56, D.M. Jones 55). Sri Lanka 168 (44.2 overs) (R.G. De Alwis 44; A.I.C. Dodemaide 7.2-0-21-5). Award: S.R. Waugh (35* and 10-2-34-3).

3 January at WACA Ground, Perth (floodlit). NEW ZEALAND beat AUSTRALIA by 1 run. Toss: New Zealand. New Zealand 232-9 (50 overs) (A.H. Jones 87, M.D. Crowe 45). Australia 231 (49.4 overs) (D.M. Jones 92, D.C. Boon 44). Award: A.H. Jones (87).

5 January at Sydney Cricket Ground (floodlit). NEW ZEALAND beat SRI LANKA by 6 wickets. Toss: Sri Lanka. Sri Lanka 174 (48.2 overs) (J.R. Ratnayeke 41; E.J. Chatfield 9.2-1-32-4). New Zealand 178-4 (48.4 overs) (M.D. Crowe 52, J.G. Wright 41). Award: E.J. Chatfield (9.2-1-32-4).

7 January at Melbourne Cricket Ground (floodlit). AUSTRALIA beat NEW ZEALAND by 6 runs. Toss: Australia. Australia 216 (49.4 overs) (S.R. Waugh 68, D.M. Jones 48). New Zealand 210-9 (50 overs) (A.H. Jones 59). Award: S.R. Waugh (68, 10-0-41-1 and 1ct).

9 January at Adelaide Oval. NEW ZEALAND beat SRI LANKA by 4 wickets. Toss: Sri Lanka. Sri Lanka 241 (49.5 overs) (R.S. Mahanama 51, P.A. De Silva 51, A. Ranatunga 42). New Zealand 242-6 (49.5 overs) (A.H. Jones 63, J.G. Wright 61). Award: R.J. Hadlee (101-35-3, 1ct, and 25).

10 January at Adelaide Oval. AUSTRALIA beat SRI LANKA by 81 runs. Toss: Australia. Australia 289-6 (50 overs) (D.C. Boon 122, D.M. Jones 69). Sri Lanka 208-8 (50 overs) (R.S. Mahanama 50, P.A. De Silva 43, A.P. Gurusinha 43). Award: D.C. Boon (122).

12 January at Bellerive Oval, Hobart. SRI LANKA beat NEW ZEALAND by 4 wickets. Toss: Sri Lanka. New Zealand 199-7 (50 overs) (R.J. Hadlee 52, T.E. Blain 49*). Sri Lanka 200-6 (46.2 overs) (R.S. Mahanama 58, P.A. De Silva 55). Award: R.S. Mahanama (58 and 1ct).

14 January at Melbourne Cricket Ground (floodlit). AUSTRALIA beat SRI LANKA by 38 runs. Toss: Australia. Australia 243-8 (50 overs) (A.R. Border 61, M.R.J. Veletta 46; G.F. Labrooy 10-1-39-4). Sri Lanka 205 (44.5 overs) (A. Ranatunga 67, R.S. Madugalle 44; P.L. Taylor 10-1-38-4). Award: P.L. Taylor (27*, 10-1-38-4, and 1ct).

16 January at Woolloongabba, Brisbane. NEW ZEALAND beat SRI LANKA by 4 wickets. Toss: New Zealand. Sri Lanka 164-8 (39 overs) (D.B.S.P. Kuruppu 47). New Zealand 167-6 (37.1 overs) (M.D. Crowe 43). Award: M.D. Crowe (43).

17 January at Woolloongabba, Brisbane. AUSTRALIA beat NEW ZEALAND by 5 wickets in a match reduced by rain to 44 overs. Toss: Australia. New Zealand 176-5 (44 overs) (A.H. Jones 65, J.J. Crowe 41). Australia 177-5 (33.2 overs) (D.C. Boon 48, S.R. Waugh 45). Award: S.R. Waugh (8-1-23-2 and 45).

19 January at Sydney Cricket Ground (floodlit). AUSTRALIA beat SRI LANKA by 3 wickets. Toss: Australia. Sri Lanka 188-9 (50 overs) (P.A. De Silva 79; S.R. Waugh 10-0-33-4, M.R. Whitney 10-2-34-4). Australia 189-7 (49.3 overs) (M.R.J. Veletta 68*). Award: M.R.J. Veletta (68*).

20 January at Sydney Cricket Ground (floodlit). AUSTRALIA beat NEW ZEALAND by 78 runs. Toss: Australia. Australia 221-8 (50 overs) (G.R. Marsh 101). New Zealand 143 (45 overs). Award: G.R. Marsh (101).

Qualifying Table	P	W	L	Run Rate	Points
AUSTRALIA	8	7	1	4.74	14
NEW ZEALAND	8	4	4	4.08	8
Sri Lanka	8	1	7	4.02	2

Final Round Results

22 January at Melbourne Cricket Ground (floodlit). AUSTRALIA beat NEW ZEALAND by 8 wickets. Toss: New Zealand. New Zealand 177 (49.5 overs) (M.D. Crowe 48). Australia 180-2 (44.5 overs) (D.M. Jones 58*, M.R.J. Veletta 57*, D.C. Boon 47).

24 January at Sydney Cricket Ground. AUSTRALIA beat NEW ZEALAND by 6 wickets in a match reduced by rain to 38 overs. Toss: Australia. New Zealand 168-5 (38 overs) (A.H. Jones

56*, J.J. Crowe 42). Australia 169-4 (34.1 overs) (D.M. Jones 53*, D.C. Boon 43).

Player of the Finals award: D.M. Jones (Australia).

Leading Averages (Qual: 8 innings or 10 wkts)

Batting and Fielding	M	I	NO	HS	R	Avge	100	50	Ct/St
D.M. Jones (A)	10	10	2	92	461	57.62	–	5	4
A.H. Jones (NZ)	9	9	1	87	416	52.00	–	5	4
M.R.J. Veletta (A)	10	10	3	68*	295	42.14	–	2	7
D.C. Boon (A)	10	10	0	122	393	39.30	1	1	6
P.A. De Silva (SL)	8	8	0	79	279	34.87	–	3	4
R.J. Hadlee (NZ)	9	8	2	52	206	34.33	–	1	1
S.R. Waugh (A)	10	8	2	68	199	33.16	–	1	3
M.D. Crowe (NZ)	9	9	0	52	298	33.11	–	1	5
A. Ranatunga (SL)	8	8	0	67	226	28.25	–	1	3
R.S. Mahanama (SL)	8	8	0	58	209	26.12	–	3	7

Bowling	O	M	R	W	Avge	Best	5wI
A.I.C. Dodemaide (A)	91.1	10	289	18	16.05	5-21	1
E.J. Chatfield (NZ)	87.1	18	300	17	17.64	4-32	–
C.J. McDermott (A)	80.5	4	321	15	21.40	3-50	–
S.R. Waugh (A)	90	3	381	17	22.41	4-33	–
C.P. Ramanayake (SL)	65	7	279	11	25.36	3-35	–
R.J. Hadlee (NZ)	80.4	10	257	10	25.70	3-35	–
M.C. Snedden (NZ)	82.4	8	362	14	25.85	3-36	–
P.L. Taylor (A)	84	5	326	12	27.16	4-38	–
J.R. Ratnayeke (SL)	72.4	2	297	10	29.70	3-33	–

Australia v Sri Lanka

Sri Lanka's lack of international exposure, particularly at Test level, was all too obvious during their heavy loss to Australia at Perth late in the 1987-88 Australian season. Australia won by an innings and 108 runs only 75 minutes into the fourth day's play. It was their biggest win for just over 15 years – since they thrashed Pakistan by an innings and 114 runs at Adelaide in December, 1972. And it was only Allan Border's sixth win in 31 Tests as Australian captain.

Sri Lanka's first Test in Australia followed a similar course to the only other Test between the countries – at Kandy in April, 1983, when Australia won by an innings and 38 runs soon after lunch on the fourth day. Like Greg Chappell, who was then in his 48th and last Test as Australia's captain, Border was able to indulge in the unaccustomed luxury of enforcing the follow-on – for only the second time in his 31-Test reign as skipper.

This was Sri Lanka's first Test since the previous April, when they had drawn with New Zealand at Colombo. It left them with just 26 Tests in six years. They had won two (against India and Pakistan), lost 14 and drawn 10.

Few Test matches anywhere have been so lacking in atmosphere. Aggregate attendance was a paltry 11,626, surely the smallest in Australian history. This was of grave concern to the Australian Cricket Board, who had invited Sri Lanka to play three Tests in Australia in 1989-90, when Pakistan also were due to play three Tests in Australia.

Batting against the Sri Lankan attack, in which only opener Ravi Ratnayeke seemed to be up to Test class, looked so easy that the Australians had to summon all their discipline and concentration to avoid being lulled into a false sense of security. Yet, having been 333 for three at the end of the first day, they were restricted to 455, of which Dean Jones contributed 102, his third century in 15 Tests. On a pitch which developed many disturbing cracks ('We had never seen a pitch like that before,' said Ranjan Madugalle, the Sri Lankan captain) and provided ample bounce and movement off the seam, the Sri Lankan batsmen were outclassed. Only tall opener Roshan Mahanama, nuggety left-hander Arjuna Ranatunga, and all-rounder Ratnayeke made an impression. In Sri Lanka's second innings, big Merv Hughes took five wickets for the first time in his seven Tests and medium-fast Tony Dodemaide, who narrowly lost the Player of the Match award to Jones, completed a seven-wicket match haul, giving him 15 wickets (avg 20.1) in his first three Tests (one each against New Zealand, England, and Sri Lanka).

The Sri Lankan's tour programme left much to be desired. In seemingly every corner of Australia, and in the centre, at Alice Springs, they played 14 one-day games, one two-day game, one three-day game, and one four-day game – 23 days out of 45 – before the Test.

Australia v Sri Lanka 1987-88

Australia won by an innings and 108 runs
Played at WACA Ground, Perth, 12, 13, 14, 15 February
Toss: Australia. Umpires: R.C. Bailhache and P.J. McConnell
Debuts: Sri Lanka – C.P. Ramanayake

Australia

G.R. Marsh	b Labrooy	53
D.C. Boon	b Ratnayeke	64
D.M. Jones	lbw b Labrooy	102
A.R. Border*	b Ratnayeke	88
M.R.J. Veletta	c De Alwis b Ratnayeke	21
S.R. Waugh	c Labrooy b Amalean	20
G.C. Dyer†	c Ramanayake b Amalean	38
P.L. Taylor	c Amalean b Ratnayeke	18
A.I.C. Dodemaide	not out	16
C.J. McDermott	c De Alwis b Amalean	4
M.G. Hughes	b Amalean	8
Extras	(LB12, W5, NB6)	23
		455

Sri Lanka

R.S. Mahanama	c Dyer b Dodemaide	41	run out (D.C. Boon)	28
D.B.S.P. Kuruppu	c Marsh b McDermott	19	c Dyer b Dodemaide	3
S.M.S. Kaluperuma	lbw b McDermott	0	c and b Hughes	6
P.A. De Silva	lbw b Waugh	6	lbw b Dodemaide	7
A. Ranatunga	c and b Waugh	55	lbw b Dodemaide	45
R.S. Madugalle*	c Border b Dodemaide	6	c Waugh b Hughes	7
J.R. Ratnayeke	c Marsh b McDermott	24	c Dyer b Dodemaide	38
R.G. De Alwis†	c Dyer b Waugh	0	c Waugh b Hughes	8
C.P. Ramanayake	c Dyer b Waugh	9	c Veletta b Hughes	0
G.F. Labrooy	c Dyer b Dodemaide	4	b Hughes	4
K.N. Amalean	not out	7	not out	0
Extras	(B1, LB6, W2, NB14)	23	(LB6, NB1)	7
		194		**153**

Sri Lanka	O	M	R	W				
Ratnayeke	40	6	98	4				
Labrooy	36	5	108	2				
Ramanayake	17	2	58	0				
Amalean	22.2	1	97	4				
Kaluperuma	13	0	62	0				
Ranatunga	8	2	18	0				
P.A. De Silva	1	0	2	0				

Australia	O	M	R	W	O	M	R	W
McDermott	20	3	50	3	4	2	8	0
Hughes	18	2	61	0	21	7	67	5
Dodemaide	22.3	6	40	3	19.1	7	58	4
Waugh	20	7	33	4	8	4	14	0
Taylor	2	1	3	0				

Fall of Wickets

Wkt	A 1st	SL 1st	SL 2nd
1st	120	51	36
2nd	133	51	42
3rd	289	60	42
4th	346	93	66
5th	346	107	83
6th	380	147	111
7th	418	148	130
8th	434	181	131
9th	443	182	153
10th	455	194	153

Statistical Highlights of the Test

Only Test, Perth. Sri Lanka lost their 1st Test in Australia after just 75 minutes' play on the fourth morning. Border captained Australia for a record 31st time and won his 6th Test. Marsh and Boon recorded their 5th hundred opening partnership. Jones scored his 3rd Test hundred and Hughes took five wickets for the first time. Ranatunga played his 23rd Test, equalling Mendis and S. Wettimuny as the most capped players for their country. Ratnayeke became the second Sri Lankan after De Mel to take 50 Test wickets when he dismissed Boon. Madugalle became the 5th Sri Lankan to reach 1,000 Test runs. Ramanayake was dropped by the wicket-keeper off his first ball in Test cricket, thus depriving Waugh of his 2nd five-wicket haul.

West Indies v Pakistan

When Pakistan's team arrived in the Caribbean for its third tour of the West Indies, Imran Khan, the captain persuaded out of retirement by pressure from public, players, and, ultimately, president for this particular assignment, said the outcome would determine the leading Test team in the game. The result was inconclusive. Two evenly matched teams produced an enthralling series that ended in one victory apiece in the three Tests with the other match excitingly drawn.

After being swept aside in all five one-day internationals, Imran managed to maintain his team's spirit and confidence and himself inspired a comfortable victory by nine wickets in the first Test, when the West Indies were seriously disadvantaged by the absence of captain Vivian Richards, recovering from a minor operation, and Malcolm Marshall, with a leg injury. With the West Indies back to full strength, both the second and third Tests were so keenly fought that neither team gained the initiative for long and, in each, either could have won even as the final ball was bowled.

As it was, the second was drawn, with Pakistan's last man, Abdul Qadir, surviving the last five balls, and the West Indies won the third to share the series. Their ninth pair, Jeffrey Dujon and Winston Benjamin, added 61 amidst tension so intense that the mercurial Qadir crossed the boundary to accost a heckling spectator to whom a monetary out-of-court settlement had to be paid.

The leading players on both sides carried enormous influence, particularly the captains. Imran, his standing as one of the game's finest all-rounders and inspirational leaders assured, dismissed the one-day results as irrelevant and proved his point with an outstanding personal performance in the Tests. He took 20 wickets in the first two Tests with high-class, fast swing bowling and, if his standards dropped in the third, fatigue appeared to have overtaken him by then, not surprising as he had been out of cricket for three months prior to the tour. His bowling and his captaincy gained him the Player of the Series award.

Richards was troubled by haemorrhoids to such an extent that he needed an operation after the first one-day international and could not appear again until the second Test. His authority, as much as his batting, was glaringly missed in the first Test, when the West Indies played without purpose or direction, and his return was emphatic. He top-scored in each innings of the second Test, including a crucial, hard-fought century in the second, took two wickets and held a vital catch in the gripping closing stages, and motivated his men to great effort. Now he, like Imran in the first Test, was Player of the Match.

Both teams also depended heavily on other experienced players. Javed Miandad, Pakistan's leading scorer in Test cricket, corrected the one omission in his otherwise imposing record by scoring his first century against the West Indies in the first Test, and followed it with another in the second. Imran's bowling support came mainly from Qadir, who bowled more overs than any other bowler, on either side.

West Indies v Pakistan 1987-88 1st Test

Pakistan won by 9 wickets
Played at Bourda, Georgetown, Guyana 2, 3, 4, 6, April
Toss: West Indies. Umpires: D.M. Archer and L.H. Barker
Debuts: West Indies – E.L.C. Ambrose

West Indies

D.L. Haynes	c Yousuf b Imran	1	b Fakih		5
P.V. Simmons	b Fakih	16	b Qadir		11
R.B. Richardson	c Shoaib b Imran	75	c Yousuf b Qadir		16
C.G. Greenidge*	c Malik b Akram	17	b Imran		43
A.L. Logie	lbw b Qadir	80	c Yousuf b Imran		24
C.L. Hooper	c Akram b Imran	33	c Malik b Qadir		30
P.J.L. Dujon†	lbw b Imran	15	c Imran b Shoaib		11
W.K.M. Benjamin	lbw b Imran	2	c Miandad b Shoaib		0
C.A. Walsh	b Imran	7	c Yousuf b Imran		14
E.L.C. Ambrose	not out	25	not out		1
B.P. Patterson	b Imran	10	b Imran		0
Extras	(B2, LB3, NB6)	11	(B4, LB8, NB5)		17
		292			**172**

Pakistan

Mudassar Nazar	b Ambrose	29	lbw b Patterson	0
Ramiz Raja	c Haynes b Patterson	5	not out	18
Shoaib Mohammad	c Greenidge b Walsh	46	not out	13
Javed Miandad	b Patterson	114		
Salim Malik	c Greendige b Patterson	27		
Ijaz Ahmed	c Haynes b Ambrose	31		
Imran Khan*	c Simmons b Benjamin	24		
Salim Yousuf†	lbw b Walsh	62		
Ijaz Fakih	b Hooper	5		
Abdul Qadir	b Walsh	19		
Wasim Akram	not out	2		
Extras	(B21, LB8, W4, NB38)	71	(NB1)	1
		435	(1 wkt)	**32**

Pakistan	O	M	R	W	O	M	R	W
Imran Khan	22.4	2	80	7	14.4	0	41	4
Wasim Akram	14	5	41	1	6	1	7	0
Ijaz Fakih	14	0	60	1	15	4	38	1
Abdul Qadir	24	2	91	1	25	5	66	3
Salim Malik	1	0	6	0				
Mudassar Nazar	5	2	9	0				
S. Mohammad					2	0	8	2

West Indies	O	M	R	W	O	M	R	W
Patterson	24	2	82	3	2	0	19	1
Ambrose	28	5	108	2	1.4	0	13	0
Walsh	27	4	80	3				
Benjamin	31	3	99	1				
Hooper	12	1	37	1				

Fall of Wickets

Wkt	WI 1st	P 1st	WI 2nd	P 2nd
1st	7	20	18	0
2nd	41	57	34	–
3rd	95	127	44	–
4th	144	217	109	–
5th	220	297	120	–
6th	244	300	145	–
7th	248	364	145	–
8th	249	383	166	–
9th	258	423	172	–
10th	292	435	172	–

West Indies v Pakistan 1987-88 2nd Test

Match Drawn
Played at Queen's Park Oval, Port-of-Spain, Trinidad 14, 15, 16, 17, 19 April
Toss: Pakistan. Umpires: L.H. Barker and C.E. Cumberbatch
Debuts: nil.

West Indies

C.G. Greenidge	c Ijaz Ahmed b Imran	1	c sub (Naveed Anjum) b Imran	29
D.L. Haynes	lbw b Akram	17	c Ijaz Ahmed b Imran	0
R.B. Richardson	c Qadir b Akram	42	c Yousuf b Imran	40
A.L. Logie	c Miandad b Qadir	18	b Imran	1
I.V.A. Richards*	c Miandad b Qadir	49	lbw b Akram	123
C.L. Hooper	c Yousuf b Qadir	0	c Ijaz Ahmed b Imran	26
P.J.L. Dujon†	c Yousuf b Imran	24	not out	106
M.D. Marshall	not out	10	b Qadir	2
E.L.C. Ambrose	lbw b Imran	4	lbw b Qadir	9
W.K.M. Benjamin	b Qadir	0	lbw b Qadir	16
C.A. Walsh	b Imran	5	st Yousuf b Qadir	12
Extras	(LB2, NB2)	4	(B9, LB14, NB4)	27
		174		**391**

Pakistan

Mudassar Nazar	c Haynes b Marshall	14	c Dujon b Benjamin	13
Ramiz Raja	c Richardson b Marshall	1	c Richards b Marshall	44
Shoaib Mohammad	c Richards b Ambrose	12	b Benjamin	0
Javed Miandid	b Benjamin	18	c Richards b Ambrose	102
Ijaz Fakih	c Richards b Benjamin	0	(10) not out	10
Salim Malik	c Logie b Hooper	66	(5) lbw b Walsh	30
Ijaz Ahmed	c Logie b Benjamin	3	st Dujon b Richards	43
Imran Khan*	c Logie b Marshall	4	(6) c Dujon b Benjamin	1
Salim Yousuf†	c Dujon b Marshall	39	(8) b Richards	35
Wasim Akram	run out (Haynes)	7	(9) c Richardson b Marshall	2
Abdul Qadir	not out	17	not out	0
Extras	(B1, LB4, NB8)	13	(B17, LB17, W2, NB25)	61
		194	(9 wkts)	**341**

Pakistan	O	M	R	W	O	M	R	W
Imran Khan	16.3	2	38	4	45	8	115	5
Wasim Akram	14	4	35	2	25	1	75	1
Abdul Qadir	19	2	83	4	47.4	6	148	4
Ijaz Fakih	3	0	13	0	4	0	22	0
Mudassar Nazar	1	0	3	0				
S. Mohammad					3	0	8	0

West Indies	O	M	R	W	O	M	R	W
Marshall	20	4	55	4	30	4	85	2
Ambrose	14	3	44	1	30	7	62	1
Walsh	8	0	23	0	29	8	52	1
Benjamin	8	0	32	3	32	9	73	3
Hooper	9	1	35	1	4	1	18	0
Richards					4	1	17	2

Fall of Wickets

Wkt	WI 1st	P 1st	WI 2nd	P 2nd
1st	2	3	1	60
2nd	25	25	54	62
3rd	80	46	66	67
4th	89	49	81	153
5th	89	50	175	169
6th	147	62	272	282
7th	157	68	284	288
8th	166	162	301	311
9th	167	170	357	341
10th	174	194	391	—

West Indies v Pakistan 1987-88 3rd Test

West Indies won by 2 wickets
Played at Kensington Oval, Bridgetown, Barbados 22, 23, 24, 26, 27 April
Toss: West Indies. Umpires: D.M. Archer and L.H. Barker
Debuts: nil.

Pakistan

Mudassar Nazar	b Ambrose	18		c Greenidge b Hooper	41
Ramiz Raja	c Greenidge b Benjamin	54		c Logie b Marshall	4
Shoaib Mohammad	c Greenidge b Ambrose	54		c and b Richards	64
Javed Miandad	c Richardson b Marshall	14		c Dujon b Marshall	34
Salim Malik	b Marshall	15		lbw b Benjamin	9
Aamir Malik	c Hooper b Benjamin	32		c Logie b Marshall	2
Imran Khan*	c Dujon b Benjamin	18		not out	43
Salim Yousuf†	retired hurt	32	(9)	c Richards b Benjamin	28
Wasim Akram	c Benjamin b Marshall	38	(8)	lbw b Marshall	0
Abdul Qadir	c Walsh b Marshall	17		c Greenidge b Marshall	2
Salim Jaffer	not out	1		b Ambrose	4
Extras	(LB7, NB9)	16		(B3, LB14, NB14)	31
		309			**262**

West Indies

C.G. Greenidge	lbw b Imran	10		c Shoaib b Jaffer	35
D.L. Haynes	c Aamir b Mudassar	48		c Malik b Akram	4
R.B. Richardson	c Aamir b Akram	3		st Aamir b Qadir	64
C.L. Hooper	b Akram	54		run out (Ramiz Raja)	13
I.V.A. Richards*	c Mudassar b Akram	67		b Akram	39
A.L. Logie	c Miandad b Mudassar	0		b Qadir	3
P.J.L. Dujon†	run out (Salim Malik)	0	(8)	not out	28
M.D. Marshall	c Aamir b Imran	48	(9)	lbw b Akram	15
E.L.C. Ambrose	lbw b Imran	7	(7)	c Jaffer b Akram	1
W.K.M. Benjamin	run out (Salim Jaffer)	31		not out	41
C.A. Walsh	not out	14			
Extras	(B5, LB11, NB8)	24		(B9, LB6, NB01)	25
		306		(8 wkts)	**268**

Salim Yousuf retired hurt at 285-7.

West Indies	O	M	R	W	O	M	R	W
Marshall	18.4	3	79	4	23	3	65	5
Ambrose	14	2	64	2	20.5	3	74	1
Benjamin	14	3	52	3	15	1	37	2
Walsh	10	1	53	0	12	1	22	0
Richards	6	0	19	0	7	3	8	1
Hooper	12	3	35	0	10	1	39	1

Pakistan	O	M	R	W	O	M	R	W
Imran Khan	25	3	108	3	6	0	34	0
Wasim Akram	27	1	88	3	31	7	73	4
Abdul Qadir	15	1	35	0	32	5	115	2
Salim Jaffer	7	1	35	0	5	0	25	1
Mudassar Nazar	10	4	24	2				
S. Mohammad					3	1	6	0

Fall of Wickets

	P	WI	P	WI
Wkt	1st	1st	2nd	2nd
1st	46	18	6	21
2nd	99	21	100	78
3rd	128	100	153	118
4th	155	198	165	128
5th	186	198	169	150
6th	215	199	169	159
7th	218	201	182	180
8th	297	225	234	207
9th	309	283	245	–
10th	–	306	262	–

Test Match Averages:
West Indies v Pakistan 1987-88

West Indies

Batting and Fielding	M	I	NO	HS	R	Avge	100s	50s	Ct/St
I.V.A. Richards	2	4	0	123	278	69.50	1	1	6
P.J.L. Dujon	3	6	2	106*	184	46.00	1	–	5/1
P.B. Richardson	3	6	0	75	240	40.00	–	2	3
C.L. Hooper	3	6	0	54	156	26.00	–	1	1
M.D. Marshall	2	4	1	48	75	25.00	–	–	–
C.G. Greenidge	3	6	0	43	135	22.50	–	–	6
A.L. Logie	3	6	0	80	126	21.00	–	1	5
W.K.M. Benjamin	3	6	1	41*	90	18.00	–	–	1
C.A. Walsh	3	5	1	14*	52	13.00	–	–	1
D.L. Haynes	3	6	0	48	75	12.50	–	–	3
E.L.C. Ambrose	3	6	2	25*	47	11.75	–	–	–

Also batted: B.P. Patterson (1 match) 10, 0; P.V. Simmons (1 match) 16, 11, 1ct.

Bowling	O	M	R	W	Avge	Best	5wI	10wM
Marshall	91.4	14	284	15	18.93	5-65	1	–
Benjamin	100	16	293	12	24.41	3-32	–	–
Ambrose	108.3	20	365	7	52.14	2-64	–	–

Also bowled: C.L. Hooper 47-1-164-3; B.P. Patterson 26-2-101-4; I.V.A. Richards 17-4-44-3; C.A. Walsh 86-15-230-4.

Pakistan

Batting and Fielding	M	I	NO	HS	R	Avge	100s	50s	Ct/St
Javed Miandad	3	5	0	114	282	56.40	2	–	4
Salim Yousuf	3	5	1	62	196	49.00	–	1	7/1
Shoaib Mohammad	3	6	1	64	189	37.80	–	2	2
Salim Malik	3	5	0	66	147	29.40	–	1	3
Ramiz Raja	3	6	1	54	126	25.20	–	1	–
Imran Khan	3	5	1	43*	90	22.50	–	–	1
Mudassar Nazar	3	6	0	41	115	19.16	–	–	1
Abdul Qadir	3	5	2	19	55	18.33	–	–	1
Wasim Akram	3	5	1	38	49	12.25	–	–	1

Also batted: Aamir Malik (1 match) 32, 2, 3ct/1st); Ijaz Ahmed (2 matches) 31, 3, 43, 3ct; Ijaz Fakih (2 matches) 5, 0, 10*; Salim Jaffer (1 match) 1*, 4, 1ct.

Bowling	O	M	R	W	Avge	Best	5wI	10wM
Imran Khan	129.5	15	416	23	18.08	7-80	2	1
Wasim Akram	117	19	319	11	29.00	4-73	–	–
Abdul Qadir	162.3	21	538	14	38.42	4-83	–	–

Also bowled: Ijaz Fakih 36-4-133-2; Mudassar Nazar 16-6-36-2; Salim Jaffer 12-1-60-1; Salim Malik 1-0-6-0; Shoaib Mohammad 8-1-22-2.

Statistical Highlights of the Tests

1st Test, Georgetown. West Indies lost their first home Test since Australia beat them at Georgetown in 1977-78. It was the 3rd win in West Indies for Pakistan. West Indies lost two consecutive Tests for the 1st time since 1975-76. Imran Khan took five wickets for the 22nd time and ten wickets for the 6th time, recording the best match analysis in a Georgetown Test. West Indies conceded a record number of extras in a Test innings, the chief offenders being Walsh (14nb) and Ambrose (12). There were 15 more no-balls scored from. The previous record was held by West Indies, also against Pakistan, at Kingston in 1976-77. Javed Miandad scored his 16th Test hundred, his 1st against West Indies. Salim Malik reached 2,000 Test runs when he scored 7 in the 1st innings. Shoaib returned his best bowling figures. Greenidge kept wicket in the 2nd innings after Dujon had injured two fingers earlier in the match.

2nd Test, Port-of-Spain. Abdul Qadir batted for the last five balls of the match to ensure a draw after Richards had Salim Yousuf lbw from the first ball of the last over. Pakistan had been set 372 to win in ten hours ten minutes. 15 wickets had fallen on the first day. Salim Malik and Salim Yousuf added 94 to set a new 8th-wicket partnership against West Indies. Richards scored his 22nd Test hundred, 2nd against Pakistan, from only 134 balls. Dujon scored his 5th Test hundred, his 1st against Pakistan. Imran Khan took five wickets for the 23rd time. Abdul Qadir reached 200 Test wickets in his 54th Test when he dismissed Marshall. He is the 25th bowler, and the second from Pakistan, to achieve this. Javed Miandad scored his 17th Test hundred, his 2nd against West Indies. Richardson reached 2,000 Test runs when he scored 5 in the 2nd innings.

3rd Test, Bridgetown. A record 9th wicket partnership of 61* saw West Indies home, thus keeping their unbroken record for Tests at Bridgetown since 1934-35, a series of 23 matches. They also preserved their unbroken home series record since 1972-73. Marshall broke Salim Yousuf's nose in two places, and so Aamer Malik kept wicket throughout the match. Ramiz Raja reached 1,000 Test runs when he scored 28 in the 1st innings. Marshall dismissed Abdul Qadir to give him 250 Test wickets in his 53rd Test. Richards became the 9th player to reach 7,000 Test runs when he scored 61 in the 1st innings. He is the 3rd West Indian after Sobers and Lloyd to achieve this. Marshall took five wickets for the 15th time in the 2nd innings.

One-Day Internationals

12 March at Sabina Park, Kingston, Jamaica. WEST INDIES beat PAKISTAN by 47 runs. Toss: Pakistan. West Indies 241-4 (46 overs) (A.L. Logie 109*, R.B. Richardson 84). Pakistan 194-7 (46 overs) (Javed Miandad 47; E.L.C. Ambrose 10-1-39-4). Award: A.L. Logie (109* and 1ct).

15 March at Recreation Ground, St John's, Antigua. WEST INDIES beat PAKISTAN by 5 wickets. Toss: West Indies. Pakistan 166-9 (46 overs) (Imran Khan 53; E.L.C. Ambrose 10-2-35-4). West Indies 167-5 (37.1 overs) (P.V. Simmons 54). Award: W.K.M. Benjamin (10-1-27-3).

18 March at Queen's Park Oval, Port-of-Spain, Trinidad. WEST INDIES beat PAKISTAN by 50 runs. West Indies 315-4 (47 overs) (D.L. Haynes 142*, R.B. Richardson 78). Pakistan 265 (43.3 overs) (Salim Malik 85, Ramiz Raja 47). Award: D.L. Haynes (142*).

20 March at Queen's Park Oval, Port-of-Spain, Trinidad, WEST INDIES beat PAKISTAN by 7 wickets. Toss: Pakistan. Pakistan 271-6 (43 overs) (Ramiz Raja 71, Javed Miandad 59, Moin-ul-Atiq 46). West Indies 272-3 (40.1 overs) (R.B. Richardson 79*, C.G. Greenidge 66, P.V. Simmons 49). Award: C.G. Greenidge (66 and 2ct).

Pakistan Tour of West Indies 1987-88

First-Class Matches: Played 6; Won 2, Lost 1, Drawn 3
All Matches: Played 11; Won 2, Lost 6, Drawn 3

First-Class Averages

Batting and Fielding	M	I	NO	HS	R	Avge	100	50	Ct/St
Javed Miandad	4	7	0	114	456	65.14	3	1	5
Shoaib Mohammad	5	10	2	208*	461	57.62	1	2	2
Ramiz Raja	5	10	1	82	338	37.55	–	3	1
Salim Yousuf	5	8	1	62	254	36.28	–	1	9/1
Salim Malik	6	11	1	86	334	33.40	–	3	8
Ijaz Ahmed	5	9	1	84	236	29.50	–	1	4
Mudassar Nazar	6	11	1	72	272	27.20	–	1	2
Aamer Malik	4	8	0	51	200	25.00	–	1	6/5
Wasim Akram	4	7	2	56*	121	24.20	–	1	1
Imran Khan	5	8	1	44	167	23.85	–	–	2
Ijaz Fakih	3	5	1	51	76	19.00	–	1	–
Abdul Qadir	5	8	2	19	72	12.00	–	–	2
Salim Jaffer	2	4	3	3*	9	9.00	–	–	1

Also batted: Haafiz Shahid (2 matches) 10, 0, 37; Moin-ul-Atiq (1 match) 38,22;
Naved Anjum (2 matches) 48, 13, 20*; Tausif Ahmed (1 match) 2, 2;
Zakir Khan (1 match) 0, 11*.

Bowling	O	M	R	W	Avge	Best	5wI	10wM
Zakir Khan	18.1	2	52	5	10.40	3-24	–	–
Salim Jaffer	34.2	2	141	7	20.14	6-67	1	–
Imran Khan	180.5	21	589	29	20.31	7-80	2	1
Abdul Qadir	214.2	36	703	26	27.03	6-42	1	–
Wasim Akram	127	20	350	12	29.16	4-73	–	–
Salim Malik	34.4	1	169	5	33.80	4-101	–	–
Ijaz Fakih	60	13	187	5	37.40	3-54	–	–

Also bowled: Aamer Malik 5-2-15-1; Haafiz Shahid 29-3-114-3; Moin-ul-Atiq 3-0-6-0;
Mudassar Nazar 30-7-87-3; Naved Anjum 34-3-99-2; Shoaib Mohammad 16.4-2-43-2;
Tausif Ahmed 35-11-69-0.

---

30 March at Bourda, Georgetown, Guyana. WEST INDIES beat PAKISTAN by 7 wickets. Toss: West
Indies. Pakistan 221-7 (43 overs) (Javed Miandad 100*, Ramiz Raja 67). West Indies 225-3 (37 overs)
(P.V. Simmons 79, R.B. Richardson 68). Award: Javed Miandad (100*).

World Youth Cup

The Australian Under-20 side won the inaugural World Youth Cup at the Adelaide Oval in March, when they beat Pakistan in the final, emulating the success of their senior side in India. The seven Test-playing countries took part, together with a composite team made up of associate members of the ICC. Each team played each other once on a round-robin basis, and the top four teams contested the semi-finals.

England, coming out of season to the heat of Australia, disappointed. They scraped through to the semi-finals by dint of a remarkable win over Pakistan, after losing their last eight wickets for 13 and registering only 126. Leicestershire's Chris Lewis, the fastest bowler in the competition (but whose pace was handicapped by a rule no-balling any delivery rising above shoulder height), took 5-39 and Pakistan were dismissed for 70.

But England's batsmen continued to struggle in the semi-final against Australia, collapsing to 194 with their last seven wickets going for 61 in 15 overs. Australia, beaten only in their last group match, by Pakistan, gained their revenge in the final. After Pakistan were bowled out for 201, opener Brett Williams scored his second hundred of the tournament to give Australia an advantage they never looked like losing.

	P	W	L	Pts	Run-rate
AUSTRALIA	7	6	1	12	4.58
PAKISTAN	7	5	2	10	3.71
WEST INDIES	7	5	2	10	3.36
ENGLAND	7	4	3	8	3.19
India	7	3	4	6	3.47
Sri Lanka	7	3	4	6	2.95
New Zealand	7	2	5	4	3.52
ICC Associates	7	0	7	0	2.97

Semi-Finals

10 March at Adelaide Oval. PAKISTAN beat WEST INDIES by 2 wickets. West Indies 203-8 (50 overs) (J. Adams 65, B.C. Lara 42), Pakistan 204-8 (47.5 overs) (Shahid Anwar 76, Zahoor Elahi 43).

11 March at Adelaide Oval. AUSTRALIA beat ENGLAND by 7 wickets. England 194 (50 overs) (N. Hussain 58, M.W. Alleyne 56). Australia 196-3 (45.2 overs) (B.D. Williams 57, L. Ferguson 40*).

Australia v Pakistan, World Youth Cup Final

Australia won by 5 wickets
Played at the Adelaide Oval, 13 March 1988 (50 overs)

Pakistan

Shahid Anwar	c Playle b Mullally	8
Basit Ali	lbw b Parker	23
Zahoor Elahi*	c Holdsworth b Mullally	35
Shahid Nawaz	c Berry b Parker	35
Imzamamul Haq	c Ferguson b Holdsworth	37
Mohammad Nawaz	c Mullally b Parker	14
Zulfiqar Butt	b Holdsworth	19
Riffaqat Ali†	c Berry b Holdsworth	4
Mushtaq Ahmed	run out	3
Zulfiqar Ali	not out	5
Shakeel Khan	not out	8
Extras	(LB4, W5, NB1)	10
	(49.3 overs)	**201**

Australia

B.D. Williams	c Mushtaq b Butt	108
D. Playle	c Riffaqat b Imzamamul	12
S.G. Law	c Zahoor b Shahid Anwar	44
L. Ferguson	b Mushtaq	9
G.R. Parker*	c & b Mushtaq	10
H. Armstrong	not out	7
J.C. Scuderi	not out	3
A.E. Tucker	did not bat	
D. Berry†	,,	
W. Holdsworth	,,	
A. Mullally	,,	
Extras	(LB1, W7, NB1)	9
	(5 wkts, 45.5 overs)	**202**

Australia	O	M	R	W
Holdsworth	9.3	1	38	3
Mullally	10	1	53	2
Scuderi	10	0	38	0
Parker	10	0	36	3
Tucker	10	0	32	0

Pakistan	O	M	R	W
Shakeel	6	0	21	0
Zulfiqar Ali	3	0	19	0
Imzamamul	6.5	0	28	1
Shahid Anwar	10	0	41	1
Mushtaq	10	0	59	2
Butt	10	1	33	1

Fall of Wickets

Wkt	P	A
1st	10	34
2nd	59	131
3rd	88	167
4th	125	192
5th	149	192
6th	171	–
7th	183	–
8th	186	–
9th	187	–
10th	201	–

Cricket in Australia

Was it simply a case of Western Australia winning the Sheffield Shield again or more a matter of Queensland losing it again? Western Australia, top of the table after each of the six teams had played 10 matches, retained the Shield by defeating Queensland by five wickets soon after lunch on the fifth day of the final at Perth's WACA Ground. It was Western Australia's 11th success in 41 years, their 10th in the past 21 years, and it was the 12th time Queensland had been runnersup in their 56 years in the competition.

Queensland's frustration at finishing second for the eighth time in 15 years was made more acute this time by the off-field drama involving Ian Botham in the week leading up to the final. Botham was fined $A800 in the Perth Magistrate's Court after pleading guilty to charges of assault and offensive behaviour during the Queenslanders' flight from Brisbane (via Melbourne) to Perth. Queensland's former Test batsman Greg Ritchie pleaded not guilty to an offensive behaviour charge, which was dropped a few months later. Botham also subsequently was fined $A5,000 by the Australian Cricket Board under the ACB's Code of Behaviour – $A3,000 for the aircraft incident and $A2,000 for allegedly wrecking a dressingroom during the QueenslandTasmania Shield match at Launceston in February. Dennis Lillee, having made a shock comeback for the second half of the season, this time for Cinderella state Tasmania, was fined $A1,800 for his involvement in the dressingroom incident. The executive of the Queensland Cricket Association terminated Botham's three-year contract after just one season, in which he had been a big, crowdpulling attraction around the country. His performances, however, were below all expectations, including his own, for a player of his renowned versatility, which often had bordered on genius at Test level. He scored 646 runs (avg 34) in 19 innings, took 29 wickets (avg 27.75) in 312.2 overs, and pulled off some fine catches.

Allan Border, the Queensland and Australian captain, conceded immediately after the Shield final that the aircraft incident had had a detrimental effect on his team. 'The investigations and subsequent police action didn't help our preparation,' Border said. 'It was not the sort of thing that is easily forgotten once in the dressing room trying to concentrate on cricket.' Border also bemoaned Queensland's now traditional fade-out after a strong start to the season. 'We've got to take a leaf out of Western Australia's book,' he said. 'They are a tremendous cricket team and are very professional in everything they do. Occasionally we let ourselves down in our preparations and in our thought processes going into a game. Western Australia are a very well organized unit, well drilled with a very good match plan they stick to. We've got to get that sort of thing into our cricket. If we can, we'll be just that bit more competitive throughout a season. I'd like to see a little more discipline in our cricket. The Australian team are successful now because they have that discipline and I think the Queensland team have got to take a lesson from Western Australia and Australia.'

Western Australia's win was another personal triumph for their captain Graeme Wood, whose 144 (run out) in the final (and a duck in the second innings) lifted his season's aggregate in 12 first-class matches to 1,050. His average of 70 put him second on the national list, behind Victorian Jamie Siddons, who made 1,077 at 71.80 in 11 matches. Wood and Siddons were rewarded with selection in the Australian team to tour Pakistan in September-October. The other four batsmen to pass 1,000 runs for the season were David Boon (1,287 at 67.74 for Tasmania and Australia), Border (1,164 at 61.26 for Queensland and Australia), David Hookes (1, 149 at 60.47 for South Australia), and Mick Taylor (1,003 at 45.59 for Tasmania).

New South Wales batsman Mark Waugh (Steve's twin) just missed Pakistan tour selection after scoring 833 at 64.08 in 10 matches. He was fourth in the national averages and tied with Queensland left-arm fast-medium bowler Dick Tazelaar for the Benson & Hedges Sheffield Shield Cricketer of the Year award. They received $A1,000 each. With 19 points (cast by umpires on a 3-2-1 basis), they finished three points ahead of Border, four clear of Taylor, and five in front of Siddons, Wood, and South Australian opening batsman Andrew Hilditch (922 at 48.53 in 11 matches). Tazelaar's 46-wicket haul (avg 22.54) was bettered only by West Australian left-hand opener Chris Matthews's 57 at 22.40. Next best was New South Wales's former Test opener Geoff Lawson, with 42 at 18.86.

Taylor was easily the most successful of the players who returned to Shield ranks after having toured South Africa in 1985-86 and 1986-87 with Kim Hughes's rebel team. But he had to leave his home State of Victoria to get an opportunity with Tasmania. Pace bowlers Terry Alderman (39 wickets at 24.20 for Western Australia) and Carl Racke-mann (31 at 23.65 for Queensland) also performed well from more limited chances. Both were prominent in the Shield final. Victoria were the only State not to recall their former rebels (Taylor, Rodney Hogg, and Graham Yallop). New South Wales's John Dyson and Steve Smith lost their places and Steve Rixon retired, South Australia dropped Michael Haysman, who had also struggled for runs, and Hughes fought his way back into the West Australian side for the final after a few mid-season appearances.

The lucky and unlucky stories of the summer belonged to Queensland wicket-keepers Peter Anderson and Ian Healy. Anderson kept wicket in the first seven Shield matches and was being tipped as the next Australian keeper, to succeed New South Wales's Greg Dyer sooner or later. But he broke a thumb in three places standing up to the stumps to medium-pacer Botham at Perth in January and missed the rest of the season. Healy played the last four matches, including the final, and impressed sufficiently, particularly against the spinners, to be picked ahead of Dyer for the Australian team's tour of Pakistan. This seemingly left Anderson without a regular future in first-class cricket. He was so disillusioned that he considered retiring, but eventually chose to move to Adelaide to play for South Australia, who were looking for a keeper because of Wayne Phillips's decision to continue playing solely as a batsman.

Western Australia v Queensland, 1987-88 Sheffield Shield Final

Western Australia won by 5 wickets
Played at WACA Ground, Perth, 18, 19, 20, 21, 22 March
Toss: Western Australia

Queensland

R.B. Kerr	c Marsh b Matthews	46		c Andrews b Alderman	2
T.J. Barsby	c Zoehrer b Matthews	48		b MacLeay	21
G.M. Ritchie	c MacLeay b Matthews	33		lbw b Alderman	34
A.R. Border*	c Andrews b MacLeay	66		c Veletta b Matthews	6
G.S. Trimble	c Zoehrer b Mullally	15		lbw b Alderman	3
I.T. Botham	c MacLeay b Matthews	9		c MacLeay b Alderman	54
D. Tazelaar	c Zoehrer b Matthews	6	(10)	c Wood b Alderman	5
T.V. Hohns	lbw b Matthews	14	(7)	not out	59
I Healy†	lbw b Matthews	14	(8)	c Zoehrer b Alderman	0
C.J. McDermott	not out	8	(9)	c Andrews b Mullally	1
C.G. Rackemann	b Matthews	0		b MacLeay	8
Extras	(B9, LB9, W8, NB4)	30		(B9, LB7, NB7)	23
		289			**216**

Western Australia

G.R. Marsh	c Healy b Rackemann	41		b Tazelaar	39
M.R.J. Veletta	c Barsby b Rackemann	23		lbw b Tazelaar	59
J. Brayshaw	c Border b Rackemann	24		c Botham b Tazelaar	4
G.M. Wood*	run out (McDermott)	141		c Healy b Tazelaar	0
K.J. Hughes	run out (Rackemann)	11		c sub (Maguire) b Botham	21
K.H. MacLeay	lbw b McDermott	2		did not bat	
W.S. Andrews	lbw b Rackemann	71	(6)	not out	20
T.J. Zoehrer†	c Healy b Rackemann	0	(7)	not out	10
C.D. Matthews	c Barsby b Hohns	2		did not bat	
T.M. Alderman	lbw b Hohns	0		,,	
A. Mullally	not out	2		,,	
Extras	(LB15, NB12)	27		(LB8, NB1)	9
		344		(5 wkts)	**162**

W. Australia	O	M	R	W	O	M	R	W
Mullally	17	2	55	1	12	6	17	1
MacLeay	27	10	53	1	17.2	6	40	2
Alderman	26	10	62	0	28	4	91	6
Matthews	32.5	7	101	8	27	9	52	1

Queensland	O	M	R	W	O	M	R	W
McDermott	24	4	80	1	7	1	21	0
Tazelaar	32	10	79	0	22.4	7	65	4
Rackemann	30	7	69	5	14	4	29	0
Botham	24	7	66	0	16	3	33	1
Hohns	19.5	7	35	2	4	1	6	0

Fall of Wickets

Wkt	Q 1st	WA 1st	Q 2nd	WA 2nd
1st	63	61	9	78
2nd	115	75	38	82
3rd	161	140	46	82
4th	200	153	49	125
5th	234	186	88	133
6th	235	322	162	–
7th	253	326	164	–
8th	266	335	169	–
9th	289	335	194	–
10th	289	344	216	–

Sheffield Shield 1987-88

Final Table	P	WO	WI	D	LI	LO	Pts
WESTERN AUSTRALIA	10	6	1	–	1	2	38
QUEENSLAND	10	5	1	–	1	3	32
New South Wales	10	4	–	1	1	4	24
Victoria	10	2	5	1	1	1	22
South Australia	10	2	2	–	2	4	16
Tasmania	10	1	–	–	3	6	5.8*

* Penalty points (0.2) for not bowling sufficient overs before 5.00 p.m. on last day of their match v South Australia at Adelaide Oval.

Outright win 6 points, 1st innings win 2 points, 1st innings win/outright loss 0 points, draw/no result 0 points.

Leading First-Class Averages

Batting (Qual. 8 innings)	State	M	I	NO	HS	R	Avge	100	50	Ct
G.M. Wood	WA	12	18	3	186*	1050	70.00	3	5	7
D.C. Boon	TAS	12	21	2	184*	1287	67.73	5	6	13
J.D. Siddons	VIC	11	18	2	241*	1077	67.31	4	5	10
M.E. Waugh	NSW	10	16	3	116	833	64.07	4	4	18
A.R. Border	Q	13	22	3	205	1164	61.26	4	2	12
D.W. Hookes	SA	11	20	1	132	1149	60.47	4	7	18
P.W. Young	VIC	9	14	5	164*	543	60.33	1	3	17
G. Watts	VIC	5	10	0	176	563	56.30	3	1	3
D.F. Whatmore	VIC	11	19	1	170	912	50.66	2	7	15
A.M.J. Hilditch	SA	11	20	1	185	992	48.52	2	5	8
M.D. Taylor	TAS	12	22	0	216	1003	45.59	2	5	5
P.L. Taylor	NSW	8	9	3	78	269	44.83	–	1	4
G.A. Bishop	SA	11	20	1	123	833	43.84	3	4	3
D.M. Jones	VIC	12	19	1	191	751	41.72	3	2	15
P.R. Sleep	SA	14	22	3	104*	775	40.78	1	6	7

Bowling	State	O	M	R	W	Avge	Best	5wI	10wM
G.F. Lawson	NSW	336.3	102	792	42	18.85	6-31	3	–
S.R. Waugh	NSW	218.3	59	499	23	21.69	5.50	1	–
C.D. Matthews	WA	443.3	83	1277	57	22.40	8-101	3	–
D. Tazelaar	Q	375	92	1036	46	22.52	6-52	3	–
G.R.J. Matthews	NSW	335	105	746	32	23.31	6-97	2	–
C.G. Rackemann	Q	280.1	68	733	31	23.64	5-69	1	–
M.R. Whitney	NSW	290.2	63	762	32	23.81	5-33	3	–
T.M. Alderman	WA	394	114	944	39	24.20	6-91	2	–
P. Reiffel	VIC	146.2	36	416	17	24.47	4-80	–	–
K.H. MacLeay	WA	271.3	78	690	28	24.64	5-99	1	–
A.I.C. Dodemaide	VIC	420.4	103	1125	45	25.00	6-58	3	–
C.J. McDermott	Q	376	77	1087	41	26.51	7-54	3	1
P.A. Capes	WA	325.1	69	887	32	27.71	4-87	–	–
I.T. Botham	Q	311.5	82	805	29	27.75	3-12	–	–

McDonald's Cup
Semi-Finals

12 March at Adelaide, Oval. SOUTH AUSTRALIA beat TASMANIA on superior run-rate. Toss: South Australia. Tasmania 220-8 (50 overs) (D.C. Boon 62). South Australia 194-3 (41.1 overs) (D.W. Hookes 57*, D. Scott 46). South Australia target 194 off 44 overs – after two breaks for rain.

13 March at Sydney Cricket Ground. NEW SOUTH WALES beat VICTORIA by 5 wickets. Toss: Victoria. Victoria 180-7 (50 overs). New South Wales 184-5 (43 overs) (G. Smith 58*).

Final

27 March at Sydney Cricket Ground. NEW SOUTH WALES beat SOUTH AUSTRALIA by 23 runs. Toss: New South Wales. New South Wales 219-7 (50 overs). South Australia 196-6 (50 overs).

Cricket in South Africa

The 1988 cricket season turned out to be a two-man contest between Clive Rice and Allan Lamb. And it was symbolic of this state of affairs that the Castle Currie Cup cricket final should be contested between their respective provinces, Transvaal and Free State.

One would be very surprised if the vote for Rice as the player of the year was not unanimous. The facts speak for themselves. He finished third in the batting averages, in spite of having to play all his home matches on the spiteful Wanderers pitch, and fifth in the bowling averages. However, as outstanding as these performances were, his greatest contribution for Transvaal was his brilliance as captain – as director of operations on the field.

Rice started the season with a team that was full of holes and looked vulnerable – as indeed it turned out to be in the first few months when losing three times, twice at home, in the Benson & Hedges night series to Eastern Province (a real annihilation), the B section Impalas, and Northern Transvaal. They were also eliminated from the Nissan Shield following another home defeat, this time by Western Province.

The holes were gaping. There was no Pollock, no Kourie, no Clarke, both Page and McKenzie had broken down with serious injuries, and Radford was there for only half a season. In addition, Estwick, the latest West Indian wonder signed to replace the lost fast bowlers, was unfit and out of form. Lesser men would have panicked. But not Clive Edward Butler Rice. He proved once again that there is no tougher fighter in a tight corner, that there is nobody who can motivate men more success-fully, and that he is still, at the age of 38, a world-class cricketer.

With the exception of Eastern Province, who eliminated themselves by preparing a succession of disastrous non-cricketing pitches, he was able to mow down every other side in the competition. By the end of the season Estwick was the leading first-class wicket-taker in the country, apart from being the safest catcher in the slips along with half-brother Sylvester Clarke, and Transvaal had the Currie Cup very safely back on the TCC's display shelf.

In the past, Rice's critics have been quick to point out that Transvaal did not need a captain. They simply had an embarrassment of riches in terms of talent that no other province, state, or county could hope to match. But not this time. Transvaal's loss of talent was made even worse when their tried and trusted opening pair of Jimmy Cook and Henry Fotheringham did not perform anywhere near their usual form.

But Rice got his youngsters moving. Brian McMillan finished top of the bowling averages and Bruce Roberts fourth in the batting averages. In addition, Louis Vorster made a memorable, match-winning century at Newlands at New Year, traditionally a difficult match and venue for the men from north of the Vaal. Thus, in many ways, this could be said to be Rice's Currie Cup, rather than Transvaal's.

As for Lamb, it is difficult to assess whether the South African-born Englishman was an asset to Free State or not. He was certainly a huge asset to South African cricket, as he achieved the remarkable feat of stepping into the retired Graeme Pollock's shoes as the biggest batting drawcard in the country as though it was the most natural development.

His initial impact on Free State was immense, setting up a first-round Currie Cup victory over Eastern Province with a superb innings of 294 and a record partnership of 355 for the fifth-wicket with Joubert Strydom. But, as the season wore on, Free State's dependence on Lamb created a complex for the rest of the batsmen, most of whom were young striplings, which they were quite unable to overcome.

Free State may care to differ, but one doubts whether their success did much long-term good. They were unable to handle the pressure of topping the southern section, let alone the Currie Cup final, and, at the end of the season, hardly any of their home-grown products, on whom they will ultimately depend, had made much progress.

In real terms, Free State were not as good a side as either of their southern rivals, Eastern Province and Western Province, and one remains convinced that a five-day final between Transvaal and Eastern province would have been the best option. The latter, through the emergence of young batting stars, such as Mark Rushmere, Philip Amm, and David Callaghan, to support the experience of Kepler Wessels, Ken McEwan, and David Richardson, had the depth and consistency to match Rice's Transvaal top-order. And, even allowing for the loss of the injured Rod McCurdy, there was not much wrong with a bowling attack that included Greg Thomas and the vastly improved Springbok spinner Tim Shaw, plus two improved youngsters in Paul Rayment and Meyrick Pringle.

Eastern Province showed what they were capable of achieving when they went through the Nissan Shield (55 overs) unbeaten. They beat Western Province twice in the semi-finals and then scored an impressive seven-wicket victory in the final over Northern Transvaal. This match had to be started twice because of rain and was finally reduced to 50 overs.

Western Province, at their best, were capable of taking on the best, but they remained mercurially erratic and they still have to learn the consistency which Rice has drilled into Transvaal and Wessels latterly into Eastern Province. Their brilliance was seen in the Benson & Hedges night series (45 overs), when they comfortably won the final against Transvaal at the Wanderers by five wickets.

Northern Transvaal, through the development of Tertius Bosch and Fanie de Villiers as a highly talented home-grown opening attack and through the spinners Rodney Ontong and Bill Morris, had the bowlers to win matches. But their batting remained terribly vulnerable, with Springbok Roy Pienaar spending most of the season on the sidelines.

The big disappointment was Natal, who could not form a power base in either batting or bowling to be effective. Their few highlights came mainly from fast bowler Trevor Packer, who managed to get through the season uninjured and finished third on the wicket-taking list.

The B section was a notable triumph for Boland, who have now won this competition twice in three seasons, and must surely be given the same chance as Free State to prove themselves in the premier league.

Transvaal v Orange Free State, 1987-88
Castle Currie Cup Final

Transvaal won by 10 wickets.
Played at the Wanderers, Johannesburg on 11, 12, 13, 14, 15 February
Umpires: S.B. Lambson and L.J. Rautenbach

Orange Free State

Batsman	1st innings		2nd innings	
R. Steyn	b Estwick	12	lbw b B. McMillan	2
L. Wilkinson	c Jennings b Estwick	30	c G. McMillan b B. McMillan	0
A. Storie	lbw b Estwick	5	c G. McMillan b Rice	9
A. Kallicharran	b McMillan	7	(5) c Fotheringham b Estwick	10
A Lamb	lbw b G McMillan	8	(6) c Vorster b Estwick	33
J. Strydom*	c Jennings b B. McMillan	3	(7) c Vorster b B. McMillan	1
J. van Heerden	c Jennings b B. McMillan	28	(4) lbw b G. McMillan	26
R. East†	c Jennings b Rice	0	not out	50
S. Clarke	b Rice	0	(10) c Jennings b Estwick	21
C. van Zyl	c Cook b Estwick	31	(9) c Jennings b Estwick	0
A. Donald	not out	0	c Vorster b Rice	10
Extras	(B6, LB9, W3, NB2)	20	(LB2, W1, NB1)	4
		144		**166**

Transvaal

Batsman	1st innings		2nd innings	
J. Cook	c Kallicharan b Clarke	11	not out	15
H. Fotheringham	c Clarke b Donald	1	not out	17
M. Yachad	c East b Donald	15		
L. Vorster	c Lamb b Donald	36		
B. Roberts	c Clarke b Van Zyl	64		
C. Rice*	c East b Van Zyl	38		
B. McMillan	c East b Van Zyl	1		
G. McMillan	c Clarke b Van Zyl	5		
R. Jennings†	c and b Van Heerden	43		
J. Hooper	c East b Donald	0		
R. Estwick	not out	43		
Extras	(B1, LB11, W5, NB5)	22	(B1, W1)	2
		279	(0 wkts)	**34**

Transvaal	O	M	R	W	O	M	R	W
Estwick	26.4	12	47	4	17	3	63	4
Rice	27	14	38	2	21.4	6	57	2
Hooper	2	1	2	0	2	0	5	0
B. McMillan	17	8	18	3	9	5	7	3
G. McMillan	13	6	18	1	10	3	32	1
Roberts	4	1	6	0				

Free State	O	M	R	W	O	M	R	W
Clarke	26	6	55	1	1	1	0	0
Donald	31	5	83	4	4	0	14	0
Van Zyl	28	6	71	4	4	1	15	0
Van Heerden	19.4	4	52	1				
Kallicharan	3	0	6	0				
Lamb					1.4	1	4	0

Fall of Wickets

Wkt	OFS 1st	T 1st	OFS 2nd	T 2nd
1st	26	16	1	–
2nd	50	18	3	–
3rd	51	65	20	–
4th	65	80	49	–
5th	70	163	59	–
6th	70	165	64	–
7th	71	183	105	–
8th	76	188	109	–
9th	144	205	149	–
10th	144	279	162	–

Castle Currie Cup Final Tables

Northern Section	P	W	L	D	1st Innings points		Total points
					Batting	Bowling	
TRANSVAAL	7	5	2	0	11	33	119
Natal	7	4	1	2	10	30	100
Northern Transvaal	7	0	2	5	9	30	39

Southern Section	P	W	L	D	1st Innings points		Total points
					Batting	Bowling	
ORANGE FREE STATE	7	2	2	3	15	27	72
Western Province	7	2	3	2	9	28	67
Eastern Province	7	1	4	2	16	22	53

Leading First-Class Averages 1987-88

Batting	M	I	NO	HS	R	Avge	100	50
A. Lamb (OFS)	6	12	2	294	878	87.80	3	3
M. Rushmere (EP)	7	12	3	140	555	61.67	3	–
C. Rice (T)	8	10	2	150*	459	57.37	2	1
B. Roberts (T)	8	10	1	174	506	56.22	2	1
M. Austen (WP)	4	7	1	202*	316	52.67	1	1
D. Callaghan (EP)	7	10	0	148	435	43.50	1	2
K. Wessels (EP)	7	11	1	130	435	43.50	2	–
P. Amm (EP)	7	12	1	129	466	42.36	1	4
K. McEwan (EP)	7	10	1	97	364	40.44	–	4
P. Kirsten (WP)	7	12	2	82	398	39.80	–	3
J. Cook (T)	8	15	4	159	422	38.64	1	1
T. Lazard (WP)	7	11	0	90	416	37.82	–	4
L. Vorster (T)	8	11	1	174	368	36.80	1	1
V. du Preez (NT)	7	13	1	92*	423	35.25	–	4
P. Visagie (NT)	4	7	0	164	229	32.71	1	–
D. Richardson (EP)	7	10	2	72	241	30.12	–	2
N. Day (NT)	7	13	1	60	360	30.00	–	3
R. East (OFS)	8	14	2	58*	356	29.87	–	4
M. Logan (N)	7	13	1	52	357	29.75	–	1

Bowling	O	M	R	W	Avge	Best	5wI	10wM
B. McMillan (T)	99.5	38	178	19	9.37	5-39	1	–
N. Radford (T)	112.5	20	313	24	13.04	6-38	2	1
S. Clarke (OFS)	231.4	59	504	32	15.75	7-48	2	–
R. Estwick (T)	233.5	68	585	36	16.25	5-17	1	–
C. Rice (T)	217.1	73	497	30	16.57	5-14	1	–
C. van Zyl (OFS)	202.2	49	471	25	18.84	4-40	–	–
D. Callaghan (EP)	70.1	13	192	10	19.20	2-16	–	–
D. Rundle (WP)	230.1	78	523	26	20.11	6-37	3	1
P. Clift (N)	209.4	58	474	23	20.61	5-53	1	–
S. Jefferies (WP)	289.2	69	793	35	22.66	10-59	2	1
T. Packer (N)	204.1	29	760	33	23.03	6-38	2	–
P. De Villiers (NT)	207.3	49	593	25	23.72	4-29	–	–
G. Le Roux (WP)	201.1	38	504	21	24.00	4-60	–	–
W. Morris (NT)	205.1	48	609	24	25.37	6-59	1	1
R. Bentley (N)	113.2	26	283	10	28.30	3-10	–	–

Nissan Shield Final

EASTERN PROVINCE beat NORTHERN TRANSVAAL by 7 wickets. Northern Transvaal 216-7 (50 overs) (R. Pienaar 62, L. Barnard 48). Eastern Province 218-3 (48.2 overs) (K. McEwan 90*, D. Callaghan 92*).

Cricket in the West Indies

It was appropriate that, in its first year under new sponsorship, the annual West Indies' first-class championship should have been won by Jamaica. After 22 seasons as the Shell Shield, the tournament became the Red Stripe Cup, sponsored by a Jamaican brewing company and named after the famous Jamaican beer.

The West Indies Cricket Board of Control (WICBC) concluded the agreement to change sponsors at its meeting in November, 1987, and said the change had been made 'purely on financial grounds'. The 1987 Shell Shield had been reduced by half because of growing losses but, according to the WICBC, the new sponsorship guaranteed a return to the full, round-robin format for five years in the first instance.

The first Red Stripe Cup proved an enormous success. Keen interest was generated by several factors, principally the closeness of the competition, the participation of the leading players once they had returned from the West Indies tour of India, and the vigorous marketing of the sponsors.

With the final two rounds remaining, four of the six teams – Barbados, Jamaica, the Leeward Islands, and Trinidad & Tobago – were all in contention and, even with the last round to go, there was a statistical possibility that there would be a three-way tie. As it was, Jamaica secured the first innings points from their match against Trinidad & Tobago to win the regional championship for the first time since 1969, when they clinched their one and only Shell Shield.

The Jamaicans, led by the all-rounder Marlon Tucker, won because of a steady, all-round performance, spoiled only by a heavy defeat to second-placed Leeward Islands. They were favoured by having three matches at Sabina Park, where their home advantage has always been strong, and, by then, they were boosted by the return of their four Test players, Jeffrey Dujon, Patrick Patterson, and Courtney Walsh from India with the West Indies team and Michael Holding from a professional contract in New Zealand. They beat the Windward Islands and Barbados outright there, and then secured the Cup with the lead over Trinidad & Tobago in a drawn match.

The Leewards, with a storming finish in which they successively defeated the Windwards, Guyana, and Barbados by massive margins, were second, just four points behind, and, with their Test players back and under the captaincy of Vivian Richards, were the best balanced and also the strongest of the six teams.

Trinidad & Tobago, hampered by the almost complete loss of their match against Guyana to the weather, were third, Barbados were fourth, after losing their last two matches to Jamaica and the Leewards. Guyana and the Windwards, both badly affected by the absence of leading players, were at the bottom of the table.

The tall Antiguan fast bowler, Curtly Ambrose, was unquestionably the Player of the Season. With just a single first-class match behind him, he wrecked opposition batting match after match with his rare ability to produce devastating yorkers. His 35 wickets (at an average of 15.51) set a new record for the regional tournament, two more than Winston Davis's mark of 1983. So direct was his method, so precise his control, that 18 of his victims were either bowled or lbw.

Of the other bowlers, only Malcolm Marshall, refreshed after missing the World Cup and West Indies' tour of India, took more than 25 wickets.

Clayton Lambert, the left-handed Guyanese opener, was the only batsman with more than 500 runs, his 549 bettering the Guyana tournament record set by Roy Fredericks in 1975.

Robert Haynes, the tall Jamaican all-rounder, advanced his claims for Test selection with a batting average of 33.71 from forthright left-handed batting and 22 wickets at 25.63 from bouncy leg-spin bowling, while Ian Bishop, yet another big, strongly built fast bowler, impressed enough in his first full season for Trinidad & Tobago to be chosen for the West Indies team to England in the summer at the age of 20.

In the final of the one-day tournament, the Geddes Grant/Harrison Line Trophy, the 15,000 spectators witnessed a match to remember. Barbados beat Jamaica when Vibert Greene hit the last ball from Courtney Walsh, his county colleague at Gloucestershire, high to mid-wicket, where the second of two substitutes dropped his second catch in the over as the batsmen scrambled two.

The season was marred by the continuing dissent shown by captains, players, and managers to umpiring decisions. Marshall, captaining Barbados for the first time, was fined the equivalent of US$250 for critical comments he made to the media about the standard of the umpiring in Barbados's match against Jamaica, claiming his team was 'robbed'. Barbados's Test opener Desmond Haynes received a suspended fine for knocking over the stumps with his bat after a decision against him in the same match, and Winston Davis, the Windwards' captain, was severely criticized in the Press, if not censured by the Board, for his attitude to the umpires in the match against Jamaica.

Of even more concern were the comments of managers Hesketh Benjamin of the Leewards and Eddison Jamies of the Windwards that imputed dishonest motive to certain umpiring decisions.

Red Stripe Cup

	P	W	D	L	ND	Points
Jamaica	5	3	1	1	–	56
Leeward Islands	5	3	1	1	–	52
Trinidad & Tobago	5	2	2	–	1	48
Barbados	5	2	1	2	–	36
Guyana	5	1	–	3	1	20
Windward Islands	5	–	1	4	–	8

Leading Red-Stripe Averages

Batting (Qual: 200 runs, 4 innings)

	M	I	NO	HS	R	Avge	100s
C.B. Lambert (G)	5	9	2	162	549	78.42	2
K.L.T. Arthurton (LI)	5	8	2	121	380	63.33	1
W.W. Lewis (J)	5	8	1	132	428	61.14	1
R. Seeram (G)	5	9	2	119	424	60.57	1
P.J.L. Dujon (J)	3	4	0	108	241	60.25	1
T.R.O. Payne (B)	5	9	0	127	461	51.22	1
C.G. Greenidge (B)	3	6	1	70	215	43.00	–
D.S. Morgan (J)	4	6	1	101*	205	41.00	–
M.D. Marshall (B)	5	9	1	77	298	37.25	–
R.S. Otto (LI)	5	8	2	74*	221	36.83	–
C.A. Best (B)	5	9	0	98	328	36.44	–
L.L. Harris (LI)	5	6	0	63	204	34.00	–
R.C. Haynes (J)	5	8	1	87	236	33.71	–
M.C. Neita (J)	5	7	0	58	231	33.00	–
D.C. Collymore (WI)	5	10	2	87*	262	32.75	–
C.B. Burnett (G)	5	7	0	63	228	32.57	–
D.A. Joseph (WI)	5	10	0	109	308	30.80	1
L.C. Sebastien (WI)	5	10	0	116	302	30.20	1
A.L. Grant (B)	5	9	1	75	223	27.87	–

Bowling (Qual: 14 wkts)

	O	M	R	W	Best	5wI
I.R. Bishop (TT)	96.0	13	260	19	13-68	–
M.A. Tucker (J)	143.1	46	298	20	14-90	2
R. Nanan (TT)	196.0	72	305	20	15-25	1
C.E.L. Ambrose (LI)	189.2	34	543	35	15-51	3
W.K.M. Benjamin (LI)	83.4	21	239	14	17-07	1
M.D. Marshall (B)	159.5	35	466	27	17-26	2
J. Garner (B)	148.5	26	450	23	19-56	–
C.A. Walsh (J)	93.0	19	286	14	20-42	1
E.T. Willett (LI)	102.0	26	248	12	20-66	–
A.H. Gray (TT)	108.0	15	349	14	24-92	–
R.C. Haynes (J)	231.0	62	564	22	25-63	2
D.C. Collymore (WI)	141.0	20	423	16	26-44	–
G.E. Charles (G)	116.2	14	430	14	30-71	2
J.T. Etienne (WI)	165.0	33	484	15	32-26	–

Geddes Grant/Harrison Line Trophy Final (1 day)
3 March, at Kingston. BARBADOS beat JAMAICA by one wicket (off the last ball). Jamaica 218-8 (46 overs) (R.C. Haynes 83, C.A. Davidson 43*). Barbados 219-9 (46 overs) (D.L. Haynes 58, T.R.O. Payne 44, A.L.Grant 40; B.P. Patterson 10-0-45-3, C.A. Walsh 10-1-46-3).

Cricket in New Zealand

In an unsatisfactory and anticlimactic finish, calculations were required to decide the Shell Trophy competition. Going into the final two matches, four teams – Auckland, Northern Districts, Wellington, and Otago – 14 points off the pace – had title aspirations.

Otago duly beat Wellington easily, taking maximum points. Auckland, working on a bizarre calculation, believed they would finish level with Otago on points, but head them off on a countback, if they played for a first-innings result against Northern on a featherbed pitch and could reach 313 for the loss of no more than four wickets. Auckland paid the penalty for taking heed of an erroneous newspaper report which stated Wellington's innings against Otago earlier in the season had ended at nine wickets down when in fact they had been all out. Thus encouraged, Auckland needlessly declared at the appointed 313 for four and claimed the trophy.

However, several days later, after a further close scrutiny of the official team cards, Otago were declared the winners by a mere 0.272 point. The winners were assessed by working out the net batting average per wicket and deducting the average runs conceded for each wicket taken.

It was Otago's fourth Shell Trophy triumph since the competition began in 1975-76, and completed an excellent season for Warren Lees' team. They had earlier won the Shell Cup one-day title. Otago were the early pace-setters with back-to-back wins over Central Districts and Auckland before rather losing their way in mid-season. In contrast, Auckland lost their first two matches outright before three consecutive wins enabled them to move rapidly up the table.

Otago's success was built around solid batting performances from Richard Hoskin, Derek Walker, and Lees, the former test wicket-keeper who is widely regarded as New Zealand's best provincial captain. Left-arm spinner Stephen Boock was the country's leading bowler.

Auckland's challenge was led by lanky opener Trevor Franklin, whose four centuries ultimately enabled him to regain his Test place. However, it was not until internationals Martin Snedden, John Bracewell, Willie Watson, and Danny Morrison returned from Australia that they began bowling teams out. That weakness proved costly.

The other four teams had patchy seasons, but some fine individual performers. Wellington captain Robert Vance pushed his way into the Tet side with 638 runs from 11 innings, while Bruce Edgar chipped in with 676 runs. Central Districts could not repeat their 1986-87 success, with Martin Crowe absent for most of the summer, although Mark Greatbatch's remarkable Test debut was born from his consistent batting performances. Northern Districts leant heavily on Graeme Hick, whose 827 runs was the competitions' highest aggregate, but it did throw up a highly promising teenage all-rounder in Shane Thomson. Canterbury, despite excellent service from Michael Holding, had an awful season, with five losses in its last seven games amid talk of unsettling disharmony within the team.

Shell Trophy 1987-88

Final Table	P	W	L	D	1st innings Points	Points
OTAGO	8	3	1	4	16	52
Auckland	8	3	2	3	16	52†
Northern Districts	8	3	1	4	12	48†
Wellington	8	2	2	4	18	42*
Central Districts	8	2	3	3	14	38*
Canterbury	8	1	5	2	20	32

12 pts for win; 4 pts 1st innings lead. * First-innings points shared in one match. † First-innings points shared in two matches.

Leading First-Class Averages 1987-88

Batting	M	I	NO	HS	R	Avge	100
R.H. Vance (Wellington)	9	14	3	121	731	66.45	3
G.A. Hick (N. Districts)	9	14	1	146	827	63.61	4
M.D. Crowe (C. Districts)	4	7	1	143	349	58.16	2
K.R. Rutherford (Otago)	7	12	1	182	629	57.18	2
B.A. Young (N. Districts)	10	14	7	94	384	54.85	0
W.K. Lees (Otago)	7	10	4	112	319	53.16	1
J.G. Bracewell (Auckland)	5	7	1	104	315	52.50	1
R.T. Latham (Canterbury)	9	16	3	141*	679	52.23	2
B.A. Edgar (Wellington)	9	15	2	103*	676	52.00	1
R.N. Hoskin (Otago)	8	14	2	157	599	49.91	2
D.J. Walker (Otago)	9	16	5	77	536	48.72	0
E.B. McSweeney (Wellington)	9	12	2	205*	459	45.90	1
M.R. Pringle (Auckland)	6	7	1	77	271	45.16	0
M.J. Greatbach (C. Districts)	10	19	1	149	795	44.16	2
J.G. Wright (Canterbury)	4	7	0	103	291	41.57	1
T.J. Franklin (Auckland)	10	16	0	120	664	41.50	4
G.R. Larsen (Wellington)	9	13	2	161	451	41.00	1
C.J. Smith (C. Districts)	8	15	2	122*	530	40.76	1
C.M. Kuggeleijn (N. Districts)	9	13	2	87	429	39.00	0
B.G. Cooper (N. Districts)	9	12	1	116*	415	37.72	1
D.J. White (N. Districts)	9	16	1	80	522	34.80	0
S.A Thomson (N. Districts)	6	6	1	84	174	34.80	0
K.J. Burns (Otago)	9	16	0	136	550	34.37	2
S.W. Duff (C. Districts)	7	11	4	70*	238	34.00	0

Qualification: 5 completed innings, average 34.

Bowling	O	M	R	W	Best	Avge
M.A. Holding (Canterbury)	258.5	87	488	29	7-52	16.82
E.J. Chatfield (Wellington)	175.1	59	320	16	4-36	20.00
W. Watson (Auckland)	181.2	50	468	23	6-55	20.34
M.C. Snedden (Auckland)	191	63	404	18	5-31	22.44
S.L. Boock (Otago)	421.2	150	948	42	6-110	22.57
W.P. Fowler (Auckland)	137.1	36	364	16	6-41	22.75
R.G. Holland (Wellington)	249.2	76	738	31	7-69	23.80
J.P. Millmow (Wellington)	264.5	67	776	31	4-19	25.03
M.W. Priest (Canterbury)	260.2	68	732	28	5-63	26.14
G.K. Robertson (C. Districts)	223.4	53	635	23	5-34	27.60
N.A. Mallender (Otago)	185.4	45	477	17	4-64	28.05
B.J. Barrett (N. Districts)	248.2	43	811	25	4-41	32.44
K. Treiber (N. Districts)	303.4	82	811	25	6-96	32.44
C.W.H. Lawrence (Canterbury)	212.5	41	684	20	4-43	34.20
D.K. Morrison (Auckland)	161	31	520	15	5-69	34.66
T.J. Wilson (Otago)	293.3	57	957	27	5-82	35.44

Qualification: 15 wickets

SUBSCRIBE TO

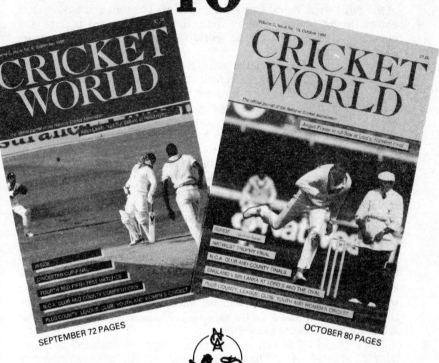

SEPTEMBER 72 PAGES

OCTOBER 80 PAGES

THE OFFICIAL JOURNAL OF
THE NATIONAL CRICKET ASSOCIATION

THE BIGGEST READ IN CRICKET

THE ONLY CRICKET MAGAZINE REPORTING THE GAME
FROM GRASS ROOTS TO SUPERSTARS.

BILL FRINDALL WRITES MONTHLY IN *CRICKET WORLD*

Cricket in India

First-class cricket in India, already relegated to a tertiary status behind Tests and one-day internationals, had to compete with the showpiece of the game – the World Cup – for attention. The tons and tons of runs scored in the Duleep Trophy went virtually unnoticed because the matches were played when the World Cup was hotting up towards its intriguing climax.

As many as 13 three-figure innings were recorded in the Duleep Trophy alone. Of them, three were double hundreds and one a big triple by Raman Lamba. How very devalued these runs can be was reflected in Lamba's making a very brief appearance in the Test series against the West Indies and beating a hasty retreat from hot Caribbean pace. Lamba made 996 runs in 12 innings and yet he is now far from the national team.

Hyderabad, which had won the Ranji Trophy after a gap of 49 years in the previous season, scored a double in winning the Irani Trophy, in which they beat the Rest of India XI by virtue of a 27-run first innings lead. Arshad Ayub's six for 105 in the match and his 11 wickets in the Duleep Trophy against North Zone pitchforked him into the Indian team. He made a bit of an impression in his first Test and then faded in the course of the series.

The lack of quality bowling is nowhere more obvious than in first-class cricket in India, much of which is played on shirtfront wickets. The only bowler to surface in the season was the leg-spinning sensation Narendra Hirwani, who equalled Bob Massie's haul of 16 wickets on a Test debut when befuddled West Indian batsmen surrendered on a doctored wicket in Madras. India, who drew the series 1-1, had beaten the West Indies in a Test for the first time in nine years.

Tamil Nadu's fine run in the Ranji Trophy culminated in a cup triumph after 33 years. The big win scored over Railways came even as India were triumphing in the Sharjah Cup. Consistent batting by the Trinidadian Robin Singh, exciting Test prospect V.B. Chandrasekhar, and L. Sivaramakrishnan was the key to the team's performance. First-season off-spinner M. Venkatramana was the state's most successful bowler with a bag of 35 wickets, while acting captain S. Vasudevan had a haul of 27 with his left-arm spin.

Tamil Nadu could get by without the services of Srikkanth and Raman, but they had been drawn so well in the knock-out part of the championship that they could not possibly fail. Delhi, Bombay, and Karnataka, all former champions, were clubbed together in one half and Delhi were knocked out by Railways in a rain-hit semi-final in which the ultimate runners-up had a better runs per wicket quotient.

There was a huge outcry about the neglect of domestic first-class cricket and the Board resolved never to let the Irani Trophy and the Duleep Trophy matches clash with international fixtures in the country again. The debate on pitches was, however, inconclusive, with no one knowing how to provide other than plumb wickets or nasty turners which pamper the spinners. The winners – North Zone (Duleep),

Hyderabad (Irani), and Tamil Nadu (Ranji) were, however, quite pleased with the way things went in another typical season of big scores.

Leading First-Class Averages 1987-88

Batting (Qualification: 600 runs)	I	NO	R	HS	Avge	100
Raman Lamba (Delhi)	12	0	996	320	83.00	4
A.D. Gaekwad (Baroda)	10	2	617	216	77.12	2
L.S. Rajput (Bombay)	14	1	905	275	69.62	4
S. Majrekar (Bombay)	14	4	678	278	67.80	1
Manu Nayyar (Delhi)	12	2	653	184	65.30	2
Arun Lal (Bengal)	12	0	777	205	64.75	2
W.V. Raman (Tamil Nadu)	13	1	637	182	53.08	1

Bowling (Qualification: 25 wickets)	O	M	R	W	Avge
D. Chopra (Punjab)	275.3	87	546	32	17.06
M. Venkatramana (T. Nadu)	239.1	55	716	35	20.45
S. Vasudevan (T. Nadu)	265.4	78	600	27	22.22
R. Bhat (Karnataka)	286	68	780	35	22.28
Naba Konwar (Assam)	177	19	592	25	23.68
N. Hirwani (Madhya Pradesh)	237.1	25	835	35	23.86
D. Sharma (Haryana)	238.3	42	628	26	24.15
A. Ayub (Hyderabad)	279.4	61	712	27	26.37
S. Yadav (Hyderabad)	286.4	65	827	28	29.54

Ranji Trophy Final

25, 26, 27, 29, 30 March, Madras. TAMIL NADU beat RAILWAYS by an innings and 144 runs. Railways 317 (Yusuf Ali Khan 87, Naresh Churi 112; M. Venkatramana 7-94) and 248 (P. Karkera 48; S. Vasudevan 7-59). Tamil Nadu 709 (V.B. Chandrasekhar 89, P.C. Prakash 50, V. Sivaramakrishnan 94, Robin Singh 131, L. Sivaramakrishnan 101, D. Girish 55; Hyder Ali 3-139).

Cricket in Pakistan

Because of the Reliance World Cup, which was jointly and successfully staged by Pakistan and India, and the subsequent Test series against England, the 1987-88 domestic season suffered. Most of the domestic contests were played, but not the PACO pentangular, for which there was hardly any time left because of the delayed start of Pakistan's major cricket championship, the Quaid-e-Azam Trophy.

The 1987-88 season began in August with an Under-19 championship, which consisted of three-day games as well as a limited-overs competition, both of which were won by the Karachi Blues. This was followed by the Wills Cup limited-overs championship, which was played as a rehearsal for the World Cup. Well contested, the tournament was won by the Pakistan International Airline (PIA), who defeated United Bank (UBL) by two wickets in a thrilling final at Lahore. PIA later went on to win the Quaid-e-Azam Trophy as well. This was PIA's fifth title win in the seven years since it was started. Aamer Malik, the man of the match in the final, was declared the best fielder, Javed Miandad the best batsman, Zahid Ali of the PIA the best bowler, and UBL's Ashraf Ali the best wicket-keeper.

In a shorter season, only 55 first-class matches were played compared with 126 last year. BCCP Patron's Trophy, which began in December, was contested between 37 teams divided into eight groups. Like last year, the group league matches were declared non-first-class. The matches from pre-quarter-final stages were given first-class status.

Habib Bank won the Patron's Trophy after a lapse of ten years. Javed Miandad's batting was the highlight of the final against the United Bank. He played two unbeaten innings of 144 and 48. Habib Bank, set to make 247, won by five wickets. PIA won the Quaid-e-Azam Trophy by beating the United Bank by 309 runs in three days. Centuries by Test batsman Asif Mujtaba and Hammad Butt set the tempo on the first day, and young pace bowlers Zulfiqar Ali and Wasim Haider ran through the UBL batsmen twice for low scores. For UBL, the 1987-88 season was heartbreaking as they lost all the finals of the domestic championships.

No batsman reached 1,000 runs, compared with six last year. The batting averages were topped by UBL's Moin-ul-Atiq, who hit three successive hundreds in the Patron's Trophy.

Only four bowlers took 50 or more wickets, compared with 17 last year. The bowling averages were topped by Test off-spinner Mohammad Nazir Jr of Railways. Test wicket-keeper Ashraf Ali finished with 40 victims.

It was a satisfying season for Pakistan cricket. The Youth team reached the final of the Youth World Cup in Australia, losing to the hosts in an exciting match. Pakistan itself did well to reach the semi-finals of the Reliance World Cup and to win the Test series against England at home. Imran Khan announced his retirement from international cricket, but later made a comeback on public and presidential demand to draw an exciting Test series in the Caribbean.

Leading First-Class Averages

Batting	M	I	NO	R	HS	Avge	100
Moin-ul-Atiq (United Bank)	4	8	1	528	157	75.42	3
Azhar Khan (Habib Bank)	6	9	3	425	73*	70.83	–
Asif Mujtaba (Pakistan Int. Airlines)	10	17	3	840	157	60.00	3
Javed Miandad (Habib Bank)	6	8	2	358	144*	59.66	1
Nasir Khan (Pakistan Int. Airlines)	4	6	2	227	64	56.75	–
Tahir Rasheed (Habib Bank)	10	11	6	275	86*	55.00	–
Nadeem Abbasi (Rawalpindi)	8	15	1	769	120*	54.92	2
Zahid Ahmed (Pakistan Int. Airlines)	9	15	1	767	179	54.78	2
Shaukat Mirza (Habib Bank)	7	11	3	424	108*	53.00	2
Nasir Wasti (PNSC)	6	11	3	417	108	52.12	1
Aamer Sohail (Habib Bank)	10	17	2	763	125	50.86	4
Rizwan-uz-Zaman (Pakistan Int. Airlines)	7	14	1	661	133*	50.84	2
Ijaz Ahmed (Habib Bank)	7	10	0	493	125	49.30	1
Saleem Taj (HBFC)	5	7	1	288	120	48.00	1
Saleem Malik (Habib Bank)	7	10	2	381	95	47.62	–
Rameez Raja (PNSC)	5	8	1	305	102	43.57	1
Mansoor Akhtar (United Bank)	10	18	3	649	132	43.26	2
Shafiq Ahmed (United Bank)	10	17	1	690	155*	43.12	1
Agha Zahid (Habib Bank)	9	16	0	679	162	42.43	2
Feroze Mehdi (Pakistan Int. Airlines)	5	8	1	295	163*	42.14	1
Mohammad Zahid (Multan)	4	7	0	295	110	42.14	1
Sajid Ali (National Bank)	6	12	1	457	100	41.54	1
Pervez Shah (Railways)	6	9	2	288	136	41.14	1
Atif Rauf (ADBP)	9	12	1	449	99	40.81	–
Rizwan Qazi (Lahore City/Lahore)	6	10	1	364	68	40.44	–
Abdullah Khan (PNSC)	7	14	1	520	155*	40.00	1
Nasir Shah (Karachi)	5	10	0	382	118	38.20	2

Qualification: 6 innings, 200 runs, avge 38.00.

Bowling	O	R	W	Avge	Best	5wI
Mohammad Nazir (Railways)	162.1	329	27	12.18	8-99	3
Shahzad Ilyas (HBFC)	68.2	209	13	16.07	4-30	–
Shahid Butt (United Bank)	77.1	163	10	16.30	3-64	–
Zulfiqar Ali (Pakistan Int. Airlines)	68.5	265	16	16.56	5-52	1
Nadeem Ghauri (Habib Bank)	492	1097	65	16.87	7-100	7
Abdul Qadir (Habib Bank)	293.1	648	36	18.00	9-56	3
Ijaz Faqih (Muslim Commercial Bank)	95.1	235	13	18.07	6-72	2
Tanvir Ali (Pakistan Int. Airlines)	90.3	216	11	19.63	4-33	–
Iqbal Qasim (National Bank)	312.5	769	39	19.71	6-40	3
Masood Anwar (United Bank)	522.3	1343	67	20.04	7-53	7
Khatib Rizwan (ADBP)	389	1004	50	20.08	7-52	5
Mohinder Kumar (HBFC)	102.2	324	16	20.25	4-50	–
Iqbal Sikander (Pakistan Int. Airlines)	227	615	30	20.50	6-50	3
Kazim Mehdi (HBFC)	179.2	580	28	20.71	5-48	3
Sajjad Akbar (PNSC)	425.2	958	46	20.82	9-59	4
Abdullah Khan (PNSC)	103.4	251	11	22.81	4-49	–
Raees Ahmed (Karachi)	210.4	626	26	24.07	6-51	2
Wasim Haider (Pakistan Int. Airlines)	137.3	537	22	24.40	5-66	2
Raja Afaq (ADBP)	374.2	980	40	24.50	7-62	2
Kamal Merchant (United Bank)	222.4	540	22	24.54	4-41	–
Asif Mujtaba (Pakistan Int. Airlines)	122.4	320	13	24.61	6-25	1
Raja Sarfraz (Rawalpindi)	430.2	1246	50	24.92	6-29	5
Rashid Khan (Pakistan Int. Airlines)	122.5	450	18	25.00	3-39	–
Zahid Ahmed (Pakistan Int. Airlines)	181.4	362	14	25.85	3-26	–
Farrukh Zaman (Muslim Commer. Bank)	277	809	31	26.09	6-78	2

Qualification: 10 wickets; avge under 27.00.
ADBP – Agricultural Development Bank of Pakistan; HBFC – House Building Finance
Corporation; PNSC – Pakistan National Shipping Corporation.

Cricket in Sri Lanka

Colombo Cricket Club won the Lakspray Trophy for the second time in four seasons, and with it the Division I interclub championships for a third time in the club's 125-year history. Easily the oldest of the 21 clubs competing for the 198788 championships, CCC made short work of Galle Cricket Club to win by an innings inside three days. Galle, who qualified to play in a final for the first time in their 112year history, were no match for the starstudded CCC side led by leftarm spinner Roger Wijesuriya and were outclassed in all departments.

CCC were spearheaded by the outstanding allround talents of the tall and powerfully built Athula Samarasekera, who followed his rich exploits in Zimbabwe with the Sri Lanka 'B' team with four wickets and a hardhit 81 off 114 balls that gave him the match award. Wicketkeeper and opening bat Ashley de Silva, another success from the Zimbabwe tour, made 74 in 4¼ hours, and with Samarasekera put on 125 for the fifth wicket. Galle CC, shot out for a moderate 77 in the first innings, folded up tamely for 155. Wijesuriya picked up five wickets in the second innings to continue from where he left off in Zimbabwe. All three CCC stars were included in the 29member pool named shortly afterwards for the tour of England.

Had either Singhalese SC or Nondescripts CC – two clubs with a number of Sri Lanka cricketers – played against CCC, the final could have been more meaningful. Ironically, Galle were responsible for keeping out both these clubs – NCC from the final round and SSC from the final.

The tournament committee's lax attitude in allowing matches to be postponed allowed Galle CC the advantage of knowing beforehand exactly the number of points they required to qualify in both instances.

The most heartening feature of the final round, where 10 clubs qualified out of 21, was the presence of four from the South – Galle CC, Moratuwa SC, Panadura SC, and debutants Singha SC. CCC, unbeaten throughout the season, topped one group, and Galle CC the other.

CCC were led admirably by Owen Mottau, a stocky Sri Lankan in his midforties, now domiciled in Australia. For most of the season he led makeshift teams, with the club losing many players on national call. Mottau was not available for the final, and the honour of leading the club to the title for a second time fell to Wijesuriya.

CCC's success during the season is marked by the presence of three of their bowlers in the top six of the averages. In the batting, Charith Senanayake, a tall stylish lefthander with the season's highest aggregate, 761, and Roshan Mahanama, who made the season's highest score, 180 against Air Force, figured in the first six.

Jayananda Warnaweera (Galle CC) not only took the season's highest number of wickets, 64, but also returned the best bowling figures, eight for 44 against Bloomfield.

Leading Lakspray Trophy Averages 1987-88

Batting	M	I	NO	HS	R	Avge	100	50
L.R.D. Mendis (SSC)	7	7	1	159	487	81.16	2	2
C.P. Senanayake (CCC)	11	15	5	133*	761	76.10	3	4
R.S. Mahanama (CCC)	5	6	1	180	341	68.20	1	1
T. Gunaratne (Kandy CC)	9	10	4	87	356	59.33	0	3
A. Ranatunga (SSC)	7	7	1	122	343	57.16	2	1
B.C. Jayawardena (Moors SC)	6	9	2	136*	343	49.00	1	2

Bowling	O	M	R	W	Avge	5wI	10wM
R.G.C.E. Wijesuriya (CCC)	110.2	33	213	27	7.88	2	0
K.I.W. Wijegunawardena (CCC)	108.4	22	318	34	9.35	2	1
M. Halangoda (SSC)	174.1	47	398	40	9.95	4	0
G.F. Labrooy (CCC)	139.4	39	373	32	11.65	3	0
V.B. John (SSC)	124	28	315	27	11.66	1	0
R. Ranjith (Singha SC)	235.5	57	593	46	12.89	4	1

Colombo CC v Galle CC

1987-88 Lakspray Trophy Final

Colombo CC beat Galle CC by an innings and 70 runs
Played at P. Saravanamuttu Stadium 28, 29, 30 April
Toss: Colombo CC.
Umpires: P.W. Vidanagamage & K.T. Francis

Galle CC

A. Seneviratne	c Senanayake b Samarasekera	14		c Senanayake b Labrooy	23
N. Ramanayake	b Jurangpathy	4	(4)	c and b Gamage	4
C. Mendis	c Wijesuriya b Samarasekera	6	(10)	c Senanayake b Wijesuriya	1
P. de Silva	c Samarasekera b Wijegunawardena	10	(6)	c Wijegunawardena b Wijesuriya	8
K. Dharmasiri	c A.M. de Silva b Labrooy	0		st A.M. de Silva b Wijesuriya	45
L. Loos†	b Samarasekera	13	(7)	c Dias b Wijesuriya	1
P. Kumara	c Senanayake b Samarasekera	0	(8)	c Seneviratne b Jurangpathy	11
G. de Silva	run out	0	(3)	c H.S.R. de Silva b Wijesuriya	4
B.P. Nilan	run out	4	(2)	b Labrooy	35
G. Pitigala*	not out	20	(9)	c Samarasekera b Wijegunawardena	17
K.P.J. Warnaweera	st A.M. de Silva b Jurangpathy	0		not out	1
Extras	(B2, NB3, W1)	6		(LB2, NB3)	5
		77			**155**

Colombo CC

A.M. de Silva†	b Warnaweera	74
H.S.R. de Silva	st Loos b Nilan	18
C.P. Senanayake	c Loos b P. de Silva	2
R.L. Dias	run out	17
M.A.R. Samarasekera	c Seneviratne b Warnaweera	81
B.R. Jurangpathy	b P. de Silva	25
A.C. Seneviratne	c Loos b Warnaweera	31
G.R. Labrooy	b Warnaweera	13
R.G.C.E. Wijesuriya*	not out	6
K.I.W. Wijegunawardena	c Loos b Warnaweera	23
J.C. Gamage	c Ramanayake b Warnaweera	4
Extras	(B3, LB2, NB1, W2)	8
		302

Colombo	O	M	R	W	O	M	R	W
Labrooy	9	3	19	1	11	4	33	2
Wijegunawardena	10	4	22	1	11	3	22	1
Samarasekera	14	5	27	4	9	2	24	0
Wijesuriya	4	1	5	0	15.5	5	33	5
Gamage					6	1	14	1
Jurangpathy	1.4	0	2	2	5	0	27	1

Galle CC	O	M	R	W
Nilan	18	1	78	1
P. de Silva	25	4	88	2
Warnaweera	33.3	8	101	6
Pitigala	12	2	30	0

Fall of Wickets

	G	C	G
Wkt	1st	1st	2nd
1st	22	25	51
2nd	34	34	66
3rd	36	62	66
4th	36	187	91
5th	37	204	97
6th	38	234	116
7th	47	259	144
8th	59	270	145
9th	77	296	151
10th	77	302	155

West Indies in England

Vivian Richards and the West Indian touring team of 1988 arrived in England with a more modest reputation than their recent predecessors from the Caribbean. On some form this could be justified. They had not reached the semi-final of the World Cup. They had only drawn a Test series in India. They had very nearly lost one at home against Pakistan.

What tended to be overlooked was that their most successful bowler, Malcolm Marshall, had withdrawn from the World Cup and the tour of India and had missed through injury the Test match in Guyana that Pakistan won. Richards himself had also missed that match. Though due respect was paid to the undoubted talent of the younger players now emerging, there was a school of thought which held that this might be a transitional period in which West Indies were vulnerable.

This view may have come under the heading of wishful thinking, but in the first month of the tour very little happened to discount it. Indeed England won the limited-overs Texaco series 3-0, a false scent if ever there was one.

It was not known then that Mike Gatting, who both as captain and as most successful batsman had done so much to win the Texaco series, would play in only two Test matches. But even in defeat West Indies had provided ominous evidence of their true strength.

The old adage that the strength of a team (or of an army) lies in its reserves must have occurred to many spectators who saw the youthful Bishop bowling in the limited-overs series. He was clearly not part of the West Indies Test plan on this tour, but he was already remarkably mature by most standards. If West Indies could do without him, they must be a strong side. The same could be said of the young Arthurton's batting form in the minor matches. When one of the batsmen, Simmonds, suffered a severe head injury and had to go home, Richards and the popular manager Jackie Hendriks did not need a replacement.

One of the many differences between limited-overs cricket and the traditional game is that the fielding captain in the former version does not have total control of his bowlers. The rules force him to use a fifth bowler, who may not be up to the standard of the other four. He may give the batsmen a chance to shake off the shackles with which the others have pinned them down and to gain a measure of confidence which had been missing previously.

Thus the policy of keeping up unrelieved pressure with four fast bowlers made this West Indian side far more menacing in the Test matches than in the rest of their programme. It may not have provided great entertainment for the purist watcher, but the frequent fall of wickets kept it from being uneventful. And if Richards did require a slow bowler in his side, he had a very fine all-round cricketer at his disposal in Roger Harper. Early in the tour Harper seemed to have lost his bowling action, but his batting and fielding made him worth his place and allowed him to find his form without undue pressure on him as a bowler.

The West Indies fast bowling on this tour clearly demonstrated two harsh facts. One was that four good fast bowlers playing together make an impact far greater than any which they can achieve as individuals. During two decades of West Indian success, most of their fast bowlers have been playing for English counties. They have taken a lot of wickets for their counties, but they have not dominated opposing batsmen as they have in the Test arena.

For this form of attack to prosper, the bowlers, of course, have to stay fit – fitter, anyhow, than most English fast bowlers. Ideally, too, one of them should be a really great bowler. Marshall met this last requirement handsomely, not only because he could come on and achieve the break-through that had been eluding the other three, but because he could cut his pace and concentrate on moving the ball about. He could lend the attack an extra element of variety.

Of the others, Walsh already had several seasons of success in English conditions behind him with Gloucestershire. Benjamin became an ever greater force as his fitness improved. Ambrose, uncannily resembling Joel Garner with his six foot eight, bowled with an accuracy and some-times a steepness of bounce that made him hard to play even on the slowest of pitches. Patterson, perhaps the fastest of them all, was scarcely needed.

By West Indian standards, the batting of the 1988 side was not up to that of their predecessors, but Logie and Dujon and sometimes Marshall gave them powers of recovery in the middle of the order that on several occasions dowsed the rising hopes of opponents.

The minor matches of the tour were a disappointment, partly because West Indies used them in an unabashed way for practice. Sometimes they made little attempt to win. In the television era, of course, the Test match is glamorized to the exclusion of the three-day county match, and the tourists are not alone in devaluing the latter. Some counties do it by using their match against the touring team to rest their main players and give experience to younger ones. It is a regrettable sign of the times.

First Test: Trent Bridge 2, 3, 4, 6, 7 June
Match Drawn.

For most of the first three days, in which play was reduced by periods of rain, England looked in danger of defeat, but they recovered after the week-end and eventually earned a draw with something to spare.

England began with an opening stand of 125 between Gooch and Broad, but once Marshall had switched to the Pavilion end, batting became vastly more complicated. The ball had done little in the morning, but after lunch it swung a lot and Marshall, relying mainly on in-swing at just under his fastest pace, ran through the leading England batsmen. Early in an accurate, superbly sustained spell of 19 overs, broken only by the tea interval, he took the first four wickets for only 14 runs. Only two overs were lost through rain, but England ended with 220 for six and it had required a resolute innings of 39 not out by Pringle to reach that.

Next day, the last five wickets fell to Ambrose and Marshall for only 25 runs. But England's problems really grew when it was revealed that their bowlers could not swing the ball as the West Indians had. After a wet afternoon, they did remove Greenidge and Richardson for 84, but West Indies ended the day at 126 for two with Richards in full flow and Haynes well established.

On the Saturday, England might well have been driven into a position from which there was no recovery, but two-thirds of the day's play was lost through rain, and, brilliantly though Richards played with the young Hooper in active and elegant support, they finished only 19 ahead at 264 for four. They had made 138 between interruptions off 29.5 overs, and Emburey's seven overs had cost 62 runs.

After the week-end, England's bowling was tidier, but they could only delay the West Indies declaration a little, and took a severe mauling from Marshall before that came with a lead of 203. There were still 31 overs of the fourth day remaining plus a possible 95 on the final day.

Gooch from the first tackled the heavy task with the utmost application and soundness. In the second hour Broad was caught at the wicket, but Gatting played through a difficult final period and for 95 minutes on the last morning when the going was still very tough.

He was out in a curious way. It had not been widely realized that Marshall was unfit, and the failure to use him in the first 75 minutes of the last morning was unexpected. However, when he did come on, it was at half-pace and he was clearly handicapped, though he produced a near unplayable ball to hit the outside of Gatting's off-stump at 116, 25 minutes before lunch.

Marshall left the field soon after lunch, and before long Gooch and Gower found themselves faced with the slow bowling of Richards and Hooper, which eased the pressure. During their stand of 161 they swiftly erased the arrears of 203, and though Gooch's magnificent innings ended at 146 after he had batted 6¾ hours, the danger was over by then.

ENGLAND v WEST INDIES   FIRST TEST   TRENT BRIDGE   June 2,3

Eng 1st

No	Batsman	How out	Bowler	Runs	Wkt	Total	6	4	Mins	Balls
1	GOOCH	b	MARSHALL	73	1	125	-	8	174	131
2	BROAD	b	MARSHALL	54	3	161	-	3	240	167
3	GATTING *	c LOGIE	MARSHALL	5	2	141	-	-	30	15
4	GOWER	c DUJON	AMBROSE	18	5	186	-	-	99	56
5	LAMB	lbw	MARSHALL	0	4	161	-	-	2	2
6	PRINGLE	b	MARSHALL	39	6	223	-	3	147	143
7	DOWNTON †	not	out	16	-	-	-	1	131	75
8	EMBUREY	c DUJON	MARSHALL	0	7	223	-	-	3	4
9	DeFREITAS	b	AMBROSE	3	8	235	-	-	17	10
10	JARVIS	b	AMBROSE	6	9	243	-	1	18	15
11	DILLEY	b	AMBROSE	2	10	245	-	-	2	2
	Extras	B - LB 13 W 5 NB 11		29					620 (101ov + 14nb)	

245

Bowler	O	M	R	W		NB	W
MARSHALL	30	4	69	6		4	2
PATTERSON	16	2	49	-		7	2
AMBROSE	26	10	53	4		1	1
WALSH	20	4	39	-		3	
HOOPER	8	1	20	-			
RICHARDS	1	-	2	-			

Wkt	Partnership between		Runs	Balls
1	Gooch	Broad	125	249
2	Broad	Gatting	16	38
3	— .. —	Gower	20	47
4	Gower	Lamb	0	2
5	— . —	Pringle	25	92
6	Pringle	Downton	37	134
7	Downton	Emburey	0	4
8	— . —	DeFreitas	12	25
9	— . —	Jarvis	8	27
10	— . —	Dilley	2	2

England won the toss & elected to bat
Lunch : 80.0 (27overs) Gooch 45* Broad 29*
Gower reached 4000 Test runs at 19
Tea : 161.3 (53.4 overs) Gower 12*
BLSP : 4.46 1 over off   BLSP : 5.48 1 over off
Close : 6.32 220.5 (88 overs) Pringle 39* Downton 9*
RSP : 11.01 after 1 ball bowled 2 overs off
England lose last 5 wickets for 25 runs in 78 balls
Marshall 5W Test/16
50th Anniversary of Test cricket at Trent Bridge
                                    (May 1938)

Umpires : H.D.Bird + J.Birkenshaw

Hrs	Balls	Runs		Runs	Balls	Last 50
1	76	44		50	93	✓
2	94	36		100	203	110
3	83	46		150	300	97
4	78	35		200	480	180
5	84	24		250		
6	97	25		300		
7	81	25		350		
8				400		
9				450		
10				500		
11				550		
12				600		
13				650		

ENGLAND v WEST INDIES FIRST TEST TRENT BRIDGE June 3, 4, 6

WI 1st

No	Batsman	How out	Bowler	Runs	Wkt	Total	6	4	Mins	Balls
1	GREENIDGE	c DOWNTON	JARVIS	25	1	54	-	4	107	86
2	HAYNES	c DOWNTON	JARVIS	60	3	159	-	5	216	133
3	RICHARDSON	c GATTING	EMBUREY	17	2	84	-	1	46	40
4	RICHARDS*	c GOOCH	DeFREITAS	80	4	231	1	12	135	98
5	HOOPER	c DOWNTON	DeFREITAS	84	7	334	-	7	228	147
6	LOGIE	c GOOCH	PRINGLE	20	5	271	-	4	42	34
7	DUJON†	c+b	DILLEY	16	6	309	-	-	69	60
8	MARSHALL	b	EMBUREY	72	8	425	3	6	137	88
9	AMBROSE	run out	(Gooch)	43	9	448	1	4	116	98
10	WALSH	not	out	3	-	-	-	-	18	7
11	PATTERSON	did not bat								
	Extras	B 6　　LB 8　　W -　　NB 14		28						791 (129.1ov + 16nb)

448-9 dec

Bowler	O	M	R	W	NB	W
DILLEY	34	5	101	1	6	
DeFREITAS	27	5	93	2	9	
JARVIS	18¹	1	63	2		
PRINGLE	34	11	82	1	1	
EMBUREY	16	4	95	2		

Wkt	Partnership between		Runs	Balls
1	Greenidge	Haynes	54	152
2	Haynes	Richardson	30	72
3	-.-	Richards	75	82
4	Richards	Hooper	72	103
5	Hooper	Logie	40	59
6	-.-	Dujon	38	102
7	-.-	Marsh	25	57
8	Marshall	Ambrose	91	136
9	Ambrose	Walsh	23	28
10				

England 245 BLSP 7 overs off To overs left June 3
Lunch: 8-0 (6 overs) Greenidge 0* Haynes 5*
RSP after lunch No play possible before tea Resume 4.15
37 overs to be bowled - play extended to 7.00
BLSP: 6.55　126-2 (42.1 overs) Haynes 53* Richards 22* 119 behind
June 4 BLSP: 11.05　Restart 2.00　33 overs off
BLSP: 3.35　Early Tea 230-3 (64.2 overs) Richards 80* Hooper 32*
BLSP: 4.40　No further play possible - called off 6.40
264.4 (72.3 overs) Hooper 47* Logie 18*　19 ahead
New Ball: 322.6 (96.3) DeFreitas
Lunch: 334-6 (101 overs) Hooper 84* Marshall 12*　89 ahead
Tea: 442.8 (128 overs) Ambrose 42* Walsh 2*　197 ahead

Greenidge/Haynes open innings 105th time in Tests

Hrs	Balls	Runs		Runs	Balls	Last 50
1	86	23		50	138	-
2	84	36		100	241	103
3	84	64		150	282	41
4	81	50		200	366	84
5	83	59		250	431	65
6	87	52		300	557	126
7	82	32		350	660	103
8	83	44		400	739	79
9	83	58		450		
10				500		
11				550		
12				600		
13				650		

ENGLAND v WEST INDIES   FIRST TEST   TRENT BRIDGE   June 6, 7

Eng 2nd

No	Batsman	How out	Bowler	Runs	Wkt	Total	6	4	Mins	Balls
1	GOOCH	c DUJON	PATTERSON	146	3	277	-	15	416	203
2	BROAD	c DUJON	AMBROSE	16	1	39	-	2	81	55
3	GATTING*	b	MARSHALL	29	2	116	-	2	140	101
4	GOWER	not	out	88	-	-	-	10	236	164
5	LAMB	not	out	6	-	-	-	-	45	32
6										
7										
8										
9										
10										
11										
	Extras	B -	LB 10 W - NB 6	16						655 (108 ov + 7nb)

301. 3

Bowler	O	M	R	W		NB	W
MARSHALL	13	4	23	1			
PATTERSON	24	6	69	1		4	
AMBROSE	23	4	56	1		1	
WALSH	25	5	84	-		2	
RICHARDS	9	1	26	-			
HOOPER	14	1	33	-			

Wkt	Partnership between		Runs	Balls
1	Gooch	Broad	39	114
2	– – –	Gatting	77	193
3	– – –	Gower	161	292
4	Gower	Lamb	24*	56
5				
6				
7				
8				
9				
10				

England 245 West Indies 448-9 dec Lead 203
31 overs left June 6
Close: 67-1 (31 overs) Gooch 38* Gatting 8*   136 behind
Marshall warned running on wicket (Bird) at 6.11
Lunch: 139-2 (57 overs) Gooch 77* Gower 10*   64 behind
Marshall left the field with injured rib muscle at 200 June 7
Tea: 241-2 (91 overs) Gooch 128* Gower 55*   38 lead
Gooch 8th Test 100, 4th v WI
New Ball taken straight after Tea - Walsh

Match Drawn

MM: M D Marshall

(R Illingworth)

Hrs	Balls	Runs		Runs	Balls	Last 50
1	84	30		50	147	-
2	85	29		100	265	118
3	81	32		150	361	96
4	77	34		200	460	99
5	93	59		250	568	108
6	104	43		300	651	83
7	76	52		350		
8				400		
9				450		
10				500		
11				550		
12				600		
13				650		

Second Test: Lord's 16, 17, 18, 20, 21 June
West Indies won by 134 runs.

The Lord's Test was played in anticyclonic weather, was on most days interrupted by bad light and on the Monday by light showers, but from the moment when the England first innings went into decline on the second afternoon, there was never much doubt that West Indies were on their way to a substantial victory. It was duly won by 134 runs.

The pitch, allowing plenty of bounce, was no hardship to the West Indies fast bowlers led by Marshall. This meant a funereal over-rate. England could not keep to the 15 overs an hour required, but West Indies, churning out only 10 or 11 an hour, over-ran by one hour 40 minutes on the Monday. The match was watched by nearly 100,000 spectators, paying a record gate of over £1 million, but many expressed their disenchantment at the pace of the proceedings, though the actual scoring rate was high.

John Emburey, captaining England for the first time, lost the toss, and after some hesitation West Indies batted. The early sunshine soon faded and they found themselves in trouble against Dilley and the swinging ball, so that five wickets were down for 54. The first of two highly important stands between Logie and Dujon then added 130 before the last five wickets fell for 25.

Broad's wicket was lost for 20 that evening, but Gooch, Moxon, and Gower played well in their different ways and England reached 112 for two in reasonably good order. However, once Gooch had been bowled by Marshall and Gower had mishooked Walsh, the rest of the batting succumbed, mostly toi Marshall, the last eight wickets falling for 53 runs. The ball swung less than on the first day, but the pace and lateral movement were too much for the England batsmen.

The third day, which West Indies began leading by 60, was sunny, and Greenidge was soon engaged in a masterly piece of batting which Richards augmented with a brilliant 72. When they were out, with the lead already approaching 300 and England's bowling missing the injured Small, Logie and Dujon took over again and added 114 that evening. If West Indies held a huge advantage in the pace and penetration of their bowling, they were no less superior in middle batting.

On the fourth morning, the last five wickets fell in an hour to Dilley and Jarvis for 43, leaving Logie five short of a well deserved 100. Marshall and Patterson soon had England 31 for three, but Lamb, with a sort of buccaneering defiance, hurled the bat at anything not requiring urgent defence and, against a close-set attacking field, prospered swiftly. Moxon was a solid partner and was unlucky to be sent back and run out when they had added 73.

England were down to 214 for seven that night, with Lamb 99 not out. On the last morning he completed his fourth Test hundred against West Indies, no mean record considering the modern stranglehold of West Indies bowlers. He was eventually rather needlessly run out, but the last wicket was not taken until after lunch. The pitch had lost a little of the life of earlier days and it seemed that with a better start to the second innings, England might have come near to holding out.

With the choice of Man of the Match to make from Marshall, who had taken 10 wickets, and Logie, Trevor Bailey opted for Logie, who had batted so well for 81 and 95 not out.

ENGLAND v WEST INDIES   SECOND TEST   LORD'S   June 16

WI 1st

No	Batsman	How out	Bowler	Runs	Wkt	Total	6	4	Mins	Balls
1	GREENIDGE	c DOWNTON	DILLEY	22	2	40	-	5	67	39
2	HAYNES	c MOXON	DILLEY	12	1	21	-	2	37	27
3	RICHARDSON	c EMBUREY	DILLEY	5	3	47	-	1	39	26
4	RICHARDS *	c DOWNTON	DILLEY	6	5	54	-	1	20	9
5	HOOPER	c DOWNTON	SMALL	3	4	50	-	-	3	4
6	LOGIE	c EMBUREY	SMALL	81	7	199	-	14	182	129
7	DUJON †	b	EMBUREY	53	6	184	-	8	149	124
8	MARSHALL	c GOOCH	DILLEY	11	8	199	-	1	33	16
9	AMBROSE	c GOWER	SMALL	0	9	199	-	-	5	6
10	WALSH	not	out	9	-	-	-	-	27	22
11	PATTERSON	b	SMALL	0	10	209	-	-	20	8
	Extras	B -	LB 6	W -	NB 1	7				410 (67.5ov +3nb)

209

Bowler	O	M	R	W		NB	W
DILLEY	23	6	55	5		1	-
JARVIS	13	2	47	-			
SMALL	18⁵	5	64	4		1	
PRINGLE	7	3	20	.		1	
EMBUREY	6	2	17	1			

Wkt	Partnership between		Runs	Balls
1	Greenidge	Haynes	21	52
2	- - -	Richardson	19	37
3	Richardson	Richards	7	10
4	Richards	Hooper	3	5
5	- - -	Logie	4	6
6	Logie	Dujon	130	228
7	- - . -	Marshall	15	34
8	Marshall	Ambrose	0	5
9	Ambrose	Walsh	0	7
10	Walsh	Patterson	10	26

West Indies won the toss + elected to bat

Lunch: 66-5 (25 overs) Logie 15* Dujon 1*

Tea: 184-6 (55.5 overs) Logie 77*

Dilley 5W Tests/6

Hrs	Balls	Runs		Runs	Balls	Last 50
1	78	35		50	102	-
2	73	31		100	205	103
3	85	58		150	278	73
4	102	60		200	390	112
5	72	25		250		
6				300		
7				350		
8				400		
9				450		
10				500		
11				550		
12				600		
13				650		

Umpires: KE Palmer + DR Shepherd

ENGLAND v WEST INDIES   SECOND TEST   LORD'S   June 16.17

Englr

No	Batsman	How out	Bowler	Runs	Wkt	Total	6	4	Mins	Balls
1	GOOCH	b	MARSHALL	44	4	129	-	5	197	106
2	BROAD	lbw	MARSHALL	0	1	13	-	·	20	9
3	MOXON	c RICHARDS	AMBROSE	26	2	58	-	4	68	48
4	GOWER	c sub (Arthurton)	WALSH	46	3	112	-	7	72	61
5	LAMB	lbw	MARSHALL	10	6	140	-	1	70	45
6	PRINGLE	c DUJON	WALSH	1	5	134	-	-	20	17
7	DOWNTON †	lbw	MARSHALL	11	8	157	-	1	56	32
8	EMBUREY *	b	PATTERSON	7	7	153	-	1	33	21
9	SMALL	not	out	5	-	-	-	1	20	5
10	JARVIS	c HAYNES	MARSHALL	7	9	165	-	1	12	13
11	DILLEY	b	MARSHALL	0	10	165	-	·	1	1
	Extras	B - LB 6 W - NB 2		8						358 (59w + 4nb)

165

Bowler	O	M	R	W	NB	W
MARSHALL	18	5	32	6		
PATTERSON	13	3	52	1	1	
AMBROSE	12	1	39	1	2	
WALSH	16	6	36	2	1	

Wkt	Partnership between		Runs	Balls
1	Gooch	Broad	13	26
2	— · —	Moxon	45	86
3	— · —	Gower	54	95
4	— · —	Lamb	17	39
5	Lamb	Pringle	5	29
6	— · —	Downton	6	21
7	Downton	Emburey	13	41
8	— · —	Small	4	5
9	Small	Jarvis	8	15
10	— · —	Dilley	0	1

West Indies 209   20 overs left June 16
BLSP: 5.48 No further play Called off at 6.50
20-1 (6.4 overs) Gooch 17* Moxon 3*   189 behind
BLSP: 12.34 -12.50 Early lunch - 1.30   4 overs off
88-2 (26 overs) Gooch 33* Gower 27*
Tea: 148-6 (52 overs) Downton 11* Emburey 2*   61 behind
Marshall 5W Tests/17 5th v Eng

BB WI v England at Lord's

Hrs	Balls	Runs		Runs	Balls	Last 50
1	74	36		50	94	-
2	77	51		100	175	81
3	75	29		150	326	151
4	70	24		200		
5				250		
6				300		
7				350		
8				400		
9				450		
10				500		
11				550		
12				600		
13				650		

ENGLAND v WEST INDIES SECOND TEST LORD'S June 17, 18, 20

WI 2nd

No	Batsman	How out	Bowler	Runs	Wkt	Total	6	4	Mins	Balls
1	GREENIDGE	c EMBUREY	DILLEY	103	3	198	-	14	246	192
2	HAYNES	c DOWNTON	DILLEY	5	1	32	-	-	57	27
3	RICHARDSON	lbw	PRINGLE	26	2	115	-	5	105	55
4	RICHARDS*	b	PRINGLE	72	4	226	1	12	112	80
5	HOOPER	c DOWNTON	JARVIS	11	5	240	-	2	52	34
6	LOGIE	not	out	95	.	-	-	†12	200	124
7	DUJON†	b	JARVIS	52	6	371	-	8	134	117
8	MARSHALL	b	JARVIS	6	7	379	-	1	8	7
9	AMBROSE	b	DILLEY	0	8	380	-	-	6	5
10	WALSH	b	DILLEY	0	9	384	-	-	7	3
11	PATTERSON	c DOWNTON	JARVIS	2	10	397	-	-	15	9
	Extras	B - LB 19 W 1 NB 5		25						653

397

† plus 1×5

(108ow +5nb)

Bowler	O	M	R	W		NB	W
DILLEY	27	6	73	4			
SMALL	19	1	76	-			1
JARVIS	26	3	107	4			
EMBUREY	15	1	62	-		2	
PRINGLE	21	4	60	2		3	

Wkt	Partnership between		Runs	Balls
1	Greenidge	Haynes	32	73
2	-.-	Richardson	83	146
3	- - -	Richards	83	114
4	Richards	Hooper	28	40
5	Hooper	Logie	14	32
6	Logie	Dujon	131	198
7	-.-	Marshall	8	13
8	-.-	Ambrose	1	7
9	- - -	Walsh	4	11
10	-.-	Patterson	13	19

West Indies 209 England 165 Lead 44
32 overs left June 17
BLSP: 5.12 7 overs off Resume 5.40
BLSP: 5.47 Resume 6.10 13 overs left
BLSP: 6.12 No further play Called off at 6.28
16-0 (6.2 overs) Greenidge 12* Haynes 4* 60 ahead
Lunch: 104.1 (33 overs) Greenidge 67* Richardson 26* 148 ahead
Tea: 219.3 (60 overs) Richards 65* Hooper 6* 263 ahead
New Ball: 307.5 (85 overs) Small
Small injured thigh + left field 5.57
Close: 354.5 (97 overs) Logie 69* Dujon 45* 398 ahead
Small unable to bowl June 20

Hrs	Balls	Runs		Runs	Balls	Last 50
1	75	32		50	108	-
2	77	40		100	195	87
3	91	58		150	269	74
4	84	60		200	344	75
5	78	50		250	394	50
6	92	50		300	510	116
7	84	63		350	580	70
8	72	44		400		
9				450		
10				500		
11				550		
12				600		
13				650		

ENGLAND v WEST INDIES   SECOND TEST   LORD'S   June 20, 21

Eng 2nd

No	Batsman	How out	Bowler	Runs	Wkt	Total	6	4	Mins	Balls
1	GOOCH	lbw	MARSHALL	16	1	27	-	3	36	26
2	BROAD	c DUJON	MARSHALL	1	2	29	-	-	48	19
3	MOXON	run out	(Patterson)	14	4	104	-	1	126	69
4	GOWER	c RICHARDSON	PATTERSON	1	3	31	-	-	10	9
5	LAMB	run out	(Hooper/Walsh)	113	9	254	-	15	338	212
6	PRINGLE	lbw	WALSH	0	5	105	-	-	8	5
7	DOWNTON †	lbw	MARSHALL	27	6	161	-	3	75	51
8	EMBUREY *	b	AMBROSE	30	7	212	-	6	48	32
9	SMALL	c RICHARDS	MARSHALL	7	8	232	-	1	37	19
10	JARVIS	not	out	29	-	-	-	3	107	64
11	DILLEY	c RICHARDSON	PATTERSON	28	10	307	-	6	52	36
	Extras	B 5 LB 20 W 2 NB 14		41						

307

542 (86.5 ov + 21 nb)

Bowler	O	M	R	W	NB	W
MARSHALL	25	5	60	4	1	
PATTERSON	21.5	2	100	2	12	
WALSH	20	1	75	1	8	
AMBROSE	20	4	47	1		

Wkt	Partnership between		Runs	Balls
1	Gooch	Broad	27	43
2	Broad	Moxon	2	12
3	Moxon	Gower	2	10
4	—.—	Lamb	73	139
5	Lamb	Pringle	1	9
6	—.—	Downton	56	90
7	—.—	Emburey	51	57
8	—.—	Small	20	45
9	—.—	Jarvis	22	65
10	Jarvis	Dilley	53	72

West Indies 209 & 397   England 165   77 overs left June 20
England need 442 to win
BLSP: 12.26 after 3 overs   Lunch 12.50 - 1.30   5 overs off
14.0 (3 overs) Gooch 11* Broad 1*   428 to win
Tea: 89-3 (27 overs) Moxon 9* Lamb 47*   353 to win
RSP Tea until 4.50   13 overs off
Close: 214-7 (59 overs) Lamb 99* Small 0*   228 to win
at 7.40!!
Lunch: 295-9 (83 overs) Jarvis 21* Dilley 16*   157 to win
Marshall low 3   1st v Eng

West Indies won by 134 runs

MM: A L Logie
(T.E. Bailey)

Hrs	Balls	Runs		Runs	Balls	Last 50
1	65	31		50	90	-
2	70	48		100	197	107
3	75	25		150	295	98
4	72	37		200	351	56
5	68	58		250	448	97
6	64	37		300	536	66
7	75	34		350		
8				400		
9				450		
10				500		
11				550		
12				600		
13				650		

Third Test: Old Trafford 30 June, 1, 2, 4, 5 July
West Indies won by an innings and 156 runs.

One of the most depressing Test matches for many years, made so both by England's feeble performance and by the frequent interruptions for rain, ended on the fifth morning with West Indies winning by an innings and 156 runs.

England, again captained by Emburey, included two spinners. John Childs, playing in his first Test at 36, replaced the injured Nick Cook, who was originally picked. DeFreitas returned in place of Small, and Broad was left out to allow the return of Gatting.

On the first day, England were bowled out in 60.2 overs for 135, never recovering from the opening thrusts by Marshall which removed Moxon and Gatting. Though the pitch was so slow, the batsmen seemed to find this a greater handicap than did the four West Indian fast bowlers, now including Benjamin for Patterson. The ball moved a little, no batsmen promised to establish himself, and the innings ended leaving West Indies to bat for nine minutes.

In those nine minutes England packed three overs, Emburey bowling the second over himself to save time and in order to bowl at Richardson who had previously been troubled by spin. On this occasion Richardson swept at Emburey's first ball which dropped from his glove only just in front of Downton. Dilley's first over had mostly comprised long hops outside the off-stump, but in his second Greenidge gave a straightforward catch which Gooch dropped at second slip.

On the second day England bowled 78 overs, and West Indies from their fortunate start advanced to 242 for five. To some extent the batsmen were contained but the day ended with Dujon and Harper giving further evidence of the strength of West Indies' middle batting. More to come in the 50 overs fitted in on the Saturday, and again when they restarted after lunch on Monday.

By this time England's only hope of salvation lay in the weather, but their second innings last only 43 overs and ended, despite further stoppages, before lunch on the fifth day.

The difference between the unruffled batting of West Indies and the lack of confidence and technique shown by the England batsmen was immense. In the England innings the ball seemed to be for ever being edged into the slips off a crooked bat. But even more marked was the far greater use which the West Indies fast bowlers, led by the brilliant Marshall with his nine for 41 in the match, made of what would once have been considered just a slow turning pitch.

Without bowling consistently at his fastest, Marshall moved the ball at a pace which cruelly exposed defensive weaknesses. And on a pitch on which the ball sometimes bounced twice before reaching the wicket-keeper, the giant Ambrose, from just short of a length, made it lift chest high, so that both Lamb and Emburey were caught at short leg fending it off. It was hard to believe that this was the same pitch on which the England bowlers had toiled with such limited success.

ENGLAND v WEST INDIES THIRD TEST OLD TRAFFORD June 30

Eng 1st

No	Batsman	How out	Bowler	Runs	Wkt	Total	6	4	Mins	Balls
1	GOOCH	c DUJON	BENJAMIN	27	4	55	-	3	109	81
2	MOXON	b	MARSHALL	0	1	12	-	-	35	22
3	GATTING	lbw	MARSHALL	0	2	14	-	-	6	4
4	GOWER	c HARPER	WALSH	9	3	33	-	2	29	20
5	LAMB	c GREENIDGE	AMBROSE	33	6	94	-	2	113	82
6	CAPEL	b	BENJAMIN	1	5	61	-	-	32	18
7	DOWNTON †	c GREENIDGE	WALSH	24	8	113	-	2	87	63
8	EMBUREY *	c DUJON	WALSH	1	7	98	-	-	18	17
9	DeFREITAS	c GREENIDGE	AMBROSE	15	9	123	-	1	31	28
10	DILLEY	c HARPER	WALSH	14	10	135	-	3	29	21
11	CHILDS	not	out	2	-	-	-	-	19	12
	Extras	B - LB 4	W - NB 5	9						368 (60.2ov +6nb)

135

Bowler	O	M	R	W	NB	W
MARSHALL	12	5	19	2		
AMBROSE	17	5	35	2	1	
WALSH	18²	4	46	4	5	
BENJAMIN	13	4	31	2		

Wkt	Partnership between		Runs	Balls
1	Gooch	Marshall	12	52
2	— . —	Gatting	2	10
3	— . —	Gower	19	41
4	— . —	Lamb	22	53
5	Lamb	Capel	6	45
6	— . —	Downton	33	64
7	Downton	Emburey	4	30
8	— . —	DeFreitas	15	33
9	DeFreitas	Dilley	10	11
10	Dilley	Childs	12	29

England won the toss & elected to bat
Lunch: 55-4 (28 overs) Lamb 16* Capel 0*
RSP: 307 Tea: 3.10 - 3.30
Tea: 97-6 (48 overs) Downton 22* Emburey 1*
Resume 5.44 Play extended until 7.00 (inns ended 6.40)

Debut: JHChilds NTPlews

Umpires: DJConstant + NT Plews

Hrs	Balls	Runs	Runs	Balls	Last 50
1	82	22	50	145	-
2	88	33	100	299	154
3	81	34	150		
4	84	34	200		
5			250		
6			300		
7			350		
8			400		
9			450		
10			500		
11			550		
12			600		
13			650		

ENGLAND v WEST INDIES THIRD TEST OLD TRAFFORD June 30, July 1, 2, 4

WI 1st

No	Batsman	How out	Bowler	Runs	Wkt	Total	6	4	Mins	Balls
1	GREENIDGE	lbw	DeFREITAS	45	3	101	-	6	155	129
2	RICHARDSON	b	DILLEY	23	1	35	-	3	35	27
3	HOOPER	lbw	CHILDS	15	2	77	-	.	82	47
4	RICHARDS *	b	CAPEL	47	4	175	1	5	104	71
5	LOGIE	lbw	DILLEY	39	5	187	-	4	83	59
6	DUJON †	c CAPEL	DILLEY	67	6	281	-	4	180	159
7	HARPER	b	DILLEY	74	7	373	-	3	307	244
8	MARSHALL	not	out	43	-	-	-	3	159	102
9	AMBROSE	not	out	7	-	-	-	1	17	8
10	BENJAMIN	} did not bat								
11	WALSH									
	Extras	B - LB 21 W - NB 3		24						846 (140.1 ov + 5nb)

384 - 7 dec

Bowler	O	M	R	W	NB	W
DILLEY	28¹	4	99	4	1	
EMBUREY	25	7	54	-		
DeFREITAS	35	5	81	1	4	
CAPEL	12	2	38	1		
CHILDS	40	12	91	1		

Wkt	Partnership between		Runs	Balls
1	Greenidge	Richardson	35	53
2	- . -	Hooper	42	118
3	- . -	Richards	24	54
4	Richards	Logie	74	101
5	Logie	Dujon	12	19
6	Dujon	Harper	94	291
7	Harper	Marshall	92	188
8	Marshall	Ambrose	11*	22
9				
10				

England 135

Close : 4.0 (3 overs) Greenidge 4* Richardson 0* 131 behind
July1 RSP - 11.24 6 overs off
Lunch : 73-1 (26 overs) Greenidge 36* Hooper 13* 62 behind
Tea : 182-4 (55 overs) Logie 34* Dujon 7* 47 ahead
RSP : 4.30 - 4.45 (4 overs off) RSP: 4.50 -5.02 (4 overs off)
RSP : 5-41 - 6.35 Play extended to 7.00
Close : 242.5 (81 overs) Dujon 35* Harper 23* 107 ahead
July2 RSP : 11.50 - 12.45 (13 overs off)
Lunch : 277-5 (103 overs) Dujon 64* Harper 25* 142 ahead
New Ball : 280 .5 (103.1 overs) Dilley
RSP : 2.38 - 4.50 Tea taken 3.40 - 4.00
Tea : 315-6 (116 overs) Harper 41* Marshall 16* 180 ahead
RSP : 6.02 No further play July2
Close : 357.6 (131 overs) Harper 61* Marshall 37* 222 ahead
July 4 No play morning session
RSP : 2.23 No play until declaration at 4.05

Hrs	Balls	Runs
1	53	35
2	84	27
3	88	39
4	88	68
5	85	47
6	108	27
7	115	37
8	74	36
9	82	34
10		
11		
12		
13		

Runs	Balls	Last 50
50	80	-
100	217	137
150	289	72
200	374	87
250	542	168
300	666	124
350	770	104
400		
450		
500		
550		
600		
650		

ENGLAND v WEST INDIES THIRD TEST OLD TRAFFORD July 4,5

Eng 2nd

No	Batsman	How out	Bowler	Runs	Wkt	Total	6	4	Mins	Balls
1	GOOCH	lbw	MARSHALL	1	1	6	-	-	11	9
2	MOXON	c RICHARDS	BENJAMIN	15	3	36	-	-	82	59
3	GATTING	c RICHARDSON	MARSHALL	4	2	22	-	-	23	25
4	GOWER	c RICHARDSON	MARSHALL	34	4	73	-	3	101	60
5	LAMB	c LOGIE	AMBROSE	9	6	73	-	1	72	53
6	CAPEL	c sub (Arthurton)	MARSHALL	0	5	73	-	-	9	7
7	DOWNTON †	c HARPER	MARSHALL	6	7	87	-	-	16	13
8	EMBUREY *	c LOGIE	AMBROSE	8	9	93	-	1	28	17
9	DeFREITAS	c HARPER	MARSHALL	0	8	87	-	-	1	2
10	DILLEY	b	MARSHALL	4	10	93	-	-	16	13
11	CHILDS	not	out	0	-	-	-	-	1	0
	Extras	B 1 LB 10 W - NB 1		12					259 (42.4 ov + 2nb)	
				93						

Bowler	O	M	R	W	NB	W
MARSHALL	15.4	5	22	7		
AMBROSE	16	4	36	2		
WALSH	4	1	10	-		
BENJAMIN	4	1	6	1		
HARPER	2	1	4	-	2	
HOOPER	1	-	4	-		

Wkt	Partnership between		Runs	Balls
1	Gooch	Moxon	6	16
2	Moxon	Gatting	16	36
3	- . -	Gower	14	63
4	Gower	Lamb	37	81
5	Lamb	Capel	0	13
6	- . -	Downton	0	7
7	Downton	Emburey	14	15
8	Emburey	DeFreitas	0	2
9	- . -	Dilley	6	21
10	Dilley	Childs	0	4

England 135   West Indies 384 . 7 dec
41 overs left July 4
RSP: 4.24 . 4.43   (9 overs off)
RSP: 4.48 - 5.18   (7 overs off)
Marshall 2 official warnings running-on wicket (Plews) 2nd at 6.15
Close: 60-3 (29 overs) Gower 24* Lamb 6*   189 behind
RSP: 11.53 - 12.08   (5 overs off)
WI won at 12.19
Marshall BB TC 5w/18 6th v Eng

West Indies won by an innings + 156 runs

MM: MD Marshall

(TW Graveney)

Hrs	Balls	Runs		Runs	Balls	Last 50
1	84	31		50	139	-
2	80	25		100		
3	78	33		150		
4				200		
5				250		
6				300		
7				350		
8				400		
9				450		
10				500		
11				550		
12				600		
13				650		

Fourth Test: Headingley, 21, 22, 23, 25, 26 July.
West Indies won by 10 wickets.

West Indies had to replace two injured batsmen, Greenidge and Richardson, and England fielded a side with seven changes and no spinner, but the outcome was no less one-sided, West Indies winning after 25 minutes' play on the fifth day by 10 wickets.

Until the fourth afternoon, the match was under frequent threat from the weather. England, under new captain Christopher Cowdrey, were put in after a delayed start, and after two overs suffered one of the more remarkable stoppages. Though the umpires had declared the ground fit, water began to seep up on the bowler's run-up at the football stand end, and two and a half hours passed before the innings was resumed.

It then followed a familiar pattern, England's early batsmen being unable to cope with the movement in the air and off the pitch achieved by the four West Indian pace bowlers. Not an over of spin was bowled in the match. Curtis, in his first Test innings, held out doggedly for 90 minutes, and Gower, in his 100th Test, played a few strokes, but four wickets were lost for 80.

At this point, Robin Smith, also in his first Test, joined Lamb, and they added 57 with relative freedom before a day's play of 49 overs ended.

Next day the partnership continued to prosper and was worth 103 when Lamb unluckily tore a calf muscle and had to retire. In 26 balls, four wickets then fell for two runs, though the changes in the England side had on paper greatly shortened the tail.

When West Indies batted, Foster, fit again after the injury that had kept him out of the previous Tests, bowled well, Curtis held a magnificent catch at square leg to remove Richards, and at 156 for five West Indies were not entirely in control.

In the 23.4 overs possible on the Saturday, Harper steered them into the lead, but lost three partners to Pringle, and at 238 for eight West Indies were still not in a winning position.

Yet on the sunnier windier fourth day, Harper and his last two partners extended the lead from 37 to 74 and, after a respectable start of 56 by Gooch and Curtis, England were swamped, losing all 10 wickets for another 82 runs. With his great height, Ambrose could produce an awkward chest-high bounce from just short of a length and the match would not have gone into a fifth day if Lamb had not limped in at number eight with a runner and, though severely restricted, made the second-top score.

This did at least give England a chance of survival if the Tuesday was wet. But though it rained again at 11.30 on the final morning, Haynes and Dujon, having made 27 of the 65 needed off seven overs on the fourth evening, had finished the job by then.

ENGLAND v WEST INDIES   FOURTH TEST   HEADINGLEY   July 21, 22

Eng 1st

No	Batsman	How out	Bowler	Runs	Wkt	Total	6	4	Mins	Balls
1	GOOCH	c DUJON	MARSHALL	9	1	14	-	2	37	27
2	CURTIS	lbw	BENJAMIN	12	2	43	-	1	94	71
3	ATHEY	lbw	AMBROSE	16	4	80	-	1	109	75
4	GOWER	c DUJON	BENJAMIN	13	3	58	-	1	17	16
5	LAMB	retired	hurt	64	-	-	-	9	158	91
6	SMITH	c DUJON	AMBROSE	38	5	183	-	5	131	91
7	COWDREY *	lbw	MARSHALL	0	6	183	-	.	14	12
8	RICHARDS †	b	AMBROSE	2	8	185	-	.	18	13
9	PRINGLE	c DUJON	MARSHALL	0	7	185	-	-	5	3
10	FOSTER	not	out	8	-	-	-	1	22	11
11	DILLEY	c HOOPER	AMBROSE	8	9	201	-	1	17	16
	Extras	B 1 LB 18 W 6 NB 6		31						426
				201						(69.1 ov + 11 nb)

Bowler	O	M	R	W	NB	W
MARSHALL	23	8	55	3		2
AMBROSE	25¹	8	58	4	5	1
BENJAMIN	9	2	27	2		
WALSH	12	4	42	-		6

Wkt	Partnership between		Runs	Balls
1	Gooch	Curtis	14	52
2	Curtis	Athey	29	83
3	Athey	Gower	15	23
4	- . -	Lamb	22	50
5	Lamb / Smith	Smith / Cowdrey	103 / 0	159 / 10
6	Cowdrey	Richards	0	11
7	Richards	Pringle	2	9
8	- . -	Foster	0	5
9	Foster	Dilley	16	24
10				

West Indies won the toss + elected to field
11.50 start (12 overs off)
Damp patch stopped play after 2 overs! 12.05
Early Lunch at 12.40 Inspection 2.00 - Start 2.30
Tea: 58-3 (25.3 overs) Athey 14*
Play extended to 7.00 but BLSP at 6.17
Close: 137-4 (49 overs) Lamb 45* Smith 23*

Lamb retired hurt at 183-4

Debut: TS Curtis KT Arthurton

Umpires: HD Bird + DR Shepherd

Hrs	Balls	Runs	Runs	Balls	Last 50
1	80	18	50	143	-
2	81	44	100	242	99
3	85	42	150	325	83
4	80	48	200	425	100
5	71	33	250		
6			300		
7			350		
8			400		
9			450		
10			500		
11			550		
12			600		
13			650		

ENGLAND v WEST INDIES   FOURTH TEST   HEADINGLEY   July 22,23,25

WI 1st

No	Batsman	How out	Bowler	Runs	Wkt	Total	6	4	Mins	Balls
1	HAYNES	lbw	PRINGLE	54	4	137	-	7	153	110
2	DUJON †	c SMITH	DILLEY	13	1	15	-	2	14	14
3	HOOPER	lbw	FOSTER	19	2	61	-	3	73	57
4	RICHARDS *	c CURTIS	FOSTER	18	3	97	-	4	25	20
5	LOGIE	c FOSTER	PRINGLE	44	5	156	-	8	59	51
6	ARTHURTON	c RICHARDS	PRINGLE	27	6	194	-	4	89	71
7	HARPER	c GOWER	FOSTER	56	10	275	-	8	161	112
8	MARSHALL	c GOOCH	PRINGLE	3	7	210	-	-	8	7
9	AMBROSE	lbw	PRINGLE	8	8	222	-	2	9	8
10	BENJAMIN	run out (sub: Fairbrother)		9	9	245	-	1	24	18
11	WALSH	not out		9	-	-	-	2	48	21
	Extras	B - LB 15 W - NB -		15						489 (91.2ov +1ab)

275

Bowler	O	M	R	W	NB	W
DILLEY	20	5	59	1		
FOSTER	32²	6	98	3	1	
PRINGLE	27	7	95	5		
COWDREY	2	-	8	-		

Wkt	Partnership between		Runs	Balls
1	Haynes	Dujon	15	18
2	—.—	Hooper	46	117
3	—.—	Richards	36	38
4	—.—	Logie	40	62
5	Logie	Arthurton	19	29
6	Arthurton	Harper	38	98
7	Harper	Marshall	16	12
8	—.—	Ambrose	12	14
9	—.—	Benjamin	23	38
10	—.—	Walsh	30	63

England 201
70 overs left July 22   Childs sub for Lamb
Tea: 107-3 (33 overs) Haynes 46* Logie 5*   94 behind
RSP: 4.48 No further play July 22
Close: 156-5 (44 overs) Arthurton 1* Harper 0*
July 23 No play possible until 2.45   46 overs left
Tea: 222-8 (64.4 overs) Harper 26*   21 ahead
BLSP: 4.43 No further play July 23
Close: 238-8 (67.5 overs) Harper 31* Benjamin 7*   37 ahead
Pringle official warning running on wicket 4.33 July 22 (Bird)

Hrs	Balls	Runs		Runs	Balls	Last 50
1	96	45		50	101	-
2	81	56		100	177	76
3	161	83		150	260	83
4	88	61		200	369	109
5				250	432	63
6				300		
7				350		
8				400		
9				450		
10				500		
11				550		
12				600		
13				650		

ENGLAND v WEST INDIES FOURTH TEST HEADINGLEY July 25

Eng 2nd

No	Batsman	How out	Bowler	Runs	Wkt	Total	6	4	Mins	Balls
1	GOOCH	c HOOPER	WALSH	50	2	80	-	6	120	100
2	CURTIS	b	AMBROSE	12	1	22	-	1	90	63
3	ATHEY	c DUJON	WALSH	11	4	85	-	.	49	22
4	GOWER	c DUJON	MARSHALL	2	3	85	-	-	13	12
5	SMITH	lbw	MARSHALL	11	5	105	-	1	42	26
6	COWDREY *	b	WALSH	5	6	105	-	-	41	36
7	RICHARDS †	b	AMBROSE	8	7	127	-	-	39	23
8	LAMB	c DUJON	AMBROSE	19	10	138	-	3	87	59
9	PRINGLE	b	BENJAMIN	3	8	132	-	-	18	13
10	FOSTER	c HOOPER	BENJAMIN	0	9	132	-	-	7	5
11	DILLEY	not	out	2	-	-	-	-	22	17
	Extras	B 3 LB 8 W - NB 4		15						376

138

(61.Sov + Snb)

Bowler	O	M	R	W		NB	W
MARSHALL	17	4	47	2			
AMBROSE	19⁵	4	40	3		3	
WALSH	20	9	38	3		2	
BENJAMIN	5	4	2	2			

Wkt	Partnership between		Runs	Balls
1	Gooch	Curtis	56	137
2	—.—	Athey	24	40
3	Athey	Gower	5	17
4	—.—	Smith	0	6
5	Smith	Cowdrey	20	55
6	Cowdrey	Richards	0	6
7	Richards	Lamb	22	44
8	Lamb	Pringle	5	26
9	—.—	Foster	0	11
10	—.—	Dilley	6	34

England 201   West Indies 275
74 overs left July 23
Lunch: 24-0 (12 overs) Gooch 17* Curtis 4*   50 behind
Rain during lunch Resume 1.50 (3 overs off)
Tea: 99-4 (36 overs) Smith 10* Cowdrey 4*   25 ahead
Smith acted as runner for Lamb

Hrs	Balls	Runs		Runs	Balls	Last 50
1	93	33		50	126	-
2	84	47		100	229	103
3	78	25		150		
4	76	27		200		
5				250		
6				300		
7				350		
8				400		
9				450		
10				500		
11				550		
12				600		
13				650		

ENGLAND v WEST INDIES   FOURTH TEST   HEADINGLEY   July 25,26

WI 2a

No	Batsman	How out	Bowler	Runs	Wkt	Total	6	4	Mins	Balls
1	HAYNES	not	out	25	-	-	-	2	54	43
2	DUJON†	not	out	40	-	-	-	7	54	44
3										
4										
5										
6										
7										
8										
9										
10										
11										
	Extras	B - LB 2 W - NB -		2						87 (14.3ov)

67-0

Bowler	O	M	R	W		NB	W
DILLEY	4	-	16	-			
FOSTER	7	1	36	-			
COWDREY	3³	-	13	-			

Wkt	Partnership between		Runs	Balls
1	Haynes	Dujon	67*	87
2				
3				
4				
5				
6				
7				
8				
9				
10				

England 201 + 138   West Indies 275
West Indies 65 to win   7 overs left July 25
Close: 27-0 (7 overs) Haynes 10* Dujon 17*
38 to win - whole day July 26
WI won at 11.25

West Indies won by 10 wickets

MM: C E L Ambrose

(ER Dexter)

Hrs	Balls	Runs	Runs	Balls	Last 50
1			50	76	-
2			100		
3			150		
4			200		
5			250		
6			300		
7			350		
8			400		
9			450		
10			500		
11			550		
12			600		
13			650		

Fifth Test: The Oval, 4, 5, 6, 8 August
West Indies won by eight wickets

Before the England team for the final Test took the field with five changes, injury had ruled out Lamb, Dilley, and the latest captain, Christopher Cowdrey. Gower and Athey were dropped, and two young batsmen, Robert Bailey and Matthew Maynard, came in to play in their first Test match.

The weather was an improvement, and the pitch, with more bounce than others elsewhere, would accommodate both good batting and good bowling. England soon lost their new captain, Graham Gooch, but reached 116 for two through the efforts of Curtis, Bailey and Robin Smith. The collapse that followed was unusual in that three of the five wickets that fell after tea were taken by the off-spinner, Harper. Having finished the first day at 203 for nine, England added two runs next morning and then embarked on their best outcricket of the series. Foster took the first five wickets, including that of Richards for nought to a smart catch by Curtis at short-leg. Once again the main resistance came from Logie and Dujon, who added 69 together from a start of 57 for four, but West Indies were bowled out for 183 in only 58 overs.

This left England to bat for 26 overs on the second evening. Gooch batted doggedly through these after a fluent start, but Curtis, Bailey, and Smith were lost and the future of the match became all too clear. Whereas West Indies could not be expected to bat so unproductively a second time, England could, and at 64 for three were poised to do so.

On the third day, England were given a robust start by the nightwatchman Foster, who rattled up 34 while Gooch was so pinned down and so short of the strike that he made only eight runs in the two hours' play before lunch. He became more active as his partners came and went, and coaxed 25 runs out of a last-wicket stand with Childs, who did not score. When Gooch was last out, West Indies had to make 225 to win.

Though this would be the highest innings of the match, West Indies had more than two days for the job on a pitch that would become slower as it aged. There was never a hint that they might find the task too much for them. Greenidge, after all, had done it all before, making 214 not out in the Lord's Test of 1984 when West Indies made 344 for one to win by nine wickets. That indeed was the last occasion when England led them on first innings.

In the 24 overs on Saturday evening Greenidge made 53 out of the 71 for no wicket. Early in the innings Gooch dislocated a finger in the slips, so that on the Monday both sides were led by deputy captains. Pringle became England's fifth captain of the summer, and Greenidge had taken over from Richards, who had gone to hospital for a minor operation. Richards was not missed. Greenidge and Haynes built their opening stand up to 131, and though Greenidge was out to the first ball after lunch, the platform had been well laid, and 20 minutes after tea West Indies had won the series 4-0.

ENGLAND v WEST INDIES   FIFTH TEST   OVAL   August 4, 5

England

No	Batsman	How out		Bowler	Runs	Wkt	Total	6	4	Mins	Balls
1	GOOCH*	c LOGIE	AMBROSE		9	1	12	-	2	35	25
2	CURTIS	c DUJON	BENJAMIN		30	2	77	-	4	155	121
3	BAILEY	c DUJON	AMBROSE		43	3	116	-	3	203	144
4	SMITH	c HARPER	MARSHALL		57	9	198	-	8	210	162
5	MAYNARD	c DUJON	AMBROSE		3	4	121	-	-	8	6
6	CAPEL	c MARSHALL	HARPER		16	5	160	-	2	49	40
7	RICHARDS†	c LOGIE	HARPER		0	6	160	-	-	5	4
8	PRINGLE	c DUJON	MARSHALL		1	7	165	-	-	17	16
9	DeFREITAS	c HAYNES	HARPER		18	8	196	-	2	31	26
10	FOSTER	c sub (Arthurton)	MARSHALL		7	10	205	-	1	15	11
11	CHILDS	not	out		0	-	-	-	-	7	5
	Extras	B - LB 6 W - NB 15			21						560 (90.3 +1w)

205

Bowler	O	M	R	W	NB	W
MARSHALL	24³	3	64	3	3	
AMBROSE	20	6	31	3	8	
WALSH	10	1	21	-	6	
BENJAMIN	14	2	33	1		
HARPER	21	7	50	3		
HOOPER	·1	1	-	-		

Wkt	Partnership between		Runs	Balls
1	Gooch	Curtis	12	50
2	Curtis	Bailey	65	180
3	Bailey	Smith	39	120
4	Smith	Maynard	5	9
5	- .. -	Capel	39	87
6	- . . -	Richards	0	10
7	- . -	Pringle	5	28
8	- . -	DeFreitas	31	56
9	- . . -	Foster	2	9
10	Foster	Childs	7	11

England won the toss + elected to bat
Lunch: 56-1 (29 overs) Curtis 20* Bailey 21*
Tea: 116-3 (56.5 overs) Smith 22*
Walsh off 5.15 Arthurton sub
Close: 203-9 (90 overs) Foster 5* Childs 0*

Debut: R J Bailey   M P Maynard
Umpires: H D Bird + K E Palmer

Hrs	Balls	Runs		Runs	Balls	Last 50
1	87	24		50	156	-
2	90	31		100	269	113
3	89	42		150	430	161
4	84	19		200	552	122
5	96	44		250		
6	94	36		300		
7				350		
8				400		
9				450		
10				500		
11				550		
12				600		
13				650		

ENGLAND v WEST INDIES   FIFTH TEST   OVAL   August 5

WI 1st

No	Batsman	How out	Bowler	Runs	Wkt	Total	6	4	Mins	Balls
1	GREENIDGE	c DeFREITAS	FOSTER	10	2	16	-	-	35	26
2	HAYNES	c RICHARDS	FOSTER	2	1	9	-	-	27	22
3	HOOPER	c GOOCH	FOSTER	11	4	57	1	-	49	27
4	RICHARDS *	c CURTIS	FOSTER	0	3	16	-	-	3	3
5	LOGIE	c GOOCH	FOSTER	47	5	126	-	5	130	79
6	DUJON †	lbw	PRINGLE	64	6	155	-	7	150	110
7	HARPER	run out (Foster/Capel/Pringle)		17	8	167	-	1	81	53
8	MARSHALL	c+b	CHILDS	0	7	156	-	-	5	7
9	AMBROSE	not	out	17	-	-	-	2	31	23
10	BENJAMIN	b	PRINGLE	0	9	168	-	-	1	1
11	WALSH	c DeFREITAS	PRINGLE	5	10	183	-	1	9	6
	Extras	B - LB 7 W 1 NB 2		10						357 (59 ov +3 nb)

183

Bowler	O	M	R	W		NB	W
FOSTER	16	2	64	5			1
DeFREITAS	13	4	33	-			
PRINGLE	17	4	45	3		3	
CAPEL	7	-	21	-			
CHILDS	6	1	13	1			

Wkt	Partnership between		Runs	Balls
1	Greenidge	Haynes	9	40
2	— . —	Hooper	7	10
3	Hooper	Richards	0	3
4	— . —	Logie	41	49
5	Logie	Dujon	69	127
6	Dujon	Harper	29	75
7	Harper	Marshall	1	9
8	— . —	Ambrose	11	25
9	Ambrose	Benjamin	1	2
10	— . —	Walsh	15	17

England 205   87 overs left August 5
Lunch: 70-4 (23 overs) Logie 36* Dujon 9*   135 behind
Tea: 155-5 (49 overs) Dujon 64* Harper 12*   50 behind
Foster Sw Test/5 1st v WI

Hrs	Balls	Runs
1	78	32
2	87	41
3	71	58
4	78	26
5		
6		
7		
8		
9		
10		
11		
12		
13		

Runs	Balls	Last 50
50	98	-
100	196	98
150	286	90
200		
250		
300		
350		
400		
450		
500		
550		
600		
650		

RIGHT: England's first and last captains of a hard season. Mike Gatting visits Graham Gooch on the players balcony at The Oval.

BELOW: Allan Border on top of the world after Australia beat England in the Reliance World Cup final in Calcutta.

LEFT: Abdul Qadir leaves the field in Lahore with two satisfied colleagues in Ashraf Ali and Wasim Akram after taking 13 wickets for 101 in England's defeat by an innings.

BELOW: Gooch at Faisalabad in a match which England might have won. Ijaz Ahmed ducks, Ashraf Ali and Iqbal Qasim watch.

ABOVE: A sorry moment in the second Test in Faisalabad. Chris Broad has refused to accept the umpire's decision that he had been caught at the wicket.

BELOW: The troubled Test in Faisalabad hangs fire while Shakoor Rana waits for an apology from England captain Mike Gatting.

ABOVE: A fine stroke by Martyn Moxon during his innings of 99 in the Auckland Test against New Zealand.

LEFT: A costly stroke in Sydney during the Bicentennial Test. Chris Broad, having batted throughout the first day and into the second morning, knocks down the stumps in irritation at having been bowled by Steve Waugh. He was fined £500.

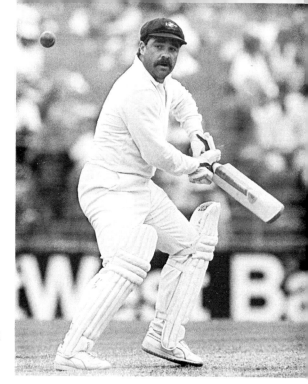

RIGHT: David Boon during his second innings of 184 not out in the drawn Bicentennial Test. Australia had followed on 211 behind.

BELOW: Bill Athey caught and bowled by the off-spinner Peter Taylor for 37 in the Bicentennial Test.

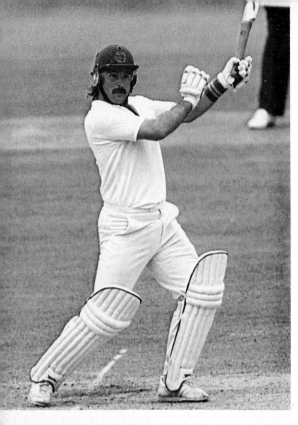

LEFT: Allan Lamb at Lord's in the course of his innings of 113, his fourth hundred against West Indies but his first in his last 26 Test matches.

BELOW: Gus Logie at Lord's, where his 81 revived West Indies after their start of 54 for five. In the second innings he made 95 not out.

ABOVE: Some 6 foot 8 inches of Curtley Ambrose at Old Trafford, where he took seven of his 22 wickets in the series.

ABOVE RIGHT: Malcolm Marshall, who was once again too much for the England batsmen, taking 35 wickets in the five-match series.

RIGHT: Allan Lamb retired hurt 64 at Headingley. He had torn a calf muscle.

ABOVE: Worcestershire, 1988 County Champions. *Back row:* G.A. Lord, P.A. Newport, G.A. Hick, M.W. Weston, S.M. McEwan, R.K. Illingworth, S.J. O'Shaughnessy. *Front row:* S.J. Rhodes, T.S. Curtis, P.A. Neale (capt), A.P. Pridgeon, N.V. Radford, D.B. D'Oliveira. *Inset:* G.R. Dilley, D.A. Leatherdale.

BELOW LEFT: Phil Newport, the country's leading wicket-taker, made his England debut in the Test against Sri Lanka at Lord's, where he was Man of the Match. He took seven wickets in the match for 164 runs.

BELOW RIGHT: Phil Neale, who made four hundreds while leading Worcestershire to the Britannic Assurance Championship.

ABOVE: Trevor Jesty during his innings of 59, which had much to do with Lancashire's victory over Worcestershire in the final of the Refuge Assurance Cup.

RIGHT: Steve Waugh making his sixth hundred of the season in his last match for Somerset, against Middlesex. His prolific English season finished early as he left to join the Australians in Pakistan.

BELOW: Steve Jefferies, the South African left-arm fast-medium swing bowler whose five for 13 in 10 overs set Hampshire on their way to their defeat of Derbyshire in the Benson & Hedges Cup final.

ABOVE: Malcolm Maynard cannot believe his misfortune, while bowler Michael Holding accepts a gift wicket with a smile. The falling helmet probably cost Glamorgan victory in their Benson & Hedges semi-final against Derbyshire at Swansea.

BELOW: The losing captain Kim Barnett congratulates his winning counterpart Mark Nicholas after Hampshire have beaten Derbyshire to win the Benson & Hedges Cup in their first ever Lord's final.

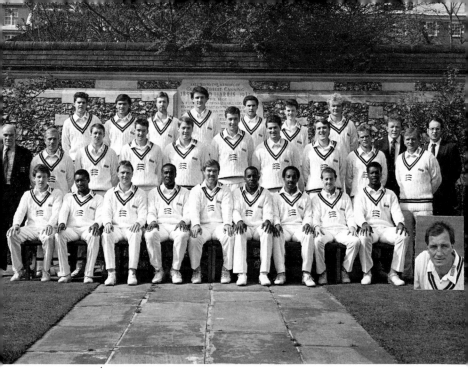

ABOVE: Middlesex, NatWest Trophy winners in 1988. *Back row:* A. Barnett, M.R. Ramprakash, A. Needham, I.J. Hutchinson, P. Weekes, T. Radford, M. Olley, J. Davis (physio), A. Jones (scorer). *Middle row:* H. Sharp (scorer), D. Bennett (coach), K.R. Brown, A.G.J. Fraser, M.A. Roseberry, A.R.C. Fraser, J.F. Sykes, P.C.R. Tufnell, N.R. Maclaurin, C.T. Radley (assistant coach). *Front row:* J.D. Carr, N.F. Williams, P.R. Downton, W.W. Daniel, M.W. Gatting (capt), W.N. Slack, R.O. Butcher, S.P. Hughes, N.G. Cowans. *Inset:* J.E. Emburey.

RIGHT: A better day for Mike Gatting at last. Middlesex win the NatWest Trophy and provide the Man of the Match, the 18-year-old Mark Ramprakash (right).

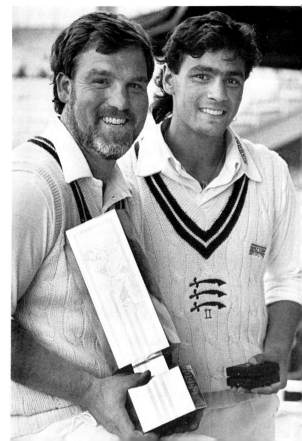

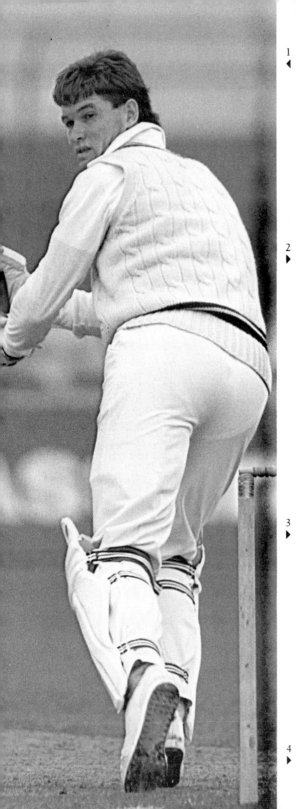

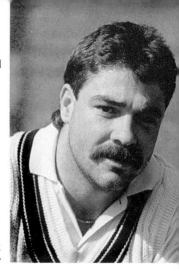

1

2

3

4

8
▶

5
◀

6
◀

The Daily Telegraph Cricketers of the Year
(see pages 19-20):

1 Graeme Hick (England)
2 David Boon (Australia)
3 Clive Rice (South Africa)
4 Vivien Richards (West Indies)
5 Martin Crowe (New Zealand)
6 Javed Miandad (Pakistan)
7 Ravi Ratnayeke (Sri Lanka)
8 Narendra Hirwani (India)

7
◀

Some of England's newcomers: Robin Smith (ABOVE) hooks his first ball for four in the fifth Test against West Indies at The Oval. Jack Russell (BELOW LEFT), the new wicketkeeper, came in against Sri Lanka at Lord's and made 94 as nightwatchman. David Lawrence (BELOW RIGHT) in action against Sri Lanka at Lord's.

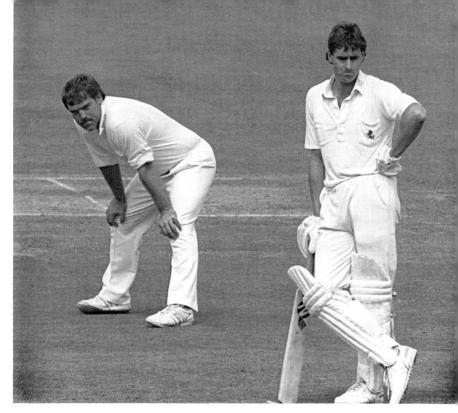

RIGHT: Two of England's captains in 1988, Mike Gatting and Christopher Cowdrey, playing for Middlesex and Kent, respectively.

BELOW: Four more England captains, past, present, and future: Pringle, Gooch, Emburey, and Gower during the second Test at Lord's. Pringle took over at The Oval when Gooch was injured.

Living legends. ABOVE LEFT: Sir Leonard Hutton at the crease at The Oval again, 50 years after he made his 364 against Australia there. ABOVE RIGHT: Denis Compton's 70th birthday celebrations were attended by an old friend and opponent, Keith Miller.
BELOW: Sir Donald Bradman on a lap of honour in Sydney during the Bicentennial Test.

ENGLAND v WEST INDIES   FIFTH TEST OVAL   August 5, 6

Eng 2nd

No	Batsman	How out	Bowler	Runs	Wkt	Total	6	4	Mins	Balls
1	GOOCH *	c GREENIDGE	AMBROSE	84	10	202	1	8	430	240
2	CURTIS	lbw	MARSHALL	15	1	50	-	2	69	50
3	BAILEY	b	BENJAMIN	3	2	55	-	-	24	18
4	SMITH	lbw	BENJAMIN	0	3	55	-	-	3	4
5	FOSTER	c LOGIE	BENJAMIN	34	4	108	-	5	106	80
6	MAYNARD	c+b	BENJAMIN	10	5	125	-	1	28	28
7	CAPEL	lbw	WALSH	12	6	139	-	2	38	33
8	RICHARDS †	c DUJON	WALSH	3	7	157	-	-	35	24
9	PRINGLE	b	HARPER	8	8	175	-	1	55	43
10	DeFREITAS	c HAYNES	HARPER	0	9	177	-	-	7	6
11	CHILDS	not	out	0	-	-	-	-	47	24
	Extras	B 3 LB 15 W - NB 15		33						550 (94.1ov + 15nb)

202

Bowler	O	M	R	W		NB	W
MARSHALL	25	6	52	1		9	
AMBROSE	24	10	50	1		5	
BENJAMIN	22	4	52	4		2	
WALSH	12	5	21	2			
HARPER	6	3	9	2			

· 16th over 5 balls

Wkt	Partnership between		Runs	Balls
1	Gooch	Curtis	50	92
2	— · —	Bailey	5	27
3	— · —	Smith	0	4
4	— · —	Foster	53	137
5	— · —	Maynard	17	39
6	— · —	Capel	14	55
7	— · —	Richards	18	50
8	— · —	Pringle	18	77
9	— · —	DeFreitas	2	8
10	— · —	Childs	25	61

England 205   West Indies 183

26 overs left August 5

Walsh off 5.41 - Close

Close: 64-3 (26 overs) Gooch 38* Foster 1*   86 ahead

Arthurton fielded for Richards August 6

Lunch: 128-5 (50 overs) Gooch 46* Capel 3*   150 ahead
Gooch faced only 49 balls in this session

Tea: 175-7 (77 overs) Gooch 67* Pringle 8*   197 ahead

Hrs	Balls	Runs		Runs	Balls	Last 50
1	79	46		50	91	-
2	71	14		100	218	127
3	69	41		150	376	158
4	80	24		200	542	166
5	84	27		250		
6	86	20		300		
7	69	24		350		
8				400		
9				450		
10				500		
11				550		
12				600		
13				650		

ENGLAND v WEST INDIES   FIFTH TEST   OVAL   August 6, 8

No	Batsman	How out	Bowler	Runs	Wkt	Total	6	4	Mins	Balls
1	GREENIDGE	c RICHARDS	CHILDS	77	1	131	-	10	219	203
2	HAYNES	not	out	77	-	-	-	6	358	237
3	HOOPER	b	FOSTER	23	2	162	1	2	55	55
4	LOGIE	not	out	38	-	-	-	6	80	59
5										
6										
7										
8										
9										
10										
11										
	Extras	B 2 LB 3 W - NB 6		11						554

226-2

(91 ov + 8nb)

Bowler	O	M	R	W	NB	W
FOSTER	18	3	52	1	1	
DeFREITAS	17	2	46	-	6	
CHILDS	40	16	79	1		
PRINGLE	13	4	24	-		
CAPEL	3	-	20	-		

Wkt	Partnership between		Runs	Balls
1	Greenidge	Haynes	131	339
2	Haynes	Hooper	31	94
3	—.—	Logie	64*	121
4				
5				
6				
7				
8				
9				
10				

England 205 + 202   West Indies 183

West Indies need 225 to win   24 overs left August 6

Gooch dislocated 4th finger left hand 2nd over August 6
NR Taylor (Kent) sub

Close: 71-0 (24 overs) Greenidge 53* Haynes 15* 154 to win

Lunch: 131-0 (55 overs) Greenidge 77* Haynes 44*   94 to win

Tea: 210-2 (86 overs) Haynes 72* Logie 28*   15 to win

WI won at 4.20 on fourth day

West Indies won by 8 wickets

West Indies won series 4-0

                    Men of Series

MM: PJL Dujon   GA Gooch

(FS Trueman)   M D Marshall

Hrs	Balls	Runs		Runs	Balls	Last 50
1	87	40		50	114	-
2	91	47		100	210	96
3	96	28		150	403	193
4	94	24		200	511	108
5	99	35		250		
6				300		
7				350		
8				400		
9				450		
10				500		
11				550		
12				600		
13				650		

Test Match Averages: England v West Indies 1988

England

Batting and Fielding	M	I	NO	HS	R	Avge	100	50	Ct/St
G.A. Gooch	5	10	–	146	459	45.90	1	3	6
A.J. Lamb	4	8	2	113	254	42.33	1	1	–
D.I. Gower	4	8	1	88★	211	30.14	–	1	2
R.A. Smith	2	4	–	57	106	26.50	–	1	1
P.R. Downton	3	5	1	27	84	21.00	–	–	9/–
P.W. Jarvis	2	3	1	29★	42	21.00	–	–	–
B.C. Broad	2	4	–	54	71	17.75	–	1	–
T.S. Curtis	2	4	–	30	69	17.25	–	–	2
N.A. Foster	2	4	1	34	49	16.33	–	–	1
M.D. Moxon	2	4	–	26	55	13.75	–	–	1
G.R. Dilley	4	7	1	28	58	9.66	–	–	1
M.W. Gatting	2	4	–	29	38	9.50	–	–	1
J.E. Emburey	3	5	–	30	46	9.20	–	–	3
D.R. Pringle	4	7	0	39	52	7.42	–	–	–
D.J. Capel	2	4	–	16	29	7.25	–	–	1
P.A.J. DeFreitas	3	5	–	18	36	7.20	–	–	2
C.J. Richards	2	4	–	8	13	3.25	–	–	3/–

Also batted: C.W.J. Athey (1 match) 16, 11; R.J. Bailey (1 match) 43, 3; J.H. Childs (2 matches) 2★, 0★, 0★, 0★ (1ct); C.S. Cowdrey (1 match) 0, 5; M.P. Maynard (1 match) 3, 10; G.C. Small (1 match) 5, 7★.

Bowling	O	M	R	W	Avge	Best	5wI	10wM
G.R. Dilley	136.1	26	403	15	26.86	5-55	1	–
N.A. Foster	73.2	12	250	9	27.77	5-64	1	–
D.R. Pringle	119	33	326	11	29.63	5-95	1	–
P.W. Jarvis	57.1	6	217	6	36.16	4-107	–	–

Also bowled: D.J. Capel 22-2-79-1; J.H. Childs 86-29-183-3; C.S. Cowdrey 5.3-0-21-0; P.A.J. DeFreitas 92-16-253-3; J.E. Emburey 62-14-228-3; G.C. Small 37.5-6-140-4.

West Indies

Batting and Fielding	M	I	NO	HS	R	Avge	100	50	Ct/St
A.L. Logie	5	7	2	95★	364	72.80	–	2	6
P.J.L. Dujon	5	7	1	67	305	50.83	–	4	20/–
R.A. Harper	3	3	–	74	147	49.00	–	2	5
D.L. Haynes	4	7	2	77★	235	47.00	–	3	3
C.G. Greenidge	4	6	–	103	282	47.00	1	1	4
I.V.A. Richards	5	6	–	80	223	37.16	–	2	3
M.D. Marshall	5	6	1	72	135	27.00	–	1	1
C.L. Hooper	5	7	–	84	166	23.71	–	1	3
C.E.L. Ambrose	5	6	2	43	75	18.75	–	–	–
R.B. Richardson	3	4	–	26	71	17.75	–	–	4
C.A. Walsh	5	5	3	9★	26	13.00	–	–	–

Also batted: K.T. Arthurton (1 match) 27; W.K.M. Benjamin (3 matches) 9, 0, 1ct; B.P. Patterson (2 matches) 0, 2.

Bowling	O	M	R	W	Avge	Best	5wI	10wM
W.K.M. Benjamin	67	17	151	12	12.58	4-52	–	–
R.A. Harper	29	11	63	5	12.60	3-50	–	–
M.D. Marshall	203.1	49	443	35	12.65	7-22	3	1
C.E.L. Ambrose	203.1	56	445	22	20.22	4-53	–	–
C.A. Walsh	157.2	40	412	12	34.33	4-46	–	–

Also bowled: C.L. Hooper 24-3-57-0; B.P. Patterson 74.5-13-270-4; I.V.A. Richards 10-1-28-0.

Statistical Highlights of the Tests

1st Test, Trent Bridge. The drawn 50th Test between the two countries stopped West Indies' unbeaten run over England at ten matches. England had now gone 14 matches without a win. Gooch scored his 8th Test hundred, his 4th against West Indies. At 29 he became the 16th English batsman to score 4,000 Test runs. Richards, at 66, reached 7,111 and passed G.S. Chappell to be 8th in the all-time list. Marshall scored his 8th Test fifty off only 88 balls, with three sixes and six fours. He had earlier taken five wickets for the 16th time, the 4th against England. With his fifth wicket he moved into second place in the West Indies' list, passing Garner (259). It was the best bowling for West Indies against England at Trent Bridge. Ambrose recorded both his highest score and his best bowling in Tests. Gower passed Barrington (6,806) in England Test runs.

2nd Test, Lord's. West Indies recorded their 11th win in 12 Tests against England. It was their 4th win in 13 matches at Lord's. Emburey captained England for the first time. Greenidge scored his 15th Test hundred, 6th against England. At 49 in the second innings he became the 19th in history, and the 5th West Indian, to score 6,000 runs. Lamb, in his 53rd Test, scored his 8th Test hundred, 4th against West Indies. His last hundred was in his 27th Test, against Sri Lanka at Lord's in 1984. Marshall took five wickets for the 17th time, 5th against England. It is the best bowling for West Indies against England at Lord's. With his 5th wicket he passed B.S. Bedi (267) to stand 10th in the world list. He completed ten wickets in a match for the third time, the first against England. Logie, at 49 in the 1st innings, reached 1,000 Test runs in his 25th Test. He and Dujon had hundred partnerships for the 6th wicket in both innings, a West Indies record. Dilley took five wickets for the 6th time, 1st against West Indies. Jarvis recorded both highest score and best bowling in Tests.

3rd Test, Old Trafford. West Indies recorded their fifth win in eleven matches at Old Trafford. England had their second-lowest total against West Indies (71 in 1976, also at Old Trafford). Childs, to be 37 on August 15, became the oldest England player to make his Test debut since R. Howorth, 38, on debut against South Africa in 1947. Richards reached 7,250 runs in Tests, passing W.R. Hammond, to stand 7th in all-time list. Gower, at 21 in 2nd innings, passed L. Hutton (6,971) in England list. Marshall took five wickets for 18th time, 6th against England, when he recorded his best Test bowling. Harper scored his best in Tests. Richardson took his 50th catch to dismiss Gower, but broke his left index finger and was unable to take any further part in the series.

4th Test, Headingley. West Indies won for the 5th time in eight matches at Headingley, in spite of the loss of over 120 overs during the first four days. Only 25 minutes' play were required. Cowdrey became the third son to join his father in captaining his country. F.T. Mann (5) and F.G. Mann (7), Nawab Pataudi Sr (3) and Jr (40) had been the only two previous instances. R.A. Smith joined his brother (C.L.) to be the 10th instance of brothers playing for England. Gower became only the 5th player to play 100 Tests. With his last stroke, he reached 7,000 runs, the 10th in the world and 4th for England. Marshall took his 100th wicket against England when he dismissed Smith. He is the 3rd West Indian to achieve this – Sobers (102) and Gibbs (100). Pringle recorded his best Test bowling, taking five wickets for the 2nd time. The previous was also against West Indies, at Edgbaston in 1984. Lamb batted with a runner (Smith) throughout the 2nd innings. (contd at bottom of page 137)

Texaco Trophy

England won the Texaco series 3-0, bringing their one-day record against West Indies up to nine wins in the last 10 meetings. Those who abused the selectors for preferring experienced players in form to untried youth or to rusty older players such as Gower and Botham were made to look, at best, ill informed and unimaginative.

All three matches were played on pitches giving opportunities to fast bowlers. This put an end to England's hopes of playing two spinners. However, on the truest, if the slowest, of the three pitches, at Edgbaston, the faster bowlers kept West Indies to 217. The most effective were Small and Pringle, whose selection had been most widely derided. Small's four for 21 brought him the Man of the Match award, one of his wickets being the vital one of Richards, who was brilliantly caught by Emburey at backward point off a full-blooded drive. After an opening stand of 70 by Gooch and Broad, England were steered home by Gatting with two overs to spare.

At Headingley, on a pitch of irregular bounce and movement, Pringle and Downton, coming together at 83 for five, helped England to 188 for eight, a not insignificant score in the conditions. West Indies were soon 11 for 2, and, before a stand between Greenidge and Richards could become menacing, Small removed both of them, Richards dragging a ball onto his stumps. Pringle took three of the remaining wickets for 30 and was named Man of the Match. Downton, another whose selection had come under fire, also had an excellent match, adding four catches to his valuable innings.

The first two matches were blessed by fine weather, but the third, before a full house at Lord's, was less favoured. Rain, infuriatingly confined to the London area, caused the first of four stoppages after one ball, and only 50 overs were bowled in the day. West Indies, having been put in, batted warily on an exacting pitch, and DeFreitas was in his sixth over before he conceded a run. Greenidge and Haynes took 17 overs to reach 40 and there was no acceleration later, Pringle bowling his last 10 for 17 runs. At the end of the 50 overs, the score was only 125 for six.

Next day, however, the skies were clear, the pitch more reliable, and Dujon and Marshall, in a rousing piece of hitting, made 53 in the remaining five overs.

This gave England a task that Gooch and Broad tackled with great care against the always formidable Marshall and three other fast bowlers who gave little away. The opening stand of 71 occupied 31 overs. But England had wickets in hand and a captain who gave a perfect exhibition of positive leadership from in front. Gatting at once set himself to attack the fifth bowler, Hooper, and sent the score racing forward. Lamb joined him in a final flurry of 56 in nine overs, which took England home with two overs to spare. DeFreitas was Man of the Match, Gatting and Marshall winning the series awards for their respective sides.

England v West Indies 1st Texaco Trophy International

England won by 6 wickets
Played at Edgbaston, Birmingham, 19 May
Toss: England. Umpires: J. Birkenshaw and B.J. Meyer
Man of the Match: G.C. Small (Ajudicator D.L. Amiss)

West Indies		Runs	Mins	Balls	6	4
C.G. Greenidge	b Small	18	52	38	–	2
P.V. Simmons	c Lamb b Dilley	22	27	16	–	3
P.B. Richardson	lbw b Pringle	11	41	22	–	–
I.V.A. Richards*	c Emburey b Small	13	9	7	–	3
A.L. Logie	c Downton b Small	51	125	96	–	3
C.L. Hooper	c Emburey b Small	51	99	96	–	5
P.J.L. Dujon†	run out (Downton/Emburey)	27	53	39	–	–
R.A. Harper	b Emburey	4	12	10	–	–
M.D. Marshall	c Lamb b DeFreitas	6	11	10	–	–
E.L.C. Ambrose	b Emburey	1	2	2	–	–
C.A. Walsh	not out	2	3	2	–	–
Extras	(LB2, W3, NB6)	11				
	(55 overs; 224 minutes)	**217**				

England		Runs	Mins	Balls	6	4
G.A. Gooch	c Harper b Ambrose	43	118	93	–	3
B.C. Broad	c Greenidge b Marshall	35	67	55	–	3
M.W. Gatting*	not out	82	136	124	–	7
M.A. Lynch	run out (Richardson/Walsh)	0	6	2	–	–
A.J. Lamb	b Hooper	12	27	22	–	–
D.R. Pringle	not out	23	49	32	–	1
P.R. Downton†	did not bat					
J.E. Emburey	,,					
P.A.J. DeFreitas	,,					
G.C. Small	,,					
G.R. Dilley						
Extras	(B2, LB9, W7, NB6)	24				
	(53 overs; 204 minutes)	**219-4**				

England	O	M	R	W
DeFreitas	11	2	45	1
Dilley	11	0	64	1
Small	11	0	31	4
Pringle	11	5	26	1
Emburey	11	1	49	2

West Indies	O	M	R	W
Ambrose	11	1	39	1
Walsh	11	1	50	0
Richards	7	1	29	0
Marshall	11	1	32	1
Harper	7	0	33	0
Hooper	6	0	25	1

Fall of Wickets

Wkt	WI	E
1st	34	70
2nd	50	119
3rd	66	121
4th	72	153
5th	169	–
6th	180	–
7th	195	–
8th	209	–
9th	212	–
10th	217	–

England v West Indies 2nd Texaco Trophy International

England won by 47 runs
Played at Headingley, Leeds, 21 May
Toss: West Indies. Umpires: D.J. Constant and D.R. Shepherd
Man of the Match: D.R. Pringle (Adjudicator D.B. Close)

England		Runs	Mins	Balls	6	4
G.A. Gooch	c Greenidge b Simmons	32	136	94	–	3
B.C. Broad	c Dujon b Ambrose	13	37	27	–	2
M.W. Gatting*	c Richards b Marshall	18	55	43	–	2
M.A. Lynch	lbw b Marshall	2	11	9	–	–
A.J. Lamb	c Dujon b Simmons	2	18	12	–	–
D.R. Pringle	b Dujon b Walsh	39	51	55	1	2
P.R. Downton†	c Dujon b Bishop	30	49	47	–	2
J.E. Emburey	c Ambrose b Bishop	8	28	20	–	1
P.A.J. DeFreitas	not out	15	38	27	–	1
G.C. Small	not out	7	16	10	–	–
G.R. Dilley	did not bat					
Extras	(B3, LB1, W3, NB13)	20				
	(55 overs; 216 minutes)	**186-8**				

West Indies		Runs	Mins	Balls	6	4
C.G. Greenidge	c Downton b Small	21	59	54	–	3
P.V. Simmons	b DeFreitas	1	7	6	–	–
P.B. Richardson	c Downton b Dilley	1	12	4	–	–
I.V.A. Richards*	b Small	31	62	29	–	6
A.L. Logie	c Lynch b Dilley	8	29	18	–	–
C.L. Hooper	lbw b Pringle	12	50	32	–	2
P.J.L. Dujon†	b Pringle	12	21	18	–	2
M.D. Marshall	c Downton b Gooch	1	4	6	–	–
E.L.C. Ambrose	c Downton b Pringle	23	76	68	–	1
C.A. Walsh	b Emburey	18	66	42	–	1
I.R. Bishop	not out	2	8	7	–	–
Extras	(LB3, W3, NB3)	9				
	(46.3 overs; 202 minutes)	**139**				

West Indies	O	M	R	W
Walsh	11	0	39	1
Ambrose	7	2	19	1
Marshall	9	1	29	2
Bishop	11	1	32	2
Simmons	9	2	30	2
Richards	8	0	33	0

England	O	M	R	W
Dilley	11	0	45	2
DeFreitas	9	2	29	1
Small	9	2	11	2
Pringle	11	0	30	3
Gooch	3	0	12	1
Emburey	3.3	0	9	1

Fall of Wickets

Wkt	E	WI
1st	29	2
2nd	64	11
3rd	72	38
4th	80	67
5th	83	67
6th	149	83
7th	154	84
8th	169	104
9th	–	132
10th	–	139

England v West Indies 3rd Texaco Trophy International

England won by 7 wickets
Played at Lord's London, 23, 24 May
Toss: England. Umpires: H.D. Bird and N.T. Plews
Man of the Match: P.A.J. DeFreitas (Ajudicator M.C. Cowdrey)
Men of the Series: M.W. Gatting and M.D. Marshall

West Indies		Runs	Mins	Balls	6	4
C.G. Greenidge	c DeFreitas b Emburey	39	118	94	1	5
D.L. Haynes	run out (Broad/Pringle)	10	69	49	–	1
P.B. Richardson	c Downton b Pringle	13	56	46	–	1
I.V.A. Richards*	c Emburey b DeFreitas	9	40	16	–	1
A.L. Logie	run out (Lamb)	0	4	4	–	–
C.L. Hooper	run out (DeFreitas/Downton)	12	51	46	–	1
P.J.L. Dujon†	not out	30	58	44	–	1
M.D. Marshall	b Emburey	41	32	30	2	3
W.K.M. Benjamin	did not bat					
C.A. Walsh	"					
I.R. Bishop	"					
Extras	(B2, LB10, W12)	24				
	(55 overs; 240 minutes)	**178-7**				

England		Runs	Mins	Balls	6	4
G.A. Gooch	st Dujon b Hooper	28	148	100	–	1
B.C. Broad	b Bishop	34	180	114	–	1
M.W. Gatting*	not out	40	90	58	–	4
M.A. Lynch	b Bishop	6	28	21	–	1
A.J. Lamb	not out	30	29	23	–	5
D.R. Pringle	did not bat					
P.R. Downton†	"					
J.E. Emburey	"					
P.A.J. DeFreitas	"					
G.C. Small	"					
N.V. Radford	"					
Extras	(B6, LB17, W5, NB14)	42				
	(50 overs; 218 minutes)	**180-3**				

England	O	M	R	W
DeFreitas	11	5	20	1
Radford	11	2	29	0
Small	10	1	34	0
Pringle	11	4	27	1
Emburey	10	1	53	2
Gooch	2	1	3	0

West Indies	O	M	R	W
Marshall	9	2	21	0
Walsh	11	5	11	0
Bishop	11	1	33	2
Benjamin	9	0	38	0
Hooper	10	0	54	1

Fall of Wickets		
Wkt	WI	E
1st	40	71
2nd	75	108
3rd	79	124
4th	79	–
5th	95	–
6th	111	–
7th	178	–
8th	–	–
9th	–	–
10th	–	–

West Indies Tour of England 1988

First-Class Matches: Played 16; Won 6, Drawn 10
All Matches: Played 23; Won 9, Lost 3, Drawn 11

First Class Averages

Batting and Fielding	M	I	NO	HS	R	Avge	100	50	Ct/St
R.A. Harper	12	13	5	217*	622	77.75	1	4	22
C.G. Greenidge	11	16	1	111	762	50.80	3	4	6
P.J.L. Dujon	12	16	4	141	601	50.08	1	5	31/–
K.T. Arthurton	10	13	3	121	499	49.90	2	2	8
D.L. Haynes	14	23	4	158	903	47.52	1	7	6
A.L. Logie	13	18	4	95*	586	41.85	–	3	9
I.V.A. Richards	13	16	1	128	624	41.60	1	5	9
C.L. Hooper	14	20	1	87	625	32.89	–	5	9
M.D. Marshall	9	10	1	76	289	32.11	–	2	3
C.E.L. Ambrose	13	15	3	59	278	23.16	–	–	1
D. Williams	8	10	1	51	182	20.22	–	1	11/1
R.B. Richardson	10	14	–	82	279	19.92	–	1	9
W.K.M. Benjamin	10	10	4	21*	102	17.00	–	–	6
I.R. Bishop	8	6	2	23	56	14.00	–	–	1
B.P. Patterson	9	7	2	23*	60	12.00	–	–	1
C.A. Walsh	9	7	3	9*	31	7.75	–	–	–

Also batted: P.V. Simmons (1 match) 53 ret hurt.

Bowling	O	M	R	W	Avge	Best	5wI	10wM
M.D. Marshall	245.4	56	553	42	13.16	7-22	3	1
W.K.M. Benjamin	183.1	43	467	33	14.15	4-20	–	–
I.R. Bishop	142	30	406	21	19.33	6-39	2	–
C.E.L. Ambrose	329.1	86	733	35	20.94	4-27	–	–
R.A. Harper	227.3	70	521	21	24.80	4-10	–	–
B.P. Patterson	196	33	632	25	25.28	5-39	1	–
C.L. Hooper	106.1	16	303	9	33.66	3-61	–	–
C.A. Walsh	232.2	55	622	18	34.55	5-49	1	–

Also bowled: K.T. Arthurton 27.1-8-80-3; I.V.A. Richards 45.4-10-122-3; R.B. Richardson 4-0-22-0.

5th Test, Oval. West Indies won their 14th Test in 15 matches against England in four days. England have now been without a win in 18 Tests. Gooch became the 4th captain for England in the series. It was only the 3rd time in history, the other times being 1884-85 (Australia v England) and 1929-30 (West Indies v England). Marshall ended the 1st innings with 34 wickets, a record for any West Indies series. He extended this to 35 in the 2nd innings. The previous record was 33, held by Marshall himself against India (1983-84), Valentine against England (1950), and Croft against Pakistan (1976-77). He also reached 104 wickets against England, a new record. England achieved a 1st innings lead over West Indies for the first time since Lord's 1984. Greenidge and Haynes opened the innings for the 109th time and recorded their 12th opening hundred partnership. When he reached 67, Greenidge had 2,000 runs against England, the 5th West Indian to achieve this. Gooch split and disclocated a finger attempting to catch Haynes in the second over of the third day and was unable to take the field again. Pringle assumed the captaincy. Richards was not present on the last day, having had to go to hospital for a minor operation.

Sri Lanka in England

Sri Lanka's short tour of England, begun in late July, followed a predictable course. They were unlikely to make the same impact as in 1984, when they took nearly all the honours from a drawn Test match against England at Lord's. Their opponents now were in much the same battered state as before, having once again been roundly defeated by West Indies. But the redoubtable Wettimuny, who made 190 in 1984, had now retired, and other players who had batted so well then had recently been very short of cricket at the top level. Political unrest had prevented several tours to Sri Lanka from taking place.

Since their entry into Test cricket, Sri Lanka's bowling has never been in the same class as their batting. It was therefore expected that Ranjan Madugalle's side would have rather more difficulty in holding England this time, even though their hosts had had a nightmare season with innumerable players being called up under four different captains.

This proved a fair assessment. Sri Lanka played some good cricket against the counties, but were unlucky to find the second half of an English season wetter and often colder than the first. The most serious influence this had on the tour came when they lost the toss in the Test match and were put in by Graham Gooch.

England, including four players new to Test cricket in Russell, Barnett, Newport, and Lawrence, bowled them out in 66 overs for 194. It is a mark of Sri Lanka's spirit in adversity that their seven-wicket defeat did not come until just after lunch on the fifth day.

Even on the first day, when the ball swung, they were able to complicate England's task. Duleep Mendis, who as captain in 1984 only missed by six runs the distinction of making a Test 100 in each innings, started a revival, from 63 for six, with Ravi Ratnayeke. This was carried on by Ratnayeke and Graeme Labrooy in a remarkable last-wicket stand of 64, lasting 90 minutes. Labrooy was the dominating partner, an unusually accomplished number 11.

England made 47 for one on the first evening. In the 75 overs possible on the second day they advanced to 278 for three, led by the nightwatchman Russell, who batted soundly for over four and a half hours for 94, his highest score in first-class cricket.

On the third day, England extended their lead to 235. But Sri Lanka replied with 95 for two and batted almost throughout the fourth day's play, with Ranatunga and Mendis sharing in an entertaining sixth-wicket stand of 104. England eventually needed 97 to win, and these were duly made on the last day for the loss of three wickets.

For several reasons, including discouraging weather, Lord's was never as much as half full, and bookings for the limited-overs international at The Oval on the following Sunday were poor. But by then the sun was shining. The ground filled while Sri Lanka were making 242 on a good pitch, and, though England always looked like winning, Sri Lanka were entitled to feel that, given luck with the toss at Lord's, they would certainly not have lost the Test match.

ENGLAND v SRI LANKA   LORD'S   August 25

SL 1st

No	Batsman	How out	Bowler	Runs	Wkt	Total	6	4	Mins	Balls
1	KURUPPU	c GOOCH	NEWPORT	46	3	52	-	6	79	58
2	SILVA†	c RUSSELL	FOSTER	1	1	7	-	-	29	22
3	SAMARASEKERA	c RUSSELL	FOSTER	0	2	44	-	-	34	19
4	De SILVA	c GOOCH	NEWPORT	3	4	53	-	.	23	18
5	MADUGALLE*	lbw	FOSTER	3	5	61	.	-	23	14
6	RANATUNGA	lbw	NEWPORT	5	6	63	-	1	18	12
7	MENDIS	c SMITH	LAWRENCE	21	7	122	.	3	70	43
8	RATNAYEKE	not out		59	.	-	-	9	175	112
9	MADURASINGHE	run out	(Lawrence)	4	8	127	-	-	10	11
10	RAMANAYAKE	lbw	PRINGLE	0	9	130	-	-	11	8
11	LABROOY	lbw	PRINGLE	42	10	194	-	6	85	83
	Extras	B 1 LB 7 W - NB 2		10						400 (65.5 overs + Sab)

194

Bowler	O	M	R	W	NB	W
FOSTER	21	5	51	3		
LAWRENCE	15	4	37	1		
NEWPORT	21	4	77	3	4	
PRINGLE	6³	1	17	2	1	
EMBUREY	2	1	4	-		

Wkt	Partnership between		Runs	Balls
1	Kuruppu	Silva	7	42
2	- . -	Samarasekera	37	49
3	- . -	De Silva	8	18
4	De Silva	Madugalle	1	13
5	Madugalle	Ranatunga	8	18
6	Ranatunga	Mendis	2	6
7	Mendis	Ratnayeke	59	94
8	Ratnayeke	Madurasinghe	5	14
9	- . -	Ramanayake	3	17
10	- . -	Labrooy	64	129

England won the toss & elected to field

Lunch: 69-6 (26 overs) Mendis 3* Ratnayeke 4*

Tea: 184-9 (61 overs) Ratnayeke 59* Labrooy 34* (Tea: 4-10)

10th wicket partnership record for Sri Lanka in all Tests

Debut: K J Barnett, D V Lawrence, P J Newport, R C Russell
WR Madurasinghe, MAR Samarasekera
JW Holder

Umpires: D J Constant & J W Holder

Hrs	Balls	Runs		Runs	Balls	Last 50
1	84	36		50	108	-
2	73	33		100	189	81
3	86	54		150	298	109
4	81	37		200		
5				250		
6				300		
7				350		
8				400		
9				450		
10				500		
11				550		
12				600		
13				650		

ENGLAND v SRI LANKA   LORD's   August 25, 26, 27

Eng 1r

No	Batsman	How out	Bowler	Runs	Wkt	Total	6	4	Mins	Balls
1	GOOCH *	lbw	RATNAYEKE	75	2	171	-	8	260	193
2	ROBINSON	c SAMARASEKERA	RATNAYEKE	19	1	40	-	1	76	58
3	RUSSELL †	c SAMARASEKERA	LABROOY	94	3	233	-	11	276	202
4	BARNETT	c RANATUNGA	LABROOY	66	4	320	-	7	170	128
5	LAMB	b	LABROOY	63	5	358	1	6	123	75
6	SMITH	b	RANATUNGA	31	6	373	-	2	77	70
7	PRINGLE	c SILVA	LABROOY	14	8	383	-	2	56	38
8	EMBUREY	c De SILVA	SAMARASEKERA	0	7	378	-	.	19	18
9	NEWPORT	c De SILVA	RAMANAYAKE	26	9	420	-	3	56	38
10	FOSTER	not	out	14	.	-	-	-	67	52
11	LAWRENCE	c MENDIS	RAMANAYAKE	4	10	429	-	-	14	12
	Extras	B 1 LB 3 W 2 NB 17		23						884

429

(143.2 overs
' 24 nb)

Bowler	O	M	R	W	NB	W
RATNAYEKE	32	3	107	2	5	
LABROOY	40	7	119	4	12	
RAMANAYAKE	27²	3	86	2	6	1
MADURASINGHE	16	4	41	-		
SAMARASEKERA	22	5	66	1	1	1
RANATUNGA	6	3	6	1		

Wkt	Partnership between		Runs	Balls
1	Gooch	Robinson	40	118
2	– . –	Russell	131	284
3	Russell	Barnett	62	133
4	Barnett	Lamb	87	103
5	Lamb	Smith	38	64
6	Smith	Pringle	15	46
7	Pringle	Emburey	5	31
8	– . –	Newport	5	7
9	Newport	Foster	37	78
10	Foster	Lawrence	9	20

Sri Lanka 194   22 overs left August 25

Close : 47-1 (22 overs) Gooch 24* Russell 2*   147 behind
lunch : 119-1 (51 overs) Gooch 54* Russell 37*   75 behind
Tea : 217-2 (81 overs) Russell 86* Barnett 25*   23 ahead
New Ball : 225-2 (85 overs) (Ratnayeke)
BLSP : 5-16 No further play August 26
Close : 278-3 (97 overs) Barnett 55* Lamb 20*   84 ahead
lunch : 377-6 (124 overs) Pringle 9* Emburey 0*   183 ahead

Hrs	Balls	Runs
1	91	35
2	93	27
3	87	45
4	98	42
5	95	45
6	77	48
7	81	53
8	80	63
9	86	26
10	87	42
11		
12		
13		

Runs	Balls	Last 50
50	148	-
100	257	109
150	372	115
200	470	98
250	548	78
300	628	80
350	694	66
400	820	126
450		
500		
550		
600		
650		

ENGLAND v SRI LANKA   LORD'S   August 27, 29

SL 2nd

No	Batsman	How out	Bowler	Runs	Wkt	Total	6	4	Mins	Balls
1	KURUPPU	c BARNETT	FOSTER	25	1	43	-	5	42	31
2	SILVA †	c RUSSELL	NEWPORT	16	2	51	-	4	58	41
3	SAMARASEKERA	lbw	EMBUREY	57	5	147	1	7	145	110
4	De SILVA	lbw	LAWRENCE	18	3	96	-	2	50	31
5	MADUGALLE*	b	FOSTER	20	4	145	-	3	70	50
6	RANATUNGA	b	NEWPORT	78	7	309	-	10	227	179
7	MENDIS	lbw	PRINGLE	56	6	251	-	8	124	97
8	RATNAYEKE	c LAMB	LAWRENCE	32	9	323	-	4	130	85
9	MADURASINGHE	b	NEWPORT	2	8	311	-	-	9	11
10	LABROOY	not out		9	-	-	-	1	37	23
11	RAMANAYAKE	c GOOCH	NEWPORT	2	10	331	-	-	12	10
	Extras	B - LB 8 W - NB 8		16						668

331

(109.3ov + 11nb)

Bowler	O	M	R	W	NB	W
FOSTER	33	10	98	2		
LAWRENCE	21	5	74	2	11	
NEWPORT	26³	7	87	4		
PRINGLE	11	2	30	1		
EMBUREY	18	9	34	1		

Wkt	Partnership between		Runs	Balls
1	Kuruppu	Silva	43	63
2	Silva	Samarasekera	8	21
3	Samarasekera	De Silva	45	74
4	-.-	Madugalle	49	101
5	-.-	Ranatunga	2	8
6	Ranatunga	Mendis	104	198
7	-.-	Ratnayeke	58	140
8	Ratnayeke	Madurasinghe	2	13
9	-.-	Labrooy	15	32
10	Labrooy	Ramanayake	8	18

Sri Lanka 194 England 429   41 overs left August 27
Tea: 22-0 (6 overs) Kuruppu 13* Silva 4*   213 behind
BLSP: 5.20 No further play August 27
Close: 92-2 (24.5 overs) Samarasekera 30* De Silva 15* 143 behind
Lunch: 161.5 (54 overs) Ranatunga 5* Mendis 10*   74 behind
Tea: 265-6 (86 overs) Ranatunga 57* Ratnayeke 2* 30 ahead
New Ball taken for ball after tea (Foster)

Hrs	Balls	Runs		Runs	Balls	Last 50
1	84	51		50	83	-
2	85	51		100	161	78
3	90	43		150	302	141
4	90	25		200	405	103
5	92	71		250	464	59
6	102	31		300	587	123
7	73	39		350		
8				400		
9				450		
10				500		
11				550		
12				600		
13				650		

ENGLAND v SRI LANKA   LORD'S   August 29, 30

Eng 2nd

No	Batsman	How out	Bowler	Runs	Wkt	Total	6	4	Mins	Balls
1	GOOCH*	c SILVA	SAMARASEKERA	36	1	73	-	5	96	70
2	ROBINSON	not	out	34	-	-	-	4	134	109
3	BARNETT	c SILVA	SAMARASEKERA	0	2	73	-	-	1	2
4	LAMB	c De SILVA	RANATUNGA	8	3	82	-	1	14	15
5	SMITH	not	out	8	-	-	-	1	17	17
6	PRINGLE									
7	EMBUREY									
8	RUSSELL †	did not bat								
9	NEWPORT									
10	FOSTER									
11	LAWRENCE									
	Extras	B - LB 8 W2 NB 4		14						

100.3

213
(34.4 ov + 5nb)

Bowler	O	M	R	W		NB	W
LABROOY	9	-	24	-		5	
RATNAYEKE	7	1	16	-			
SAMARASEKERA	10	-	38	2			
RANATUNGA	8.9	4	14	1			

Wkt	Partnership between		Runs	Balls
1	Gooch	Robinson	73	158
2	Robinson	Barnett	0	2
3	— . —	Lamb	9	26
4	— . —	Smith	18*	27
.5				
.6				
7				
.8				
.9				
.10				

Sri Lanka 194 + 331   England 429

England need 97 to win   3 overs left August 29

Close: 8-0 (3 overs) Gooch 1* Robinson 4*   89 to win

Lunch: 96-3 (34 overs) Robinson 34* Smith 4* Scores level

England won at 1.42 (4 balls after lunch)

England won by 7 wickets

Men of Series: P J Newport
RJ Ratnayeke

Hrs	Balls	Runs		Runs	Balls	Last 50
1	94	42		50	108	-
2	97	40		100		
3				150		
4				200		
5				250		
6				300		
7				350		
8				400		
9				450		
10				500		
11				550		
12				600		
13				650		

Sri Lanka Tour of England 1988

First-Class Matches: Played 8; Drawn 7, Lost 1
All Matches: Played 12; Drawn 10, Lost 2

First-Class Averages

Batting and Fielding	M	I	NO	HS	R	Avge	100	50	Ct/St
J.R. Ratnayeke	8	10	5	60*	311	62.20	–	2	1
P.A. De Silva	6	9	3	117*	333	55.50	1	2	3
D.S.B.P. Kuruppu	6	10	1	158	438	48.66	1	2	1/1
R.S. Madugalle	8	11	2	97	403	44.77	–	3	4
L.R.D. Mendis	9	12	2	124	362	36.20	1	2	2
A. Ranatunga	8	9	1	84	271	33.87	–	2	3
M.A.R. Samarasekera	9	15	2	104	401	30.84	1	2	5
R.S. Mahanama	5	8	2	46*	179	29.83	–	–	1
S.A.R. Silva	8	14	1	112	338	26.00	1	1	15/-
G.F. Labrooy	7	4	1	42	73	24.33	–	–	2
H.P. Tillekeratne	5	6	1	50*	121	24.20	–	1	4
W.R. Madurasinghe	6	7	2	30	75	15.00	–	–	2
H.C.P. Ramanayake	4	3	0	18	20	6.66	–	–	–

Also batted: F.S. Ahangama (5 matches) 0*, 3*, 1ct; S.D. Anurasiri (3 matches) 4*, 1ct.
B.E.A. Rajadurai played in two matches but did not bat.

Bowling	O	M	R	W	Avge	Best	5wI	10wM
F.S. Ahangama	99.2	22	321	12	26.75	4-51	–	–
G.F. Labrooy	201.5	30	665	20	33.25	6-61	1	–
M.A.R. Samarasekera	127.4	14	406	10	40.60	3-31	–	–
H.C.P. Ramanayake	87.2	11	315	7	45.00	2-36	–	–
J.R. Ratnayeke	231.5	36	687	15	45.80	3-47	–	–
W.R. Madurasinghe	144.4	35	376	6	62.66	3-50	–	–

Also bowled: S.D. Anurasiri 62-16-175-2; P.S. DeSilva 14-5-42-1; B.E.A. Rajadurai; 20-3-65-1;
A. Ranatunga 50.4-11-153-2; H.P. Tillekeratne 9-1-35-1.

Statistical Highlights of the Test

Only Test, The Oval. England recorded their first Test win since December 28
at Melbourne. They had played 18 Tests since then to the start of this match.
Gooch, at 73 in 1st innings, reached 4,503 runs and passed E.R. Dexter in the
England list. At 33 in the 2nd innings he reached 4,538 and passed P.B.H. May.
This left him 13th in the England list. He finished the summer with 4,541, only
14 behind H. Sutcliffe. Ratnayeke and Labrooy put on 64 for the 10th wicket, a
record for Sri Lanka in any Test. Mendis and Ranatunga played in their 24th
Test, a Sri Lankan record. Ranatunga, at 41 in 2nd innings, became the first Sri
Lankan to reach 1,500 Test runs.

England v Sri Lanka, Texaco Trophy International

England won by 5 wickets
Played at Kennington Oval, London, 4 September
Toss: England. Umpires: J.A. Holder and K.E. Palmer
Men of the Match: K.J. Barnett and L.R.D. Mendis (Adjudicator: A.V. Bedser)

Sri Lanka		Runs	Mins	Balls	6	4
D.S.B.P. Kuruppu†	lbw b Gooch	38	92	66	–	5
M.A.R. Samarasekera	b Small	10	32	29	–	1
P.A. De Silva	b Gooch	16	36	28	–	1
A. Ranatunga	run out (Barnett)	37	72	62	–	3
L.R.D. Mendis	b Small	60	88	66	1	6
R.S. Madugalle*	c Foster b Pringle	17	31	25	–	–
J.R. Ratnayeke	c Pringle b Small	19	33	19	–	3
H.P. Tillekeratne	not out	15	42	27	–	–
G.F. Labrooy	,,	10	11	11	–	–
S.D. Anurasiri	did not bat					
W.R. Madurasinghe	,,					
Extras	(B1, LB10, W8, NB1)	20				
	(55 overs; 226 minutes)	**242-7**				

England		Runs	Mins	Balls	6	4
G.A. Gooch*	c De Silva b Labrooy	7	8	10	–	1
R.T. Robinson	lbw b Ratnayeke	13	44	33	–	–
K.J. Barnett	run out (Samarasekera)	84	179	143	–	5
A.J. Lamb	c sub (Rajadurai) b Labrooy	66	86	71	1	3
R.A. Smith	c Kuruppu b Labrooy	9	17	15	–	1
R.J. Bailey	not out	43	53	34	1	3
D.R. Pringle	,,	19	15	11	1	1
R.C. Russell†	did not bat					
V.J. Marks	,,					
G.C. Small	,,					
N.A. Foster	,,					
Extras	(W3, NB1)	4				
	(52.4 overs; 206 minutes)	**245-5**				

England	O	M	R	W
Foster	11	0	47	0
Small	11	1	44	3
Gooch	11	1	35	2
Pringle	11	0	46	1
Marks	11	0	59	0

Sri Lanka	O	M	R	W
Ratnayeke	9.4	3	37	1
Labrooy	10	0	40	3
Samarasekera	11	0	52	0
Ranatunga	11	0	42	0
Anurasiri	6	0	31	0
De Silva	2	0	19	0
Madurasinghe	3	0	24	0

Fall of Wickets

Wkt	SL	E
1st	21	9
2nd	54	22
3rd	75	140
4th	144	154
5th	190	213
6th	193	–
7th	224	–
8th	–	–
9th	–	–
10th	–	–

1988

ENGLISH SEASON

Britannic Assurance Championship

Worcestershire's victory in the Britannic Assurance Championship was won over Kent by only one point, but always seemed likely in a season when they were proving hard to beat in all four competitions. They also won the Refuge Assurance Sunday League, reached the final of the NatWest Trophy , in which Middlesex beat them, and lost in the Benson & Hedges Cup semi-final to the eventual winners Hampshire.

In 1987, the first season with Ian Botham and Graham Dilley in their ranks, they had only finished ninth in the championship. In 1988, almost from the start they were without Botham, who departed for a back operation. During the season they lost to the England selectors not only Dilley, but at various times Radford, Newport, and Curtis. But they had at Worcester a square that was more likely than many to reward good bowling, and they had the brilliant Graeme Hick, who set new batting records for a championship reduced to 22 matches.

In their last match but one, they beat Gloucestershire at Bristol to edge one point in front of Kent. And though Kent made a spirited effort to take maximum points off Surrey at Canterbury by lunch on the third day of a four-day match, Worcestershire within three hours did the same at Worcester to Glamorgan.

Essex had been only five points behind starting the last series of matches, and provided another instance of the 1987 form being turned upside-down. Worcestershire had then finished ninth, Kent 14th, and Essex 12th. In 1987, Middlesex and Warwickshire were trying to avoid bottom place when they met at Uxbridge in late August. This year at the same time and place they had fourth place in their sights.

Middlesex, with only two wins in 1987, did in fact start 1988 best of all, winning all three of their early four-day matches, against Notts, Essex, and Surrey. With their three Test players absent they then won a remarkable victory at Leicester, largely thanks to a fine innings on a testing pitch by John Carr. Their bowlers, notably Cowans and Angus Fraser, were now bowling sides out. But Carr became short of runs, Gatting, though more often available, was not as consistent as usual in a troubled season, and it was August before they won again.

The big surprise was no doubt the finish in fifth place of Nottinghamshire, of whom not much had been expected in the immediate aftermath of the retirement of Clive Rice and Richard Hadlee. However, they produced instead the 29-year-old Barbadian all-rounder Franklyn Stephenson, who performed the nowadays unlikely double of 1,000 runs and 100 wickets, rounding his season off in an astonishing last match against Yorkshire (which Notts lost) by taking 11 wickets and making a hundred in each innings.

Worcestershire had made almot as good a start to the season as Middlesex, but Kent mustered only 13 points from their first three four-day matches. From this point, however, Kent, starting with a three-wicket win over Yorkshire at Canterbury, began a surge upwards. This was the first of six successive victories, and when they beat Warwickshire by an innings in two days at Edgbaston on June 20 they pushed Worcestershire off the top. Their captain, Christopher Cowdrey, was in form with both bat and ball, Tavaré was consistent, Ellison fitter than for several seasons and taking wickets again. So was Penn. Pienaar was proving an invaluable all-rounder.

From then until September the weather became a big factor. Some counties were luckier than others, but for a time Kent went on prospering. When they beat Northants at Northampton by one wicket it was their eighth win in 10 matches, and they were 35 points clear of Worcestershire, who were just ahead of Essex. Kent played Worcestershire at Folkestone in late July, but rain cut the match by a third. Bonus points were keenly contested, though no one could have guessed their ultimate significance. Worcestershire indeed took one more than Kent from the match.

Kent were brought down to earth with a bump during the Canterbury Week, when Somerset beat them by an innings, losing only four wickets in the process. By August 10, Worcestershire had cut Kent's lead to 11 points, and when they beat Glamorgan at Abergavenny in a match of three declarations by making 344 for five in the last innings, Hick 159, they were in front by three points with five matches left.

However, in the next week Essex won a fine victory at Worcester, and Kent, having beaten Hampshire at Bournemouth, were 16 points ahead again with three four-day matches remaining.

Rain was the winner of Worcestershire's match with Warwickshire, but Kent misses their chance in a crucial match againt Sussex at Maidstone. Having had the better of the first innings, they ran up against stiff resistance from the Sussex batsmen in the second and lost by 63 runs.

But, in the dismal August weather no one had come from behind to challenge them, and they still led Worcestershire by 16 points with two matches left.

It was Kent's next match, against Middlesex at Lord's, that was to prove decisive. Worcestershire were clearly going to beat Gloucestershire, but in a splendid match at Lord's, Kent, having led Middlesex by 122 on first innings, still seemed to have the match under control after three days.

Middlesex began the last day only 108 ahead and lost Gatting to the first ball. But then Kent were cruelly held up by local showers. With less time to have to hold out, Middlesex's later batsmen put their heads down, and when the innings ended, with a last-wicket stand of 46 in 17 overs between Downton and Tufnell as the final frustration, Middlesex were 229 ahead with only 29 overs left. Kent made a despairing effort, but lost wickets in the process and only avoided defeat with their last pair together.

Worcestershire were in the lead again – by just the one point. But it was enough.

Britannic Assurance County Championship 1988

Final Table	P	W	L	D	1st Innings Points Batting	Bowling	Total Points
1 WORCESTERSHIRE (9)	22	10	3	9	55	75	290
2 Kent (14)	22	10	5	7	57	72	289
3 Essex (12)	22	9	5	8	61	69	282†
4 Surrey (4)	22	7	5	10	57	72	241
5 Nottinghamshire (1)	22	8	8	6	34	71	229‡
6 Warwickshire (15)	22	6	8	8	48	74	218
7 Leicestershire (3)	22	6	3	13	56	63	215
8 Middlesex (16)	22	7	3	12	49	54	215
9 Lancashire (2)	22	6	7	9	41	67	212†
10 Gloucestershire (10)	21*	6	7	8	52	59	207
11 Somerset (11)	22	5	6	11	48	65	201†
12 Northamptonshire (7)	22	5	7	10	48	71	199
13 Yorkshire (8)	22	4	6	12	48	65	177
14 Derbyshire (6)	22	4	3	15	53	54	171
15 Hampshire (5)	22	4	6	12	33	69	166
16 Sussex (17)	22	3	11	8	37	65	150
17 Glamorgan (13)	21*	1	8	12	42	53	111

1987 positions are shown in brackets. * No play possible in one match. †includes 8 points for drawn match in which scores finished level. ‡ includes 12 points for win in one-innings match.

Points

For a win: 16 points, plus any first innings points. For winning a match reduced to a single innings because it started with less than eight hours' playing time remaining: 12 points. First innings points are awarded during the first 100 overs of each first innings:

Batting		Bowling	
150 to 199 runs	1	3 or 4 wickets	1
200 to 249 runs	2	5 or 6 wickets	2
250 to 299 runs	3	7 or 8 wickets	3
300 runs and over	4	9 or 10 wickets	4

Final Positions 1890-1988

	D	E	Gm	Gs	H	K	La	Le	M	Nh	Nt	Sm	Sy	Sx	Wa	Wo	Y
1890	—	—	—	6	—	3	2	—	7	—	5	—	1	8	—	—	3
1891	—	—	—	9	—	5	2	—	3	—	4	5	1	7	—	—	8
1892	—	—	—	7	—	7	4	—	5	—	2	3	1	9	—	—	6
1893	—	—	—	9	—	4	2	—	3	—	6	8	5	7	—	—	1
1894	—	—	—	9	—	4	4	—	3	—	7	6	1	8	—	—	2
1895	5	9	—	4	10	14	2	12	6	—	12	8	1	11	6	—	3
1896	7	5	—	10	8	9	2	13	3	—	6	11	4	14	12	—	1
1897	14	3	—	5	9	12	1	13	8	—	10	11	2	6	7	—	4
1898	9	5	—	3	12	7	6	13	2	—	8	13	4	9	9	—	1
1899	15	6	—	9	10	8	4	13	2	—	10	13	1	5	7	12	3
1900	13	10	—	7	15	3	2	14	7	—	5	11	7	3	6	12	1
1901	15	10	—	14	7	7	3	12	2	—	9	12	6	4	5	11	1
1902	10	13	—	14	15	7	5	11	12	—	3	7	4	2	6	9	1
1903	12	8	—	13	14	8	4	14	1	—	5	10	11	2	7	6	3
1904	10	14	—	9	15	3	1	7	4	—	5	12	11	6	7	13	2
1905	14	12	—	8	16	6	2	5	11	13	10	15	4	3	7	8	1
1906	16	7	—	9	8	1	4	15	11	11	5	11	3	10	6	14	2
1907	16	7	—	10	12	8	6	11	5	15	1	14	4	13	9	2	3
1908	14	11	—	10	9	2	7	13	4	15	8	16	3	5	12	6	1
1909	15	14	—	16	8	1	2	13	6	7	10	11	5	4	12	8	3
1910	15	11	—	12	6	1	4	10	3	9	5	16	2	7	14	13	8
1911	14	6	—	12	11	2	4	15	3	10	8	16	5	13	1	9	7
1912	12	15	—	11	6	3	4	13	5	2	8	14	7	10	9	16	1
1913	13	15	—	9	10	1	8	14	6	4	5	16	3	7	11	12	2
1914	12	8	—	16	5	3	11	13	2	9	10	15	1	6	7	14	4

	D	E	Gm	Gs	H	K	La	Le	M	Nh	Nt	Sm	Sy	Sx	Wa	Wo	Y
1919	9	14	—	8	7	2	5	9	13	12	3	5	4	11	15	—	1
1920	16	9	—	8	11	5	2	13	1	14	7	10	3	6	12	15	4
1921	12	15	17	7	6	4	5	11	1	13	8	10	2	9	16	14	3
1922	11	8	16	13	6	4	5	14	7	15	2	10	3	9	12	17	1
1923	10	13	16	11	7	5	3	14	8	17	2	9	4	6	12	15	1
1924	17	15	13	6	12	5	4	11	2	16	6	8	3	10	9	14	1
1925	14	7	17	10	9	5	3	12	6	11	4	15	2	13	8	16	1
1926	11	9	8	15	7	3	1	13	6	16	4	14	5	10	12	17	2
1927	5	8	15	12	13	4	1	7	9	16	2	14	6	10	11	17	3
1928	10	16	15	5	12	2	1	9	8	13	3	14	6	7	11	17	4
1929	7	12	17	4	11	8	2	9	6	13	1	15	10	4	14	16	2
1930	9	6	11	2	13	5	1	12	16	17	4	13	8	7	15	10	3
1931	7	10	15	2	12	3	6	16	11	17	5	13	8	4	9	14	1
1932	10	14	15	13	8	3	6	12	10	16	4	7	5	2	9	17	1
1933	6	4	16	10	14	3	5	17	12	13	8	11	9	2	7	15	1
1934	3	8	13	7	14	5	1	12	10	17	9	15	11	2	4	16	5
1935	2	9	13	15	16	10	4	6	3	17	5	14	11	7	8	12	1
1936	1	9	16	4	10	8	11	15	2	17	5	7	6	14	13	12	3
1937	3	6	7	4	14	12	9	16	2	17	10	13	8	5	11	15	1
1938	5	6	16	10	14	9	4	15	2	17	12	7	3	8	13	11	1
1939	9	4	13	3	15	5	6	17	2	16	12	14	8	10	11	7	1
1946	15	8	6	5	10	6	3	11	2	16	13	4	11	17	14	8	1
1947	5	11	9	2	16	4	3	14	1	17	11	11	6	9	15	7	7
1948	6	13	1	8	9	15	5	11	3	17	14	12	2	16	7	10	4
1949	15	9	8	7	16	13	11	17	1	6	11	9	5	13	4	3	1
1950	5	17	11	7	12	9	1	16	14	10	15	7	1	13	4	6	3
1951	11	8	5	12	9	16	3	15	7	13	17	14	6	10	1	4	2
1952	4	10	7	9	12	15	3	6	5	8	16	17	1	13	10	14	2
1953	6	12	10	6	14	16	3	3	5	11	8	17	1	2	9	15	12
1954	3	15	4	13	14	11	10	16	7	7	5	17	1	9	6	11	2
1955	8	14	16	12	3	13	9	6	5	7	11	17	1	4	9	15	2
1956	12	11	13	3	6	16	2	17	5	4	8	15	1	9	14	9	7
1957	4	5	9	12	13	14	6	17	7	2	15	8	1	9	11	16	3
1958	5	6	15	14	2	8	7	12	10	4	17	3	1	13	16	9	11
1959	7	9	6	2	8	13	5	16	10	11	17	12	3	15	4	14	1
1960	5	6	11	8	12	10	2	17	3	9	16	14	7	4	15	13	1
1961	7	6	14	5	1	11	13	9	3	16	17	10	15	8	12	4	2
1962	7	9	14	4	10	11	16	17	13	8	15	6	5	12	3	2	1
1963	17	12	2	8	10	13	15	16	6	7	9	3	11	4	4	14	1
1964	12	10	11	17	12	7	14	16	6	3	15	8	4	9	2	1	5
1965	9	15	3	10	12	5	13	14	6	2	17	7	8	16	11	1	4
1966	9	16	14	15	11	4	12	8	12	5	17	3	7	10	6	2	1
1967	6	15	14	17	12	2	11	3	7	9	16	8	4	13	10	5	1
1968	8	14	3	16	5	2	6	9	10	13	4	12	15	17	11	7	1
1969	16	6	1	2	5	10	15	14	11	9	8	17	3	7	4	12	13
1970	7	12	2	17	10	1	3	15	16	14	11	13	5	9	7	6	4
1971	17	10	16	8	9	4	3	5	6	14	12	7	1	11	2	15	13
1972	17	5	13	3	9	2	15	6	8	4	14	11	12	16	1	7	10
1973	16	8	11	5	1	4	12	9	13	3	17	10	2	15	7	6	14
1974	17	12	16	14	2	10	8	4	6	3	15	5	7	13	9	1	11
1975	15	7	9	16	3	5	4	1	11	8	13	12	6	17	14	10	2
1976	15	6	17	3	12	14	16	4	1	2	13	7	9	10	5	11	8
1977	7	6	14	3	11	1	16	5	1	9	17	4	14	8	10	13	12
1978	14	2	13	10	8	1	12	6	3	17	7	5	16	9	11	15	4
1979	16	1	17	10	12	5	13	6	14	11	9	8	3	4	15	2	7
1980	9	8	13	7	17	16	15	9	1	12	3	5	2	4	14	11	6
1981	12	5	14	13	7	9	16	8	4	15	1	3	6	2	17	11	10
1982	11	7	16	15	3	13	12	2	1	9	4	6	5	8	17	14	10
1983	9	1	15	12	3	7	12	4	2	6	14	10	8	11	5	16	17
1984	12	1	13	17	15	5	16	4	3	11	2	7	8	6	9	10	14
1985	13	4	12	3	2	9	14	16	1	10	7	17	6	7	15	5	11
1986	11	1	17	2	6	8	15	7	12	9	4	16	3	14	13	5	10
1987	6	12	13	10	5	14	2	3	16	7	1	11	4	17	15	9	8
1988	14	3	17	10	15	2	9	7	8	12	5	11	4	16	6	1	13

Derbyshire

No season in which you reach the Benson & Hedges Cup final can be counted wholly disappointing, but Derbyshire's heavy defeat by Hampshire on their big day at Lord's, their slump to 14th in the Championship and ineffectiveness on Sundays meant that the summer ended with mounting concern about standards. Conspicuous individual successes were neutralized by the failures of others, and the banality of pitches in the county undoubtedly contributed to the under-achievements of a seam attack expected to be the side's strong suit.

Kim Barnett, the captain, fully justified his promotion to Test cricket with more than 1,600 first-class runs, including five centuries, and occasional glimpses of his leg-spin convinced many members that this was an under-employed weapon. Peter Bowler, released by Leicestershire, immediately established himself as one of the major successes of the summer, for Derbyshire or anybody else, making a century on his debut and passing 1,700 runs to finish third highest scorer of the season behind Graeme Hick and Graham Gooch. Bowler, like Barnett, passed 50 on 13 occasions in first-class games, and his ability to apply intense concentration for long periods provided a marked contrast to the depressing decline of Bruce Roberts and the too-frequent flimsiness of the contribution from the gifted but inconsistent John Morris.

Steve Goldsmith, jettisoned by Kent, responded to greater opportunity with more than 1,000 runs, most made at an entertaining gallop, and Bernie Maher complemented sound form behind the stumps by finishing only 26 runs short of 1,000 in first-class fixtures.

In limited-overs matches, however, only Barnett seemed regularly capable of making big scores at the required tempo.

The Derbyshire staff contained no fewer than eleven seamers, but only Olé Mortensen enhanced his reputation, and Michael Holding's form was especially modest. His meagre haul of only 24 first-class wickets took the gloss off his world limited-overs record of 8-21 against Sussex in the NatWest Trophy. Though Devon Malcolm occasionally excited with his vivid pace, his inaccuracy led to some spectacularly expensive analyses and the conclusion that a Ferrari is of limited value without a steering wheel.

With Newman renewing his season-ticket for the physio's couch and neither Allen Warner nor Simon Base consistently effective, it was left to the fiercely committed Mortensen to provide an example of genuine quality which kept him at the top of the national bowling averages for much of the summer. He evoked fond memories of the great swing and seam merchants of the county's golden era of fast-medium bowling, but persistent back and leg injuries limited his availability and confined him to 34 first-class wickets, another factor in Derbyshire's disappointing collection of bowling points. Only bottom-placed Glamorgan earned fewer. Tim O'Gorman and Frank Griffith did well enough with limited exposure to suggest each might develop, but with Barnett graduating to the England squad the future cannot be viewed with unqualified

Britannic Assurance County Championship: 14th; Won 4, Lost 3, Drawn 15
All First-Class Matches: Won 5, Lost 3, Drawn 16
NatWest Bank Trophy: Lost to Hampshire in quarter-final
Benson & Hedges Cup: Lost to Hampshire in final
Refuge Assurance League: 13th; Won 5, Lost 8, Tied 1, No Result 2

Championship Averages

Batting and Fielding	M	I	NO	HS	R	Avge	100	50	Ct/St
K.J. Barnett	17	27	2	239*	1406	56.24	4	7	14
R.J. Finney	3	5	2	52*	142	47.33	–	1	–
P.D. Bowler	22	40	4	159*	1563	43.41	3	9	12
J.G. Wright	11	20	1	154*	815	42.89	1	5	1
J.E. Morris	21	35	5	175	1163	38.76	2	6	5
S.C. Goldsmith	22	37	4	89	956	28.96	–	5	16
B.J.M. Maher	22	38	6	121*	920	28.75	1	4	51/1
B. Roberts	22	37	4	71	903	27.36	–	7	13
R. Sharma	9	13	2	80	275	25.00	–	1	5
T.J.E. O'Gorman	4	8	0	78	152	19.00	–	1	5
F.A. Griffith	4	6	1	37	87	17.40	–	–	2
A.E. Warner	18	25	6	45	300	15.78	–	–	3
P.G. Newman	14	18	5	39	174	13.38	–	–	1
M.A. Holding	11	12	2	30*	129	12.90	–	–	7
O.H. Mortensen	12	12	8	15	46	11.50	–	–	6
S.J. Base	7	9	3	15	51	8.50	–	–	2
D.E. Malcolm	19	21	5	22	119	7.43	–	–	1
M. Jean-Jacques	3	4	0	5	5	1.25	–	–	1

Also batted: C.J. Adams (1 match) 21 (1ct).

Hundreds (11)

4 K.J. Barnett: 175 v Glos, Derby; 239* v Leics, Leicester; 109 v Yorks, Chesterfield; 157 v Lancs, Derby
3 P.D. Bowler: 159* v Essex, Chesterfield; 158 v Surrey, Oval; 134 v Lancs, Derby
2 J.E. Morris: 175 v Glam, Swansea; 106 v Notts, Trent Bridge
1 B.J.M. Maher: 121* v Leics, Derby
  J.G. Wright: 154* v Warwicks, Derby

Bowling	O	M	R	W	Avge	Best	5wI	10wM
O.H. Mortensen	233.3	73	464	34	13.64	6-35	4	–
P.G. Newman	306.5	70	877	32	27.40	8-29	1	–
A.E. Warner	416	92	1091	37	29.48	4-36	–	–
F.A. Griffith	80.3	17	268	9	29.77	4-47	–	–
K.J. Barnett	158.1	35	411	13	31.61	3-63	–	–
M. Jean-Jacques	84.1	14	262	8	32.75	3-49	–	–
D.E. Malcolm	468	85	1642	50	32.84	6-68	2	–
M.A. Holding	279.1	49	827	24	34.45	4-74	–	–
B. Roberts	99	21	300	8	37.50	2-17	–	–
S.J. Base	165	12	654	17	38.47	4-74	–	–
R. Sharma	208.2	47	559	7	79.85	1-0	–	–
P.D. Bowler	169.5	28	577	7	82.42	2-63	–	–

Also bowled: R.J. Finney 45-8-131-0; S.C. Goldsmith 43-8-125-0; J.E. Morris 5.1-0-19-0.

confidence.

The retirement from county cricket of New Zealand opener John Wright deprives them of a shining example of high skill and exemplary professional commitment, but consolation is available in Derbyshire's success, amid strong competition, in persuading the impressive young West Indian fast bowler Ian Bishop to join them in 1989.

Essex

The plaintive lament 'This nearly was mine' about sums up Essex in 1988, as they came reasonably close to success in all four competitions, but finished with nothing. Although this represented a marked improvement on the previous summer, a side containing two world-class batsmen, three members of the current England attack, and a centurion, East, batting at number nine, and who could afford to omit Fletcher, Hardie, and Topley from their team and possessed an unusually well-balanced bowling line-up, should, despite international calls and injuries, have done even better.

To some extent this stemmed from the lack of a killer instinct, as illustrated when they failed to go for the jugular at Southend and Colchester, and, although fielding their strongest XI, allowed Lancashire and Notts to climb back off the floor. If Fletcher and Lever had been three years younger, they would have carried off the County Championship comfortably. They were one match-winning pace bowler short, which was especially noticeable when Foster and Pringle were missing. As the former, and possibly the latter, is likely to be on Test duty next summer, the signing of M. Waugh, a talented batsman, is somewhat surprising.

The Essex batting was very strong. Gooch and Border provided large quantities of runs and entertainment to demonstrate the enormous gap between a true Test player and a county batsman, but what long term could prove far more important was the big advance made by Stephenson and Hussain. The former seized on the injury to Hardie and the frequent absences of Gooch to indicate the arrival of a talented opener, while the much younger Hussain looks an even more exciting prospect. Although not quite back to his 1986 form, Prichard is almost there and his technique remains impressive. Lilley, who fielded magnificently and bravely, benefited from his promotion in the order without ever scoring quite enough runs.

After missing the first month through injury, Foster quickly regained his position as England's most accomplished opening bowler. This was Pringle's most impressive season with the ball; in addition to his control and natural lift, he did just enough off the pitch. Unfortunately, his batting remains an enigma. On occasions he played delightfully and on others he looked as if he could not bat at all. Topley never stopped trying, and earned, somewhat belatedly, his cap as a useful third seamer. At the start of the summer nobody seriously imagined that Childs would be selected for England, though most of the umpires reckoned that he was the best available slow left-armer. Miller enjoyed a much improved all-round season, and has decided to stay.

What of the future? The difference in ability between the 17 counties has never been less, so that 1989 could prove highly successful for Essex, provided their players can achieve a five per cent improvement. However, they cannot afford any complacency, and must avoid a tendency to become depressed when things are going wrong. This was when the odd

Britannic Assurance County Championship: 3rd; Won 9, Lost 5, Drawn 8
All First-Class Matches: Won 10, Lost 5, Drawn 9
NatWest Bank Trophy: Lost to Glamorgan in 2nd round
Benson & Hedges Cup: Lost to Hampshire in semi-final
Refuge Assurance League: 11th; Won 6, Lost 8, Tied 1, No Result 1

Championship Averages

Batting and Fielding	M	I	NO	HS	R	Avge	100	50	Ct/St
G.A. Gooch	14	23	0	275	1631	70.91	5	9	19
A.R. Border	19	30	7	169*	1361	59.17	6	4	25
N. Hussain	8	11	3	165*	469	58.62	1	2	5
M.E. Waugh	3	4	0	86	178	44.50	–	1	2
P.J. Prichard	22	36	7	80	1051	36.24	–	7	12
K.W.R. Fletcher	12	14	3	58	303	27.54	–	2	9
J.P. Stephenson	17	29	3	99	707	27.19	–	5	10
A.W. Lilley	19	30	2	80*	730	26.07	–	4	16
D.R. Pringle	13	17	0	128	446	26.23	1	3	5
D.E. East	18	26	2	134	580	24.16	1	1	53/4
B.R. Hardie	12	19	3	58	353	22.06	–	2	9
G. Miller	17	19	4	77	329	21.93	–	1	18
I.L. Pont	6	6	2	29	76	19.00	–	–	1
T.D. Topley	15	20	6	56*	233	16.64	–	1	8
J.H. Childs	16	15	8	25*	71	10.14	–	–	4
N.A. Foster	13	16	2	22	108	7.71	–	–	7
A.D. Brown	4	5	3	6*	13	6.50	–	–	9/2
J.K. Lever	13	13	1	20	53	4.41	–	–	2

Also batted: M.C. Ilott (1 match) 6.

Hundreds (14)

6 A.R. **Border:** 169* v Derbys, Chesterfield; 112 v Warwicks, Edgbaston; 161 v Sussex, Ilford; 168 v Kent, Canterbury; 110* v Northants, Northampton; 130* v Notts, Colchester

5 G. A. **Gooch:** 275 v Kent, Chelmsford; 139 v Surrey, Chelmsford; 113 v Sussex, Ilford; 123 v Surrey, Oval; 108 v Northants, Chelmsford

1 D.E. **East:** 134 v Glos, Ilford
  N. **Hussain:** 165* v Leics, Chelmsford
  D.R. **Pringle:** 128 v Kent, Chelmsford

Bowling	O	M	R	W	Avge	Best	5wI	10wM
N.A. Foster	471.1	95	1423	66	21.56	6-53	4	2
T.D. Topley	500.1	81	1521	62	24.53	7-75	4	1
D.R. Pringle	352.3	71	1031	41	25.14	6-39	3	–
J.H. Childs	506.2	161	1262	49	25.75	6-92	3	1
J.K. Lever	422.4	90	1120	43	26.04	4-61	–	–
G. Miller	375	95	1001	35	28.60	5-76	1	–
I.L. Pont	158	16	591	16	36.93	5-103	1	–
G.A. Gooch	135	37	342	9	38.00	2-29	–	–

Also bowled: A.R. Border 28-8-74-1; N. Hussain 9-0-47-0; M.C. Ilott 15-1-48-0; A.W. Lilley 11-0-119-0; P.J. Prichard 1-0-7-0; J.P. Stephenson 59.2-12-187-4; M.E. Waugh 12-0-75-0.

lapse in the Essex fielding, generally very good, frequently brilliant, did occur.

Glamorgan

Glamorgan's disappointment at finishing last in the County Championship during their Centenary season was tempered by their improved form in the one-day competitions. They finished sixth in the Refuge Assurance League, reached the semi-final of the Benson & Hedges competition for the first time and were quarter-finalists in the NatWest Trophy.

Nevertheless, a solitary victory in the County Championship, gained against Warwickshire in early September, was disappointing for a side who appeared well balanced in both batting and bowling, but who failed to produce the level of consistency required to win matches.

Glamorgan also suffered more than any other county from the abysmal weather. Nearly a third of playing time in home matches was affected by rain compared with five per cent away from home. One three-day match was totally washed out, while nearly three days were lost in the four-day match at Neath.

Matthew Maynard, who played for England against the West Indies in the final Test, was again Glamorgan's leading run-scorer. He scored five centuries in all competitions, was voted Young Cricketer of the Year, and pledged his allegiance to Glamorgan by signing a new five-year contract.

Butcher was the only other batsman to score over 1,000 runs, Holmes was only one run short, while Morris would assuredly have reached that target had he not missed the final three matches because of a knee injury. Thomas, who developed into a capable all-rounder, scored two centuries in the last month of the season, including a match-winning effort of 110 at Edgbaston.

Glamorgan obtained fewer bowling points than any other county, although Watkin, their 23-year-old seam bowler, took 46 wickets in his first full season, including 8-59 against Warwickshire. He impressed many with his high arm action and the ability to bowl long accurate spells on unresponsive wickets. Thomas was more effective on the quicker wickets away from home, while Barwick missed a number of matches through injury.

Ontong and Shastri, Glamorgan's spinners, were the least effective of the bowlers, taking only 46 wickets between them, and despite contributing significantly in one-day matches, their inability to dismiss sides on turning pitches was a major disappointment. Ontong and Barwick were hurt in a car accident towards the end of the season, and Ontong's knee was so badly injured that it is doubtful whether he will be able to resume his first-class career.

Metson, who joined Glamorgan from Middlesex in 1987, emulated the high wicket-keeping standards he had set the previous year. He equalled the Glamorgan record for the number of dismissals during a season in the Sunday League and also equalled Eifion Jones' record of six catches in a championship innings.

John Hopkins, who scored over 13,000 runs during his 18-year career, retired at the end of the season. Todd, formerly of Nottinghamshire, and

Britannic Assurance County Championship: 17th; Won 1, Lost 8, Drawn 12, No Play 1
All First-Class Matches: Won 1, Lost 8, Drawn 14, No Play 1
NatWest Bank Trophy: Lost to Surrey in quarter-final
Benson & Hedges Cup: Lost to Derbyshire in semi-final
Refuge Assurance League: Won 8, Lost 5, Tied 1, No Result 2

Championship Averages

Batting and Fielding	M	I	NO	HS	R	Avge	100	50	Ct/St
M.P. Maynard	19	35	6	126	1361	46.93	3	11	22
R.C. Ontong	16	24	8	120*	734	45.87	1	4	7
R.J. Shastri	12	19	2	157	575	33.82	1	2	5
G.C. Holmes	18	30	3	117	912	33.77	4	3	6
A.R. Butcher	21	38	2	93	1098	30.50	–	9	12
H. Morris	18	32	3	87	820	28.27	–	6	13
P.D. North	5	7	3	41*	107	26.75	–	–	2
P.A. Cottey	12	21	3	73	443	24.61	–	3	4
J.G. Thomas	15	25	4	110	515	24.52	2	–	5
J.A. Hopkins	11	20	1	71	368	19.36	–	2	8
C.P. Metson	21	29	7	48	347	15.77	–	–	49/6
P.G.P. Roebuck	2	4	0	46	60	15.00	–	–	1
S. Bastien	4	6	2	36*	57	14.25	–	–	1
M.J. Cann	6	7	0	28	78	11.14	–	–	4
J. Derrick	19	26	5	50*	212	10.09	–	1	8
S.L. Watkin	15	19	7	23	115	9.58	–	–	1
S.R. Barwick	12	7	2	30	40	8.00	–	–	2
C.J.P.G. Van Zyl	3	5	1	11	30	7.50	–	–	1

Also batted: S. Monkhouse (2 matches) 0*.

Hundreds (11)

4 **G.C. Holmes:** 117 v Glos, Bristol; 108 v Somerset, Cardiff; 100* & 107 v Somerset, Taunton
3 **M.P. Maynard:** 126 v Glos, Bristol; 122 v Somerset, Cardiff; 108* v Worcs, Abergavenny
2 **J.G. Thomas:** 100* v Worcs, Abergavenny; 110 v Warwicks, Edgbaston
1 **R.C. Ontong:** 120* v Kent, Cardiff
  R.J. Shastri: 157 v Somerset, Cardiff

Bowling	O	M	R	W	Avge	Best	5wI	10wM
S.L. Watkin	505.3	113	1347	44	30.61	8-59	2	–
J.G. Thomas	400.2	60	1444	47	30.72	6-68	2	–
J. Derrick	506.1	123	1418	45	31.51	6-54	1	–
S.R. Barwick	383.5	102	1014	32	31.68	5-37	1	–
A.R. Butcher	47	8	172	5	34.40	2-28	–	–
R.J. Shastri	304.2	91	709	20	35.45	7-49	1	1
S. Bastien	119.1	35	289	8	36.12	5-90	1	–
P.D. North	64.5	12	195	5	39.00	3-24	–	–
G.C. Holmes	116.2	12	440	11	40.00	5-38	1	–
R.C. Ontong	376.1	88	1078	24	44.91	4-38	–	–

Also bowled: M.J. Cann 14-2-63-4; J.A. Hopkins 5-1-46-0; M.P. Maynard 5-2-13-0; S. Monkhouse 44-8-118-2; H. Morris 4.3-0-58-0; C.J.P.G. Van Zyl 99.1-27-291-2.

Monkhouse, formerly of Warwickshire, were released, while Van Zyl, the South African fast bowler, terminated his contract with the county.

Gloucestershire

Gloucestershire occupied the same 10th position in the County Championship as they did last year, and despite finishing second in the Refuge Assurance League, their lack of success in recent years prompted the cricket committee to relieve David Graveney of the captaincy. The decision caused much ill-feeling among members and sponsors, and the club faced a winter of discontent. The county had made an encouraging start to the season, winning four of their Championship matches, but thereafter a combination of inconsistent batting and rain-affected matches meant that they won only two of their remaining 15 games. The weather deprived them of probable wins in three matches, while the game against Glamorgan was abandoned without a ball bowled.

Stovold, Wright, Bainbridge, Athey, and Curran reached 1,000 runs for the season, but Lloyds, Gloucester's leading scorer the previous season, was injured at the end of July and did not reappear until the last week of the season. Athey, whose name was linked with the captaincy, was also injured, and missed the final two months of the season.

Romaines played some notable innings, while Russell, who had been overlooked for the Test series against the West Indies, answered those who had doubted his batting ability by scoring 94 in his first Test Match, against Sri Lanka.

The leading wicket-takers were Lawrence, Alderman, and Curran, who took over 200 wickets between them. Lawrence, whose whole-hearted effort and endeavour were an example to others, took 81 wickets at 26, twice the number he took last year. He was rewarded with a first cap against Sri Lanka and was chosen for the Indian tour. Alderman, who replaced Walsh as Gloucestershire's overseas signing, was most effective, taking 75 wickets at 22, and despite Walsh's return in 1989, Alderman has intimated that he would welcome another season. Consequently it is likely that if Gloucester accede to his request, Greene, another West Indian fast bowler, will be released.

Curran's medium pace supplemented the fast bowlers, and the injured back that had inhibited him from bowling in 1987 withstood the rigours of a county season and he finished with 65 wickets.

Graveney achieved the season's best match figures when he took 14-165 in the final home game against Worcestershire on a turning wicket at Bristol. He took 53 wickets during the season, when pitches throughout the land were not conducive to the quicker bowlers.

Lloyds, Gloucestershire's other spin bowler, bowled only 240 overs during the season, and his 13 wickets proved expensive at over 58 runs per wicket.

It was encouraging to see Gloucestershire give opportunities to younger players on the staff, and Ball, a promising 18-year-old off-spinner, made his Championship debut against Hampshire, while Pooley, a former Young England player, played six Championship matches. Andy Brassington, a former wicket-keeper and a loyal

Britannic Assurance County Championship: 10th; Won 6, Lost 7, Drawn 8, No Play 1
All First-Class Matches: Won 6, Lost 7, Drawn 11, No Play 1
NatWest Bank Trophy: Lost to Worcestershire in quarter-final
Benson & Hedges Cup: Failed to qualify for quarter-final (3rd in Group D)
Refuge Assurance League: 2nd; Won 10, Lost 4, No Result 2
Refuge Assurance Cup: Lost to Lancashire in semi-final

Championship Averages

Batting and Fielding	M	I	NO	HS	R	Avge	100	50	Ct/St
C.W.J. Athey	11	20	6	168*	1037	74.07	2	6	19
K.M. Curran	19	34	7	142	1005	37.22	2	4	15
A.W. Stovold	21	39	2	136	1296	35.02	2	6	14
P. Bainbridge	21	36	1	169	1213	34.65	3	6	7
K.B.K. Ibadulla	3	6	2	77	122	30.50	–	1	1
R.C. Russell	19	30	6	72	658	27.41	–	4	45/9
A.J. Wright	21	38	0	136	1023	26.92	1	4	13
P.W. Romaines	18	34	2	101*	859	26.84	1	5	12
M.W. Pooley	6	12	4	38	146	18.25	–	–	4
J.W. Lloyds	14	22	2	68	331	16.55	–	1	20
D.A. Graveney	20	23	8	47	227	15.13	–	–	3
M.W. Alleyne	12	19	1	56	224	12.44	–	1	11/1
T.M. Alderman	20	22	11	43*	135	12.27	–	–	12
D.V. Lawrence	20	24	3	29	217	10.33	–	–	3

Also batted: M.J.C. Ball (1 match) 2; A.J. Brassington (1 match) 1 (1ct/1st); I.P. Butcher
(1 match) 11, 8 (2ct); V.S. Greene (1 match) 2; K.B.S. Jarvis (1 match) 1*; D.J. Thomas
(1 match) 7, 3.

Hundreds (11)

3 P. Bainbridge: 119 v Warwicks, Cheltenham; 169 v Yorks, Cheltenham; 124 v Worcs, Bristol
2 C.W.J. Athey: 123 v Glam, Bristol; 168* v Northants, Bristol
  K.M. Curran: 101 v Surrey, Cheltenham; 142 v Middx, Lord's
  A.W. Stovold: 136 v Sussex, Bristol; 133 v Somerset, Taunton
1 P.W. Romaines: 101* v Lancs, Old Trafford
  A.J. Wright: 136 v Derbys, Derby

Bowling	O	M	R	W	Avge	Best	5wI	10wM
K.M. Curran	414.2	86	1385	65	21.30	7-54	4	3
T.M. Alderman	600	135	1711	75	22.81	8-59	3	–
D.A. Graveney	562.5	163	1268	49	25.87	8-127	2	1
D.V. Lawrence	580.2	94	2037	77	26.45	7-47	4	–
M.W. Pooley	104.4	25	311	11	28.27	4-80	–	–
M.W. Alleyne	61	11	206	6	34.33	4-48	–	–
P. Bainbridge	284.4	58	913	12	76.08	3-85	–	–
J.W. Lloyds	214.3	37	696	9	77.33	2-84	–	–

Also bowled: C.W.J. Athey 5-0-20-0; M.J.C. Ball 5-3-2-1; V.S. Greene 18-3-49-0;
K.B.K. Ibadulla 26.2-6-94-3; K.B.S. Jarvis 22-1-104-1; P.W. Romaines 0.1-0-6-0;
D.J. Thomas 24.4-5-66-3.

clubman, retired at the end of the season and was appointed to the
marketing staff.

Hampshire

Hampshire at last laid the jinx of never appearing in a Lord's final. Not only did they break this barrier in the Benson & Hedges Cup, but won the title and further proved themselves by reaching the last four of the NatWest Trophy competition. But in the final analysis, it is by performance in the Championship that a county's season is remembered. By that yardstick, Hampshire disappointed.

Dropping ten places from 1987, Hampshire finished 15th. The last time they sank to such low reaches was in 1984, and before that, 1980 was a year of similar depression. It is not coincidental that all these summers were the ones in which the West Indies toured England, depriving Hampshire of the services of two great match-winners, Gordon Greenidge, from whom they are now parted for good, and Malcolm Marshall.

To emphasize sufficiently the influence of the two Barbadians on Hampshire's fortunes it must be recorded that, in the three years separating the two West Indies tours, the county's final positions were second, sixth, and fifth. Rules forbade the replacement of both the stars with other overseas players, but Hampshire tried to fill the void left by Marshall by signing the left arm pace bowler from Western Australia, Bruce Reid. He, however, incurred a long-term injury during the Australian season and could not fulfil his commitment.

In that, Hampshire were desperately unlucky. There were not many options left to them when Reid's unavailability became known, and they had to make do with a stand-in of lesser stature – although a very great trier – in South African Stephen Jefferies, formerly of Lancashire. Jefferies, left-arm, was in the forefront of Hampshire's win in their first-ever Cup final, but much less of a force in the Championship.

Moreover, he broke down in early August and missed all of the rest of the season. Just before then, however, he took only his second haul of five wickets or more. His first was an impressive eight for 67 at Gloucester. Jefferies' injury was by no means the only one to deplete Hampshire's attack. They suffered right through the season. Except for Rajesh Maru, their spinner, every front-line bowler was out of action at some time or another, the worst casualty being their young pace bowler Stephen Andrew, with stress fractures in the back. Tremlett, who for many seasons has carried a high workload, had an assortment of injuries. At one stage, he missed ten matches in a row, and in all played in only seven.

Five batsmen, the brothers Smith, Turner, Terry, and Nicholas, scored over a thousand runs, but none averaged above 40, and Hampshire's striking rate, as reflected in their batting bonus points, was lower than all the other counties' except Notts. There was one very direct explanation for Hampshire's batsmen being unable to give full expression to their talents, and that was the quality of pitches, including their own.

Their meagre tally of batting points, 33, is not necessarily indicative of

Britannic Assurance County Championship: 15th; Won 4, Lost 6, Drawn 12
All First-Class Matches: Won 4, Lost 6, Drawn 14
NatWest Bank Trophy: Lost to Worcestershire in semi-final
Benson & Hedges Cup: Winners
Refuge Assurance League: 9th; Won 7, Lost 8, No Result 1

Championship Averages

Batting and Fielding	M	I	NO	HS	R	Avge	100	50	Ct/St
N.G. Cowley	4	5	2	55	139	46.33	–	1	1
C.L. Smith	22	43	3	124*	1436	35.90	3	8	14
D.R. Turner	21	38	5	150*	1121	33.96	2	5	5
S.T. Jefferies	14	19	5	60	462	33.00	–	2	4
R.A. Smith	16	32	4	141*	912	32.57	2	2	10
M.C.J. Nicholas	22	42	3	132*	1146	29.38	2	4	18
V.P. Terry	22	42	3	126*	992	25.43	2	5	30
J.R. Ayling	18	31	4	88*	667	24.70	–	4	5
S.J.W. Andrew	10	9	7	12*	41	20.50	–	–	1
R.J. Scott	7	13	0	58	255	19.61	–	2	9
P.J. Bakker	10	11	8	16	50	16.66	–	–	1
R.J. Parks	22	33	8	38*	392	15.68	–	–	59/10
K.D. James	10	19	2	77	238	14.00	–	1	2
T.M. Tremlett	6	10	2	38	111	13.87	–	–	3
R.J. Maru	21	28	5	74	302	13.13	–	1	30
C.A. Connor	17	22	4	24	135	7.50	–	–	3

Hundreds (11)

3 C.L. Smith: 124* v Lancs, Liverpool; 117 v Notts, Southampton; 103* v Essex, Portsmouth
2 M.C.J. Nicholas: 132* v Glam, Bournemouth; 102 v Essex, Portsmouth
  R.A. Smith: 141* v Glos, Gloucester; 119 v Sussex, Southampton
  V.P. Terry: 106 v Somerset, Southampton; 126* v Surrey, Guildford
  D.R. Turner: 100* v Somerset, Southampton; 150* v Middx, Basingstoke

Bowling	O	M	R	W	Avge	Best	5wI	10wM
T.M. Tremlett	105.3	29	281	13	21.61	4-19	–	–
P.J. Bakker	293.4	86	670	30	22.33	5-54	1	–
J.R. Ayling	409.1	84	1065	45	23.66	4-57	–	–
K.D. James	250.5	55	639	26	24.57	5-25	1	–
S.J.W. Andrew	233.3	58	681	26	26.19	4-52	–	–
C.A. Connor	470.5	86	1451	53	27.37	5-70	1	–
N.G. Cowley	96.1	22	246	8	30.75	3-49	–	–
C.L. Smith	49	1	171	5	34.20	5-69	1	–
S.T. Jefferies	355.1	52	1216	34	35.76	8-97	2	–
R.J. Maru	622	173	1618	45	35.95	5-69	1	–

Also bowled: M.C.J. Nicholas 33-3-114-1; R.J. Scott 13.3-2-52-0; R.A. Smith 5.1-1-34-0; D.R. Turner 0.2-0-8-0.

the approach of their captain, Mark Nicholas. As always, he tried to be positive, but could ot only manoeuvre within the limitations of his team. Nevertheless, Hampshire won four matches, only one of them at home. Two of their victories were against counties that finished in the frame – Kent, whom they beat with a day to spare, and Surrey, who, at their early season meeting, had demolished them in two days.

Kent

The single point that separated Kent from a share in the County Championship was the subject of some heartburning at Canterbury as, on the penultimate day of the first-class season, Chris Cowdrey's men vanquished Surrey by an innings and 66 runs. Conversation turned to the match at Edgbaston, in June, when Kent were denied a richly deserved fourth point because Warwickshire, with two men absent, lost only eight wickets in their first innings.

The fact remains that Kent would have won the Championship outright had they not stumbled three fences from the post in losing to lowly Sussex at Maidstone. This, indeed, was one of the few occasions when lethargy clouded their otherwise extraordinarily inspired summer.

Having lost, or dispensed with, the services of Derek Underwood, Eldine Baptiste, and Kevin Jarvis, Kent's only concession to the need for replacement was the signing of Hartley Alleyne, once with Worcestershire and, more recently, Natal. In the event, the season began disastrously, as most uncommitted observers had predicted.

Injuries to Alan Igglesden, Chris Penn, and Richard Ellison compounded the gloom as Kent lost the first three Championship matches and languished 15th in the table.

It was at this point that Cowdrey called a team conference which proved so uplifting that, by the end of June, Kent were firmly established as Championship leaders.

As the remarkable renaissance continued, it became clear that the transformation was due entirely to team effort. All the bowlers, supported by excellent catching, performed heroically – notably Penn and Ellison, who ran neck and neck as leading wicket-takers, with Cowdrey, Pienaar, and Davis close behind.

Such was the corporate success that, in the space of six weeks, Kent achieved as many Championship victories as they had in the previous two seasons. That against Warwickshire – despite the 'missing' point – exemplified the method, as Tavaré, Cowdrey, and Benson led the charge with 327, then Penn, Ellison, and Cowdrey shared 15 wickets as Kent romped home by an innings and 46 runs.

The batting, as ever, had plenty of depth, and Tavaré's return to century-making form, after a couple of relatively lean seasons, was a bonus. But perhaps the most significant contributions came from Pienaar, originally engaged as a seam bowler, who cruised past his 1,000 runs with a series of excellent innings.

On July 22, Kent's typically audacious win at Northampton, where they reached 288 in 63 overs with two balls to spare, found them 35 points clear of Worcester. But, in the next match at Folkestone, they could only draw against their closest rivals. When they subsequently lost to Somerset, at Canterbury, the gap began to narrow.

By August 9, Worcestershire were a mere 11 points behind, and when Kent, despite a first innings of 466 for nine declared (Cowdrey 108 and Tavaré 119), failed to beat Derbyshire, Worcestershire took the lead by

Britannic Assurance County Championship: 2nd; Won 10, Lost 5, Drawn 7
All First-Class Matches: Won 10, Lost 6, Drawn 8
NatWest Bank Trophy: Lost to Middlesex in quarter-final
Benson & Hedges Cup: Failed to qualify for quarter-final (3rd in Group C)
Refuge Assurance League: 7th; Won 7, Lost 6, No Result 3

Championship Averages

Batting and Fielding	M	I	NO	HS	R	Avge	100	50	Ct/St
C.J. Tavaré	21	35	1	129*	1292	38.00	3	5	29
R.F. Pienaar	19	32	2	144	1070	35.66	2	7	5
M.R. Benson	21	37	1	110	1227	34.08	2	8	13
G.R. Cowdrey	18	29	4	145	790	31.60	1	4	10
N.R. Taylor	20	36	2	114	915	26.91	2	4	15
S.G. Hinks	14	24	1	92	611	26.56	–	3	11
C.S. Cowdrey	19	33	6	108	714	26.44	1	2	31
T.R. Ward	9	15	0	72	345	23.00	–	3	9
C. Penn	19	30	12	40	407	22.61	–	–	7
D.J.M. Kelleher	4	5	1	43*	86	21.50	–	–	2
S.A. Marsh	22	34	5	120	613	21.13	1	1	51/5
A.P. Igglesden	7	8	2	41	103	17.16	–	–	1
R.M. Ellison	19	27	6	50*	345	16.42	–	1	7
M.D. Harman	10	11	6	17*	71	14.20	–	–	6
R.P. Davis	17	19	6	23	103	7.92	–	–	12
H.L. Alleyne	3	5	1	9	16	4.00	–	–	–

Hundreds (12)

3 C.J. Tavaré: 129* v Glam, Cardiff; 103 v Warwicks, Edgbaston; 119 v Derbys, Chesterfield
2 M.R. Benson: 110 v Essex, Chelmsford; 110 v Middx, Tunbridge Wells
  R.F. Pienaar: 144 v Yorks, Canterbury; 128 v Leics, Canterbury
  N.R. Taylor: 112* v Glam, Cardiff; 114 v Surrey, Guildford
1 C.S. Cowdrey: 108 v Derbys, Chesterfield
  G.R. Cowdrey: 145 v Essex, Chelmsford
  S.A. Marsh: 120 v Essex, Chelmsford

Bowling	O	M	R	W	Avge	Best	5wI	10wM
A.P. Igglesden	234.3	46	805	37	21.75	6-34	3	1
R.M. Ellison	571.4	156	1652	69	23.94	7-75	3	–
C. Penn	629.1	141	1918	80	23.97	7-70	6	–
H.L. Alleyne	74.3	13	260	10	26.00	5-54	1	–
M.D. Harman	238.4	76	537	20	26.85	5-68	1	–
D.J.M. Kelleher	72	18	188	7	26.85	4-24	–	–
C.S. Cowdrey	384.5	92	1114	39	28.56	5-46	1	–
R.F. Pienaar	368.2	90	1055	32	32.96	5-27	1	–
R.P. Davis	529.2	163	1333	34	39.20	5-132	1	–
G.R. Cowdrey	88.4	17	351	5	70.20	1-5	–	–

Also bowled: M.R. Benson 3.3-0-39-0; S.G. Hinks 2-0-28-0; N.R. Taylor 8-4-7-1; T.R. Ward 4-1-4-0.

three points.
    Success at Bournemouth was essential, and Igglesden, recently restored after weeks of inactivity, bowled Kent to victory with match figures of 10 for 91. Back on top, Kent were disappointed not to beat Gloucestershire at Bristol, and, after that defeat by Sussex and a draw against Middlesex, they went on to the final match that crucial one point behind.

Lancashire

Lancashire could be satisfied with a season in which they were third in the Refuge Assurance League and also became the first Refuge Assurance Cup winners, even though they were less successful in other competitions.

Failure to qualify for the Benson & Hedges quarter-finals and a minimal impact in the NatWest competition represented disappointment in areas where the club has glorious traditions, while a drop from second to ninth in the Britannic Assurance Championship was unwelcome.

There was, however, much to enthuse about, for though some individuals fell on leaner times spirit remained generally high. Attractive and positive cricket was played and interest in the Britannic Assurance Championship prize money remained right up to the last few matches.

Of the batsmen, only Fairbrother improved his aggregate, though his average dropped from 43 to just over 30. Fowler's tally of runs was over 600 down on his rich harvest of 1987, and his average dropped accordingly.

Mendis was consistent, though even he was not quite the force he had been in the previous season. Jesty, signed from Surrey during the winter, could not at 40 years of age provide all that was needed at number three, and later lost his place to the Cambridge Blue Atherton, who again batted splendidly.

Nor did the lower middle order make its accustomed impact. Certainly, useful runs came from Watkinson, Allott, and Hegg, but there was not the complete dependability that marked their efforts in 1987.

On the bowling front, Allott, now operating profitably at around medium-fast pace, had another excellent season. But, sadly, the Pakistan Test all-rounder Wasim Akram, of whom so much had been expected, was restricted by a groin injury to under 300 overs.

Watkinson was therefore given more work and responded willingly, though he was rather expensive. Simmons's off-spinners were as effective as ever, but Folley, though still given plenty of bowling by skipper Hughes, seemed to have lost something in control.

These circumstances meant increased opportunities for the young all-rounders Hayhurst and Austin. Both looked natural cricketers, bowling at a brisk medium-pace and striking the ball cleanly. Much can be expected of them in the future.

In the field, Lancashire maintained their customary high standards. Fairbrother's ground fielding was outstanding, some fine close catches were taken by Hughes, Allott, Fowler, and Atherton, while Hegg's wicket-keeping justified his growing reputation.

Though the season brought fewer individual triumphs, teamwork was of a high order, while the continued optimism and friendliness of Old Trafford's atmosphere reflected credit on the whole club.

Chairman Bob Bennett and his committee continue to look to the

Britannic Assurance County Championship: 9th; Won 6, Lost 7, Drawn 9
All First-Class Matches: Won 6, Lost 7, Drawn 11
NatWest Bank Trophy: Lost to Glamorgan in 2nd round
Benson & Hedges Cup: Failed to qualify for quarter-final (4th in Group A)
Refuge Assurance League: 3rd; Won 10, Lost 4, No Result 2
Refuge Assurance Cup: Winners

Championship Averages

Batting and Fielding	M	I	NO	HS	R	Avge	100	50	Ct/St
M.A. Atherton	8	14	2	152*	456	38.00	2	–	5
G.D. Mendis	22	40	4	151	1166	32.38	1	7	9
Wasim Akram	10	18	2	116*	496	31.00	1	3	2
I.D. Austin	6	9	2	64	216	30.85	–	2	–
G. Fowler	20	36	1	172	1061	30.31	2	4	18
N.H. Fairbrother	22	40	3	111	1090	29.45	2	6	9
T.E. Jesty	13	25	3	73	587	26.68	–	2	3
A.N. Hayhurst	12	21	2	107	477	25.10	1	2	1
M. Watkinson	22	37	4	85*	725	21.96	–	6	13
J. Simmons	20	26	9	57*	335	19.70	–	1	9
D.P. Hughes	21	33	3	62	465	15.50	–	2	25
W.K. Hegg	22	32	5	76	406	15.03	–	1	50/8
I. Folley	17	19	13	30	90	15.00	–	–	7
P.J.W. Allott	19	28	4	31*	308	12.83	–	–	13
C.D. Matthews	2	3	0	31	38	12.66	–	–	–
A.J. Murphy	2	3	0	3	3	1.00	–	–	1

Also batted: J. Abrahams (1 match) 9,1 (1ct); J.D. Fitton (1 match) 36; N.J. Speak (1 match) 35, 10 (2ct); G.D. Lloyd (1 match) 22, 0 (1ct).

Hundreds (9)

2 M.A. Atherton: 152* v Sussex, Hove; 115* v Derbys, Old Trafford
  N.H. Fairbrother: 101 v Notts, Trent Bridge; 111 v Essex, Southend
  G. Fowler: 104 v Essex, Southend; 172 v Derbys, Derby
1 A.N. Hayhurst: 107 v Derbys, Derby
  G.D. Mendis: 151 v Glos, Old Trafford
  Wasim Akram: 116* v Somerset, Old Trafford

Bowling	O	M	R	W	Avge	Best	5wI	10wM
J.D. Fitton	42	13	77	7	11.00	6-59	1	–
P.J.W. Allott	590.2	161	1378	67	20.56	6-59	5	–
Wasim Akram	291.4	76	666	31	21.48	7-53	2	–
J. Simmons	585	150	1457	60	24.28	5-53	2	–
I.D. Austin	137.1	43	367	15	24.46	5-79	1	–
I. Folley	547.3	142	1544	52	29.69	6-20	2	–
M. Watkinson	600.3	149	1632	50	32.64	6-43	2	–
A.N. Hayhurst	159.3	31	518	15	34.53	4-45	–	–
C.D. Matthews	60	16	177	5	35.40	4-47	–	–

Also bowled: M.A. Atherton 89.5-23-262-4; N.H. Fairbrother 10.1-0-59-0;
T.E. Jesty 25-10-56-0; G.D. Mendis 8-0-35-0; A.J. Murphy 47.1-7-184-3.

future, and were notably quick to sing Phil DeFreitas, the gifted but controversial England all-rounder released by Leicestershire at the end of the season.

Leicestershire

Leicestershire, among the favourites for honours in 1988, further shortened their odds with some emphatic victories early in the season. But they tailed off in the last few weeks of the summer to end up in joint seventh place, four places lower than in 1987.

The general impression of under-achievement was reinforced by rather poor performances in limited-overs matches, and it was the batting that did most to dissipate early-season confidence. The simmering disaffection of Philip DeFreitas, who was first dropped and then released, undoubtedly bruised morale, but it was the batting that most often frustrated supporters.

David Gower's late flourish produced fine centuries against Essex and Notts to carry him past 1,100 runs, but otherwise he endured a patchy season, and James Whitaker plunged into a mid-summer trough just when it seemed he was rediscovering international quality.

The flimsy form of Peter Willey, who had looked forward to a summer devoid of captaincy responsibilities, was a major puzzle. He failed to reach 1,000 runs in the Championship for the first time in five seasons with the county, but Nigel Briers compiled the highest aggregate of his career as well as leading the side with evident relish and tactical aplomb in Gower's absences.

While Tim Boon and Russ Cobb had disappointing seasons, the former failing to rediscover good early form after breaking an arm, Laurie Potter's tighter batting technique earned him his county cap.

DeFreitas, who made close to 500 runs in 20 first-class innings, topped the bowling averages with 61 victims in 14 matches. But it was Jon Agnew who again took the most wickets, adding 93 to the 101 he claimed in 1987 to impress everybody, it seemed, except the England selectors. Word filtered through from high places that Agnew was deemed too reliant on helpful pitches at Grace Road and too injury-prone, though his three best returns were all achieved away from home and he has not missed a Championship game in two years.

With the consistently hostile George Ferris claiming 62 wickets and Chris Lewis and Les Taylor adding 77 between them, the seam attack was as strong as expected, but spin seemed to find employment only as a last resort or an afterthought and yielded only 37 championship victims.

Leicestershire's one-day form was a source of despair. The wash-out of their Benson & Hedges zonal match in Scotland denied them a quarter-final place, but convincing excuses were not forthcoming for short-comings in the NatWest Trophy or the Refuge Assurance Sunday League.

Leicestershire must hope that the return of Winston Benjamin after a highly successful tour with the West Indies will compensate for the departure of DeFreitas, and they have also taken Gordon Parsons back onto their staff after his spell with Warwickshire.   .

Amid all the fluctuations of form in 1988, that of wicket-keeper Phil Whitticase remained consistently good. His 74 first-class victims

Britannic Assurance County Championship: 7th; Won 6, Lost 3, Drawn 13
All First-Class Matches: Won 7, Lost 3, Drawn 14
NatWest Bank Trophy: Lost to Gloucestershire in 2nd round
Benson & Hedges Cup: Failed to qualify for quarter-final (3rd in Group A)
Refuge Assurance League: 16th; Won 4, Lost 9, No Result 3

Championship Averages

Batting and Fielding	M	I	NO	HS	R	Avge	100	50	Ct/St
D.I. Gower	17	29	3	172	1081	41.57	2	4	14
J.J. Whitaker	21	36	5	145	1160	37.41	3	4	12
N.E. Briers	22	38	2	125*	1231	34.19	2	8	14
L. Potter	21	31	4	107	796	29.48	1	4	13
P.A.J. DeFreitas	12	17	1	113	458	28.62	1	3	5
P. Willey	22	37	1	130	946	26.27	2	3	11
T.J. Boon	13	20	1	131	459	24.15	1	2	7
R.A. Cobb	11	20	2	65	432	24.00	–	2	10
P. Hepworth	4	6	0	51	132	22.00	–	1	–
P.J. Whitticase	21	30	9	71	453	21.57	–	2	61/4
C.C. Lewis	14	20	3	40	337	19.82	–	–	9
J.P. Agnew	22	28	8	38	263	13.15	–	–	1
L.B. Taylor	15	15	6	60	111	12.33	–	1	3
G.J.F. Ferris	18	20	8	36*	139	11.58	–	–	1
P.M. Such	6	5	2	6	7	2.33	–	–	–

Also batted: J.D.R. Benson (1 match) 3; L. Tennant (1 match) 3,0*. M.A. Garnham played in one match but did not bat (2ct).

Hundreds (12)

3 J.J. Whitaker: 145 v Derbys, Derby; 100 v Worcs, Leicester; 126 v Glam, Neath
2 N.E. Briers: 125* v Derbys, Leicester; 119 v Essex, Leicester
  D.I. Gower: 146 v Notts, Leicester; 172 v Essex, Leicester
  P. Willey: 130 v Sussex, Leicester; 104 v Yorks, Headingley
1 T.J. Boon: 131 v Kent, Leicester
  P.A.J. DeFreitas: 113 v Notts, Worksop
  L. Potter: 107 v Derbys, Derby

Bowling	O	M	R	W	Avge	Best	5wI	10wM
P.A.J. DeFreitas	412.3	91	1188	54	22.00	5-38	5	–
G.J.F. Ferris	452.1	82	1380	62	22.25	5-47	2	–
J.P. Agnew	718.5	156	2139	88	24.30	7-61	8	1
L.B. Taylor	283 3	60	850	31	27.41	6-49	1	–
C.C. Lewis	342.2	68	1102	31	35.54	5-73	1	–
P.M. Such	115	20	331	8	41.37	4-81	–	–
P. Willey	333	104	775	18	43.05	4-153	–	–
L. Potter	93.1	25	269	6	44.83	2-32	–	–

Also bowled: L. Tennant 7-2-19-1.

strengthened local conviction that he ought to be in contention for an England career.

Middlesex

Middlesex, whose season began with a remarkable all-round flourish, were ultimately grateful for the NatWest Trophy, a semi-final appearance in the new Refuge League Cup, and a much improved position in the County Championship.

Having comfortably won their first four Championship fixtures, there was confidence at Lord's that the grim summers of 1986 and '87 could be forgotten. In the sense that, by May 15, Middlesex had already won twice as many matches as they did in the whole of the previous season, this was justifiable. But suddenly the spectre rose again, and not until August 9 were they to win another Championship game.

Certainly there were matches in which the dreadful summer played its part in foreclosing a promising situation, but there were other reasons, too. When the battery of seam bowlers that had brushed aside the early opposition began to lose steam, a lack of depth and consistency was exposed in the county's batting.

Not unnaturally, this was particularly evident when Mike Gatting, John Emburey, and Paul Downton were on international duty, on which occasions a further factor came into play. In the absence of the three senior professionals, the captaincy passed to Roland Butcher, whose lack of tactical experience was emplified in the match against Yorkshire, at Lord's, when the pursuit of a luxurious first innings advantage left Middlesex with insufficient time to win.

However, excuses were hard to find when Gatting led the full side beaten by struggling Notts at Trent Bridge. The simple reason was batting failure.

After 11 consecutive Championship matches without a win, the sequence was finally broken at Old Trafford, where Middlesex actually beat Lancashire by 10 wickets. Meanwhile, they had been hanging tenuously onto pole position in the Sunday League and, with a competent victory over Surrey, were through to the final of the NatWest Trophy competition.

Even though the Championship title had now become a lost cause, the season had not been without encouragement. John Carr had well and truly confirmed his class and reliability as Wilf Slack's opening partner. Gatting and Downton had not allowed disappointment at a higher level to affect their response to the county's needs, and Butcher, as he re-affirmed in the NatWest semi-final, was still, on his day, an exciting batsman.

Ramprakash, approaching his 19th birthday, averaged 57 in eight championship matches, and other young players were at last beginning to assume maturity – not least spinner Jamie Sykes, whose batting, on several occasions, justified his recognition as a genuine all-rounder. Angus Fraser, like Norman Cowans in the top dozen of the first-class averages, had certainly come of age as a fast bowler – to ease the general regret that Wayne Daniel, who made only two injury-stricken appearances, had been forced to stand down.

Britannic Assurance County Championship: 8th; Won 7, Lost 3, Drawn 12
All First-Class Matches: Won 7, Lost 3, Drawn 14
NatWest Bank Trophy: Winners
Benson & Hedges Cup: Lost to Derbyshire in quarter-final
Refuge Assurance League: 4th; Won 9, Lost 3, No Result 4
Refuge Assurance Cup: Lost to Worcestershire in semi-final

Championship Averages

Batting and Fielding	M	I	NO	HS	R	Avge	100	50	Ct/St
M.R. Ramprakash	8	11	4	68*	401	57.28	–	3	1
M.W. Gatting	18	29	2	210	1431	53.00	3	9	14
W.N. Slack	19	32	5	163*	1228	45.48	3	6	10
J.E. Emburey	15	20	4	102	584	36.50	1	4	19
J.D. Carr	22	39	6	144	1194	36.18	2	7	20
P.R. Downton	14	18	4	120	506	36.14	1	2	30/5
A. Needham	7	10	3	66*	231	33.00	–	2	5
R.O. Butcher	17	25	2	134	673	29.26	1	3	13
K.R. Brown	19	30	4	131*	668	25.69	1	2	28
M.A. Roseberry	12	18	3	67	357	23.80	–	1	5
N.F. Williams	8	11	2	63*	186	20.66	–	1	1
S.P. Hughes	16	18	5	34	248	19.07	–	–	3
J.F. Sykes	7	10	1	86	164	18.22	–	1	3
I.J.F. Hutchinson	3	4	0	25	48	12.00	–	–	–
M.W.C. Olley	3	3	0	16	36	12.00	–	–	8/–
A.R.C. Fraser	22	26	9	17	182	10.70	–	–	1
N.G. Cowans	20	21	7	27*	119	8.50	–	–	5
P.C.R. Tufnell	9	10	2	20	41	5.12	–	–	4

Also batted: A.A. Barnett (1 match) 10; W.W. Daniel (2 matches) 0, 0.

Hundreds (12)

3 M.W. Gatting: 210 v Notts, Lord's; 104 v Hants, Basingstoke, 180 v Glam, Lord's
 W.N. Slack: 144 v Yorks, Lord's; 163* & 105* v Glam, Lord's
2 J.D. Carr: 106 v Notts, Lord's; 144 v Leics, Leicester
1 K.R. Brown: 131* v Notts, Lord's
 R.O. Butcher: 134 v Sussex, Hove
 P.R. Downton: 120 v Lancs, Old Trafford
 J.E. Emburey: 102 v Warwicks, Uxbridge

Bowling	O	M	R	W	Avge	Best	5wI	10wM
N.F. Williams	178.3	33	511	30	17.03	6-42	2	–
N.G. Cowans	491.5	124	1290	71	18.16	6-49	3	1
A.R.C. Fraser	674.1	190	1484	77	19.27	6-68	6	2
J.E. Emburey	543.1	167	1201	49	24.51	6-24	2	–
J.D. Carr	65.1	15	154	5	30.80	1-4	–	–
P.C.R. Tufnell	349.2	89	876	19	46.10	4-88	–	–
A. Needham	113.4	19	399	8	49.87	5-125	1	–
S.P. Hughes	385.3	70	1136	22	51.63	3-45	–	–

Also bowled: A.A. Barnett 27-8-65-0; K.R. Brown 1-1-0-0; W.W. Daniel 16-2-37-2; M.W. Gatting 96-22-287-4; M.R. Ramprakash 8-0-53-0; M.A. Roseberry 11.4-1-61-2; W.N. Slack 2-1-14-0; J.F. Sykes 30-0-142-0.

Northamptonshire

There is much of 1988 that Northants will want to forget, finishing in the lower half of the County Championship table, being knocked out of the NatWest Trophy by Cheshire, failing to qualify for the later stages of the Benson & Hedges Cup, and, as usual, making no impact on the Sunday League. Yet they possessed the talent to have aachieved more.

There were several reasons why they failed to do so. First, injuries and international calls meant they were able to field their strongest team in only four of the 22 first-class matches. Second, their batting, which looked so impressive on paper, failed to provide sufficient runs on dodgy pitches, of which there were more than usual. Their tail seldom wagged effectively, and their support bowlers rather lacked penetration. Finally, they were short of confidence, not helped by the Cheshire disaster and several players experiencing lean spells. This led to insufficient bite in some of their play, and was reflected by the large number of dropped catches.

Despite the disappointments, the season did contain several highly satisfactory features, which suggest that good times may be just around the corner. What Northants require is some luck and a greater belief in themselves, which new leadership may bring, though Geoff Cook, who has resigned, has been a good skipper.

In the batting, Bailey tightened up his defence and, with Capel, excelled on the poor pitches when runs were in short supply. His just reward was an England cap, which many felt overdue, and selection for India. Although Capel gained international recognition as an all-rounder, his figures this summer reveal that he is essentially a dependable batsman with a good temperament who can bowl.

Lamb again demonstrated that he is at least one class better than any of his colleagues, with numerous memorable innings for both England and Northants, not only a fine player with an individual style, but also a natural fighter.

Although Larkins, one of the most exciting strokemakers in the country, struggled on bad wickets, his two centuries in better conditions emphasized that he had not lost his skill, merely some confidence.

It will never be known whether Lillee would have taken a large haul of wickets, because a serious injury early in the season, followed by typically courageous recovery, restricted his number of matches. But he proved himself to be an outstanding coach and a tonic for his adopted county.

Fortunately, in Davis the club had one of the best strike bowlers on the circuit, who would be even more effective with fewer no-balls. Nick Cook, who, despite encountering few helpful pitches, has probably never bowled better, was unlucky to have to withdraw from the England squad. Williams enjoyed another good all-round summer, although he certainly should have bowled more.

The success of Northants in 1989 could in no small way depend upon Robinson, who was possibly the most promising fast, as distinct from

Britannic Assurance County Championship: 12th; Won 5, Lost 7, Drawn 10
All First-Class Matches: Won 6, Lost 7, Drawn 11
NatWest Bank Trophy: Lost to Cheshire in 1st round
Benson & Hedges Cup: Failed to qualify for quarter-final (3rd in Group B)
Refuge Assurance League: 14th; Won 4, Lost 9, No Result 3

Championship Averages

Batting and Fielding	M	I	NO	HS	R	Avge	100	50	Ct/St
A.J. Lamb	9	15	2	155	731	56.23	3	3	4
D.J. Capel	17	29	4	92	981	39.24	–	7	4
R.J. Bailey	20	36	1	127*	1203	34.37	2	8	19
R.G. Williams	18	31	7	119	770	32.08	1	4	8
G. Cook	17	29	1	203	836	29.85	2	3	9
A. Fordham	15	28	6	125*	627	28.50	1	3	13
W. Larkins	20	37	2	134	905	25.85	2	2	23
A. Walker	16	19	10	40*	208	23.11	–	–	7
M.R. Gouldstone	7	12	1	71	239	21.72	–	2	4
W.W. Davis	15	18	3	43	306	20.40	–	–	5
N.A. Stanley	6	10	2	62	142	17.75	–	1	3
D.J. Wild	17	26	1	75	408	16.32	–	2	3
D. Ripley	22	30	5	49	390	15.60	–	–	66/6
D.K. Lillee	7	10	2	22	98	12.25	–	–	3
S.J. Brown	3	6	1	25*	34	6.80	–	–	2
N.G.B. Cook	20	24	1	24	133	5.78	–	–	12
M.A. Robinson	13	16	7	19*	32	3.55	–	–	3

Hundreds (11)

3 A.J. Lamb: 117 v Glos, Bristol; 104* v Glam, Wellingborough; 155 v Essex, Chelmsford

2 R.J. Bailey: 127* v Sussex, Northampton; 110 v Derbys, Northampton

G. Cook: 124* v Middx, Luton; 203 v Yorks, Scarborough

W. Larkins: 134 v Glos, Bristol; 112* v Kent, Northampton

1 A. Fordham: 125* v Surrey, Oval

R.G. Williams: 119 v Essex, Northampton

Bowling	O	M	R	W	Avge	Best	5wI	10wM
W.W. Davis	538.2	92	1614	73	22.10	7-52	7	2
M.A. Robinson	347.4	72	932	42	22.19	4-19	–	–
N.G.B. Cook	632.2	228	1285	56	22.94	6-56	2	–
A. Walker	406.1	81	1240	46	26.95	5-64	1	–
R.G. Williams	295	61	888	31	28.64	5-86	1	–
D.J. Wild	164.5	33	486	16	30.37	4-18	–	–
D.J. Capel	371.4	68	1235	34	36.32	4-40	–	–
D.K. Lillee	232	42	731	20	36.55	6-68	1	–
R.J. Bailey	59.1	8	201	5	40.20	3-27	–	–

Also bowled: S.J. Brown 65-13-176-4; G. Cook 5-1-7-0; W. Larkins 5-1-18-0.

fast-medium, bowler in the country, while Fordham has the defence and the temperament to become the eventual successor to Geoff Cook as opener.

Nottinghamshire

Notts, County Champions and NatWest Trophy winners the previous year, ended the 1988 season fifth in the Championship and failed to produce an effective challenge in any of the limited-overs competitions. But there were still strong feelings of satisfaction around Trent Bridge as predictions of a spectacular decline in standards were emphatically confounded.

Even pronouncements from within the club before the season began conceded that their first summer without Richard Hadlee and Clive Rice was likely to be a severely testing one, and a sequence of bad results early on provided an extra test of nerve. The season was redeemed, however, by a master-stroke. Franklyn Stephenson, previously of Gloucestershire, was recruited from League cricket, and did the 'double' of 1,000 runs and 100 wickets, completing an inspired summer with a flourish by scoring two centuries and taking eleven wickets in the final Championship fixture against Yorkshire. Only George Hirst and Bernard Bosanquet had previously achieved such a feat.

Stephenson, whose hostility on the field was matched by his amiability off it, eclipsed the persuasive claims of Worcestershire's prolific Graeme Hick to be voted the Britannic Assurance Player of the Year, and his final total of 125 wickets was the best for Notts since Bruce Dooland 31 years earlier. A badly broken nose in mid-season failed to deflect Stephenson and an impressive number of his victims fell for a delivery which became the talk of the circuit, a slow, looping full-toss which reduced many batsmen to flailing mystification and spectators to guffaws.

Kevin Cooper, who broke a leg playing football during the winter, recovered so splendidly that he became the only other player to top 100 wickets. Kevin Evans and David Millns stepped up to hint at genuine potential, and Chris Cairns, a 19-year-old New Zealander at Trent Bridge on a scholarship, impressed so much that he was registered as their second overseas player for 1989.

The spin department suffered major problems. The highly promising left-arm spinner Andy Afford was able to bowl only 83 overs before succumbing to a back injury which later required surgery. And Eddie Hemmings was considerably inhibited by a persistent groin strain.

It was the batting, however, that prevented Notts from maintaining a bid to retain the Championship title. Chris Broad rarely seemed at peace with things as he laboured through a second season without a Championship century and well under 1,000 runs. And he was for a time suspended following a confrontation with Tim Robinson that provoked the new captain's resignation, albeit a temporary one.

A century against Derbyshire in September hardly compensated for Mick Newell's struggle to recapture 1987's prosperity, but Robinson overcame a run of low scores and that test of his authority with match-winning hundreds against Worcestershire and Essex.

Paul Johnson, though still erratic, confirmed abundant talent with close to 1,400 runs, Derek Randall as ever mixed the mundane with the

Britannic Assurance County Championship: 5th; Won 8, Lost 8, Drawn 6
All First-Class Matches: Won 8, Lost 8, Drawn 10
NatWest Bank Trophy: Lost to Worcestershire in 2nd round
Benson & Hedges Cup: Lost to Glamorgan in quarter-final
Refuge Assurance League: 17th; Won 3, Lost 11, No Result 2

Championship Averages

Batting and Fielding	M	I	NO	HS	R	Avge	100	50	Ct/St
D.W. Randall	21	37	4	237	1286	38.96	2	9	9
R.T. Robinson	18	30	3	134*	988	36.59	3	4	17
P. Johnson	21	37	0	140	1104	29.83	2	4	10
F.D. Stephenson	20	34	0	117	962	28.29	2	6	9
P. Pollard	7	13	0	142	323	24.84	1	–	6
B.C. Broad	16	27	0	68	647	23.96	–	3	13
M. Newell	16	30	1	105	619	21.34	1	2	28
K.P. Evans	13	22	3	54	359	18.89	–	1	18
J.D. Birch	20	36	2	75	596	17.52	–	2	12
E.E. Hemmings	16	25	10	31*	245	16.33	–	–	8
R.A. Pick	2	3	1	19	31	15.50	–	–	–
B.N. French	6	11	1	28	135	13.50	–	–	12/–
C.W. Scott	16	25	4	47*	273	13.00	–	–	39/2
D.J.R. Martindale	6	10	0	46	125	12.50	–	–	3
K.E. Cooper	22	33	9	39	263	10.95	–	–	7
C.L. Cairns	2	4	1	15	29	9.66	–	–	–
K. Saxelby	7	12	1	17	41	3.72	–	–	4
D.J. Millns	8	11	5	7*	19	3.16	–	–	4
J.A. Afford	4	8	3	3	4	0.80	–	–	2

Also batted: M.K. Bore (1 match) 5,0.

Hundreds (11)

3 R.T. Robinson: 115 v Lancs, Trent Bridge; 107* v Worcs, Trent Bridge; 134* v Essex, Colchester
2 P. Johnson: 140 v Hants, Southampton; 124 v Yorks, Sheffield
  D.W. Randall: 134 v Leics, Worksop; 237 v Derbys, Trent Bridge
  F.D. Stephenson: 111 & 117 v Yorks, Trent Bridge
1 M. Newell: 105 v Derbys, Trent Bridge
  P. Pollard: 142 v Kent, Dartford

Bowling	O	M	R	W	Avge	Best	5wI	10wM
F.D. Stephenson	776.1	191	2161	121	17.85	7-56	10	3
K.E. Cooper	776	213	2035	99	20.55	5-41	5	–
C.L. Cairns	49	6	179	8	22.37	4-70	–	–
J.A. Afford	83	19	270	9	30.00	3-60	–	–
E.E. Hemmings	495.5	137	1265	41	30.85	4-50	–	–
D.J. Millns	101	13	374	12	31.16	3-37	–	–
K.P. Evans	201.5	34	665	18	36.94	3-22	–	–
J.D. Birch	68.4	16	226	5	45.20	2-52	–	–
R.A. Pick	51	7	236	5	47.20	2-62	–	–
K. Saxelby	193	29	690	12	57.50	3-30	–	–

Also bowled: M.K. Bore 9-2-41-0; M. Newell 1-0-11-0; R.T. Robinson 4-0-38-0.

brilliant, and Chris Scott, granted an extended chance by Bruce French's hand operation, added some valuable batting contributions to his efficient displays with the gloves. Renewed carping about Trent Bridge pitches could not wholly be discounted as 'sour grapes'. Notts claimed less batting bonus points than any other county, while only Worcs, similarly accused, collected more batting points.

Somerset

Somerset's modest results in 1988 – 11th place in the Britannic Assur-ance Championship, as in 1987, 12th in the Refuge Assurance Sunday League, and failure in the one-day knock-out competitions – should not be allowed to mask some positive developments.

The loss of Martin Crowe with a back injury after he had played only nine first-class innings gave the young Australian Steve Waugh the opportunity to display batting of a calibre that clearly established him in world class. Waugh's fluency and power of stroke made him a formid-able opponent in all types of cricket. With Crowe's future with the club doubtful at present, Waugh's availability is a real bonus.

Though much of the rest of the batting was disappointing, allowance must be made for the persistent injuries that prevented Roebuck from giving his usual solid foundation and cut his run tally by more than half. Injuries were undoubtedly a factor in his decision to stand down as captain in favour of Marks.

Hardy, at his best an elegant and attractive left-hander, still lacked a little steel in his play. His failure to reach 1,000 runs was unaccountable bearing in mind his undoubted gifts.

Felton did not develop as hoped, but, ironically, having heard that he was not to be retained, made a marvellous 127 in his final innings for the County, on a difficult pitch and in a losing situation.

Wyatt had his moments without ever quite looking the part, an accusa-tion that could not be levelled at young Bartlett, whose timing and range of stroke made him a player to watch in the future.

The lower middle order was called on regularly to cover deficiencies nearer the top and with Burns, an improving wicket-keeper, Marks, and Rose batting effectively could be complimented on their efforts.

The seam bowlers were, at times, a highly efficient force. Mallender, though not always fit, enjoyed some remarkably destructive spells, and Rose, less troubled by injury than in 1987, was most reliable. Jones, strong and willing, did not always command the necessary control and was the most expensive of the main quick bowlers. Marks, as reliable as ever with his off-spin, was once again the leading wicket-taker.

Of the younger bowlers, Cleal, only 19, showed distinct promise. Strongly built and with a good side-on action, he regularly moved the ball away from the right-hander at a brisk pace.

Somerset were notable for their unwillingness to concede defeat and for their obvious team spirit, qualities for which Roebuck can take much credit for instilling during three difficult years of captaincy.

Britannic Assurance County Championship: 11th; Won 5, Lost 6, Drawn 11
All First-Class Matches: Won 5, Lost 7, Drawn 11
NatWest Bank Trophy: Lost to Hampshire in 2nd round
Benson & Hedges Cup: Failed to qualify for quarter-final (4th in Group D)
Refuge Assurance League: 12th; Won 6, Lost 9, No Result 1

Championship Averages

Batting and Fielding	M	I	NO	HS	R	Avge	100	50	Ct/St
S.R. Waugh	14	22	6	161	1286	80.37	6	4	19
M.D. Crowe	4	7	1	136*	473	78.83	2	2	4
N.A. Felton	13	25	2	127	706	30.69	1	4	6
R.J. Harden	6	11	1	78	295	29.50	–	3	3
P.M. Roebuck	12	19	3	112*	454	28.37	1	1	6
N.D. Burns	22	32	7	133*	708	28.32	1	2	55/2
J.J.E. Hardy	21	37	3	97	902	26.52	–	6	23
V.J. Marks	22	29	2	68	673	24.92	–	3	8
R.J. Bartlett	18	29	3	102*	648	24.92	1	2	12
J.G. Wyatt	14	24	1	69	532	23.13	–	3	9
N.J. Pringle	8	15	4	54	244	22.18	–	1	8
G.D. Rose	19	23	6	69*	359	21.11	–	1	10
C.H. Dredge	2	4	0	37	73	18.25	–	–	–
D.J. Foster	12	12	7	20	64	12.80	–	–	–
N.A. Mallender	16	19	6	44	157	12.07	–	–	8
A.N. Jones	20	21	8	38	130	10.00	–	–	8
M.W. Cleal	8	10	1	13	72	8.00	–	–	1
H.R.J. Trump	8	10	1	48	62	6.88	–	–	7

Also batted: G.V. Palmer (1 match) 0, 23; T.J.A. Scriven (2 matches) 7,4.

Hundreds (12)

6 S.R. Waugh: 115* v Hants, Southampton; 103* v Warwicks, Bath; 137 v Sussex, Bath; 101* v Glam, Taunton; 161 v Kent, Canterbury; 112 v Middx, Uxbridge
2 M.D. Crowe: 132 v Worcs, Worcester; 136* v Lancs, Old Trafford
1 R.J. Bartlett: 102* v Kent, Canterbury
  N.D. Burns: 133* v Sussex, Hove
  N.A. Felton: 127 v Glos, Taunton
  P.M. Roebuck: 112* v Glam, Taunton

Bowling	O	M	R	W	Avge	Best	5wI	10wM
N.A. Mallender	411.3	108	969	47	20.61	5-12	1	–
G.D. Rose	483.5	112	1456	54	26.96	6-47	1	–
H.R.J. Trump	258	70	653	23	28.39	4-17	–	–
V.J. Marks	856.5	220	2201	76	28.96	7-118	5	1
A.N. Jones	512	85	1658	55	30.14	7-30	1	–
M.W. Cleal	153	22	541	16	33.81	3-16	–	–
D.J. Foster	282.3	44	967	25	38.68	4-46	–	–

Also bowled: R.J. Bartlett 30-4-145-4; C.H. Dredge 53.5-15-181-3; R.J. Harden 16-1-61-0; J.J.E. Hardy 0.3-0-12-0; G.V. Palmer 18.2-2-54-1; N.J. Pringle 13-1-40-1; P.M. Roebuck 28.4-2-106-1; T.J.A. Scriven 96-25-237-3; S.R. Waugh 23-5-60-3; J.G. Wyatt 9-4-30-1.

Surrey

Though Surrey once again narrowly failed to achieve a *médallon d'or*, they were entitled to regard 1988 as a vintage summer inasmuch as, given a little time to mature, the wine will undoubtedly be of *premier cru* class. This will be the ultimate endorsement of a pre-season policy committed to grafting young stock on to the established vine.

Given the departure of Trevor Jesty and David Thomas, the doubtful availability of Tony Gray, and the increasing girth of Sylvester Clarke, it was a bold decision not to seek experienced replacements outside the county but to rely on fledgling resources – particularly in the bowling department.

As things transpired, that the policy did not totally succeed had less to do with the individual capabilities of the newcomers than their lack of corporate consistency. On the one hand, there were marvellous occasions – as when Nick Peters claimed match figures of 10 for 67 in the defeat of Warwickshire, early in July. On the other, the disappointment was justifiable when, two weeks later, indifferent bowling allowed Hampshire to score a match-winning 299 for two at Guildford.

Similarly, high hopes when Keith Medlycott's four for 19 helped hustle out Yorkshire for 142, at Harrogate, were frustrated when, second time around, the home side sauntered to 310 for six and a draw.

A defeat and a draw, then, resulted in matches that had illustrated the excellence of Surrey's batting: against Hants, 301 for two declared in the first innings (Smith 157 not out, Stuart 72, Lynch 48 not out) and 122 for three in the second; against Yorks, 342 for four declared in the only innings (Clinton 101, Richards 60 not out, Medlycott 54 not out).

Indeed, Surrey's season was resplendent with excellent batting throughout the order. Jack Richards, opening in the Sunday League at Chelmsford – 105 not out in a winning total of 138. In the innings victory over Sussex, Richards, at number six – 102 not out to follow David Smith's 131 in a total of 467 for five.

There were more centuries for Grahame Clinton – 100 against Middlesex at Lord's; 102 in the next match against Gloucestershire at Cheltenham. But, none of this could overshadow splendidly consistent contributions from Alec Stewart, Monte Lynch, and David Ward.

Even so, Surrey's progress in the championship and the Sunday League seemed to be dogged by a 'two steps forward, one step back' routine. In the Benson & Hedges, they were tantalizingly inconsistent. Badly beaten by Essex at Chelmsford, they savaged Kent at The Oval by nine wickets. Then, having lost to Middlesex by one run, they were humbled at Hove, of all places.

The NatWest offered high hopes, especially when they were drawn at home in the semi-final. But, ironically, on this occasion it was the batting that let them down. In response to a Middlesex total of 258, Stewart hit a magnificent 107 not out, but the next highest score was Clinton's 17 and Surrey fell 70 runs short.

Britannic Assurance County Championship: 4th; Won 7, Lost 5, Drawn 10
All First-Class Matches: Won 8, Lost 6, Drawn 11
NatWest Bank Trophy: Lost to Middlesex in semi-final
Benson & Hedges Cup: Failed to qualify for quarter-final (5th in Group C)
Refuge Assurance League: 5th; Won 8, Lost 5, Tied 1, No Result 2

Championship Averages

Batting and Fielding	M	I	NO	HS	R	Avge	100	50	Ct/St
C.J. Richards	17	21	4	102*	861	50.64	1	6	58/1
D.M. Smith	10	17	5	157*	585	48.75	2	1	2
G.S. Clinton	17	28	5	158	980	42.60	4	3	7
A.J. Stewart	20	30	3	133	992	36.74	2	6	22/1
M.A. Lynch	20	28	3	103	893	35.72	1	4	17
D.M. Ward	22	31	5	126	835	32.11	1	7	17
P.D. Atkins	5	9	0	99	235	26.11	–	1	–
M.A. Feltham	20	24	9	74	352	23.46	–	1	9
K.T. Medlycott	21	27	4	77*	483	21.00	–	3	26
J. Robinson	2	4	2	20	37	18.50	–	–	1
I.A. Greig	22	27	1	47	462	17.76	–	–	15
G.P. Thorpe	2	4	1	19	50	16.66	–	–	1
Zahid Sadiq	2	3	0	37	50	16.66	–	–	–
D.J. Bicknell	9	16	1	50	247	16.46	–	1	3
S.T. Clarke	12	10	1	28	141	15.66	–	–	11
N.H. Peters	11	14	7	25*	83	11.85	–	–	4
C.K. Bullen	9	11	1	24	101	10.10	–	–	5
M.P. Bicknell	15	12	3	25	60	6.66	–	–	3
M. Frost	2	3	0	4	4	1.33	–	–	1

Also batted: J. Boiling (1 match) 1, 8*; G.E. Brown (1 match) 0 (1ct/1st); C.S. Mays (2 matches) 13* (2ct).

Hundreds (11)

4 **G.S. Clinton:** 101 v Yorks, Harrogate; 100 v Middx, Lord's; 102 v Glos, Cheltenham; 158 v Sussex, Hove
2 **D.M. Smith:** 131 v Sussex, Oval; 157* v Hants, Guildford
  A.J. Stewart: 133 v Essex, Oval; 119 v Sussex, Hove
1 **M.A. Lynch:** 103 v Lancs, Oval
  C.J. Richards: 102* v Sussex, Oval
  D.M. Ward: 126 v Glam, Swansea

Bowling	O	M	R	W	Avge	Best	5wI	10wM
S.T. Clarke	396.4	108	913	63	14.49	6-52	4	2
K.T. Medlycott	522.1	143	1445	62	23.30	8-52	6	3
I.A. Greig	371.3	74	1082	41	26.39	6-56	1	–
N.H. Peters	263.2	48	907	34	26.67	6-31	1	1
M.A. Feltham	521.4	116	1536	51	30.11	5-45	2	–
M.P. Bicknell	439.2	115	1280	36	35.55	4-34	–	–
C.K. Bullen	60.1	7	209	5	41.80	1-10	–	–

Also bowled: D.J. Bicknell 1-0-18-0; J. Boiling 15-3-40-0; G.S. Clinton 0.4-0-16-0; M. Frost 28-4-115-2; M.A. Lynch 29.2-8-88-4; C.S. Mays 25-2-102-1; C.J. Richards 4-1-26-0; J. Robinson 13-1-67-3; A.J. Stewart 13.1-2-45-1; G.P. Thorpe 24-2-60-3; D.M. Ward 5-0-31-0.

Sussex

Poor Sussex. They were the chopping block of the Championship, being beaten in half their matches. Still, they had a better season than 1987, winning three matches and at least managing to keep off the bottom of the table. For all their tribulations, Sussex did partly influence the destiny of the Championship by beating Kent, leaders at the time, only three matches away from the winning post.

To be fair, little more could have been expected from Sussex than they achieved, for they had not managed to make up the shortfall of experience on their playing staff. However, the chaos which reigned for so long after the palace revolution of 1986 was ended and order restored with Paul Parker, personable and a player of stature, appointed to the captaincy. Another positive step was the engagement of John Jameson to fill the post of coach.

Again, though, Sussex's season did not pass without rumblings in the dressing-room. Their discontent arose from the leniency the club showed to Imran Khan who, by the terms of his contract, was to play in the one-day competitions and make only limited appearances in the Championship.

Imran, in his last season for the county, arrived too late to play in a Sunday match at Eastbourne, claiming to have been held up in traffic. His explanation was accepted by the committee, who contemplated no further action. For his part, Imran offered compensation by way of two extra appearances in the Championship. This compromise was not acceptable to his team-mates, who refused to play if Imran did. No criticism can be levelled at Imran over the terms of his unusual contract, but the committee should have seen the pitfalls of engaging him as a part-time star.

The Imran chapter, however, is now closed. That Sussex, on their present strength, cannot afford to start another campaign without a good overseas player is beyond question, and the net was already cast as the season was finishing. Negotiations with David Smith, released by Surrey, were also at an advanced stage.

With Imran unavailable to play regularly, Le Roux retired, and Reeve gone to Warwickshire, Sussex's dilemma at the start of the season was their bowling strength. But, supported by superb fielding for which the captain set an example, their bowlers stood them in good stead and they had a very respectable tally of 65 bowling points at the season's end.

The responsibility of leading the attack did wonders for Tony Pigott. So injury-prone in the past, he missed only two matches and was the county's main wicket-taker. Batting in the middle order, he also played many useful innings.

Between them, Babington, who had played only 20 matches in his two previous seasons, and Bunting, a new acquisition from Norfolk, took 90 wickets. If Sussex made a contribution to the few pleasures of the summer, it was in introducing to the scene an unknown leg-spinner in Andy Clarke, of whom they made extensive and advantageous use.

Britannic Assurance County Championship: 16th; Won 3, Lost 11, Drawn 8
All First-Class Matches: Won 3, Lost 11, Drawn 9
NatWest Bank Trophy: Lost to Derbyshire in 1st round
Benson & Hedges Cup: Failed to qualify for quarter-final (4th in Group C)
Refuge Assurance League: 15th; Won 4, Lost 9, Tied 2, No Result 1

Championship Averages

Batting and Fielding	M	I	NO	HS	R	Avge	100	50	Ct/St
P.W.G. Parker	20	39	5	124	1270	37.35	5	4	14
A.P. Wells	22	41	5	120	1269	35.25	1	9	17
I.J. Gould	18	30	4	82*	842	32.38	–	6	28
C.M. Wells	22	39	4	109*	906	25.88	1	4	8
A.C.S. Pigott	20	34	8	56	668	25.69	–	3	16
N.J. Lenham	17	31	2	74	721	24.86	–	3	7
A.M. Green	15	28	2	68	607	23.34	–	4	10
Imran Khan	4	6	1	55	116	23.20	–	1	–
R.I. Alikhan	9	18	0	98	400	22.22	–	3	8
M.P. Speight	7	13	0	58	258	19.84	–	2	5
P. Moores	14	24	2	97*	395	17.95	–	1	30/3
N.J. Falkner	7	14	0	55	232	16.57	–	1	4
M.W. Pringle	4	6	0	35	90	15.00	–	–	1
A.R. Clarke	20	31	8	68	336	14.60	–	1	5
S.J.S. Kimber	4	7	3	32*	54	13.50	–	–	2
R.A. Bunting	16	20	4	17*	92	5.75	–	–	2
A.M. Babington	18	25	8	12	85	5.00	–	–	7

Also batted: P.A.W. Heseltine (2 matches) 6, 8; D.K. Standing (2 matches) 0, 9, 4.
P.W. Threlfall played in one match but did not bat.

Hundreds (7)

5 P.W.G. Parker: 101* v Somerset, Hove; 101* v Somerset, Bath; 117 v Kent, Hastings; 104* v Hants, Eastbourne; 124 v Kent, Maidstone
1 A.P. Wells: 120 v Warwicks, Hove
  C.M. Wells: 109* v Surrey, Oval

Bowling	O	M	R	W	Avge	Best	5wI	10wM
Imran Khan	109.3	26	255	13	19.61	5-50	1	–
A.C.S. Pigott	624	109	2078	74	28.08	6-100	2	–
R.A. Bunting	351	63	1088	36	30.22	5-44	2	–
A.M. Babington	514.5	106	1496	48	31.16	4-66	–	–
C.M. Wells	495.4	109	1359	42	32.35	4-43	–	–
A.R. Clarke	577	153	1481	42	35.26	5-60	2	–
A.M. Green	148.5	39	387	10	38.70	6-82	1	–
S.J.S. Kimber	83	19	272	7	38.85	3-44	–	–
M.W. Pringle	98	19	323	6	53.83	2-51	–	–

Also bowled: R.I. Alikhan 0.3-0-7-0; I.J. Gould 21-2-84-2; P.A.W. Heseltine 28-5-106-1; N.J. Lenham 19.5-2-60-3; P. Moores 1-0-6-0; P.W.G. Parker 1-0-1-1; M.P. Speight 0.3-0-2-1; P.W. Threlfall 17-6-31-0; A.P. Wells 5-1-11-0.

It is said that ill-luck always strikes the underdog and, indeed, Sussex suffered from injuries to their batsmen, principally Green, who, on his comeback, made runs regularly, and Lenham. Parker and Alan Wells were the only two to score above 1,000, and Colin Wells, by his own standards, had a lean season.

Warwickshire

Warwickshire finished sixth in the Britannic County Championship. It was their highest position for five years, but still there was some frustration at Edgbaston. Quite simply they were disappointed not to finish much closer to their neighbours and champions, Worcestershire.

The new-look club – chairman Bob Evans, manager Bob Cottam, and captain Andy Lloyd took office during the previous winter – welcomed a total of six wins but could have pointed to three defeats – Northants (by 6 runs), Leicestershire (1 wicket), and Glamorgan (4 runs) – which might have been turned into victories.

The strength of the side was easily identifiable. Only Worcestershire captured more bowling bonus points, and Warwickshire had no fewer than six pace bowlers, sharing 269 wickets, in the top 40 in the national averages. Gladstone Small, fitter than in the previous year but selected for only one Test, claimed 10 or more wickets in a match on two occasions, including a personal best of 12 for 121 against Glamorgan.

The hostility of Tony Merrick undoubtedly unsettled opposing batsmen, and there was much satisfaction in the progress made by Tim Munton and Paul Smith. Even though Dermot Reeve was plagued by a shoulder injury, which eventually required surgery, the pace attack compared with any in the country, especially on the lively pitches at Edgbaston.

The county were full of good intentions in attempting to quicken the pitches, but the bounce became uneven. This worked for and against Warwickshire. They were beaten in two days by Kent, but overcame both Essex and Northants when conditions were at their worst.

While their own batsmen had less than a cushy ride in home matches, this was not used as an excuse for a general shortage of runs. Lloyd, who had every reason to be pleased with his first year as captain, and Asif Din, who made the No. 3 position his own, were the only players to top 1,000, but nobody averaged even 40.

Andy Moles would have reached 1,000 but for breaking a thumb in August. Alvin Kallicharran, in his first season as an English-qualified player, was out for ten weeks with a fractured finger, and there were broken bones for Reeve, Smith, and David Banks, a former Worcestershire batsman who was engaged on a two-year contract.

Equally damaging was the decline in the batting form of wicket-keeper Geoff Humpage. Potentially a 1,500-runs-a-year man, he scored only 411 in 26 innings and was omitted from the last six Championship matches. On the plus side, David Thorne, a former Oxford University captain, had his longest and most encouraging run with the county, and younger players began to emerge from the team which won the Birmingham League and the national Under-25 competition.

Pirran Holloway, 17, a Cornish-born batsman/wicket-keeper from Taunton School, played in three Championship matches, and there was a move towards the future with debuts for batsmen Jason Ratcliffe, 19, and Simon Green, 18.

Britannic Assurance County Championship: 6th; Won 6, Lost 8, Drawn 8
All First-Class Matches: Won 6, Lost 8, Drawn 10
NatWest Bank Trophy: Lost to Kent in 2nd round
Benson & Hedges Cup: Lost to Essex in quarter-final
Refuge Assurance League: 10th; Won 6, Lost 8, No Result 2

Championship Averages

Batting and Fielding	M	I	NO	HS	R	Avge	100	50	Ct/St
T.A. Lloyd	22	41	2	160*	1439	36.89	4	3	7
Asif Din	21	39	3	131	1208	33.55	1	7	18
A.J. Moles	17	30	2	115	873	31.17	1	4	10
G.C. Small	17	26	5	70	521	24.80	–	3	7
D.A. Thorne	14	24	1	76	561	24.39	–	4	17
P.A. Smith	15	27	4	84*	542	23.56	–	3	3
D.A. Reeve	16	23	3	103	431	21.55	1	–	11
A.I. Kallicharran	8	14	0	63	301	21.50	–	2	3
G.J. Parsons	8	12	3	52	174	19.33	–	1	1
D.A. Banks	6	8	1	47	134	19.14	–	–	4
G.A. Tedstone	4	8	0	50	151	18.87	–	1	7/1
A.C. Storie	8	16	2	68	233	16.64	–	1	6
G.W. Humpage	15	25	1	80	397	16.54	–	3	52/1
S.D. Myles	3	6	0	39	90	15.00	–	–	–
T.A. Merrick	15	21	3	34*	256	14.22	–	–	5
A.R.K. Pierson	8	12	7	18*	57	11.40	–	–	1
A.A. Donald	6	10	3	29	74	10.57	–	–	4
T.A. Munton	16	22	7	24*	131	8.73	–	–	2
P.C.L. Holloway	3	5	0	16	40	8.00	–	–	8/1
J.D. Ratcliffe	2	4	0	16	31	7.75	–	–	2
N. Gifford	17	25	11	23*	104	7.42	–	–	3

Also batted: S.J. Green (1 match) 0, 28.

Hundreds (7)

4 T.A. Lloyd: 151 v Somerset, Bath; 160* v Hants, Edgbaston, 121 v Northants, Edgbaston; 101 v Middx, Uxbridge
1 Asif Din: 131 v Northants, Northampton
A.J. Moles: 115 v Lancs, Nuneaton
D.A. Reeve: 103 v Northants, Northampton

Bowling	O	M	R	W	Avge	Best	5wI	10wM
G.C. Small	550.2	146	1380	75	18.40	7-15	8	2
A.A. Donald	167.4	36	507	26	19.50	5-57	1	–
T.A. Merrick	451	104	1416	64	22.12	6-29	5	1
T.A. Munton	425.1	126	1047	46	22.76	6-21	2	–
P.A. Smith	157.3	20	525	22	23.86	3-7	–	–
G.J. Parsons	203	62	513	21	24.42	3-17	–	–
D.A. Reeve	292	71	750	24	31.25	4-50	–	–
N. Gifford	422.1	120	971	31	31.32	3-66	–	–
A.R.K. Pierson	148.5	35	431	9	47.88	3-33	–	–
Asif Din	91	16	326	6	54.33	3-57	–	–

Also bowled: G.W. Humpage 3-0-10-0; T.A. Lloyd 31-1-208-2; S.D. Myles 6-0-28-0; A.C. Storie 6-2-20-0; D.A. Thorne 3-0-11-0.

Norman Gifford, the oldest player in county cricket at the age of 48, retired after 29 seasons in which he took 2,068 wickets. Although his spin bowling was hardly required at Edgbaston, his departure leaves a big gap in the attack. Much will depend on the progress of off-spinner Adrian Pierson when he becomes the senior slow bowler next summer.

Worcestershire

Ian Botham's claim that Worcestershire have the best squad of players in the country was put to the test when the England all-rounder withdrew from active service after playing in the opening three victories in the Britannic County Championship. While Botham spent the summer convalescing after major back surgery, the team lived up to his highest expectations. They won the Championship for the first time since 1974, retained the Refuge Assurance League title, and reached the final of the NatWest Trophy and the new Refuge Assurance Cup.

Throughout the decisive last six weeks in the pursuit of Kent at the top of the Championship, Worcestershire constantly resorted to the depth of their squad. The extraordinary Graeme Hick may have given them the impetus, but their challenge would have diminished without players like Martin Weston, who came in for Botham, David Leatherdale, a promising 20-year-old batsman, and long-serving paceman Paul Pridgeon.

Others filled vacancies as Worcestershire grappled with the problems of injuries and Test calls. Tim Curtis and Phil Newport graduated to the Test arena for the first time, and when Steve Rhodes was named for the winter tour, he became the sixth Worcestershire player to be selected by England in 13 months. Perhaps the greatest satisfaction was that Worcestershire refuted the charge that they bought success when signing Botham and Graham Dilley, who played only 13 Championship matches between them. However, Dilley's willingness to play through the discomfort in the wins against Gloucestershire and Glamorgan in the final week was a testimony to the spirit within the squad.

Obviously, the season will be remembered elsewhere for the astonishing performances by Hick. Ten centuries – including a mind-boggling 405 not out against Somerset – equalled the county record, and his first-class aggregate of 2,713 was the highest by any player since the championship programme was reduced in 1969. After becoming the first batsman since 1973 to score 1,000 runs by the end of May, Hick continued to demolish all types of bowling in all conditions. He never went longer than seven innings without a century, and he scored almost as many runs on unreliable pitches at New Road as he did elsewhere.

Curtis and Phil Neale, an admirable captain who made four centuries, each in a crisis situation, were the only other batsmen to score more than 1,000 runs. But Gordon Lord became a reliable opening partner for Curtis with a dozen innings of 40 or more, including a vital century in the penultimate match in the Championship.

Rhodes, an excellent wicket-keeper throughout the season, scored a maiden first-class century against Derbyshire, and no partnership was more important than that of 113 by Richard Illingworth and Neal Radford against Notts in July. They began at 39 for 8 and secured a bonus point that meant everything in the final table.

Illingworth was the leading spin bowler in the national averages, and won two matches by ten wickets on turning pitches. Newport and Radford bore the brunt of the work, and there were valuable supporting

Britannic Assurance County Championship: 1st; Won 10, Lost 3, Drawn 9
All First-Class Matches: Won 10, Lost 3, Drawn 10
NatWest Bank Trophy: Lost to Middlesex in final
Benson & Hedges Cup: Lost to Hampshire in quarter-final
Refuge Assurance League: 1st; Won 12, Lost 3, No Result 1
Refuge Assurance Cup: Lost to Lancashire in final

Championship Averages

Batting and Fielding	M	I	NO	HS	R	Avge	100	50	Ct/St
G.A. Hick	22	34	2	405*	2443	76.34	9	4	27
T.S. Curtis	18	31	4	131	1155	42.77	2	6	19
P.A. Neale	21	31	5	167	1036	39.84	4	2	8
G.J. Lord	19	32	2	101	862	28.73	1	4	4
M.J. Weston	17	24	5	95*	514	27.05	–	3	14
P.J. Newport	20	24	8	77*	421	26.31	–	1	8
S.J. Rhodes	22	33	10	108	597	25.95	1	1	68/8
R.K. Illingworth	22	22	4	60	404	22.44	–	2	18
N.V. Radford	18	15	6	65	200	22.22	–	1	14
P. Bent	3	6	1	50	111	22.20	–	1	–
D.A. Leatherdale	10	15	1	34*	255	18.21	–	–	3
D.B. D'Oliveira	8	11	1	37	132	13.20	–	–	6
G.R. Dilley	9	8	1	36	89	12.71	–	–	1
R.M. Ellcock	4	4	1	13	27	9.00	–	–	1
S.J. O'Shaughnessy	10	17	0	44	133	7.82	–	–	5
I.T. Botham	4	4	0	7	18	4.50	–	–	4
A.P. Pridgeon	10	11	3	11	31	3.87	–	–	3

Also batted: S.M. McEwan (5 matches) 0*, 6 (1ct).

Hundreds (17)

9 **G.A. Hick:** 212 v Lancs, Old Trafford; 405* v Somerset, Taunton; 177 v Hants, Worcester; 198 v Yorks, Worcester;
   132 v Northants, Worcester; 159 v Glam, Abergavenny; 127 v Surrey, Oval; 121 v Glos, Bristol; 197 v Glam, Worcester
4 **P.A. Neale:** 125 v Derbys, Derby; 108* v Kent, Folkestone; 167 v Sussex, Kidderminster; 102* v Glos, Bristol
2 **T.S. Curtis:** 108 v Middx, Lord's; 131 v Hants, Worcester
1 **G.J. Lord:** 101 v Glos, Bristol
   S.J. Rhodes: 108 v Derbys, Derby

Bowling	O	M	R	W	Avge	Best	5wI	10wM
P.J. Newport	544	115	1640	85	19.29	8-52	7	1
G.R. Dilley	251	44	695	34	20.44	5-46	3	–
R.K. Illingworth	578.4	184	1229	56	21.94	5-46	4	2
N.V. Radford	570.5	100	1770	71	24.92	7-73	3	–
M.J. Weston	120	31	316	12	26.33	4-24	–	–
G.A. Hick	204	43	642	21	30.57	4-114	–	–
A.P. Pridgeon	266.3	58	662	21	31.52	3-68	–	–
S.M. McEwan	79	7	289	8	36.12	4-43	–	–
R.M. Ellcock	81.1	8	328	7	46.85	3-86	–	–

Also bowled: I.T. Botham 43-11-125-1; T.S. Curtis 14.5-1-74-1; D.A. Leatherdale 7-3-20-1;
P.A. Neale 14-1-62-0; S.J. O'Shaughnessy 34-3-152-4.

contributions from Weston, Pridgeon, and Hick with his underrated off-breaks.

If Botham and Dilley are fully fit next summer – and Worcestershire are confident they will be stronger than at any time since joining the county – there is every reason to believe that the New Road club are only at an early stage in a dominant era.

Yorkshire

The 1988 season was another one of disappointment for Yorkshire, who finished 13th in the Britannic Assurance Championship, 8th in the Refuge Assurance League, failed to qualify for the Benson & Hedges quarter-finals, and were eliminated at the first real hurdle in the NatWest competition.

Yorkshire's faithful followers, while troubled by continued poor results, were increasingly concerned at the county's lack of any coherent policy directed towards countering the weaknesses that have become more and more evident in recent seasons.

Certainly, the bowling was crucially weakened by injury to Paul Jarvis, which limited his first-class output to 233 overs (in which he took 37 wickets), but little imagination was shown in the selection or handling of what remained. Sidebottom, mercifully injury-free in his benefit season, provided the sharpest cutting edge, and Fletcher, lively and spirited, improved in tally of wickets and average, but Yorkshire still looked unlikely to bowl sides out twice on good pitches.

The medium-pacers Shaw and Peter Hartley were steady enough, but, with skipper Carrick's main virtue as a slow left-armer being containment rather than penetration, defensive field settings and attritional attitudes held sway. The introduction of the young left-armer Booth late in the season brought welcome variety and resurrected the hope that Yorkshire might one day regularly field two spinners rather than one.

The selection of the batting was inconsistent. Metcalfe survived a long run of modest scores to enjoy a profitable late run spree which took his total past 1,300, treatment differing sharply from Blakey's. Having been the county's leading scorer in 1987, when he also topped their averages, Blakey spent five separate spells out of a side in which he was far from the only player struggling, and also moved up and down the batting order like a yo-yo.

The experiment of playing the off-spinner Swallow at No. 3 in Blakey's place was unsuccessful, so it was fortunate for Yorkshire that Moxon was so consistent and that Robinson responded well when given a long run.

The left-hander Byas showed promise, but it was as well that the lower middle order, and in particular Carrick himself and Sidebottom, batted so reliably in view of the inconsistency of Love and Sharp.

Bairstow, out of form with the bat and troubled by damaged fingers, lost his wicket-keeping place to Blakey. It seems, sadly, that the days of this great-hearted cricketer may be numbered.

Though they have considerable individual talents, Yorkshire appeared to play the game without noticeably enterprise. They will not return to the heights without a change in approach – until, in particular, they are prepared to risk defeat in the pursuit of victory.

Britannic Assurance County Championship: 13th; Won 4, Lost 6, Drawn 12
All First-Class Matches: Won 5, Lost 6, Drawn 13
NatWest Bank Trophy: Lost to Middlesex in 2nd round
Benson & Hedges Cup: Failed to qualify for quarter-final (4th in Group B)
Refuge Assurance League: 8th; Won 7, Lost 7, No Result 2

Championship Averages

Batting and Fielding	M	I	NO	HS	R	Avge	100	50	Ct/St
M.D. Moxon	18	33	3	191	1297	43.23	2	8	21
A.A. Metcalfe	21	39	5	216*	1268	37.29	2	7	4
P.E. Robinson	22	37	3	129*	1132	33.29	1	8	19
P.J. Hartley	13	17	6	127*	364	33.09	1	–	7
P. Carrick	21	32	7	81	795	31.80	–	2	6
S.N. Hartley	·2	3	1	26*	60	30.00	–	–	–
J.D. Love	17	27	2	93*	744	29.76	–	6	11
A. Sidebottom	18	24	5	55	517	27.21	–	2	5
D. Byas	12	22	1	112	515	24.52	1	3	8
D.L. Bairstow	14	23	3	94*	416	20.80	–	2	38/1
I.G. Swallow	11	19	2	48*	352	20.70	–	–	5
R.J. Blakey	14	21	2	51	347	18.26	–	1	24/2
K. Sharp	11	17	0	57	297	17.47	–	1	9
P.A. Booth	4	7	2	33*	82	16.40	–	–	1
C. Shaw	21	25	12	31	170	13.07	–	–	2
S.D. Fletcher	16	14	3	18	79	7.18	–	–	7
S.J. Dennis	2	3	1	14*	14	7.00	–	–	–
P.W. Jarvis	5	9	1	13	55	6.87	–	–	–

Hundreds (7)

2 A.A. Metcalfe: 115 v Derbys, Chesterfield; 216* v Middx, Headingley
  M.D. Moxon: 106 v Worcs, Worcester; 191 v Northants, Scarborough
1 D. Byas: 112 v Glos, Cheltenham
  P.J. Hartley: 127* v Lancs, Old Trafford
  P.E. Robinson: 129* v Notts, Sheffield

Bowling	O	M	R	W	Avge	Best	5wI	10wM
P.W. Jarvis	176.1	46	434	31	14.00	6-40	2	1
A. Sidebottom	513.2	135	1303	63	20.68	7-89	3	–
S.D. Fletcher	384.4	59	1252	53	23.62	8-58	2	–
P.A. Booth	109.4	27	281	9	31.22	5-98	1	–
C. Shaw	507.5	110	1522	46	33.08	4-17	–	–
P. Carrick	546	163	1447	42	34.45	5-46	2	–
P.J. Hartley	307.3	32	1219	34	35.85	5-85	1	–
S.J. Dennis	63	9	196	5	39.20	3-35	–	–

Also bowled: D. Byas 9.2-0-49-0; S.N. Hartley 5-1-25-0; J.D. Love 2.3-0-11-1; A.A. Metcalfe 2.5-0-7-0; M.D. Moxon 6-2-15-0; P.E. Robinson 1.2-0-12-0; K. Sharp 1-0-11-0; I.G. Swallow 88-15-311-2.

Oxford and Cambridge

As their records for the season make plain, neither Oxford nor Cambridge was a team of rich vintage in 1988, but their annual match at Lord's, the oldest on the fixture list, was unique, in that it was the first in a series of 144 to be abandoned without a ball being bowled.

The captains, Michael Kilborn and Michael Atherton, did not even toss, much to the agony of those picked to play in the grand old match for the first time: S.A. Almaer, G.D. Reynolds, M.R. Sygrove, T. Jack, M. Brown (Oxford) and J.C.M. Atkinson, R. Turner, S. Noyes, S.D. Heath, R. Bate, N.C.W. Fenton (Cambridge). But tradition was waived and, after consultations with committees, Blues were awarded to the unfortunates.

It is hard to judge on the basis of their performances against the counties which way the Lord's match would have gone, had it taken place, except that the presence in the Cambridge ranks of the one batsman of true class on either side, Atherton, should have given the Light Blues the edge.

Atherton, who joined forces with Lancashire after the end of term, scored 1,121 runs for the season, finishing with a higher average (48.73) than all English-born batsmen save Athey, Gooch, and Barnett. He aggregated 665 (avge 60.45) for Cambridge, including unbeaten centuries against Surrey and Middlesex, besides scoring one and 45 in the two-day match against the West Indies.

Besides his two centuries, Atherton had three scores of well over 50 during the Cambridge part of his season. The burdens of captaining a side frequently overwhelmed rested lightly on his shoulders, and his consistency was commendable because pitches at Fenner's were nothing like they used to be, even if they showed an improvement on 1987. In the circumstances, runs were hard to come by for Atherton's fellow batsmen, even those with a fair amount of experience, notably Bail and Atkinson, both of Somerset. Atkinson's 73 against Surrey, at The Oval, was the only score of over 50 by any batsman other than Atherton.

Despite helpful pitches, Cambridge struggled to take wickets. Only twice did they bowl out the opposition, Middlesex and Yorkshire, both playing below strength. The only bowler to achieve any measure of success was Nigel Fenton, a post-graduate student from Durham. So desperate did Cambridge become that at one stage they recruited Alastair Scott, who had gone down in 1987 and happened to be in Cambridge looking for a job.

Cambridge lost five of their eight matches, winning none. If Oxford ostensibly fared better, with only two defeats in seven outings, it was either because rain saved them or because their opponents preferred to take batting practice rather than go for the kill.

No Oxford batsman made a hundred. The nearest anyone came to this distinction was the captain-elect Michael Crawley, Atherton's contemporary at Manchester Grammar School, with 98 against Nottinghamshire. Crawley's season was marred by a cycling accident which left

Cambridge University

Results: Played 8; Lost 5, Drawn 3

First-Class Averages

Batting	M	I	NO	HS	R	Avge
M.A. Atherton†	8	13	2	151*	665	60.45
J.C.M. Atkinson†	7	12	0	73	257	21.41
P.A.C. Bail†	4	6	0	44	102	17.00
R. Bate†	7	12	2	45	160	16.00
S.D. Heath†	5	8	1	33*	100	14.28
S.J. Noyes†	8	14	1	38	170	13.07
R.J. Turner†	8	14	1	27	155	11.92
G.A. Pointer†	7	12	2	18*	114	11.40
J.M. Tremellem†	7	12	0	33	131	10.91
J.N. Perry†	7	9	1	26	73	9.12
A.M.G. Scott	3	5	1	8	9	2.25
R.J. Hart	3	5	1	6	7	1.75
N.C.W. Fenton†	7	9	3	2	4	0.66

Also batted: A.K. Golding (1 match) 18*;
R. Heap (1 match) 0, 15; A.M. Hooper
(2 matches) 3, 2, 0; R.A. Pyman (2 matches)
3, 0, 4; J.M.C. Stenner (1 match) 10, 13.

Hundreds (2)

2 M.A. Atherton: 100* v Surrey, Cambridge;
151* v Middlesex, Cambridge.

Bowling	O	M	R	W	Avge	Best
Fenton	271.4	65	726	21	34.57	4-64
Scott	120	26	385	11	35.00	4-66
Perry	211	44	643	10	64.30	3-72
Atherton	179.2	19	565	7	80.71	2-38
Pointer	184.5	24	663	7	94.71	3-31

Also bowled: Atkinson 17-1-86-1;
Bail 14-1-71-1; Golding 23-11-43-0;
Hart 67-11-231-4; Tremellem 5-0-13-1.

Fielding

10 Atherton, Turner (9ct/2st); 4 Atkinson;
3 Perry, Tremellem; 2 Golding, Heap,
Heath, Pyman; 1 Bail, Bate, Fenton

Oxford University

Results: Played 7; Lost 2, Drawn 5

First-Class Averages

Batting	M	I	NO	HS	R	Avge
M.A. Crawley†	4	7	2	98	177	35.40
D.A. Hagan†	7	13	2	59	306	27.81
M.J. Kilborn†	7	13	0	78	351	27.00
D.A. Polkinghorne	3	4	1	45*	72	24.00
M.E.O. Brown†	3	5	2	47	71	23.66
S.A. Almaer†	6	11	0	67	256	23.27
G.D. Reynolds†	6	9	1	69	147	18.37
S.D. Weale†	6	9	0	40	136	15.11
J.D. Nuttall†	5	6	2	35	52	13.00
I.M. Henderson†	5	7	1	21*	55	9.16
P.G. Edwards†	5	7	3	9	32	8.00
M.R. Sygrove†	7	8	3	8*	29	5.80
R.E. Morris	4	8	0	21	39	4.87
A.N.S. Hampton	3	6	0	12	22	3.66

Also batted: N.H. Green (1 match) 9;
M. Heppel (1 match) 14*; T. Jack†
(2 matches) 29, 5, 23; A.M. Searle (1 match) 2.
J.E.B. Cope played in one match but did not bat.

Hundreds (0)

Bowling	O	M	R	W	Avge	Best
Kilborn	41.5	8	185	5	37.00	3-37
Sygrove	215.4	34	848	18	47.11	3-91
Nuttall	116	20	410	7	58.57	2-64
Edwards	171.3	43	560	9	62.22	3-88
Henderson	71	10	316	5	63.20	3-104
Weale	200	41	681	8	85.12	3-130

Also bowled: Crawley 38-7-136-0; Hagan
3-0-21-0; Heppel 14-0-74-0; Searle 17-2-76-0.

Fielding

6 Reynolds; 5 Kilborn; 3 Hagan, Weale;
2 Almaer, Crawley, Edwards, Nuttall,
Polkinghorn, 1 Cope, Green, Henderson, Jack,
Morris.

* not out † Blue 1988

him with an injured collar-bone.

The Dark Blues' runs came from wider sources than Cambridge's, however, with Hagan, Kilborn, Reynolds, and Crawley all passing 50 at least once. In common with Cambridge, they had only one bowler who had a strike rate worth the name, Malcolm Sygrove, a freshman.

Between the two, Oxford and Cambridge provided only five players (ratio one to four) for the 13-strong Combined Universities squad for the Benson & Hedges Cup competition. In the two-day match against the West Indies, at Fenner's, Oxbridge were bowled out for only 38 in the first innings, but had the resilience to fight back in the second. However, the students did inflict on the West Indies one of the poorest starts to their innings on the tour – 17 for two.

First-Class Averages 1988

Batting (Qual: 8 inn, avge 10.00)	M	I	NO	HS	Runs	Avge	100s	50s
R.A. Harper	12	13	5	217*	622	77.75	1	4
G.A. Hick	24	37	2	405*	2713	77.51	10	5
S.R. Waugh	15	24	6	161	1314	73.00	6	4
C.W.J. Athey	13	22	6	168*	1064	66.50	2	6
G.A. Gooch	21	37	1	275	2324	64.55	6	15
J.R. Ratnayeke	8	10	5	60*	311	62.20	–	2
M.D. Crowe	5	9	1	136*	487	60.87	2	2
A.R. Border	20	32	8	169*	1393	58.04	6	4
K.J. Barnett	19	30	2	239*	1623	57.96	5	8
P.A. De Silva	6	9	3	117*	333	55.50	1	2
A.J. Lamb	16	27	5	155	1163	52.86	5	5
C.G. Greenidge	11	16	1	111	762	50.80	3	4
P.J.L. Dujon	12	16	4	141	601	50.08	1	5
K.T. Arthurton	10	13	3	121	499	49.90	2	2
M.A. Atherton	16	27	4	152*	1121	48.73	4	3
D.S.B.P. Kuruppu	6	10	1	158	438	48.66	1	2
N. Hussain	9	13	3	165*	486	48.60	1	2
D.M. Smith	11	18	5	157*	630	48.46	2	1
M.W. Gatting	20	33	2	210	1469	47.38	3	9
M.R. Ramprakash	9	13	4	68*	421	46.77	–	3
P.D. Bowler	24	42	5	159*	1725	46.62	4	9
D.L. Haynes	15	25	4	158	964	45.90	1	7
W.N. Slack	19	32	5	163*	1228	45.48	3	6
R.S. Madugalle	8	11	2	97	403	44.77	–	3
G.S. Clinton	18	29	5	158	1054	43.91	4	4
R.C. Ontong	17	25	8	120*	734	43.17	1	4
J.G. Wright	11	20	1	154*	815	42.89	1	5
C.J. Tavaré	22	36	2	138*	1430	42.05	4	5
A.L. Logie	13	18	4	95*	586	41.85	–	3
C.J. Richards	20	25	4	102*	874	41.61	1	6
I.V.A. Richards	13	16	1	128	624	41.60	1	5
M.P. Maynard	23	42	6	126	1485	41.25	3	11
M.D. Moxon	21	39	3	191	1485	41.25	3	8
R.A. Smith	21	42	8	141*	1356	39.88	4	4
P.A. Neale	21	31	5	167	1036	39.84	4	2
M.A. Lynch	21	29	4	103*	996	39.84	2	4
T.S. Curtis	22	38	4	131	1337	39.32	2	7
D.W. Randall	21	37	4	237	1286	38.96	2	9
P.W.G. Parker	21	40	5	124	1359	38.82	5	5
P.J. Prichard	24	39	8	97	1202	38.77	–	9
D.I. Gower	22	38	4	172	1318	38.76	2	5
Asif Din	23	41	4	158*	1425	38.51	2	8
R.T. Robinson	21	35	4	134*	1194	38.51	4	4
A.A. Metcalfe	22	40	5	216*	1320	37.71	2	8
J.E. Morris	23	37	5	175	1204	37.62	2	6
K.M. Curran	19	34	7	142	1005	37.22	2	4
R.F. Pienaar	21	35	2	144	1228	37.21	3	7
T.A. Lloyd	24	43	3	160*	1448	36.20	4	3
R.J. Bailey	24	42	2	127	1448	36.20	3	8
L.R.D. Mendis	9	12	2	124	362	36.20	1	2

Batting (contd)	M	I	NO	HS	Runs	Avge	100s	50s
P. Bainbridge	23	38	1	169	1334	36.05	4	6
J.J. Whitaker	23	39	5	145	1223	35.97	3	5
C.L. Smith	22	43	3	124*	1436	35.90	3	8
G.D. Mendis	24	42	4	151	1364	35.89	2	8
P.D. Atkins	6	11	1	114*	357	35.70	1	1
G.C. Holmes	20	32	4	117	999	35.67	4	4
P. Johnson	24	42	3	140	1389	35.61	3	7
D.R. Turner	22	40	6	150*	1204	35.41	2	6
J.D. Carr	24	43	6	144	1297	35.05	2	7
A.W. Stovold	21	39	2	136	1296	35.02	2	6
A.P. Wells	23	42	5	120	1286	34.75	1	9
A.J. Stewart	22	32	3	133	1006	34.68	2	6
N.E. Briers	24	41	2	125*	1335	34.23	2	9
M.R. Benson	21	37	1	110	1227	34.08	2	8
A. Ranatunga	8	9	1	84	271	33.87	–	2
R.J. Shastri	12	19	2	157	575	33.82	1	2
A.R. Butcher	23	40	2	166	1282	33.73	1	9
R.G. Williams	20	34	9	119	842	33.68	1	4
D.J. Capel	21	36	5	92	1040	33.54	–	7
A.J. Moles	18	31	2	115	968	33.37	1	5
P.J. Hartley	13	17	6	127*	364	33.09	1	–
S.T. Jefferies	14	19	5	60	462	33.00	–	2
C.L. Hooper	14	20	1	87	625	32.89	–	5
L. Potter	23	34	7	107	885	32.77	1	5
A. Needham	8	12	3	66*	293	32.55	–	2
I.J. Gould	19	31	4	82*	875	32.40	–	6
P.R. Downton	18	24	5	120	614	32.31	1	2
M.D. Marshall	9	10	1	76	289	32.11	–	2
P.E. Robinson	24	40	3	129*	1173	31.70	1	8
D.M. Ward	25	36	6	126	942	31.40	1	8
R.C. Russell	24	36	8	94	870	31.07	–	6
Wasim Akram	10	18	2	116*	496	31.00	1	3
A.J. Wright	24	42	1	137	1268	30.92	2	5
I.D. Austin	6	9	2	64	216	30.85	–	2
M.A.R. Samarasekera	9	15	2	104	401	30.84	1	2
N.H. Fairbrother	23	41	4	111	1134	30.64	2	6
G. Fowler	21	38	1	172	1134	30.64	2	5
R.O.Butcher	19	29	3	134	796	30.61	1	4
S.C. Goldsmith	24	39	4	89	1071	30.60	–	7
P. Carrick	23	34	7	81	815	30.18	–	2
P.A. Cottey	13	23	3	92	603	30.15	–	5
A.I. Kallicharran	9	15	1	117*	418	29.85	1	2
R.S. Mahanama	5	8	2	46*	179	29.83	–	–
M.C.J. Nicholas	25	47	3	132*	1301	29.56	2	5
V.P. Terry	23	43	3	190	1182	29.55	3	5
B.J.M. Maher	24	39	6	121*	974	29.51	1	5
R.J. Harden	6	11	1	78	295	29.50	–	3
S.G. Hinks	16	27	1	138	764	29.38	1	3
G. Cook	18	30	1	203	850	29.31	2	3
J.P.Stephenson	18	31	4	99	791	29.29	–	6
J.E. Emburey	20	27	4	102	673	29.26	1	4
F.D. Stephenson	22	35	0	117	1018	29.08	2	7
C.S. Cowdrey	21	36	7	124*	843	29.06	2	2
J.D. Love	18	28	2	93*	751	28.88	–	6
T.E. Jesty	15	27	3	73	693	28.87	–	3
N.A. Felton	14	27	2	127	720	28.80	1	4
R. Sharma	10	14	3	80	315	28.63	–	1

Batting (contd)	M	I	NO	HS	Runs	Avge	100s	50s
G.R. Cowdrey	20	33	4	145	830	28.62	1	4
P.M. Roebuck	12	19	3	112*	454	28.37	1	1
K.R. Brown	21	34	5	131*	822	28.34	2	2
D.A. Hagan	7	13	2	59	306	27.81	–	1
G.J. Lord	20	33	2	101	862	27.80	1	4
H. Morris	19	33	3	87	832	27.73	–	6
A. Fordham	16	29	6	125*	637	27.69	1	3
K.W.R. Fletcher	12	14	3	58	303	27.54	–	2
A. Sidebottom	18	24	5	55	517	27.21	–	2
N.R. Taylor	21	37	3	114	925	27.20	2	4
M.J. Weston	18	24	5	95*	514	27.05	–	3
M.J. Kilborn	7	13	0	78	351	27.00	–	2
A.W. Lilley	21	33	3	80*	803	26.76	–	5
P. Pollard	9	17	1	142	428	26.75	1	1
P.W. Romaines	21	39	3	101*	955	26.52	1	6
N.A. Stanley	8	12	2	66	263	26.30	–	3
P.J. Newport	22	25	8	77*	447	26.29	–	1
B. Roberts	24	39	4	71	919	26.25	–	7
W. Larkins	23	41	2	134	1024	26.25	2	4
N.D. Burns	23	34	7	133*	708	26.22	1	2
S.A.R. Silva	8	14	1	112	338	26.00	1	1
S.J. Rhodes	23	33	10	108	597	25.95	1	1
J.J.E. Hardy	22	39	3	97	927	25.75	–	6
A.C.S. Pigott	20	34	8	56	668	25.69	–	3
B.C. Broad	20	34	0	73	872	25.64	–	5
R.J. Bartlett	19	31	3	102*	707	25.25	1	3
G.C. Small	20	29	7	70	554	25.18	–	3
P. Willey	24	40	1	130	978	25.07	2	3
R.J. Scott	9	16	1	107*	374	24.93	1	2
I.L. Pont	8	8	2	68	149	24.83	–	1
V.J. Marks	23	31	2	68	719	24.79	–	3
D. Byas	14	25	1	112	592	24.66	1	4
S.A. Marsh	23	35	6	120	713	24.58	2	1
C.M. Wells	24	41	4	109*	908	24.54	1	4
J.G. Thomas	16	26	5	110	515	24.52	2	–
J.R. Ayling	19	33	4	88*	711	24.51	–	4
N.J. Lenham	18	32	2	74	733	24.43	–	3
D.A. Banks	7	9	1	61	195	24.37	–	1
J.F. Sykes	9	13	1	88	292	24.33	–	2
J.A. Hopkins	13	23	1	87	534	24.27	–	4
R.A. Cobb	11	20	2	65	432	24.00	–	2
D.E. East	20	30	2	134	669	23.89	1	2
A.M. Green	16	29	2	68	639	23.66	–	4
D.A. Thorne	15	25	1	76	566	23.58	–	4
P.A. Smith	16	27	4	84*	542	23.56	–	3
A.N. Hayhurst	14	23	2	107	492	23.42	1	2
S.A. Almaer	6	11	0	67	256	23.27	–	1
C.E.L. Ambrose	13	15	3	59	278	23.16	–	1
J.G. Wyatt	15	26	1	69	578	23.12	–	3
K.T. Medlycott	23	29	5	77*	554	23.08	–	4
T.J. Boon	15	23	1	131	505	22.95	1	2
C. Penn	20	31	12	40	436	22.94	–	–
M.A. Feltham	22	25	9	74	367	22.93	–	1
R.I. Alikhan	10	19	0	98	429	22.57	–	3
K. Sharp	12	19	0	128	428	22.52	1	1
R.K. Illingworth	23	22	4	60	404	22.44	–	2

Batting (contd)	M	I	NO	HS	Runs	Avge	100s	50s
R.J. Blakey	16	24	4	85*	446	22.30	–	2
N.V. Radford	18	15	6	65	200	22.22	–	1
N.J. Pringle	8	15	4	54	244	22.18	–	1
J.D. Birch	24	39	4	114*	776	22.17	1	2
G. Miller	19	21	4	77	377	22.17	–	1
B.R. Hardie	13	20	3	58	377	22.17	–	2
M. Newell	20	37	3	105	740	21.76	1	2
C.K. Bullen	12	14	2	59*	261	21.75	–	2
M.R. Gouldstone	7	12	1	71	239	21.72	–	2
M. Watkinson	24	39	4	85*	759	21.68	–	6
D.A. Reeve	16	23	3	103	431	21.55	1	–
P.A.J. DeFreitas	17	25	1	113	517	21.54	1	3
M.A. Roseberry	14	21	3	67	386	21.44	–	1
J.C.M. Atkinson	7	12	0	73	257	21.41	–	1
P.J. Whitticase	23	32	10	71	469	21.31	–	2
A. Walker	18	20	10	40*	213	21.30	–	–
T.R. Ward	10	17	0	72	362	21.29	–	3
C.C. Lewis	16	23	4	40	400	21.05	–	–
D.L. Bairstow	14	23	3	94*	416	20.80	–	2
I.G. Swallow	11	19	2	48*	352	20.70	–	–
N.F. Williams	8	11	2	63*	186	20.66	–	1
J.W. Lloyds	16	24	3	102*	433	20.61	1	1
S.J.W. Andrew	11	9	7	12*	41	20.50	–	–
W.W. Davis	15	18	3	43	306	20.40	–	–
K.P. Evans	15	24	4	54	406	20.30	–	1
G.D. Rose	20	25	6	69*	385	20.26	–	1
D. Williams	8	10	1	51	182	20.22	–	1
J. Simmons	21	27	9	57*	362	20.11	–	1
D.J.R. Martindale	9	14	1	52*	261	20.07	–	1
S.P. Hughes	18	21	5	53	321	20.06	–	1
R.B. Richardson	10	14	0	82	279	19.92	–	1
M.P. Speight	7	13	0	58	258	19.84	–	2
I.A. Greig	23	28	1	67	529	19.59	–	1
G.J. Parsons	10	13	4	52	174	19.33	–	1
D.R. Pringle	19	27	0	128	516	19.11	1	3
D.J. Bicknell	11	19	1	62	343	19.05	–	2
G.A. Tedstone	4	8	0	50	151	18.87	–	1
M.W. Pooley	8	13	5	38	149	18.62	–	–
G.D. Reynolds	6	9	1	69	147	18.37	–	1
D.A. Leatherdale	10	15	1	34*	255	18.21	–	–
P. Moores	14	24	2	97*	395	17.95	–	1
D.P. Hughes	22	34	4	62	522	17.40	–	3
A.P. Igglesden	7	8	2	41	103	17.16	–	–
I. Folley	19	20	14	30	102	17.00	–	–
W.K.M. Benjamin	10	10	4	21*	102	17.00	–	–
A.C. Storie	9	17	2	68	255	17.00	–	1
C.W. Scott	19	27	6	63*	356	16.95	–	1
T.J.E. O'Gorman	5	9	0	78	152	16.88	–	1
D. Ripley	25	33	6	49	451	16.70	–	–
P.J. Bakker	10	11	8	16	50	16.66	–	–
N.J. Falkner	7	14	0	55	232	16.57	–	1
R.M. Ellison	20	27	6	50*	345	16.42	–	1
G.W. Humpage	17	26	1	80	411	16.44	–	3
E.E. Hemmings	17	25	10	31*	245	16.33	–	–
D.J. Wild	18	27	1	75	423	16.26	–	2
W.K. Hegg	24	34	5	76	467	16.10	–	1

Batting (contd)	M	I	NO	HS	Runs	Avge	100s	50s
K.D. James	12	22	2	77	320	16.00	–	1
R. Bate	7	12	2	45	160	16.00	–	–
P.A. Booth	5	8	2	33*	96	16.00	–	–
C.P. Metson	23	30	8	48	351	15.95	–	–
A.E. Warner	19	25	6	45	300	15.78	–	–
S.T. Clarke	12	10	1	28	141	15.66	–	–
R.J. Parks	23	35	8	38*	420	15.55	–	–
D.A. Graveney	23	24	9	47	231	15.40	–	–
S.D. Weale	6	9	0	40	136	15.11	–	–
M.W. Alleyne	14	21	1	56	300	15.00	–	1
T.D. Topley	16	22	6	56*	235	14.68	–	1
D.J. Foster	13	14	9	20	72	14.40	–	–
P.G. Newman	16	19	6	39	187	14.38	–	–
S.D. Heath	5	8	1	33*	100	14.28	–	–
T.A. Merrick	16	21	3	34	256	14.22	–	–
A.R. Clarke	21	32	8	68	337	14.04	–	1
T.M. Tremlett	7	10	2	38	111	13.87	–	–
B.N. French	7	11	1	28	135	13.50	–	–
D.K. Lillee	8	11	2	22	120	13.33	–	–
D.B.D'Oliveira	8	11	1	37	132	13.20	–	–
C. Shaw	21	25	12	31	170	13.07	–	–
S.J. Noyes	8	14	1	38	170	13.07	–	–
J.P. Agnew	24	29	8	38	271	12.90	–	–
M.A. Holding	11	12	2	30*	129	12.90	–	–
P.J.W. Allott	19	28	4	31*	308	12.83	–	–
R.J. Maru	23	29	5	74	302	12.58	–	1
A.R.C. Fraser	23	27	9	41	223	12.38	–	–
T.M. Alderman	20	22	11	43*	135	12.27	–	–
N.A. Mallender	17	20	7	44	158	12.15	–	–
N.H. Peters	12	15	8	25*	85	12.14	–	–
R.J. Turner	8	14	1	27	155	11.92	–	–
G.J.F. Ferris	18	20	8	36*	139	11.58	–	–
O.H. Mortensen	12	12	8	15	46	11.50	–	–
M.D. Harman	12	13	6	17*	80	11.42	–	–
A.R.K. Pierson	9	12	7	18*	57	11.40	–	–
G.A. Pointer	7	12	2	18*	114	11.40	–	–
G.R. Dilley	13	15	2	36	147	11.30	–	–
K.E. Cooper	24	34	9	39	282	11.28	–	–
L.B. Taylor	17	16	6	60	111	11.10	–	1
J.M. Tremellem	7	12	0	33	131	10.91	–	–
A.A. Donald	7	10	3	29	74	10.57	–	–
J.H. Childs	20	19	12	25*	73	10.42	–	–
J. Derrick	21	28	6	50*	229	10.40	–	1
N.A. Foster	16	21	4	34	171	10.05	–	–
A.N. Jones	20	21	8	38	130	10.00	–	–

Bowling

(Qual: 10 wkts in 10 inns)	O	M	R	W	Avge	Best	5wI	10wM
M.D. Marshall	245.4	56	553	42	13.16	7-22	3	1
O.H. Mortensen	233.3	73	464	34	13.64	6-35	4	–
W.K.M. Benjamin	183.1	43	467	33	14.15	4-20	–	–
S.T. Clarke	396.4	108	913	63	14.49	6-52	4	2
N.F. Williams	178.3	33	511	30	17.03	6-42	2	–
P.W. Jarvis	233.2	52	651	37	17.59	6-40	2	1

Bowling (contd)	O	M	R	W	Avge	Best	5wI	10wM
N.G. Cowans	491.5	124	1290	71	18.16	6-49	3	1
F.D. Stephenson	819.1	196	2289	125	18.31	7-56	10	3
G.J. Parsons	228	69	553	29	19.06	7-16	1	–
I.R. Bishop	142	30	406	21	19.33	6-39	2	–
A.R.C. Fraser	697.1	195	1550	80	19.37	6-68	6	2
P.J. Newport	600.3	127	1844	93	19.82	8-52	7	1
G.C. Small	628.1	170	1605	80	20.06	7-15	8	2
A.A. Donald	180.4	40	534	26	20.53	5-57	1	–
P.J.W. Allott	590.2	161	1378	67	20.56	6-59	5	–
A. Sidebottom	513.2	135	1303	63	20.68	7-89	3	–
N.A. Mallender	433.3	111	1037	50	20.74	5-12	1	–
C.E.L. Ambrose	329.1	86	733	35	20.94	4-27	–	–
K.M. Curran	414.2	86	1385	65	21.30	7-54	4	3
Wasim Akram	291.4	76	666	31	21.48	7-53	2	–
K.E. Cooper	816	220	2179	101	21.57	5-41	5	–
A.P. Igglesden	234.3	46	805	37	21.75	6-34	3	1
K.D. James	298.5	72	763	35	21.80	5-25	2	–
R.K. Illingworth	597.4	189	1274	58	21.96	5-46	4	2
W.W. Davis	538.2	92	1614	73	22.10	7-52	7	2
T.A. Merrick	458.3	105	1437	65	22.10	6-29	5	1
S.D. Fletcher	412	66	1308	59	22.16	8-58	2	–
G.J.F. Ferris	452.1	82	1380	62	22.25	5-47	2	–
P.J. Bakker	293.4	86	670	30	22.33	5-54	1	–
G.R. Dilley	387.1	70	1098	49	22.40	5-46	4	–
T.A. Munton	425.1	126	1047	46	22.76	6-21	2	–
N.A. Foster	598.3	122	1822	80	22.77	6-53	5	2
T.M. Alderman	600	135	1711	75	22.81	8-59	3	–
M.A. Robinson	402.4	85	1055	46	22.93	4-19	–	–
T.M. Tremlett	125.3	35	326	14	23.28	4-19	–	–
I.A. Greig	402.3	83	1143	49	23.32	6-34	2	–
J.R. Ayling	432.1	97	1098	47	23.36	4-57	–	–
P.A. Smith	164.3	20	540	23	23.47	3-7	–	–
M.D. Harman	266.4	86	593	25	23.72	5-55	2	–
R.M. Ellison	603.4	171	1697	71	23.90	7-75	3	–
D.J. Capel	768.2	264	1635	68	24.04	6-56	2	–
K.T. Medlycott	593.1	159	1660	69	24.05	8-52	6	3
P.A.J. DeFreitas	557.3	127	1555	64	24.29	5-38	5	–
C. Penn	646.1	143	1989	81	24.55	7-70	6	–
J. Simmons	629	159	1548	63	24.57	5-53	2	–
S.J.W. Andrew	268.5	66	765	31	24.67	5-36	1	–
R.A. Harper	227.3	70	521	21	24.80	4-10	–	–
N.V. Radford	570.5	100	1770	71	24.92	7-73	3	–
B.P. Patterson	196	33	632	25	25.28	5-39	1	–
J.P. Agnew	783.5	166	2367	93	25.45	7-61	8	1
D.A. Graveney	613.2	179	1353	53	25.52	8-127	2	1
A. Walker	465.5	98	1380	54	25.55	5-64	1	–
T.D. Topley	538.4	87	1664	65	25.60	7-75	4	1
J.H. Childs	655.5	209	1605	62	25.88	6-92	4	1
J.K. Lever	422.4	90	1120	43	26.04	4-61	–	–
A.E. Warner	445	104	1151	44	26.15	4-22	–	–
D.R. Pringle	515.2	111	1492	57	26.17	6-39	4	–
J.E. Emburey	671.5	215	1543	58	26.60	6-24	2	–
M.J. Weston	124	31	320	12	26.66	4-24	–	–
G.D. Rose	504.5	116	1527	57	26.78	6-47	1	–
P.G. Newman	339.5	81	950	35	27.14	8-29	1	–

Bowling (contd)	O	M	R	W	Avge	Best	5wI	10wM
C.A. Connor	495.3	92	1497	55	27.21	5-70	1	–
D.V. Lawrence	647.2	103	2296	84	27.33	7-47	4	–
L.B. Taylor	324.3	72	967	35	27.62	6-49	1	–
N.H. Peters	278.2	50	954	34	28.05	6-31	1	1
A.C.S. Pigott	624	109	2078	74	28.08	6-100	2	–
C.K. Bullen	107.1	25	316	11	28.72	4-56	–	–
C.C. Lewis	391.4	83	1210	42	28.80	6-22	2	1
H.R.J. Trump	270	74	696	24	29.00	4-17	–	–
M.W. Cleal	168	25	582	20	29.10	4-41	–	–
V.J. Marks	862.5	222	2214	76	29.13	7-118	5	1
C.S. Cowdrey	391.2	92	1141	39	29.25	5-46	1	–
I. Folley	614.3	168	1681	57	29.49	6-20	2	–
M.W. Pooley	128.4	30	384	13	29.53	4-80	–	–
G. Miller	433	106	1153	39	29.56	5-76	1	–
K.J. Barnett	161.1	37	414	14	29.57	3-63	–	–
R.G. Williams	331	72	980	33	29.69	5-86	1	–
D.E. Malcolm	488.1	93	1676	56	29.92	6-68	2	–
M.A. Feltham	584.1	135	1679	56	29.98	5-45	2	–
A.N. Jones	512	85	1658	55	30.14	7-30	1	–
M.P. Bicknell	516.2	136	1511	50	30.22	9-45	1	–
G.A. Hick	204	43	642	21	30.57	4-114	–	–
S.L. Watkin	527.3	117	1423	46	30.93	8-59	2	–
P. Carrick	593	179	1551	50	31.02	5-46	2	–
E.E. Hemmings	508.5	139	1312	42	31.23	4-50	–	–
D.A. Reeve	292	71	750	24	31.25	4-50	–	–
D.J. Wild	187.5	37	563	18	31.27	4-18	–	–
N.A. Gifford	425.1	121	976	31	31.48	3-66	–	–
A.P. Pridgeon	266.3	58	662	21	31.52	3-68	–	–
J.G. Thomas	422.2	62	1531	48	31.89	6-68	2	–
J. Derrick	542.1	138	1511	47	32.14	6-54	1	–
R.A. Bunting	400	66	1320	41	32.19	5-44	3	–
R.F. Pienaar	404.2	99	1162	36	32.27	5-27	1	–
A.N. Hayhurst	181.3	41	553	17	32.52	4-45	–	–
C. Shaw	507.5	110	1522	46	33.08	4-17	–	–
I.L. Pont	220	30	795	24	33.12	5-103	1	–
A.M. Babington	554.5	110	1628	49	33.22	4-66	–	–
S.R. Barwick	408.5	112	1064	32	33.25	5-37	1	–
G.F. Labrooy	201.5	30	665	20	33.25	6-61	1	–
S.J. Base	195	20	735	22	33.40	4-74	–	–
P.M. Such	123.5	22	340	10	34.00	4-81	–	–
C.M. Wells	534.4	119	1469	43	34.16	4-43	–	–
M. Watkinson	647.3	153	1779	52	34.21	6-43	2	–
M.A. Holding	279.1	49	827	24	34.45	4-74	–	–
C.A. Walsh	232.2	55	622	18	34.55	5-49	1	–
N.C.W. Fenton	271.4	65	726	21	34.57	4-64	–	–
D.J. Capel	436.1	76	1451	41	35.39	4-40	–	–
R.J. Shastri	304.2	91	709	20	35.45	7-49	1	1
S.T. Jefferies	355.1	52	1216	34	35.76	8-97	2	–
R.J. Maru	701	203	1792	50	35.84	5-69	1	–
P.J. Hartley	307.3	32	1219	34	35.85	5-85	1	–
D.J. Millns	179	22	683	19	35.94	3-37	–	–
D.K. Lillee	245	45	778	21	37.04	6-68	1	–
R.P. Davis	563	177	1409	38	37.07	5-132	1	–
D.J. Foster	299.3	46	1044	28	37.28	4-46	–	–
A.R. Clarke	618	156	1650	44	37.50	5-60	2	–

Bowling (contd)	O	M	R	W	Avge	Best	5wI	10wM
K.P. Evans	258.5	49	829	22	37.68	3-22	–	–
G.A. Gooch	152	39	401	10	40.10	2-29	–	–
G.C. Holmes	121.2	15	445	11	40.45	5-38	1	–
M.A.R. Samarasekera	127.4	14	406	10	40.60	3-31	–	–
P. Willey	341	106	803	19	42.26	4-153	–	–
P.C.R. Tufnell	433.2	119	1058	25	42.32	4-88	–	–
R.C. Ontong	395.1	94	1128	26	43.38	4-38	–	–
J.R. Ratnayeke	231.5	36	687	15	45.80	3-47	–	–
S.P. Hughes	441.3	84	1258	27	46.59	4-39	–	–
M.R. Sygrove	215.4	34	848	18	47.11	3-91	–	–
K. Saxelby	245.2	42	837	17	49.23	3-21	–	–
J.W. Lloyds	239.3	42	757	13	58.23	2-22	–	–
P. Bainbridge	324	62	1054	17	62.00	5-33	1	–
J.N. Perry	211	44	643	10	64.30	3-72	–	–
M.A. Atherton	269.1	42	827	11	75.18	3-32	–	–

The following bowlers took 10 wickets but bowled in fewer than 10 innings:

	O	M	R	W	Avge	Best	5wI	10wM
Imran Khan	122.3	27	310	13	23.84	5-50	1	–
I.D. Austin	137.1	43	367	15	24.46	5-79	1	–
C.L. Cairns	109	16	384	15	25.60	4-70	–	–
F.S. Ahangama	99.2	22	321	12	26.75	4-51	–	–
H.L. Alleyne	94.3	17	322	12	26.83	5-54	1	–
N.G. Cowley	157.1	47	337	11	30.63	3-39	–	–
M. Frost	99.5	23	326	10	32.60	4-56	–	–
P.A. Booth	135.4	35	361	11	32.81	5-98	1	–
F.A. Griffith	99.3	20	347	10	34.70	4-47	–	–
A.M.G. Scott	120	26	385	11	35.00	4-66	–	–
A.M. Green	151.5	40	392	10	39.20	6-82	1	–

Fielding Statistics (Qualification: 20 dismissals)

87 D. Ripley (80c, 7s)
77 S.J. Rhodes (69c, 8s)
74 P.J. Whitticase (70c, 4s)
73 R.J. Parks (63c, 10s)
68 R.C. Russell (56c, 12s)
66 D.E. East (60c, 6s)
64 C.J. Richards (63c, 1s)
61 B.J.M. Maher (60c, 1s)
61 S.A. Marsh (56c, 5s)
60 W.K. Hegg (52c, 8s)
59 N.D. Burns (57c, 2s)
58 C.P. Metson (50c, 8s)
57 G.W. Humpage (56c, 1s)
51 C.W. Scott (49c, 2s)
45 P.R. Downton (40c, 5s)
39 D.L. Bairstow (38c, 1s)

33 C.S. Cowdrey
33 P. Moores (30c, 3s)
33 V.P. Terry
32 K.R. Brown
32 I.J. Gould
31 P.J.L. Dujon
31 R.J. Maru
29 C.J. Tavaré
28 R.J. Blakey (26c, 2s)
28 G.A. Gooch
28 G.A. Hick
28 K.T. Medlycott
28 M. Newell
26 A.R. Border
26 A.J. Stewart (25c, 1s)

25 D.P. Hughes
24 J.E. Emburey
23 R.J. Bailey
23 J.J.E. Hardy
23 W. Larkins
23 M.P. Maynard
22 R.A. Harper
22 M.D. Moxon
22 D.M. Ward
21 J.D. Carr
21 T.S. Curtis
21 G. Miller
21 P.E. Robinson
20 J.W. Lloyds
20 S.R. Waugh

Benson & Hedges Cup

The Benson and Hedges Cup final, which Hampshire won by seven wickets having needed only 118 to beat Derbyshire, may have been one of the most one-sided, but it was not uneventful.

Before it started, it was a historic occasion, for this was the first time that Hampshire had reached a Lord's final. Not even in the days of Barry Richards and Andy Roberts, and more recently of Gordon Greenidge and Malcolm Marshall, had they done it. Now they had, despite Greenidge and Marshall's absence on the West Indies tour.

From the first, almost everything went Hampshire's way, starting with the toss. Derbyshire's strength had seemed to lie in their five fast and fast-medium bowlers, but now they were put in and forced to face up to Hampshire's four bowlers of medium pace and above, plus the seasoned off-spinner Nigel Cowley. The sky was overcast, the ball swung and, beginning with the last ball of his third over, the left-arm fast-medium Stephen Jefferies demolished the early Derbyshire batting.

An accurate left-arm bowler with genuine late inswing is always a handful. Jefferies pitched the ball up, and within eight deliveries took the first four wickets for one run. That one run came from a hard chance to first slip on one of relatively few occasions when he moved the ball away from the batsman.

A dogged partnership between Morris and Maher halted the collapse but without suggesting that Derbyshire would ever make enough runs. In the event, Cowley bowled his 11 overs for 17 runs, Jefferies returned to bring his figures up to five for 13, and the other batsmen were removed without much trouble and with 8.5 of Derbyshire's 55 overs unused.

Early in Hampshire's innings, Terry was caught at second slip off Malcolm, but Nicholas stood firm against Holding and others, Robin Smith played the few robust strokes of the day, and Hampshire won with no less than 23 overs to spare. The most notable contribution from the luckless Derbyshire was a magnificent catch by Steven Goldsmith, who raced more than 30 yards to catch, near the ground, a steepling, swirling top-edged mishook from Robin Smith.

Derbyshire had come unbeaten through to the final, recording a particularly impressive quarter-final win at Derby over Middlesex, who at that time were carrying all before them. In the rain-interrupted semi-final at Swansea, they always had the measure of Glamorgan.

Hampshire qualified less easily. Few at Southampton on May 10 could have guessed that it was the ultimate Cup-winners whom they were seeing Gloucestershire dispose of by six wickets. But Hampshire won a difficult quarter-final at Worcester. Needing 170 on an unpredictable pitch, they were 114 for seven, but were taken home by Robin Smith's brilliant 87 not out and Cowley's support in an unbroken eighth-wicket stand. When called on to make 239 to beat Essex in the semi-final at Chelmsford, they did so in style by seven wickets, after an opening stand of 118 between Terry and Chris Smith and Terry's 109.

Zonal Results

Group A	P	W	L	NR	Pts	Group C	P	W	L	NR	Pts
DERBYSHIRE	4	3	0	1	7	ESSEX	4	3	1	–	6
WARWICKSHIRE	4	2	1	1	5	MIDDLESEX	4	3	1	–	6
Leicestershire	4	2	1	1	5	Kent	4	2	2	–	4
Lancashire	4	1	3	–	2	Sussex	4	1	3	–	2
Scotland	4	0	3	1	1	Surrey	4	1	3	–	2

Group B	P	W	L	NR	Pts	Group D	P	W	L	NR	Pts
WORCESTERSHIRE	4	2	1	1	5	GLAMORGAN	4	3	1	–	6
NOTTINGHAMSHIRE	4	2	1	1	5	HAMPSHIRE	4	3	1	–	6
Northamptonshire	4	2	1	1	5	Gloucestershire	4	3	1	–	6
Yorkshire	4	1	1	2	4	Somerset	4	1	3	–	2
Minor Counties	4	0	3	1	1	Combined Universities	4	0	4	–	0

Note: Where two or more teams in a group have equal points, their positions are determined by runs faced per 100 balls (runs scored by 100, divided by balls faced) in all zonal matches.

Final Rounds

Quarter-Finals 25, 26, 27 May	Semi-Finals 8, 9, 10 June	Final 9 July

Derbyshire†
Middlesex
(£2,500)
⎬ Derbyshire

Glamorgan†
Nottinghamshire
(£2,500)
⎬ Glamorgan†
(£5,000)

⎬ Derbyshire
(£10,500)

Essex†
Warwickshire
(£2,500)
⎬ Essex†
(£5,000)

Worcestershire†
(£2,500)
Hampshire
⎬ Hampshire

⎬ Hampshire

⎬ HAMPSHIRE
(£21,000)

† Home team.
  Prize money in brackets.

Benson & Hedges Cup Winners

1972	Leicestershire	1978	Kent	1984	Lancashire
1973	Kent	1979	Essex	1985	Leicestershire
1974	Surrey	1980	Northamptonshire	1986	Middlesex
1975	Leicestershire	1981	Somerset	1987	Yorkshire
1976	Kent	1982	Somerset	1988	Hampshire
1977	Gloucestershire	1983	Middlesex		

Derbyshire v Hampshire
1988 Benson & Hedges Cup Final

Hampshire won by 7 wickets
Played at Lord's, 9 July
Toss: Hampshire. Umpires: D.J. Constant and N.T. Plews
Man of the Match: S.T. Jefferies (Adjudicator: C.H. Lloyd)

Derbyshire		Runs	Mins	Balls	6	4
K.J. Barnett*	b Jefferies	13	22	19	–	1
P.D. Bowler	c Nicholas b Jefferies	4	29	22	–	1
B. Roberts	c Nicholas b Jefferies	0	9	5	–	–
J.E. Morris	run out (Cowley/Parks)	42	108	79	–	4
S.C. Goldsmith	lbw b Jefferies	0	5	2	–	–
B.J.M. Maher†	b Ayling	8	67	52	–	–
M.A. Holding	c Turner b Cowley	7	8	16	–	1
P.G. Newman	b Connor	10	62	56	–	–
A.E. Warner	b Jefferies	4	31	25	–	–
O.H. Mortensen	not out	0	9	5	–	–
D.E. Malcolm	b Connor	0	1	1	–	–
Extras	(LB14, W12, NB3)	29				
	(46.3 overs; 183 minutes)	**117**				

Hampshire		Runs	Mins	Balls	6	4
V.P. Terry	c Roberts b Malcolm	2	15	13	–	–
C.L. Smith	c Maher b Mortensen	20	70	51	–	3
M.C.J. Nicholas*	not out	35	108	88	–	4
R.A. Smith	c Goldsmith b Warner	38	30	27	–	7
D.R. Turner	not out	7	21	17	–	–
J.R. Ayling	did not bat					
S.T. Jefferies	,,					
R.J. Parks†	,,					
N.G. Cowley	,,					
C.A. Connor	,,					
S.J.W. Andrew	,,					
Extras	(LB8, W3, NB5)	16				
	(31.5 overs; 125 minutes)	**118-3**				

Hampshire	O	M	R	W
Connor	7.3	1	27	2
Jefferies	10	3	13	5
Andrew	9	0	25	0
Ayling	9	2	21	1
Cowley	11	2	17	1

Derbyshire	O	M	R	W
Holding	11	2	36	0
Malcolm	7	2	25	1
Newman	3	1	11	0
Mortensen	5	1	19	1
Warner	5.5	0	19	1

Fall of Wickets		
Wkt	D	H
1st	27	10
2nd	28	44
3rd	29	90
4th	32	–
5th	71	–
6th	80	–
7th	101	–
8th	114	–
9th	117	–
10th	117	–

NatWest Bank Trophy

Even though the corporate form of their batsmen was erratic, Middlesex were too good a side to finish the season empty-handed. And it was the premier one-day competition they won to provide their captain, Mike Gatting, with one pleasant memory of his benefit summer which, from other viewpoints, including a personal one, was distressing.

Right through to the final, in which they beat Worcestershire, Middlesex contemptuously set aside Hertfordshire, Yorkshire, Kent, and Surrey, whom they outplayed at The Oval, where they had lost all their five previous matches in this competition.

Middlesex seemed half-way to winning the final when Gatting won the toss and earned the option of bowling first on a pitch retaining moisture from its preparation. The issue looked virtually settled when Worcestershire, having consumed almost a third of their overs, were 21 for three. Although a captain's innings of 64 from Phil Neale, with noble support from David Leatherdale and Martin Weston, revived them, Worcestershire, with a total of only 161, were on the ropes.

But Middlesex directed their knock-out blows at themselves, rather than at their opponents, and would have laid themselves out but for Mark Ramprakash, 18 and playing his maiden NatWest match. Out when Middlesex, who won by three wickets, were only three runs from their objective, Ramprakash's 56 was as much a triumph of temperament as skill.

The value of the toss cannot be exaggerated, nor the problems posed by a 10.30 start. But Worcestershire's early plight also reflected new-ball bowling of superlative quality by Norman Cowans and Angus Fraser. Their accuracy permitted Worcestershire only four scoring shots in their first 12 overs, and the great Graeme Hick just one in 26 balls.

Cheshire became only the sixth minor county to get to the second round beating 1987 runners-up, Northants. Last year's winning captain, Clive Rice, could work no wonders for Scotland against Glamorgan. In the one first-round clash between first-class counties, Michael Holding took 8 Sussex wickets for 21, a new record in limited-overs cricket.

In the second round, badly disrupted by the weather, Cheshire gave Derbyshire a fright – through a hat-trick by left-arm spinner John O'Brien – but did no more. At the quarter-finals stage, Derbyshire were the only side unable to exploit home advantage. In a repeat of the Benson & Hedges final, played three weeks earlier, they were beaten by Hampshire by four wickets.

Conversely, the semi-finals were both won by sides batting first, Middlesex – who chose to do so – and Worcestershire, against whom Hampshire suffered from having to bat on a very murky evening.

It was precisely because the forecast was for a morning of settled weather and bright sunshine that Gatting took the calculated risk of batting first against Sylvester Clarke on a fresh Oval pitch. Alec Stewart scored the only century of the round, but it served only to give Surrey respectability in defeat.

Gillette Cup Winners

1963	Sussex	1969	Yorkshire	1975	Lancashire
1964	Sussex	1970	Lancashire	1976	Northamptonshire
1965	Yorkshire	1971	Lancashire	1977	Middlesex
1966	Warwickshire	1972	Lancashire	1978	Sussex
1967	Kent	1973	Gloucestershire	1979	Somerset
1968	Warwickshire	1974	Kent	1980	Middlesex

NatWest Bank Trophy Winners

1981 Derbyshire   1982 Surrey   1983 Somerset   1984 Middlesex   1985 Essex
1986 Sussex   1987 Notts   1988 Middlesex

1988 Tournament

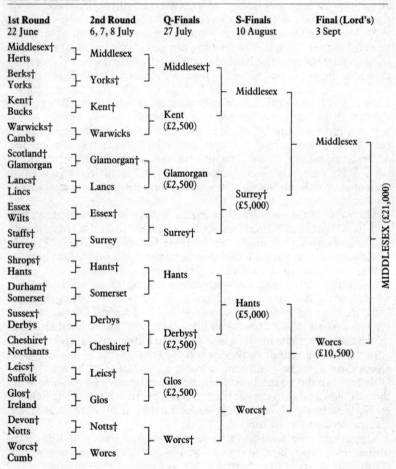

1st Round 22 June	2nd Round 6, 7, 8 July	Q-Finals 27 July	S-Finals 10 August	Final (Lord's) 3 Sept
Middlesex† Herts	Middlesex	Middlesex†	Middlesex	Middlesex
Berks† Yorks	Yorks†			
Kent† Bucks	Kent†	Kent (£2,500)		
Warwicks† Cambs	Warwicks		Surrey† (£5,000)	
Scotland† Glamorgan	Glamorgan†	Glamorgan (£2,500)		
Lancs† Lincs	Lancs			
Essex Wilts	Essex†	Surrey†		
Staffs† Surrey	Surrey			
Shrops† Hants	Hants†	Hants	Hants (£5,000)	
Durham† Somerset	Somerset			Worcs (£10,500)
Sussex† Derbys	Derbys	Derbys† (£2,500)		
Cheshire† Northants	Cheshire†			
Leics† Suffolk	Leics†	Glos (£2,500)		
Glos† Ireland	Glos		Worcs†	
Devon† Notts	Notts†	Worcs†		
Worcs† Cumb	Worcs			

MIDDLESEX (£21,000)

†Home team.
Amounts in brackets show prize-money won by that county.

Middlesex v Worcestershire, 1988 NatWest Bank Trophy Final

Middlesex won by 3 wickets
Played at Lord's, 3 September
Toss: Middlesex. Umpires: H.D. Bird and D.R. Shepherd
Man of the Match: M.R. Ramprakash (Adjudicator: G. Boycott)

Worcestershire		Runs	Mins	Balls	6	4
T.S. Curtis	b Fraser	4	6	7	–	–
S.J. O'Shaughnessy	c Downton b Cowans	1	31	23	–	–
G.A. Hick	b Fraser	4	36	26	–	1
D.A. Leatherdale	b Needham	29	97	89	–	–
P.A. Neale*	b Hughes	64	144	143	–	5
M.J. Weston	c Downton b Fraser	31	46	41	–	3
S.J. Rhodes†	c Emburey b Hughes	1	3	5	–	–
P.J. Newport	b Hughes	4	9	8	–	–
N.V. Radford	b Hughes	5	8	8	–	–
R.K. Illingworth	not out	6	10	7	–	–
G.R. Dilley	,,	2	4	5	–	–
Extras	(LB7, W1, NB2)	10				
	(60 overs; 206 minutes)	**161-9**				

Middlesex		Runs	Mins	Balls	6	4
W.N. Slack	b Dilley	14	59	47	–	2
J.D. Carr	c Rhodes b Dilley	1	9	5	–	–
A. Needham	b Dilley	6	37	22	–	–
M.W. Gatting*	run out (O'Shaughnessy/Rhodes)	0	1	0	–	–
R.O. Butcher	run out (Hick/Illingworth)	24	65	47	–	2
M.R. Ramprakash	c Radford b Dilley	56	154	123	–	4
J.E. Emburey	b Dilley	35	87	78	–	2
P.R. Downton†	not out	8	14	11	–	1
S.P. Hughes	not out	0	5	3	–	–
A.R.C. Fraser	did not bat					
N.G. Cowans						
Extras	(B4, LB5, W7, NB2)	18				
	(55.3 overs; 222 minutes)	**162-7**				

Middlesex	O	M	R	W
Cowans	12	6	23	1
Fraser	12	5	36	3
Carr	4	1	9	0
Hughes	8	0	30	4
Needham	12	1	25	1
Emburey	12	3	31	0

Worcestershire	O	M	R	W
Dilley	12	3	29	5
Radford	11.3	3	37	0
Illingworth	12	4	24	0
Newport	10	1	20	0
Weston	2	0	9	0
Hick	5	0	19	0
O'Shaughnessy	3	0	15	0

Fall of Wickets

Wkt	Wo	M
1st	5	3
2nd	8	21
3rd	9	21
4th	71	25
5th	137	64
6th	140	149
7th	145	159
8th	148	–
9th	153	–
10th	–	–

Refuge Assurance League

Worcestershire, the holders, comfortably retained the Sunday League Championship, but it was Lancashire, who finished in third place, who went on to win the four-team 'play-off' for the new Refuge Assurance Cup.

The League competition started particularly well for the three Metropolitan counties, of whom only Surrey (7th) had finished in the top half of the 1987 table. After five Sundays, Middlesex and Surrey shared the lead with three wins and one no-result, while Essex were equal third with Glamorgan – three wins and two defeats each.

With the onset of the international season, however, Essex suffered from a growing demand on their key players, Gooch, Pringle, Foster, and Childs, while, conversely, Gatting, Emburey, and Downton were subsequently 'released' and returned to full-time duty with Middlesex.

Surrey, meanwhile, having struck a barren patch as June went into July – a tie against Derby, a washout against Warwicks, and defeat by Worcestershire – began, like Essex, to slip out of contention. Their most significant lapse came on August 7, at Ebbw Vale, when a side lacking Clinton, Smith, Lynch, Richards, and Clarke was beaten by Glamorgan, who thereby moved effectively into fifth place.

On the same day, Gloucestershire, who had never been out of the top six, beat Yorkshire at Cheltenham, to slide into joint third place with Lancashire, who, at the half-way stage, had been neck and neck with Middlesex. Lancashire's worst hiccup came in mid-July when they lost consecutive games – against Somerset and Essex – and it ultimately proved decisive.

In the meantime, what of Notts, the 1987 runners-up? Alas, nowhere was the retirement of Hadlee and Rice more keenly felt than in the Sunday League where, as the season drew to its close, they languished at the bottom of the table with their Leicestershire neighbours.

With three weeks to go, Worcestershire were on 38 points, Lancashire and Gloucestershire 36 each, while Middlesex, though technically ahead with 40 points, had only two games to play – the first against Gloucestershire at Lord's.

This they narrowly managed to win on faster scoring rate, but Lancashare and Worcestershire also won, and when both collected four more points, the following week, Worcester went top with 46 points with Lancs and Middlesex joint second and Gloucestershire fourth. Worcester duly won the league title by six clear points, and when Lancs and Middlesex lost their final matches, Gloucestershire joined Worcestershire as hosts in the Cup semi-finals.

Final Table

	P	W	L	T	NR	Pts	6s	4w
1 WORCESTERSHIRE (1)	16	12	3	0	1	50	27	6
2 Gloucestershire (3)	16	10	4	0	2	44	31	2
3 Lancashire (9)	16	10	4	0	2	44	25	2
4 Middlesex (10)	16	9	3	0	4	44	24	1
5 Surrey (7)	16	8	5	1	2	38	28	3
6 Glamorgan (14)	16	8	5	1	2	38	30	2
7 Kent (6)	16	7	6	0	3	34	27	3
8 Yorkshire (12)	16	7	7	0	2	32	29	5
9 Hampshire (7)	16	7	8	0	1	30	11	3
10 Essex (14)	16	6	8	1	1	28	24	3
11 Warwickshire (8)	16	6	8	0	2	28	14	3
12 Somerset (4)	16	6	9	0	1	26	23	1
13 Derbyshire (5)	16	5	8	1	2	26	30	1
14 Northamptonshire (10)	16	4	9	0	3	22	23	0
15 Sussex (14)	16	4	9	2	1	22	15	1
16 Leicestershire (12)	16	4	9	0	3	22	13	3
17 Nottinghamshire (2)	16	3	11	0	2	16	13	1

The final positions for teams finishing with equal points are decided by (a) most points, (b) most wins, (c) most away wins, (d) run-rate.
The first four teams also qualified for the Refuge Assurance Cup. 1987 positions are shown in brackets.

Sunday League Winners

1969	Lancashire	1976	Kent	1983	Yorkshire
1970	Lancashire	1977	Leicestershire	1984	Essex
1971	Worcestershire	1978	Hampshire	1985	Essex
1972	Kent	1979	Somerset	1986	Hampshire
1973	Kent	1980	Warwickshire	1987	Worcestershire
1974	Leicestershire	1981	Essex	1988	Worcestershire
1975	Hampshire	1982	Sussex		

1988 Awards

£21,000 and League Trophy to champions WORCESTERSHIRE; £10,500 to runners-up Gloucestershire; £4,750 to third-placing Lancashire; £2,750 to fourth-placing Middlesex; £275 to winner of each match (shared in the event of 'no results' and ties). £400 to the batsman hitting most sixes in the season: R.J. Shastri (Glamorgan) 14; £400 to the bowler taking four or more wickets most times in the season: S.D. Fletcher (Yorkshire) 3; £250 to the batsman scoring the fastest 50 in a match televised on BBC2: D.B. D'Oliveira (Worcestershire) – 31 balls v Nottinghamshire at Worcester on May 1.

Refuge Assurance Cup

Lancashire reached the final at Edgbaston, on September 18, by narrowly beating Gloucestershire in a low-scoring match at Bristol. Accordingly, Worcestershire – having disposed of Middlesex fairly competently in the other semi-final, at Worcester, were warm favourites to win the Cup – especially when they won the toss.

Worcester's prospects seemed even brighter when Lancs made a disastrous start by losing Mendis and Hayhurst for four runs. However, after Fowler and Fairbrother had steadied the ship, in came Jesty to hit 59 off 60 balls and, in company with Watkinson, spur Lancs to a useful 201 for five.

In reply, Worcester also lost two cheap wickets – the most telling, perhaps, that of Hick, bowled by Watkinson for two. But, unlike Lancashire, there followed no substantial consolidation, so that Leather-dale, Curtis, and the gallant Neale all subsequently surrendered their wickets to the mounting strike-requirement.

In the event, Hayhurst cashed in with four for 46 and Worcestershire were beaten by 52 runs in 35.5 overs.

Semi-finals (played on September 7)
LANCASHIRE beat GLOUCESTERSHIRE by 3 wickets at Bristol. Toss: Lancashire. Gloucestershire 117-9 (40 overs) (A.W. Stovold 40, J. Simmons 8-1-14-3). Lancashire 121-7 (39.5 overs). Award: P.J.W. Allott (8-4-14-2 and 16*).

WORCESTERSHIRE beat MIDDLESEX by 7 wickets at Worcester. Toss: Worcestershire. Middlesex 146-9 (40 overs) (P.R. Downton 30*; N.V. Radford 8-1-23-4, R.K. Illingworth 8-0-29-3). Worcestershire 147-3 (38.4 overs) (G.A. Hick 74*, D.A. Leatherdale 41). Award: G.A. Hick (74*).

Final (played on September 18 at Edgbaston)
LANCASHIRE beat WORCESTERSHIRE by 52 runs. Toss: Worcestershire. Lancashire 201-5 (40 overs) (T.E. Jesty 59, M. Watkinson 42*, N.H. Fairbrother 38). Worcestershire 149 (35.5 overs) (P.A. Neale 42, T.S. Curtis 32, D.A. Leatherdale 30; A.N. Hayhurst 8-0-46-4, I.D. Austin 7.5-0-51-3). Award: M. Watkinson (42*, 6-2-10-1, and 1ct).

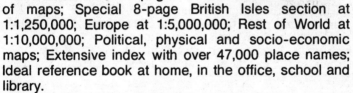

Second XI Competition

Surrey won their final match against Sussex at Hove to take the 2nd XI championship and deny Worcestershire, the Britannic Assurance champions, a first and second team double.

Mark Frost, a Staffordshire fast-bowler plucked out of minor county cricket at the age of 25, rewarded Surrey's judgement with 48 wickets, despite missing nearly half the games with an ankle injury. Neil Kendrick, slow left-arm, and James Boiling, the Durham University off-spinner who won the *Daily Telegraph* bowling award when at Rutlish School, added balance to a very effective attack. Surrey's batting was dominated by Darren Bicknell (883 runs at an average of 49.06), Zahid Sadiq, and Graham Thorpe, an 18-year-old who scored a maiden first-team century against Cambridge University.

David Callaghan, a South African on a cricket scholarship with Nottinghamshire, scored heavily to finish with 934 runs, including five hundreds.

Simon Kellett, 21 in October, marked himself as a good Yorkshire prospect with 916 runs (average 41.63). Two first-teamers, Kevin Sharp (238 not out) and David Bairstow (130 not out), rediscovered their batting form by putting on 242 for the fourth wicket in a total of 514 for three against Somerset at Taunton.

Yorkshire won the 55-over Bain Clarkson Trophy, beating Kent by seven wickets in the Headingley final. Simon Hinks (88) helped Kent, last year's championship titleholders, to 270 for eight, but David Byas (91) took Yorkshire home with two overs to spare.

There was a huge 55-over game match aggregate of 632 runs at Canterbury in the qualifiers: Kent 360 for seven (Trevor Ward 129), Middlesex 272 (45.2 overs).

Second XI Championship Final Table

					Bonus Pts		Total	
	P	W	L	D	Bat	Bowl	Pts	Avge
1 SURREY (8)	17	8	0	9	45	48	221	13.00
2 Worcestershire (12)	15	7	2	6	38	34	184	12.27
3 Nottinghamshire (15)	15	6	3	6	29	41	166	11.07
4 Essex (11)	15	4	5	6	40	50	154	10.27
5 Lancashire (3)	20	6	2	12	42	57	195	9.75
6 Warwickshire (6)	17	5	3	9	31	47	158	9.29
7 Hampshire (5)	14	4	2	8	24	39	127	9.07
8 Middlesex (14)	15	4	0	11	38	32	134	8.93
9 Yorkshire (1)	16	4	1	11	43	28	135	8.44
10 Sussex (4)	14	2	5	7	28	52	112	8.00
11 Northamptonshire (13)	17	3	4	10	37	41	126	7.41
12 Glamorgan (7)	12	2	5	5	20	27	79	6.58
13 Kent (1)	16	1	6	9	37	52	105	6.56
14 Derbyshire (17)	14	1	5	8	16	39	71	5.07
15 Leicestershire (10)	18	1	6	11	27	48	91	5.06
16 Somerset (9)	15	0	5	10	36	35	71	4.73
17 Gloucestershire (16)	14	0	4	10	19	35	54	3.86

Glamorgan had two matches abandoned without a ball being bowled.
Nottinghamshire and Warwickshire each had one match abandoned. Figures in parentheses denote last season's position.

Warwick Under-25 Competition

Zonal Group A	P	W	L	NR	Pts		Zonal Group C	P	W	L	T	Pts
LANCASHIRE	3	3	0	0	12		SURREY	3	3	0	0	12
Derbyshire	3	2	1	0	8		Kent	3	1	1	1	6
Yorkshire	3	1	2	0	4		Sussex	3	0	1	2	4
Nottinghamshire	3	0	3	0	0		Hampshire	3	0	2	1	2

Zonal Group B	P	W	L	NR	Pts		Zonal Group D	P	W	L	NR	Pts
MIDDLESEX	3	2	0	1	10		WARWICKSHIRE	4	4	0	0	16
Leicestershire	3	2	1	0	8		Glamorgan	4	3	1	0	12
Essex	3	1	1	1	6		Worcestershire	4	2	2	0	8
Northamptonshire	3	0	3	0	0		Somerset	4	1	3	0	4
							Gloucestershire	4	0	4	0	0

Semi-Finals
LANCASHIRE beat Middlesex by 9 wickets
WARWICKSHIRE beat Surrey by 6 wickets

Final
WARWICKSHIRE beat Lancashire by 5 runs

Bain Clarkson Trophy

North Zone	P	W	L	NR	Pts		South-East Zone	P	W	L	NR	Pts
YORKSHIRE	10	7	2	1	15		KENT	10	6	1	3	15
Lancashire	10	6	3	1	13		Surrey	10	7	2	1	15
Derbyshire	10	6	4	0	12		Middlesex	10	5	5	0	10
Northamptonshire	10	4	4	2	10		Sussex	10	3	5	2	8
Nottinghamshire	10	3	7	0	6		Hampshire	10	3	6	1	7
Leicestershire	10	2	8	0	4		Essex	10	2	7	1	5

South-West Zone	P	W	L	NR	Pts
WORCESTERSHIRE	8	6	2	0	12
Warwickshire	8	4	3	1	9
Somerset	8	3	4	1	7
Glamorgan	8	3	4	1	7
Gloucestershire	8	2	5	1	5

Round Robin
Kent beat Worcestershire by 46 runs
Worcestershire beat Yorkshire by 8 wickets
Yorkshire beat Kent by 8 wickets

Final
Warwickshire beat Lancashire by 5 runs

Minor Counties

It was Cheshire's turn in 1988 to make the headlines in the NatWest Trophy, not only with their thrilling victory over Northamptonshire but by virtue of one of their strong hand of spinners – John O'Brien – performing the hat-trick in the second round match with Derbyshire. Cheshire then, having comfortably headed the Western Division of the Championship, set the seal on a splendid season by defeating Cambridgeshire in the play-off at Worcester to take the Carphone Group Trophy and Championship. Dorset, too, had a notable success, taking the Holt Cup – the first ever title in the county's history. Sympathy must be expressed for Cambridgeshire who for the second year in succession lost in both finals.

Earlier in the season the Representative XI, while not causing any upsets in the Benson & Hedges zonal matches, nonetheless played their full part in providing good cricket at Darlington (against Northamptonshire) and at Headingley. Later they played West Indies, but weather interference gave them only a token five overs' response to the predictably mammoth visitors' total. In contrast, against Sri Lanka, in two days of glorious sunshine and excellent batting, they had rather the better of a drawn match.

Minor Counties Championship

E. Division	P	W	L	Drawn U	T	B	NR	Pts		W. Division	P	W	L	Drawn U	T	B	NR	Pts
1 Cambs*	9	5	0	1	0	2	1	57		1 Cheshire*	9	5	1¹	1	0	1	0	62
2 Durham*	9	3	1	4	0	1	0	43		2 Berks*	9	3	2	4	0	0	0	42
3 Staffs*	9	3	2¹	2	0	1	1	42		3 Dorset*	9	3	1	2	1	2	0	40
4 Suffolk*	9	2	2¹	5	0	0	0	38		4 Oxon*	9	1	1¹	4	1	0	0	33
5 Herts*	9	2	2²	0	0	3	2	33		5 Wilts*	9	2	2	1	0	3	1	28
6 C'berland*	9	2	1¹	1	1	4	0	32		6 Shrops*	9	1	1¹	3	0	4	0	26
7 N'berland*	9	1	3	3	1	1	0	25		7 Devon	9	1	1	2	1	3	1	23
8 Norfolk	9	1	2	2	0	4	0	20		8 Bucks	9	1	3¹	2	0	3	0	22
9 Beds	9	0	2²	2	0	5	0	17		9 Wales	9	0	3²	3	1	1	1	20
10 Lincs	9	0	4¹	2	0	1	2	14		10 Cornwall	9	1	3	0	0	4	1	16

Points: 10 for win; 2 for no result (NR); 1st innings points – U = up (3 pts), T = tied (2), B = Behind (1); 3 for 1st innings lead in match lost – superior figure in lost (L) column indicates number of times points gained in matches lost. *Qualified for 1989 NatWest Bank Trophy.

Leading Averages

Batting	I	NO	HS	Runs	Avge		Bowling	O	M	R	W	Avge
P.R. Oliver	11	5	136*	459	76.50		S. Dyson	107.3	38	206	23	8.96
T.A. Lester	16	6	97*	679	67.90		P.J. Lewington	302.5	94	658	54	12.19
I. Cockbain	15	4	119	681	61.91		S. Turner	346.4	90	763	58	13.16
I.S. Lawrence	17	4	144	787	60.54		G. Edwards	126.4	52	283	20	14.15
S.G. Plumb	16	1	204*	830	55.33		R.C. Green	206.2	51	614	39	15.74
A.R. Harwood	10	2	142*	434	54.25		R. Ellwood	189	52	491	31	15.84
N.A. Riddell	12	5	63	367	52.43		D. Surridge	156	42	387	23	16.83
M.J. Roberts	8	1	155*	338	48.29		D. Marshall	206.5	53	509	30	16.97
N.G. Roberts	·15	2	103*	617	47.46		J. Thompson	135	38	360	21	17.14
P.J. Garner	16	3	94*	601	46.23		M.G. Boocock	139.5	43	363	21	17.29

Knock-out Competition

Holt Cup Final: At Weymouth, 24th July. DORSET beat CAMBRIDGESHIRE by 2 wickets (50 overs). Cambridgeshire 123-9 (Stuart 3-32); Dorset 127-8 (49.2 overs) (Stone 34*, Turner 3-12, Collard 3-26).

Cheshire v Cambridgeshire, Minor Counties Championship Play-off

Cheshire won by 13 runs
Played at the County Ground, Worcester, 11 September 1988 (55 overs)
Match sponsored by The Carphone Group
Toss: Cambridgeshire. Umpires: C. Smith, R.T. Wilson. *Captain   †Wicket-keeper

Cheshire

B. Wood	b Benson	24
J.J. Hitchmough	run out	9
I. Cockbain	b Collard	26
D.W. Varey	b Turner	67
*N.T. O'Brien	lbw b Benson	2
S.T. Crawley	c Collard b Lethbridge	16
† S. Bramhall	lbw b Lethbridge	9
J.S. Hitchmough	c Lethbridge b Collard	19
S. Dyson	c Garnham b Lethbridge	0
A.J. Murphy	c Dicks b Lethbridge	5
J.F.M. O'Brien	not out	2
Extras		12
	(53.3 overs)	**191**

Cambridgeshire

*N.T. Gadsby	b Dyson	28
I.S. Lawrence	c & b Dyson	18
†M.A. Garnham	c & b J.S. Hitchmough	4
J.D.R. Benson	B J.M.F. O'Brien	30
P.A. Redfarn	c Dyson b Murphy	37
N.J. Adams	not out	1
S. Turner	run out	1
P.J. Dicks	c Dyson b Murphy	37
C. Lethbridge	b Dyson	0
D.C. Collard	b Murphy	3
M.G. Stephenson	not out	1
Extras		18
	(54.2 overs)	**178-9**

Cheshire	O	M	R	W
Turner	10	2	34	1
Lethbridge	10.3	2	47	4
Benson	11	1	34	2
Collard	11	2	54	2
Stephenson	11	3	18	0

Cambridgeshire	O	M	R	W
Murphy	10.2	1	41	3
J.S. Hitchmough	11	2	29	1
Dyson	11	1	30	3
J.F.M. O'Brien	11	0	27	1
N.T. O'Brien	6	1	20	0
Wood	5	1	19	0

Fall of Wickets

Wkt	Ch	C
1st	13	40
2nd	54	51
3rd	78	63
4th	81	107
5th	123	115
6th	135	116
7th	176	166
8th	183	168
9th	187	171
10th	191	–

Village and Club Cricket

Both national 'grass roots' finals at Lord's suffered from atrocious weather conditions, despite tremendous care by Mick Hunt and his staff. The four captains concerned with the 'headquarters' finals rightly decided each match should be fully played out – or abandoned to another venue and date. Unfortunately this happened on both days. However, each replayed final provided a fine match, with Enfield of Middlesex winning the Cockspur Cup, the senior club competition, and Wiltshire's heroic Goatacre emerging as national village club champions in the Hydro Trophy.

At Lord's on 19 August, Enfield, put in by Wolverhampton, had scored 104 for two wickets in 31 overs before torrential rain ended all hope of resumption. The final was transferred to Edgbaston on 24 August when Wolverhampton chose to bat.

After an opening stand of 50, only Jones, their captain, offered any real resistance. Heavy rain intervened but the Warwickshire ground staff coped quickly, and Enfield, needing 165, still had time for a full innings. This was launched by Allen and Sandrock with an opening stand of 141, and Enfield won by 9 wickets with 10 overs to spare. They received £1,250, the runners-up £750.

The Cockspur Cup (45 overs). Edgbaston, 24 August. Wolverhampton won toss. Wolverhampton 164-9 (R. Griffin 48, D. Lampitt 30; A. Roach 3-35, A. Higgs 3-40). Enfield 165-1 (J.A. Allen 119 not out, G.W. Sandrock 30). **Enfield won by 9 wickets.**

The Hydro National Village Championship met similar misfortune at Lord's. Himley, seven miles from Wolverhampton, were put in and completed their 40 overs, making 207 for six wickets. The rain allowed only one over to Goatacre and the abandoned final was rearranged at the Midland Bank ground at Beckenham.

Kevin Iles, captain of Goatacre and grandson of the club's founder, started a day of personal triumph by again winning the toss and putting Himley in. Walker scored a good 75, but Iles stepped in to take four wickets and the West Midlanders were all out for 192. Goatacre started badly and fell behind the required run rate until Iles took command. His unbeaten 91 included six sixes, and at the start of the final over Goatacre needed eight runs to win. Iles remained at the non-striker's end as Butler hit successive boundaries. Goatacre won £700, Himley £400. During 1988, Iles set a competition record of five centuries in this competition, which was founded in 1972 and is organized by *The Cricketer*.

Hydro National Village Championship (40 overs). Beckenham, Kent, 21 August. Goatacre won toss. Himley 192 (S. Walker 75; K. Iles 4-46). Goatacre 193-6 (K. Iles 91 not out). **Goatacre won by four wickets.**

Schools and Youth Cricket

The demands of the new GCSE examination caused some diminution in mid-week fixture lists and many schools who advanced the end of term to very early July lost some Saturday games. Fortunately, post-term festival matches are more and more popular and helped bridge the gap before the start of MCC Schools Festival at Oxford in the middle of the month.

Any number of promising young cricketers were on show, many, of course, not exam-tied, but auguring well for the future – though some behavioural standards often suffered from attempted 'replays' of the televised ill manners of their seniors. Nicholas Knight, captain of Felsted, was far and away the outstanding schoolboy batsman of the season and led his sides well. From Ipswich School, Nadim Shahid was again the best young bowler, showing remarkable maturity of control of flight and spin with leg-breaks, top-spinner, and googly. Both he and Knight are on Essex's books.

Others who caught the eye were Kellaway of Eastleigh, a very fine young wicket-keeper-batsman, the Erith twins – James, captain of Eton, and Edward of Haileybury – whose fast-bowling actions are almost identical, including a knack of taking equal numbers of wickets, often seven, in different matches. Fleming, also of Eton, not only bowled slow left-arm with skill, but got through his overs in a shade under two minutes apiece – *not* as seen on TV. Impressive fast bowlers were Ellison (Rugby), Headley (RGS, Worcester), Cousins (Wellington), Ilott (Francis Combe, Watford), Challinor (RGS, Guildford), Houseman (Harrogate GS), and Derbyshire (Ampleforth).

Many festivals suffered from early July rain. But one beautiful day at Eastbourne, Felsted had a splendid win by four wickets over Tonbridge, overtaking 264-5 with one ball and four wickets to spare. And to this high-scoring match on the large Memorial Ground, Knight, hero of Felsted, contributed only two runs. One of the more enterprising events was the Royal Grammar Schools festival, where Worcester played hosts in 1988 to Guildford, High Wycombe, and Colchester.

MCC's Schools Festival at Oxford is much valued, combining as it does the best of the English Schools Cricket Association and Headmasters Conference Schools players. The first two days are separate ESCA and HMC trials. Then 44 boys, selected regardless of school, play two one-day trial games, the best 22 going forward to the final trial on the Christ Church ground to determine a side to move on to Lord's. In the trials, Aftab Habib of Taunton scored 100, 53, and 41 – each not out – and Knight of Felsted was chosen to lead MCC Schools at Lord's against MCC and a National Association of Young Cricketers XI on 20 and 21 July. The team:

N.V. Knight (Felsted, captain), J.J. Lewis (King Edward VI, Chelmsford), D.A. Graham (Chipping Campden), A. Habib (Taunton), N. Shahid and J. Gregory (Ipswich), B.C.A. Ellison (Rugby), M.J. Kellaway (Eastleigh Coll. of Education, wicket-keeper), M.J.C. Ball (Bath C of E), I.J. Houseman (Harrogate GS), M.C. Ilott (Francis Combe, Watford); N.A. Derbyshire (Ampleforth) replaced Houseman against NAYC.

Against the Club, MCC Schools received a salutary lesson in the art of slow left-arm bowling from head coach Don Wilson (England and Yorkshire). MCC batted first on a rain-affected pitch and were bowled out for 137. Ball of Bath, bowling off-spin round the wicket, took five wickets and Shahid picked up two more with leg-spin. Kellaway, as always, kept wicket impeccably. The Schools seemed to have few problems against a modest target, until Wilson came on at the Nursery End after Knight and Lewis had opened with 45. The head coach then bowled unchanged to have figures of 18.4-9-22-6 and the boys were all out for 114, losing by 23.

Lord's, 20 July. MCC won toss. MCC 137 (S. Mohammed 37; M.J.C. Ball 5-42). MCC Schools 114 (D. Wilson 6-22). MCC won by 23 runs.

The following day NAYC won the toss and batted first, only to find Shahid and Ilott, fast left-arm, in top form. The Ipswich School leg-spinner took four for 51 and Ilott, already with Essex successes to his credit, three for 72. Bailey of Staffordshire top-scored with 34 in a total of 191. Knight and Lewis again gave MCC Schools a good start, Habib hit a splendidly controlled 60 and victory by six wickets came in the 48th over.

Lord's 21 July. National Association of Young Cricketers XI won toss. NAYC 191 (N. Shahid 4-51; M. Ilott 3-72). MCC Schools 192-4 (A. Habib 60). MCC Schools won by 6 wickets.

The match between a National Cricket Association YC XI, captained by Knight, and Combined Services was abandoned as a draw following mid-afternoon rain. NCA YC won the toss and fielded, Services making 228-5 declared. NCA had time for only 28 overs, during which they made 113-4, with Simmonite of Lancashire well established with 62 not out.

To celebrate the 40th anniversary of their Schools Cricket Associations, Sri Lanka sent an Under-17 side to tour England, and for the first time in this age group English Schools played at international level; the tour was not blessed by good weather. Each country won a one-day international, but the decider, at The Oval, was washed out. Rain ruined the first three-day match at Taunton. The second three-day 'Test' was a splendid match at Canterbury, where in a thrilling last day Sri Lanka set England a target of 291 at a rate of about five runs an over. The match ended for bad light when England were 43 short of the target with four wickets in hand. Earlier Toby Radford, 107, and Russell Warren, 99, shared an opening stand of 200. Radford, of Park House, Newbury, winner of *The Daily Telegraph* Under-15 batting award for 1987, added a mature century to his first-innings 55.

Canterbury 24, 25, 26 August. Sri Lanka Under-17 174 (J. Silva 54; J. Hallett 5-35) & 303-6 dec (N. Silva 90, J. Silva 60 not out; R. Irani 3-34). England Under-17 187 (T. Radford 55) & 247-6 (T. Radford 107, R. Warren 99; S. Jayawardhana 4-43). Match drawn.

Esso Youth Sport sponsored for the third year the NAYC Under-19 County Festivals at Oxford and Cambridge, when teams from 30 counties took part in 54-overs matches on a round-robin basis. Surrey, winners of the Cambridge section, travelled to Oxford for the final on the Christ Church ground on 13 August against Warwickshire. Surrey put Warwicks in and dismissed them for 162 in the last over. Surrey's innings was dominated by MacMillan of Charterhouse, who was out after scoring 82. Surrey fell behind the rate and needed eight runs from the last over. The last man was run out and Warwickshire had won by seven runs.

ESSO/NAYC Under-19 County Final. Christ Church, Oxford, 13 August. Surrey won toss. Warwickshire 162 (G. Steer 48; C. Cowell 3-43). Surrey 155 (G. MacMillan 82). Warwickshire won by 7 runs.

Women's Cricket

The England Women's Cricket Association's 1988 season saw the creation of a new national league for clubs, the first official county championships, the introduction of a territorial championship, and the nomination of a new England captain.

Jane Powell (31) became England's ninth captain in 54 years of women's Test cricket – a refreshing contrast in length of office compared with the England men's cricket!

Powell (Yorkshire) succeeds Carole Hodges (Lancs & Cheshire), captain since 1985, who made it known at the beginning of the season that she did not wish to be considered. Hodges was in charge against the 1987 touring Australians, when England lost their first ever Test series at home and inferred that she did not have the support of senior players in the dressing-room and on the field.

Powell will lead England in the fourth Women's Cricket World Cup in Australia in November/December, with the final played at the famous Melbourne Cricket Ground. The World Cup will be sponsored by Shell (Australia), and other participants, apart from England and the hosts, will be New Zealand, Holland, and Ireland.

The England World Cup party is: Jane Powell (Yorks, captain) Janette Brittin (Surrey, vice-captain), Jan Aspinall (Yorks), Caroline Barrs (Surrey), Jo Chamberlain (East Midlands), Karen Hicken (East Midlands), Carole Hodges (Lancs & Cheshire), Suzie Kitson (East Anglia), Pat Lovell (Surrey), Denise Maybury (Yorks), Lisa Nye (Middlesex, wicket-keeper), Gill Smith (Middlesex), Claire Taylor (Yorks), Wendy Watson (East Midlands). Maybury is just 17; Chamberlain, Hicken, and Kitson are 19.

The team selection caused unrest among members, and they called for the sacking of selectors who had curiously omitted Avril Starling (Middlesex), holder of the world record number of wickets taken in a Test series, and Amanda Stinson (Yorks), who had made such a fine wicket-keeping debut two years ago against India. The call for an extraordinary meeting was defeated, so now the Association waits to see whether the relatively inexperienced side will seriously challenge Australia's hold on the world cup.

The County Championships were played over five days on various university grounds at Cambridge. Ten teams took part. Yorkshire won Pool A and Surrey took Pool B after beating East Midlands in the deciding match. Batsman of the tournament was deposed England captain Carole Hodges, who scored 293 runs (including one century) for once out in four innings. Pace bowler Jo Chamberlain took 15 wickets at an average of 5.46.

The final was played three weeks later at Chigwell. Yorkshire made 162-6 off 55 overs; Surrey had a rain-reduced target of 148. In the end they needed 20 runs off six overs with 5 wickets in hand, but they failed by two runs. Janette Brittin top-scored for Surrey with 41, and took four catches and two wickets.

In the inaugural Territorial Championship at Oxford, spanning three days, North, led by Powell, dominated, winning all their matches. Only two half-centuries were scored in six games – by Brittin (South) and Watson (Mid-West). Sarah Cook (East), who has been handicapped by deafness since birth, was the pick of the bowlers.

Twenty-four teams contested the first ever national league title zoned into four regions. The group winners were Wakefield, Redoubtables (Surrey), Vagabonds (Herts), and Somerset Wanderers. Torrential rain washed out the semi-finals at Berkhamsted. Somerset and Redoubtables progressed to the final on the highest number of bonus points in the regional matches, but again the weather won the day at the final and the trophy was shared.

Wolverhampton won the National Clubs Knock-Out for the first time in the 15 years of the competition. They beat holders Vagabonds in a low-scoring final on an under-prepared wicket at Brunel University, Uxbridge, to register a triumph for their new captain, Rachel Kirk, who formerly played for Vagabonds.

County Championships

Pool A: Yorkshire 79, Middlesex 63½, East Anglia 52, West 35½, Thames Valley 24½.

Pool B: Surrey 83½, East Midlands 70, Kent 49½, Lancs & Cheshire 39, Sussex 18.

Final

August 21, Chigwell (Metropolitan Police CG). YORKSHIRE beat SURREY by 2 runs. Yorkshire 162-6 (55 overs) (J. Powell 42). Surrey 146-7 (rain-reduced to 50 overs; target 148) (Jo Brittin 41)

National Club Knock-Out Final

September 3, Brunel University, Uxbridge. WOLVERHAMPTON beat VAGABONDS by 30 runs. Wolverhampton 85-9 (40 overs). Vagabonds 55 (36.1 overs) (J. Crump 3-5).

Trial Matches

September 10, Brinton's CG, Kidderminster. JUNIOR ENGLAND beat YOUNG ENGLAND by 5 wickets. Young England 85 (L. Chapman 4-12, A. Cram 3-9). Junior England 86-5 (D. Maybury 34*).

September 11, Mitchell's & Butlers CG, Edgbaston, Birmingham. PROBABLES beat POSSIBLES by 67 runs. Probables 186-7 (55 overs) (C. Hodges 88). Possibles 119 (54.3 overs) (D. Maybury 3-18).

EXTRAS

Test Career Records

The following individual career averages include all official Test matches to the end of the 1988 English season.

Australia

Batting / Fielding	M	I	NO	HS	R	Avge	100	50	Ct/St
D.C. Boon	28	50	3	184★	1896	40.34	6	9	18
A.R. Border	94	164	27	205	7343	53.59	22	34	102
A.I.C. Dodemaide	3	4	2	50	81	40.50	–	1	1
G.C. Dyer	6	6	0	60	131	21.83	–	1	22/2
M.G. Hughes	7	9	0	16	44	4.88	–	–	4
D.M. Jones	15	27	3	210	1181	49.20	3	5	7
C.J. McDermott	22	29	2	36	277	10.25	–	–	5
G.R. Marsh	19	34	2	118	1210	37.81	3	5	12
T.B.A. May	1	1	1	14★	14	–	–	–	–
B.A. Reid	15	18	9	13	58	6.44	–	–	1
P.R. Sleep	11	17	0	90	401	23.58	–	3	3
P.L. Taylor	3	4	0	42	91	22.75	–	–	1
M.R.J. Veletta	5	6	0	39	127	21.16	–	–	9/–
S.R. Waugh	18	27	4	79★	676	29.39	–	6	18
M.R. Whitney	3	6	2	4	6	1.50	–	–	–

Bowling	Balls	R	W	Avge	Best	5wI	10wM
D.C. Boon	12	5	0	–	–	–	–
A.R. Border	1781	699	16	43.68	3-20	–	–
A.I.C. Dodemaide	757	302	15	20.13	6-58	1	–
M.G. Hughes	1491	792	21	37.71	5-67	1	–
D.M. Jones	90	29	1	29.00	1-5	–	–
C.J. McDermott	4564	2484	73	34.02	8-141	3	–
T.B.A. May	504	202	4	50.50	3-68	–	–
B.A. Reid	3301	1482	48	30.87	4-64	–	–
P.R. Sleep	2419	1153	22	52.40	5-72	1	–
P.L. Taylor	546	241	12	20.08	6-78	1	–
S.R. Waugh	1940	885	28	31.60	5-69	1	–
M.R. Whitney	789	383	9	42.55	4-92	–	–

England

Batting/Fielding	M	I	NO	HS	R	Avge	100	50	Ct/St
C.W.J. Athey	23	41	1	123	919	22.97	1	4	13
R.J. Bailey	1	2	0	43	46	23.00	–	–	–
K.J. Barnett	1	2	0	66	66	33.00	–	1	1
B.C. Broad	23	40	2	162	1579	41.55	6	6	8
D.J. Capel	10	16	0	98	272	17.00	–	2	4
J.H. Childs	2	4	4	2*	2	–	–	–	1
N.G.B. Cook	12	20	1	26	134	7.05	–	–	5
C.S. Cowdrey	6	8	1	38	101	14.42	–	–	5
T.S. Curtis	2	4	0	30	69	17.25	–	–	2
P.A.J. DeFreitas	12	17	1	40	182	11.37	–	–	4
G.R. Dilley	39	55	18	56	479	12.94	–	2	10
P.R. Downton	30	48	8	74	785	19.62	–	4	70/5
J.E. Emburey	56	83	17	75	1409	21.34	–	7	33
N.H. Fairbrother	4	4	0	3	5	1.25	–	–	3
N.A. Foster	25	37	5	39	342	10.68	–	–	6
B.N. French	16	21	4	59	308	18.11	–	1	38/1
M.W. Gatting	67	115	14	207	3848	38.09	9	18	51
G.A. Gooch	68	123	4	196	4541	38.15	8	27	39
D.I. Gower	100	172	13	215	7000	44.02	14	35	68
E.E. Hemmings	8	12	3	95	207	23.00	–	1	4
P.W. Jarvis	4	6	2	29*	76	19.00	–	–	–
A.J. Lamb	56	98	9	137*	2969	33.35	8	12	53
D.V. Lawrence	1	1	0	4	4	4.00	–	–	–
M.P. Maynard	1	2	0	10	13	6.50	–	–	–
M.D. Moxon	9	15	1	99	437	31.21	–	3	10
P.J. Newport	1	1	0	26	26	26.00	–	–	–
D.R. Pringle	19	33	3	63	479	15.96	–	1	7
N.V. Radford	3	4	1	12*	21	7.00	–	–	–
C.J. Richards	8	13	0	133	285	21.92	1	–	20/1
R.T. Robinson	28	47	5	175	1589	37.83	4	6	7
R.C. Russell	1	1	0	94	94	94.00	–	1	3/–
G.C. Small	5	7	3	21*	61	15.25	–	–	1
R.A. Smith	3	6	1	57	145	29.00	–	1	2

Bowling	Balls	R	W	Avge	Best	5wI	10wM
B.C. Broad	6	4	0	–	–	–	–
D.J. Capel	1112	527	10	52.70	2-13	–	–
J.H. Childs	516	183	3	61.00	1-13	–	–
N.G.B. Cook	3551	1407	47	29.93	6-65	4	1
C.S. Cowdrey	399	309	4	77.25	2-65	–	–
P.A.J. DeFreitas	2339	1080	23	46.95	5-86	1	–
G.R. Dilley	7682	3789	133	28.48	6-38	6	–
J.E. Emburey	13195	4725	129	36.62	7-78	6	–
N.H. Fairbrother	12	9	0	–	–	–	–
N.A. Foster	5079	2376	76	31.26	8-107	5	1
M.W. Gatting	752	317	4	79.25	1-14	–	–
G.A. Gooch	1431	550	13	42.30	2-12	–	–
D.I. Gower	36	20	1	20.00	1-1	–	–
E.E. Hemmings	2332	876	16	54.75	3-53	–	–
P.W. Jarvis	931	418	12	34.83	4-107	–	–
A.J. Lamb	30	23	1	23.00	1-6	–	–
D.V. Lawrence	216	111	3	37.00	2-74	–	–
M.D. Moxon	48	30	0	–	–	–	–
P.J. Newport	285	164	7	23.42	4-87	–	–
D.R. Pringle	3232	1501	43	34.90	5-95	2	–
N.V. Radford	678	351	4	87.75	2-131	–	–
R.T. Robinson	6	0	0	–	–	–	–
G.C. Small	1083	454	20	22.70	5-48	2	–

West Indies

Batting / Fielding	M	I	NO	HS	R	Avge	100	50	Ct/St
C.E.L. Ambrose	8	12	4	43	122	15.25	–	–	–
K.T. Arthurton	1	1	0	27	27	27.00	–	–	–
W.K.M.Benjamin	7	9	1	41*	117	14.62	–	–	3
C.G. Butts	7	8	1	38	108	15.42	–	–	2
W.W. Davis	15	17	4	77	202	15.53	–	1	10
P.J.L. Dujon	55	76	9	139	2607	38.91	5	14	174/5
C.G. Greenidge	87	146	14	233	6186	46.86	15	31	83
R.A. Harper	23	29	3	74	503	19.34	–	3	34
D.L. Haynes	76	129	15	184	4523	39.67	9	28	47
C.L. Hooper	11	17	1	100*	469	29.31	1	2	5
A.L. Logie	28	41	4	130	1295	35.00	2	7	28
M.D. Marshall	58	72	6	92	1278	19.36	–	8	24
B.P. Patterson	13	15	8	21*	56	8.00	–	–	2
I.V.A. Richards	99	147	9	291	7268	52.66	22	33	99
R.B. Richardson	36	59	6	185	2173	41.00	6	8	50
P.V. Simmons	2	4	0	16	49	12.25	–	–	1
C.A. Walsh	25	30	11	18*	189	9.94	–	–	4

Bowling	Balls	R	W	Avge	Best	5wI	10wM
C.E.L. Ambrose	1905	810	29	27.93	4-53	–	–
W.K.M. Benjamin	1182	537	26	20.65	4-52	–	–
C.G. Butts	1554	595	10	59.50	4-73	–	–
W.W. Davis	2773	1472	45	32.71	4-19	–	–
C.G. Greenidge	26	4	0	–	–	–	–
R.A. Harper	3243	1166	45	25.91	6-57	1	–
D.L. Haynes	18	8	1	8.00	1-2	–	–
C.L. Hooper	655	323	5	64.60	2-42	–	–
A.L. Logie	7	4	0	–	–	–	–
M.D. Marshall	13047	5921	290	20.41	7-22	18	3
B.P. Patterson	2203	1354	47	28.80	5-24	2	–
I.V.A. Richards	3826	1383	28	49.39	2-17	–	–
R.B. Richardson	42	9	0	–	–	–	–
C.A. Walsh	4816	2190	87	25.17	5-54	3	–

New Zealand

Batting/Fielding	M	I	NO	HS	R	Avge	100	50	Ct/St
S.L. Boock	29	40	8	37	199	6.21	–	–	14
J.G. Bracewell	30	45	10	110	809	23.11	1	3	24
E.J. Chatfield	38	46	30	21*	160	10.00	–	–	6
J.J. Crowe	35	59	4	128	1441	26.20	3	6	38
M.D. Crowe	42	70	6	188	2774	43.34	9	9	46
T.J. Franklin	5	8	0	62	134	16.75	–	1	1
E.J. Gray	9	14	0	50	245	17.50	–	1	5
M.J. Greatbach	2	3	1	107*	186	93.00	1	1	–
R.J. Hadlee	74	118	17	151*	2770	27.42	2	13	36
P.A. Horne	3	5	0	27	59	11.80	–	–	1
A.H. Jones	5	9	1	150	423	52.87	1	2	6
D.K. Morrison	6	6	1	14*	16	3.20	–	–	2
D.N. Patel	6	12	0	62	265	22.08	–	1	2
K.R. Rutherford	14	23	3	107*	331	16.55	1	2	6
I.D.S. Smith	43	59	13	113*	1037	22.54	1	2	120/7
M.C. Snedden	16	18	3	32	196	13.06	–	–	3
R.H. Vance	1	1	0	47	47	47.00	–	–	–
J.G. Wright	58	103	4	141	3343	33.76	7	14	26

Bowling	Balls	R	W	Avge	Best	5wI	10wM
S.L. Boock	6178	2335	73	31.98	7-87	4	–
J.G. Bracewell	6033	2464	72	34.22	6-32	2	1
E.J. Chatfield	9016	3454	115	30.03	6-73	3	1
J.J. Crowe	18	9	0	–	–	–	–
M.D. Crowe	1239	607	13	46.69	2-25	–	–
E.J. Gray	1770	719	14	51.35	3-73	–	–
R.J. Hadlee	19135	8379	373	22.46	9-52	32	8
D.K. Morrison	1092	623	16	38.93	5-69	1	–
D.N. Patel	187	103	0	–	–	–	–
K.R. Rutherford	112	65	1	65.00	1-38	–	–
I.D.S. Smith	18	5	0	–	–	–	–
M.C. Snedden	2847	1344	36	37.33	5-68	1	–
J.G. Wright	30	5	0	–	–	–	–

India

Batting/Fielding	M	I	NO	HS	R	Avge	100	50	Ct/St
M. Amarnath	69	113	10	138	4378	42.50	11	24	47
Arshad Ayub	4	7	2	57	133	26.60	–	1	–
Arun Lal	9	16	0	93	513	32.06	–	6	6
M. Azharuddin	24	36	3	199	1646	49.87	6	5	21
N. Hirwani	1	1	0	1	1	1.00	–	–	–
Kapil Dev	92	133	12	163	3889	32.14	6	21	48
R.Lamba	4	5	0	53	102	20.40	–	1	5
Maninder Singh	31	35	12	15	88	3.82	–	–	9
S.V. Manjrekar	1	2	1	10*	15	15.00	–	–	–
K.S. More	17	22	5	49	397	23.35	–	–	29/11
W.V. Raman	1	2	0	83	92	46.00	–	1	1
A. Sharma	1	2	0	30	53	26.50	–	–	1
C. Sharma	19	21	7	54	310	22.14	–	1	5
R.J. Shastri	58	86	12	142	2568	34.70	7	9	27
K.Srikkanth	32	51	1	123	1590	31.80	2	9	26
D.B. Vengsarkar	98	158	22	166	6256	46.00	17	30	65

Bowling	Balls	R	W	Avge	Best	5wI	10wM
M. Amarnath	3676	1782	32	55.68	4-63	–	–
Arshad Ayub	936	400	6	66.66	4-72	–	–
Arun Lal	16	7	0	–	–	–	–
M. Azharuddin	6	8	0	–	–	–	–
N. Hirwani	203	136	16	8.50	8-61	2	1
Kapil Dev	19225	9454	319	29.63	9-83	19	2
Maninder Singh	7318	2878	79	36.43	7-27	3	2
W.V. Raman	6	7	1	7.00	1-7	–	–
A. Sharma	24	9	0	–	–	–	–
C. Sharma	2930	1797	53	33.90	6-58	4	1
R.J. Shastri	13051	4911	127	38.66	5-75	2	–
K. Srikkanth	150	68	0	–	–	–	–
D.B. Vengsarkar	47	36	0	–	–	–	–

Pakistan

Batting / Fielding	M	I	NO	HS	R	Avge	100	50	Ct/St
Aamer Malik	3	4	1	98*	137	45.66	–	1	7/1
Abdul Qadir	54	64	7	61	916	16.07	–	3	15
Ashraf Ali	8	8	3	65	229	45.80	–	2	17/5
Asif Mujtaba	3	5	0	12	39	7.80	–	–	3
Ijaz Ahmed	10	11	0	69	285	25.90	–	2	7
Ijaz Fakih	5	8	1	105	183	26.14	1	–	–
Imran Khan	73	106	18	135*	2860	32.50	4	11	25
Iqbal Qasim	47	53	14	56	482	12.35	–	1	38
Javed Miandad	92	141	18	280*	6621	53.82	17	35	80/1
Mudassar Nazar	71	109	8	231	3991	39.51	10	17	44
Ramiz Raja	22	36	3	122	1030	31.21	2	5	16
Salim Jaffer	5	7	2	9	22	4.40	–	–	1
Salim Malik	47	65	11	119*	2140	39.62	6	11	42
Salim Yousuf	19	26	4	91*	698	31.72	–	3	55/6
Shoaib Mohammad	17	25	2	101	661	28.73	1	4	7
Tausif Ahmed	24	25	14	23*	166	15.09	–	–	8
Wasim Akram	25	31	6	66	410	16.40	–	2	8

Bowling	Balls	R	W	Avge	Best	5wI	10wM
Aamer Malik	60	46	0	–	–	–	–
Abdul Qadir	14424	6483	205	31.62	9-56	14	5
Asif Mujtaba	18	2	0	–	–	–	–
Ijaz Fakih	534	299	4	74.75	1-38	–	–
Imran Khan	17137	7319	334	21.91	8-58	23	6
Iqbal Qasim	12397	4630	159	29.11	7-49	7	2
Javed Miandad	1470	682	17	40.11	3-74	–	–
Mudassar Nazar	5469	2358	58	40.65	6-32	1	–
Salim Jaffer	899	418	10	41.80	3-79	–	–
Salim Malik	212	92	4	23.00	1-3	–	–
Shoaib Mohammad	126	62	3	20.66	2-8	–	–
Tausif Ahmed	5524	2177	75	29.02	6-45	3	–
Wasim Akram	4974	2098	76	27.60	6-91	4	1

Sri Lanka

Batting/Fielding	M	I	NO	HS	R	Avge	100	50	Ct/St
K.N. Amalean	2	3	2	7*	9	9.00	–	–	1
R.G. De Alwis	11	19	0	28	152	8.00	–	–	21/2
P.A. De Silva	15	28	2	122	660	25.38	2	1	8
S.M.S. Kaluperuma	4	8	0	23	88	11.00	–	–	6
D.B.S.P. Kuruppu	3	5	1	201*	294	73.50	1	–	1/–
G.F. Labrooy	3	5	2	42	64	21.33	–	–	1
R.S. Madugalle	21	39	4	103	1029	29.40	1	7	9
W.R. Madurasinghe	1	2	0	4	6	3.00	–	–	–
R.S. Mahanama	4	7	0	41	148	21.14	–	–	1
L.R.D. Mendis	24	43	1	124	1329	31.64	4	8	9
C.P. Ramanayake	2	4	0	9	11	2.75	–	–	1
A. Ranatunga	24	43	2	135*	1537	37.48	2	12	11
J.R. Ratnayke	20	35	6	93	667	23.00	–	3	1
M.A.R. Samarasekera	1	2	0	57	57	28.50	–	1	2
S.A.R. Silva	9	16	2	111	353	25.21	2	–	33/1

Bowling	Balls	R	W	Avge	Best	5wI	10wM
K.N. Amalean	244	156	7	22.28	4-97	–	–
P.A. De Silva	36	24	0	–	–	–	–
S.M.S Kaluperuma	240	124	2	62.00	2-17	–	–
G.F. Labrooy	720	415	7	59.28	4-119	–	–
R.S. Madugalle	84	38	0	–	–	–	–
W.R. Madurasinghe	96	41	0	–	–	–	–
C.P. Ramanayake	266	144	2	72.00	2-86	–	–
A. Ranatunga	1441	614	11	55.81	2-17	–	–
J.R. Ratnayeke	3576	1832	55	33.30	8-83	4	–
M.A.R. Samarasekera	192	104	3	34.66	2-38	–	–

Guide to Newcomers

Record in English First-Class Cricket 1988

Batting/Fielding		M	I	NO	HS	R	Avge	100	50	Ct/St
Derbyshire	C.J. Adams	1	1	0	21	21	21.00	–	–	1
	F.A. Griffith	5	7	1	37	105	17.50	–	–	2
Essex	M.C. Ilott	2	1	0	6	6	6.00	–	–	–
	R.N. Pook	1	1	0	6	6	6.00	–	–	3
	A.C. Seymour	1	1	1	33*	33	–	–	–	–
	M.E. Waugh	3	4	0	86	178	44.50	–	1	2
Glamorgan	S. Bastien	4	6	2	36*	57	14.25	–	–	1
Gloucestershire	M.J.C. Ball	2	1	0	1	2	2.00	–	–	–
	M.W. Pooley	8	13	5	38	149	18.62	–	–	4
Hampshire	J.R. Ayling	19	33	4	88*	711	24.51	–	4	5
	A.D. Mullally	1	–	–	–	–	–	–	–	1
	R.J. Scott	9	16	1	107*	374	24.93	1	2	10
Kent	D.J. Sabine	1	2	0	7	8	4.00	–	–	1
	V.J. Wells	1	2	0	6	6	3.00	–	–	1
Lancashire	C.D. Matthews	3	3	0	31	38	12.66	–	–	–
	N.J. Speak	1	2	0	35	45	22.50	–	–	2
Leicestershire	J.D.R. Benson	1	1	0	3	3	3.00	–	–	–
	P. Hepworth	4	6	0	51	132	22.00	–	1	–
Middlesex	A.A. Barnett	1	1	0	10	10	10.00	–	–	–
	I.J.F. Hutchinson	3	4	0	25	48	12.00	–	–	–
	N.R.C. MacLaurin	1	2	0	35	37	18.50	–	–	–
	M.W.C. Olley	4	5	1	27*	69	17.25	–	–	9/–
Northamptonshire	N.A. Stanley	8	12	2	66	263	26.30	–	3	4
Nottinghamshire	C.L. Cairns	4	5	1	15	31	7.75	–	–	–
	D. Callaghan	1	1	0	29	29	29.00	–	–	–
	D.J. Millns	11	12	5	7*	20	2.85	–	–	4
Somerset	M.W. Cleal	9	12	1	19	97	8.81	–	–	2
	T.J.A. Scriven	2	2	0	7	11	5.50	–	–	–
	H.R.J. Trump	9	11	1	48	62	6.20	–	–	7
Surrey	P.D. Atkins	6	11	1	114*	357	35.70	1	1	–
	J. Boiling	1	2	1	8*	9	9.00	–	–	–
	M. Frost	4	4	0	7	11	2.75	–	–	1
	N.M. Kendrick	1	1	1	8*	8	–	–	–	1
	N.H. Peters	12	15	8	25*	85	12.14	–	–	5
	J. Robinson	3	5	2	20	55	18.33	–	–	1
	Zahid Sadiq	4	6	0	64	135	22.50	–	1	2
	G.P. Thorpe	3	6	2	100*	158	39.50	1	–	3
Sussex	R.A. Bunting	17	21	5	17*	96	6.00	–	–	2
	A.R. Clarke	21	32	8	68	337	14.04	–	1	7
	P.W. Threlfall	1	–	–	–	–	–	–	–	–
Warwickshire	J.E. Benjamin	1	–	–	–	–	–	–	–	–
	S.J. Green	1	2	0	28	28	14.00	–	–	–
	P.C.L. Holloway	3	5	0	16	40	8.00	–	–	8/1
	J.D. Ratcliffe	2	4	0	16	31	7.75	–	–	2

Batting / Fielding		M	I	NO	HS	R	Avge	100	50	Ct/St
Worcestershire	D.A. Leatherdale	10	15	1	34*	255	18.21	–	–	3
	L.P. Vorster	1	1	1	16*	16	–	–	–	–
Yorkshire	P. Anderson	1	1	0	0	0	–	–	–	1
	N.G. Nicholson	2	4	1	16	47	15.66	–	–	3
	D.A. Towse	1	1	0	1	1	1.00	–	–	1
Cambridge Univ.	N.C.W. Fenton	7	9	3	2	4	0.80	–	–	1
	R. Heap	1	2	0	15	15	7.50	–	–	2
	S.J. Noyes	8	14	1	38	170	13.07	–	–	–
	R.A. Pyman	2	3	0	4	7	2.33	–	–	2
	J.M.C. Stenner	1	2	0	13	23	11.50	–	–	–
	R.J. Turner	8	14	1	27	155	11.92	–	–	9/2
Oxford Univ.	S.A. Almaer	6	11	0	67	256	23.27	–	1	2
	M.E.O. Brown	3	5	2	47	71	23.66	–	–	–
	N.H. Green	1	1	0	9	9	9.00	–	–	1
	A.N.S. Hampton	3	6	0	12	22	3.66	–	–	–
	M. Heppel	1	1	1	14*	14	–	–	–	–
	T. Jack	2	3	0	29	57	19.00	–	–	1
	D.A. Polkinghorne	3	4	1	45*	72	24.00	–	–	2
	G.D. Reynolds	6	9	1	69	147	18.37	–	1	6/–
	A.M. Searle	1	1	0	2	2	2.00	–	–	–

Bowling		O	M	R	W	Avge	Best	5wI	10wM
Derbyshire	F.A. Griffith	99.3	20	347	10	34.70	4-47	–	–
Essex	M.C. Ilott	49	15	111	3	37.00	2-23	–	–
	M.E. Waugh	12	0	75	0	–	–	–	–
Glamorgan	S. Bastien	119.1	35	289	8	36.12	5-90	1	–
Gloucestershire	M.J.C. Ball	34	8	90	2	45.00	1-2	–	–
	M.W. Pooley	128.4	30	384	13	29.53	4-80	–	–
Hampshire	J.R. Ayling	432.1	97	1098	47	23.36	4-57	–	–
	A.D. Mullally	20	5	52	0	–	–	–	–
	R.J. Scott	19.3	3	66	0	–	–	–	–
Kent	D.J. Sabine	10	4	29	0	–	–	–	–
	V.J. Wells	14	4	51	1	51.00	1-51		
Lancashire	C.D. Matthews	77.2	18	225	7	32.14	4-47	–	–
Middlesex	A.A. Barnett	27	8	65	0	–	–	–	–
	N.R.C. MacLaurin	1	0	4	0	–	–	–	–
Nottinghamshire	C.L. Cairns	109	16	384	15	25.60	4-70	–	–
	D. Callaghan	17	1	59	1	59.00	1-59	–	–
	D.J. Millns	179	22	683	19	35.94	3-37	–	–
Somerset	M.W. Cleal	168	25	582	20	29.10	4-41	–	–
	T.J.A. Scriven	96	25	237	3	79.00	1-40	–	–
	H.R.J. Trump	270	74	696	24	29.00	4-17	–	–
Surrey	J. Boiling	15	3	40	0	–	–	–	–
	M. Frost	99.5	23	326	10	32.60	4-56	–	–
	N.M. Kendrick	28.5	7	97	1	97.00	1-92	–	–
	N.H. Peters	278.2	50	954	34	28.05	6-31	1	1
	J. Robinson	22	4	105	3	35.00	2-41	–	–
	G.P. Thorpe	30	3	77	4	19.25	2-33	–	–

Bowling (contd)		O	M	R	W	Avge	Best	5wI	10wM
Sussex	R.A. Bunting	400	66	1320	41	32.19	5-44	3	–
	A.R. Clarke	618	156	1650	44	37.50	5-60	2	–
	P.W. Threlfall	17	6	31	0	–	–	–	–
Warwickshire	J.E. Benjamin	17	6	53	0	–	–	–	–
Worcestershire	D.A. Leatherdale	7	3	20	1	20.00	1-12	–	–
Yorkshire	P. Anderson	17.3	4	47	1	47.00	1-47	–	–
	D.A. Towse	20	7	50	3	16.66	2-26	–	–
Cambridge Univ.	N.C.W. Fenton	271.4	65	726	21	34.57	4-64	–	–
Oxford Univ.	M. Heppel	14	0	74	0	–	–	–	–
	A.M. Searle	17	2	76	0	–	–	–	–

County caps awarded in 1988

Essex: G. Miller, T.D. Topley
Glamorgan: J. Derrick, R.J. Shastri
Hampshire: C.A. Connor
Kent: G.R. Cowdrey, R.F.Pienaar
Leicestershire: G.J.F. Ferris, L. Potter
Middlesex: A.R.C. Fraser
Nottinghamshire: C.W. Scott, F.D. Stephenson
Somerset: G.D. Rose, S.R. Waugh
Surrey: K.T. Medlycott
Warwickshire: T.A. Merrick

Deloitte Ratings
by Richard Lockwood

The Deloitte Ratings, which became Test cricket's first computerized rating system when they were launched in June 1987, provide a method of showing accurately the current form of all Test cricketers in a similar way to golf and tennis ratings. They are a unique method of assessing the relative abilities of Test players as, unlike traditional Test career records which measure a player's performance over his whole career, Deloitte Ratings measure his current form, emphasizing his most recent Test performances with bat or ball.

The Ratings were born out of an idea by Ted Dexter, former England captain, who felt that traditional averages were too simple – they did not give enough credit to either batsman or bowler for an outstanding Test performance in 'unfavourable' conditions. He conceived a system by which a player's performance would be rated according to the strength of the opposition and the conditions of the match.

Produced by computer after each Test match, the Deloitte Ratings take into account a whole variety of factors, not simply wickets and runs, to make them a realistic guide to current Test form. These factors are: (1) the quality of the opposition batsmen and bowlers; (2) the comparative performance of all players in the match; (3) the result of the match; (4) whether the match was high- or low-scoring; (5) new players have to establish themselves in Test cricket before being allowed a full rating; (6) players not selected for one of their country's Test matches lose 1% of their rating; (7) players coming back after a long absence have to re-establish themselves; (8) a player's most recent performances count for most; his last performance has far greater importance than those 15 or 20 Tests before; (9) each player is ranked on a scale from 0 to 1000 – new players starting from nought.

How they work in practice

The effect of each of the factors involved in the calculation of the Deloitte Ratings can best be seen in selected examples from the past year's Test cricket. In the opening Test of the series between India and West Indies at Delhi, for example, Viv Richards made a brilliant undefeated 109 to bring West Indies to victory. The Indian bowling attack was a strong one, the match was relatively low-scoring (18 wickets fell on the first day), and his innings was decisive in taking his side to victory. Thus his Rating rose by 77 points and he jumped from 5th to 2nd in the world. By contrast, when Martin Crowe made his 143 against England at Wellington, his Rating improved by only 7 points. He made his runs against a weak bowling side in ideal batting conditions (only eight wickets fell in the match) and the game finished in a draw.

Similar criteria apply to bowlers who have done best in the Deloitte Ratings. Malcolm Marshall in England this summer and Imran Khan at Georgetown, in Pakistan's historic win, played a major part in their side's victories.

September 1987 to September 1988

The lists of the World Top 30 batsmen and bowlers show at a glance the relative merits of the leading Test players over the year covered by *The Daily Telegraph Year Book*. A total of 24 Tests were played and many dramatic changes have occurred.

Although Dillip Vengsarkar has not been dislodged from first place in the batting, the top five have a different look about them. Allan Border has gained four places to move into 2nd place, while Viv Richards has risen two places to move into 3rd and Javed Miandad is up four places to 5th. Further down the list the fluctuations are more marked: Jeff Dujon, thanks to his magnificent series with the bat against England, and Graham Gooch, bravely resisting the West Indies fast bowlers, have both moved up 12 places into the world's top 10. Even more dramatic were the improvements of David Boon and Gus Logie. The former made big 100s against New Zealand and England to move up 29 places to 11th and the latter was the best of the West Indian batsmen in the series against England, leaping up 34 places to 13th. New Zealand's Andrew Jones was the best of the newcomers, gaining steadily throughout last winter to finish in 19th place.

The changes in the bowling rankings are even more marked, with a new leader, Malcolm Marshall, and four impressive newcomers. Marshall missed West Indies' series in India and the first Test against Pakistan, but he was back at his best to defeat Pakistan at Bridgetown and was even more destructive against England. He actually overtook Richard Hadlee after his performance in the Lord's Test, and at the end of the series has a 20-point lead. Narendra Hirwani produced the performance of the year when he took 16 wickets on his debut for India to bowl West Indies to a crushing defeat. Not surprisingly he immediately gained a rating of 709 and is in 5th place in the bowling Ratings; had his Rating not been held down because this was his first Test, he would be the leading bowler! Conventional averages would have him at number one, which is surely unrealistic.

Winston Benjamin made his debut in West Indies' series in India and enjoyed such success against Pakistan and England that he has made his way up to 4th place – although still a long way behind Imran in 3rd. Curtly Ambrose's rating improved by an impressive 392 points during the series against England, and he stands in 21st place. Australia's Tony Dodemaide is the fourth newcomer to create a good impression for himself, finishing the year in 20th place.

Graham Dilley is England's highest rated bowler, and he moved up five places over the course of the year to 11th. Other climbers in the bowling ratings are Steve Waugh (up 10 places to 9th), Abdul Qadir (up four places to 16th), Ravi Shastri (up 14 places to 19th), and Peter Taylor (up nine places to 23rd).

Team Comparisons

Deloitte Ratings can also be used to compare the relative strengths of all the Test-playing countries at any time in the last seven years. The positions at the end of the 1988 English season are given in the table overleaf:

	Team Batting	Team Bowling
West Indies	499.70	523.37
Pakistan	437.09	474.12
Australia	492.87	412.77
India	395.00	456.28
New Zealand	358.75	463.57
England	341.80	261.00
Sri Lanka	344.09	155.25

The figures in the table show the average Rating of each side's specialist batsmen and bowlers selected to play in any Test match between September 1987 and September 1988. West Indies come out well on top following their demolition of England, with Pakistan, who pushed them so hard in the Caribbean last winter, and Australia, who improved so much last year, challenging for second place. England come second bottom – the result of having neither a settled nor a successful side: 33 players were selected during the year, yet only the last of the 13 Tests was won.

Top 30 Deloitte Ratings

Batting Rating		Rating*	Change†	Bowling Rating		Rating*	Change†
1	Vengsarkar (I)	911	(+18)	1	Marshall (WI)	902	(+49)
2	Border (A)	826	(+29)	2	Hadlee (NZ)	882	(–20)
3	Richards (WI)	804	(+8)	3	Imran Khan (P)	851	(+11)
4	Crowe, M. (NZ)	750	(–90)	4	Benjamin (WI)	709	(NEW)
5	Miandad (P)	739	(+4)	5	Hirwani (I)	670	(NEW)
6	Greenidge (WI)	678	(–162)	6	Akram (P)	665	(+34)
7	Ranatunga (SL)	678	(+22)	7	Chatfield (NZ)	652	(+4)
8	Jones (A)	671	(–81)	8	Sharma, C. (I)	641	(+51)
9	Dujon (WI)	663	(+89)	9	Waugh (A)	636	(+97)
10	Gooch (E)	649	(+106)	10	Reid (A)	621	(+34)
11	Boon (A)	646	(+194)	11	Dilley (E)	616	(+74)
12	Haynes (WI)	628	(–183)	12	Kapil Dev (I)	586	(+12)
13	Logie (WI)	620	(+257)	13	Walsh (WI)	584	(–75)
14	Richardson (WI)	609	(–123)	14	Ratnayeke (SL)	580	(–19)
15	Azharuddin (I)	590	(–16)	15	Foster (E)	573	(+10)
16	Salim (P)	589	(–29)	16	Qadir (P)	571	(+52)
17	Gower (E)	580	(–96)	17	McDermott (A)	569	(+19)
18	Wright (NZ)	574	(–13)	18	Tauseef (P)	535	(–45)
19	Jones (NZ)	570	(+450)	19	Shastri (I)	524	(+77)
20	Yousuf (P)	567	(+70)	20	Dodemaide (A)	508	(NEW)
21	Broad (E)	556	(–7)	21	Ambrose (WI)	497	(NEW)
22	Imran Khan (P)	555	(–55)	22	Boock (NZ)	494	(–16)
23	Kapel Dev (I)	542	(+34)	23	Taylor (A)	493	(+42)
24	Hadlee (NZ)	539	(–62)	24	Mudassar (P)	486	(+28)
25	Mudassar (P)	526	(–81)	25	Harper (WI)	484	(–56)
26	Marsh, G. (A)	519	(–15)	26	Qasim (P)	480	(–23)
27	Gatting (E)	519	(–230)	27	Maninder (I)	474	(–93)
28	Kuruppu (SL)	508	(+84)	28	Bracewell J. (NZ)	470	(–44)
29	Lamb (E)	498	(+112)	29	Davis (WI)	460	(+3)
30	Ramiz Raja (P)	497	(–29)	30	Patterson (WI)	451	(–4)

* Ratings after Test 201 (E v SL, Lord's, 26 August 1988).
† Changes since Test 177 (E v P, The Oval, 6 August 1987).

Honeywell Bull Fielding Awards

Several television viewers noticed that the BBC commentators spent more time analysing catches and run-outs during the matches between England and West Indies last summer. They were adjudicating for the Honeywell Bull Fielding performance awards. The commentators took their responsibilities seriously, and each dismissal generated much discussion in the commentary box.

Honeywell Bull computers have provided the statistics to BBC/TV for the past ten years, and to mark this anniversary Honeywell Bull sponsored a novel fielding performance award for the best overall performance over the one-day internationals and five Test matches between England and West Indies.

Each catch, run-out, or stumping was assessed by Tony Lewis, Jack Bannister, and Richie Benaud and awarded up to 10 points for degree of difficulty, giving 30 points maximum for each dismissal. Where two fielders or fielder and wicket-keeper were involved, points were shared according to each individual's contribution. Wicket-keepers' points totals were then halved (statistics show that wicket-keeping records of dismissals are approximately double those of other key fielders). The cumulative score through the series determined the top fielder for each team and the overall winner.

John Emburey was the early leader after the one-day internationals and he also gained high points for his catch in the gully to dismiss Viv Richards. Phil DeFreitas was second, his low boundary catch to dismiss Gordon Greenidge at Lord's a major factor in his score. Gower's flying catch in the gully to dismiss Ambrose on the first day of the second Test remained the best effort until Curtis matched his score with his memorable catch to dismiss Richards in the fourth Test, when we also saw the best run-out, Fairbrother's direct hit to dismiss Benjamin.

It was Dujon's late run of dismissals in the fourth and fifth Tests that gave him the overall award of £500, and a silver salver. Graham Gooch also received a silver salver as the best England fielder. During the Sri Lanka Test, BBC/TV showed the highest rated dismissals and the presentation of awards by Ted Dexter.

Overall Performance

England		West Indies	
Graham Gooch	112	Jeff Dujon	129.5
John Emburey	99	Roger Harper	92
Paul Downton	90.5	Ritchie Richardson	77
Philip DeFreitas	72	Gordon Greenidge	73
Tim Curtis	46	Gus Logie	65
		Carl Hooper	63

Highest Rated Dismissals

David Gower	26	Ambrose c Gower b Small	2nd Test
Tim Curtis	26	Richards c Curtis b Foster	4th Test
John Emburey	25	Richards c Emburey b Small	1st one-day
Jeff Dujon	25	Emburey c Dujon b Marshall	1st Test
Philip DeFreitas	24	Greenidge c DeFreitas b Emburey	3rd one-day
Graham Gooch	24	Marshall c Gooch b Pringle	4th Test

Obituary 1987-88

by E.W. Swanton

No one would claim that the period under review was anything but a dark blot in the history of cricket. At least, however, we were spared a heavy toll of deaths: only eight Test cricketers, for instance, as against 16 a year ago and 17 two years ago. Of Englishmen there were two – *C. Gladwin* (72) of Derbyshire and *R.A. Sinfield* (87) of Gloucestershire. That persevering and ever-cheerful trundler, Cliff Gladwin, will be remembered for his reputed remark when he went in to join Alec Bedser at the crux of the England-South Africa Test at Durban in 1948-49: 'Coometh the hour, coometh the man.' And the man was as good as his world – victory by a leg-bye off his thigh from the last ball of the match! Reg Sinfield had Bradman caught at the wicket in his only Test. He had a solid all-round county record and an even worthier one as a much-loved coach for forty-odd years, first at Clifton and, up until a few months of his death, at Colston's School, Bristol.

V.M. Merchant (76) was the finest of the first crop of Indian Test cricketers, and with a career average of 71 for 13,248 runs ranks only behind Sir Donald Bradman, ahead of W.H. Ponsford's 65. *Dr Jahangir Khan* (78), father of Majid, uncle of Imran, played for India on the first two Test tours to England, in 1932 and 1936, a splendid all-round cricketer, who had much to do after partition with the rise of Pakistan as a cricket power.

Two South African Test bowlers, *E.S. Newson* (77) and *J.T. Partridge* (55), died, the latter, a Zimbabwean from Bulawayo, tragically by his own hand. Newson, afterwards a high-class golfer, was one of the attack that endured the 10-day Test at Durban in 1938-39. *C.A. Roach* (84) of Trinidad opened the West Indian batting when they were given Test status in the late 1920s, and for some years was second only to the great George Headley. *T.B. Burtt* (69) bowled flighty left-arm slows in the popular New Zealand side that toured England under W.A. Hadlee in 1949.

Pride of place among others to have passed on must go to *Jack Mercer*, Sussex and Glamorgan bowler, then Northamptonshire coach and scorer (until his 87th year), who died at 92, an ever-popular fellow who gave his life to cricket. Other county stalwarts included *Jim Bailey*, of Hampshire, the last man to do the double for them, which he managed when 40 in 1948. He served many years on the county committee. *Stuart Leary* (another sad suicide, in his native Cape) gave good service to Kent, as did *S.M. Brown* in the palmy years of Middlesex as J.D. Robertson's opening partner. Another Glamorgan bowling import was *Norman Hever*, who arrived at Cardiff just in time to help the Welshmen to their first highly surprising Championship title in 1948. Another man involved in a first-ever Championship win was *Mervyn Burden*, of Hampshire, in 1961.

H.T. Bartlett, captain successively of Dulwich (for three years!), Cambridge, and Sussex, was a left-handed bat of legendary hitting powers whom the war probably deprived of a Test cap. His 175 in

Gentlemen and Players and 100 in 57 minutes against the Australians in 1938 were innings never to be forgotten. Another county captain was *G.E.S. Woodhouse,* of Somerset in 1948 and subsequently of Dorset, a cricketer whose potential was affected by the war.

One University captain and several other Blues died, the former, *C.H. Knott* aged 87 of Tonbridge, Oxford, and Kent. John Knott, an unusually hard hitter who once made 261 for the Harlequins against the 1928 West Indians, had an unbroken association with Tonbridge of more than 70 years. He is one of several notable cricket coaches mentioned here, along with Sinfield, Mercer, and a Cambridge Blue and headmaster in turn of Cranbrook School, Sydney, and All Hallows, Honiton, *G.E. Hewan.* Other Blue deaths were *A.K. Judd,* known as Peter, who made 124 for Cambridge in the 1927 University match and later assisted Hampshire; *R.I.F. McIntosh* (Oxford), *R.H. Cobbold* (Cambridge), and *R.W. Skene* (Oxford), who became head of the scholastic agency Gabbitas and Thring.

Other overseas deaths included *Wendell Bill,* an early New South Wales contemporary of Bradman's, and *S.K. Wankhede,* a lawyer and politician who, although not a cricketer of any note, has his name perpetuated in the Wankhede Stadium at Bombay. Following years of squabble, this ground was built in the 1970s within sight of the Cricket Club of India, whose ground it supplanted as a Test venue.

Career Details
(b – born; d – died; F-c – first-class career)

BURTT, Thomas Browning; b Christchurch, New Zealand, 22.1.1915; d Christchurch, 24.5.88. Canterbury and New Zealand. F-c (1943-55): 1,644 runs (17.30); 408 wkts (22.19) 53ct.

GLADWIN, Clifford; b Doe Lea, Derbyshire, 3.4.1916; d Chesterfield, 10.4.88. Derbyshire and England. F-c (1939-58): 6,285 runs (17.36), 1,653 wkts (18.30); 134ct.

JAHANGIR KHAN, Dr Mohammed; b Jullundur, India, 1.2.1910; d Lahore, 23.7.88. Muslims, Northern India, South Punjab, Punjab Governor's XI, Punjab, India. F-c (1928/29-1955/56): 3,319 runs (22.12); 326 wkts (25.06); 79ct.

MERCHANT, Vijaysingh Madhavji; b Bombaby, India, 12.10.1911; d Bombay, 27.10.87. Hindus, Bombay, and India. F-c (1929/30-1950/1): 13,340 (71.33); 65 wkts (32.12); 115ct.

NEWSON, Edward Serrurier; b Cape Town, South Africa, 2.12.1910; d Durban, 24.4.88. Transvaal and South Africa. F-c (1929/30-1949/50): 533 runs (17.83); 60 wkts; 13ct.

PARTRIDGE, Joseph Titus; b Bulawayo, Rhodesia, 9.12.1932; d Harare 7.6.88. Rhodesia and South Africa. F-c (1951-1966): 376 wkts (20.77).

ROACH, Clifford Archibald; b Port-of-Spain, Trinidad, 13.3.1904; d 16.4.88. Trinidad and West Indies. F-c (1925-1935): 4,851 runs (28.04); 5 wkts (105.20); 43ct.

SINFIELD, Reginald Albert; b Stevenage, Hertfordshire, 24.12.1900; d Bristol, 17.3.88. Gloucestershire and England. F-c (1921-39): 15,674 runs (25.70); 1,173 wkts (24.49); 178ct.

Their Record in Tests

Batting/Fielding	Career	M	I	NO	HS	R	Avge	100	50	Ct/St
T.B. Burtt (NZ)	1946/7-1952/3	10	15	3	42	252	21.00	–	–	2
C. Gladwin (Eng)	1947-49	8	11	5	51	170	28.33	–	1	2
M.J. Khan (Ind)	1932-36	4	7	–	13	39	5.57	–	–	4
V.M. Merchant (Ind)	1933/4-1951/2	10	18	–	154	859	47.72	3	–	7
E.S. Newson (SA)	1930/1-1938/9	3	–	–	0	30	7.5	–	–	3
J. Partridge (SA)	1963/4	11	–	–	0	73	10.42	–	–	6
C.A. Roach (WI)	1928-1934/5	16	32	1	209	952	30.70	2	–	5
R.A. Sinfield (Eng)	1938	1	1	–	6	6	6.00	–	–	0

Bowling	Balls	R	W	Avge	Best	5wI	10wM
T.B. Burtt (NZ)	2593	1170	33	33.45	6-162	3	–
C. Gladwin (Eng)	2129	571	15	38.06	3-21	–	–
M.J. Khan (Ind)	606	255	4	63.75	4-60	–	–
V.M. Merchant (Ind)	54	40	0	–	–	–	–
E.S. Newson (SA)	874	265	4	66.25	–	–	–
J. Partridge (SA)	3684	1373	44	31.20	7-91	–	–
C.A. Roach (WI)	222	103	2	51.50	1-18	–	–
R.A. Sinfield (Eng)	378	123	2	61.50	1-51	–	–

1989

LOOKING FORWARD

England's Cancelled Tour

The team chosen in September for England's tour of India which was cancelled in October was: G.A. Gooch (captain), J.E. Emburey (vice-captain), R.J. Bailey, K.J. Barnett, J.H. Childs, G.R. Dilley, N.A. Foster, D.I. Gower, E.E. Hemmings, A.J. Lamb, D.V. Lawrence, P.J. Newport, S.J. Rhodes, R.T. Robinson, R.C. Russell, R.A. Smith. Of these only Rhodes has yet to play in a Test match.

This is not the first team to be chosen for a tour of India which did not take place. In 1939-40 an MCC team was prevented from going by the outbreak of World War II. Three Tests were scheduled to be played, in Bombay, Calcutta, and Madras.

Of the party of 16 chosen, Wyatt, Nichols, Gimblett, and Wellard had played Test cricket (Bob Wyatt 40 times). Griffith, Dollery, George Pope, and Peter Smith played in Tests after the war. The other eight lost their chance with the cancellation of the tour.

The 1939-40 team was: A.J. Holmes (Sussex, capt), H.T. Bartlett (Sussex), J.M. Brocklebank (Lancashire), S.C. Griffith (Sussex), R.H.C. Human (Worcestershire), R.E.S. Wyatt (Warwickshire), E. Davies (Glamorgan), H.E. Dollery (Warwickshire), H. Gimblett (Somerset), G.H. Pope (Derbyshire), John Langridge (Sussex), G. Mobey (Surrey), M.S. Nichols (Essex), J.F. Parker (Surrey), P. Smith (Essex), A.W. Wellard (Somerset).

The 1989 Season

A year ago one looked forward to the 1988 season with guarded optimism. The optimism was inspired not only by England's highly successful winter in Australia but by signs that the forthcoming series against West Indies might not be the complete disaster of recent series. The optimism was guarded because in the two previous summers England had been beaten at home by India, New Zealand, and Pakistan.

The best one can offer about 1989 and the series for the Ashes against Australia is guarded pessimism. It is guarded because Australia have brought the best out of England in the last two series. Some might say that this was because their bowling was of rare friendliness. Certainly, after losing the one-day Texaco series, England made a lot of runs in 1985, exceeding 450 five times.

The gloom sets in when one remembers that England's bowling then was not very effective until Richard Ellison came on the scene and swung the ball about to take 17 wickets in the last two Test matches, both of which England won by an innings. Alas, despite a much better season in 1988, Ellison has never recovered the form and fitness of those matches at Edgbaston and The Oval.

Further reflection will bring the thought that Australia are nothing if not resilient and are always likely to bounce back at their most dangerous when emerging from a sticky period with young players. On arrival in England they search the newspapers for a reference to them as one of the weakest sides ever to leave Australia. There is usually someone who will oblige. If not, they will imagine that some such slur is intended. Then they are very hard to beat.

One can play down Australia's World Cup win on the grounds of the irrelevance of one-day results to a Test series. England's 3-0 defeat of West Indies in 1988 is a nice example of this. It may also be held against Australia that it was only an almost equally unfancied England whom they beat by seven runs in the final in Calcutta.

The firmest evidence of Australian strength, and the most depressing in English eyes, surely came during the recent summer of 1988. While England were in all sorts of trouble in a season of many uneven pitches and poor weather, Stephen Waugh, to be found no higher than number seven in recent Australian batting orders, was coming into the Somerset side as a replacement for Martin Crowe and in 15 matches was averaging 73, six and a half runs more than the leading English batsman. And when Allan Border, averaging nearly 60, had to stop making runs for Essex in order to lead Australia in Pakistan, he was replaced by Waugh's twin brother to good effect. Glimpses of Dean Jones suggested that his extra experience of English conditions will have done him no harm.

Meanwhile, England may hope that some of the young players tried in 1988, especially the bowlers, will move up a class and that Mike Gatting, who averaged 87 against Australia in 1985, will reappear refreshed after a winter's rest.

Fixtures 1989

Duration of Matches (*including play on Sunday)

Cornhill Insurance Tests	5 days		Texaco Trophy	1 day
Britannic Assurance			Benson & Hedges Cup	1 day
County Championship	3 days or as stated		NatWest Bank Trophy	1 day
Tourist matches	3 days or as stated		Refuge Assurance League/Cup	1 day
Universities v Counties	3 days		Other matches	as stated

APRIL 15, SATURDAY
Fenners	*Cambridge U v Glamorgan
The Parks	Oxford U v Northants
Lord's	MCC v Champions (Worcs)

APRIL 19, WEDNESDAY
Fenners	Cambridge U v Glos
The Parks	Oxford U v Surrey

APRIL 20, THURSDAY
Britannic Assurance Championship (4 days)
Derby	Derbyshire v Northants
Southampton	Hampshire v Somerset
Canterbury	Kent v Essex
Leicester	Leics v Glamorgan
Lord's	Middlesex v Yorkshire
Trent Bridge	Notts v Worcs
Edgbaston	Warwickshire v Lancashire

APRIL 23, SUNDAY
Refuge Assurance League
Derby	Derbyshire v Northants
Southampton	Hampshire v Somerset
Canterbury	Kent v Essex
Leicester	Leics v Glamorgan
Lord's	Middlesex v Yorkshire
Trent Bridge	Notts v Worcs
The Oval	Surrey v Glos
Edgbaston	Warwickshire v Lancashire

APRIL 25, TUESDAY
Benson & Hedges Cup
Edgbaston	Warwickshire v Northants
Old Trafford	Lancashire v Leics
Cardiff	Glamorgan v Kent
Hove	Sussex v Essex
Fenners	Combined Univs v Surrey
Lord's	Middlesex v Worcs
Derby	Derbyshire v Somerset
Jesmond	Minor Counties v Yorkshire

APRIL 27, THURSDAY
Britannic Assurance Championship (4 days)
Chelmsford	Essex v Middlesex
Bristol	Glos v Northants
Old Trafford	Lancashire v Notts
The Oval	Surrey v Hampshire
Hove	Sussex v Kent
Edgbaston	Warwickshire v Worcs

Other Matches
Fenners	Cambridge U v Leics
The Parks	Oxford Univ v Derbyshire

APRIL 28, FRIDAY
Britannic Assurance Championship (4 days)
Taunton	*Somerset v Glamorgan

APRIL 30, SUNDAY
Refuge Assurance League
Chelmsford	Essex v Middlesex
Old Trafford	Lancashire v Notts
Leicester	Leicestershire v Derbyshire
The Oval	Surrey v Hampshire
Hove	Sussex v Kent

MAY 2, TUESDAY
Benson & Hedges Cup
Leicester	Leicestershire v Warwicks
Perth (N. Inch)	Scotland v Lancashire
Chelmsford	Essex v Hampshire
Canterbury	Kent v Sussex
Bristol	Glos v Middlesex
The Oval	Surrey v Worcs
Taunton	Somerset v Minor Counties
Trent Bridge	Notts v Derbyshire

MAY 4, THURSDAY
Britannic Assurance Championship (4 days)
Chelmsford	Essex v Derbyshire
Cardiff	Glamorgan v Glos
Southampton	Hampshire v Kent
Lord's	Middlesex v Surrey
Northampton	Northants v Leics
Taunton	Somerset v Sussex
Worcester	Worcs v Lancashire
Headingley	Yorkshire v Notts

Other Match
Fenners	Cambridge U v Warwickshire

MAY 5, FRIDAY
Tourist Match
West Bromwich Dartmouth	League Cricket Conf v Australia (1 day)

MAY 7, SUNDAY
Refuge Assurance League
Chelmsford	Essex v Derbyshire
Cardiff	Glamorgan v Glos
Southampton	Hampshire v Kent
Lord's	Middlesex v Surrey
Northampton	Northants v Warwicks
Taunton	Somerset v Sussex
Worcester	Worcs v Lancashire
Headingley	Yorkshire v Notts

Tourist Match

Arundel	Lavinia, Duchess of Norfolk's XI v Australia (1 day)

MAY 9, TUESDAY

Benson & Hedges Cup

Leicester	Leics v Scotland
Northampton	Northants v Lancs
Canterbury	Kent v Essex
Southampton	Hampshire v Glamorgan
Worcester	Worcs v Glos
The Parks	Combined Univs v Middlesex
Headingley	Yorkshire v Somerset
Oxton (Birkenhead)	Minor Counties v Notts

Tourist Match

Hove	Sussex v Australia (1 day)

MAY 11, THURSDAY

Benson & Hedges Cup

Northampton	Northants v Leics
Edgbaston	Warwicks v Scotland
Chelmsford	Essex v Glamorgan
Hove	Sussex v Hampshire
The Oval	Surrey v Glos
Worcester	Worcs v Combined Univs
Trent Bridge	Notts v Yorkshire
Derby	Derbyshire v Minor Counties

Tourist Match

Lord's	MCC v Australia (1 day)

MAY 13, SATURDAY

Benson & Hedges Cup

Glasgow (Hamilton Cres)	Scotland v Northants
Old Trafford	Lancashire v Warwicks
Southampton	Hampshire v Kent
Swansea	Glamorgan v Sussex
Lord's	Middlesex v Surrey
Bristol	Glos v Combined Univs
Headingley	Yorkshire v Derbyshire
Taunton	Somerset v Notts

Tourist Match

Worcester	*Worcs v Australia

MAY 14, SUNDAY

Refuge Assurance League

Leek	Derbyshire v Lancs
Chelmsford	Essex v Hampshire
Bristol	Glos v Middlesex
Canterbury	Kent v Surrey
Leicester	Leics v Yorkshire

MAY 16, TUESDAY

Britannic Assurance Championship (4 days)

Northampton	Northants v Yorkshire

MAY 17, WEDNESDAY

Britannic Assurance Championship

Chesterfield	Derbyshire v Leics
Old Trafford	Lancs v Warwicks
Lord's	Middlesex v Hampshire
Hove	Sussex v Surrey

Tourist Match

Taunton	Somerset v Australia

Other Matches

Fenners	Cambridge Univ v Kent
The Parks	Oxford Univ v Notts

MAY 20, SATURDAY

Britannic Assurance Championship

Swansea	Glamorgan v Northants
Bristol	Glos v Essex
Dartford	*Kent v Derbyshire
Trent Bridge	*Notts v Hampshire
Taunton	Somerset v Lancashire
Edgbaston	Warwicks v Surrey

Tourist Match

Lord's	*Middlesex v Australia

MAY 21, SUNDAY

Refuge Assurance League

Ebbw Vale	Glamorgan v Northants
Bristol	Glos v Essex
Taunton	Somerset v Lancs
Hove	Sussex v Leics
Worcester	Worcs v Surrey
Headingley	Yorkshire v Warwicks

MAY 23, TUESDAY

Tourist Match

Headingley	Yorkshire v Australia (1 day)

MAY 24, WEDNESDAY

Britannic Assurance Championship

Leicester	Leicester v Kent
The Oval	Surrey v Lancashire
Worcester	Worcs v Notts
Headingley	Yorkshire v Derbyshire

Other Matches

Fenners	Cambridge Univ v Essex
The Parks	Oxford Univ v Middlesex

MAY 25, THURSDAY

Texaco Trophy (1st 1-day international)

Old Trafford	England v Australia

MAY 27, SATURDAY

Texaco Trophy (2nd 1-day International)

Trent Bridge	England v Australia

Britannic Assurance Championship

Chelmsford	Essex v Somerset
Cardiff	Glamorgan v Notts
Bristol	Glos v Worcs
Bournemouth	Hampshire v Leics
Liverpool	Lancashire v Sussex
The Oval	Surrey v Yorkshire
Edgbaston	Warwicks v Middlesex

MAY 28, SUNDAY

Refuge Assurance League

Chelmsford	Essex v Somerset
Llanelli	Glamorgan v Notts
Bristol	Glos v Worcs
Bournemouth	Hampshire v Leics
Canterbury	Kent v Northants
Old Trafford	Lancashire v Sussex
The Oval	Surrey v Yorkshire
Edgbaston	Warwicks v Middlesex

MAY 29, MONDAY

Texaco Trophy   (3rd 1-day international)
Lord's   England v Australia

MAY 31, WEDNESDAY

Benson & Hedges Cup
Quarter-finals

Tourist Match
Old Trafford
  or Edgbaston   Lancs or Warwicks v Australia

JUNE 3, SATURDAY

Britannic Assurance Championship

Tunbridge Wells	Kent v Hampshire
Northampton	Northants v Surrey
Trent Bridge	Notts v Yorkshire
Edgbaston	Warwickshire v Sussex
Worcester	Worcs v Glamorgan

Tourist Match
Derby   *Derbyshire v Australia

JUNE 4, SUNDAY

Refuge Assurance League

Leicester	Leics v Lancs
Lord's	Middlesex v Hampshire
Northampton	Northants v Surrey
Trent Bridge	Notts v Somerset
Edgbaston	Warwicks v Sussex
Worcester	Worcs v Glamorgan

JUNE 7, WEDNESDAY

Britannic Assurance Championship

Cardiff	Glamorgan v Somerset
Basingstoke	Hampshire v Surrey
Tunbridge Wells	Kent v Sussex
Leicester	Leics v Yorks
Lord's	Middlesex v Notts
Northampton	Northants v Glos
Nuneaton	
(Griff & Coton)	Warwicks v Derbyshire

Other Match
The Parks   Oxford Univ v Lancs

JUNE 8, THURSDAY

First Cornhill Test
Headingley   ENGLAND v AUSTRALIA

JUNE 10, SATURDAY

Britannic Assurance Championship

Abergavenny	Glamorgan v Middlesex
Leicester	Leics v Glos
Trent Bridge	Notts v Kent
Taunton	Somerset v Yorkshire
The Oval	Surrey v Essex
Hove	Sussex v Northants
Worcester	Worcs v Derbyshire

Other Match
The Parks   Oxford Univ v Hampshire

JUNE 11, SUNDAY

Refuge Assurance League

Merthyr Tydfil	Glamorgan v Middlesex
Basingstoke	Hampshire v Warwicks
Leicester	Leics v Glos
Trent Bridge	Notts v Kent
Taunton	Somerset v Yorkshire
The Oval	Surrey v Essex
Hove	Sussex v Northants
Worcester	Worcs v Derbyshire

JUNE 14, WEDNESDAY

Benson & Hedges Cup
Semi-finals

Tourist Match
Edgbaston or
  Old Trafford   Warwicks or Lancs v Australia

Other Matches
Harrogate   Tilcon Trophy.(3 days)

JUNE 17, SATURDAY

Britannic Assurance Championship

Derby	Derbyshire v Sussex
Chelmsford	Essex v Leics
Old Trafford	Lancs v Glamorgan
Bath	Somerset v Kent
The Oval	Surrey v Middlesex
Harrogate	Yorkshire v Glos

Tourist Match
Northampton   *Northants v Australia

Other Match
Fenners   *Cambridge Univ v Notts

JUNE 18, SUNDAY

Refuge Assurance League

Derby	Derbyshire v Sussex
Chelmsford	Essex v Leics
Blackpool	Lancashire v Glamorgan
Bath	Somerset v Kent
Edgbaston	Warwicks v Worcs
Headingley	Yorkshire v Glos

JUNE 21, WEDNESDAY

Britannic Assurance Championship

Ilford	Essex v Hampshire
Southport	Lancs v Northants
Bath	Somerset v Glos
Edgbaston	Warwicks v Glamorgan
Sheffield	Yorkshire v Worcs

Other Match

Hove	Sussex v Cambridge Univ

JUNE 22, THURSDAY

Second Cornhill Test

Lord's	ENGLAND v AUSTRALIA

JUNE 24, SATURDAY

Britannic Assurance Championship

Ilford	Essex v Warwicks
Southampton	Hampshire v Sussex
Old Trafford	Lancs v Kent
Leicester	Leics v Notts
Luton	Northants v Somerset
The Oval	Surrey v Glos
Worcester	Worcs v Middlesex
Headingley	Yorkshire v Glamorgan

JUNE 25, SUNDAY

Refuge Assurance League

Ilford	Essex v Warwicks
Southampton	Hampshire v Sussex
Old Trafford	Lancs v Kent
Luton	Northants v Leics
Trent Bridge	Notts v Derbyshire
Bath	Somerset v Glos
Worcester	Worcs v Middlesex
Hull	Yorkshire v Glamorgan

JUNE 28, WEDNESDAY

NatWest Bank Trophy (1st round)

March	Cambs v Worcs
Chester	
(Boughton Hall)	Cheshire v Hampshire
Carlisle	Cumberland v Lancs
Derby	Derbyshire v Ireland
Darlington	Durham v Middlesex
Cardiff	Glamorgan v Staffs
Hitchin	Herts v Notts
Canterbury	Kent v Dorset
Jesmond	Northumberland v Surrey
Oxford (Christ	
Church College	Oxfordshire v Glos
Telford	
(St George's)	Shropshire v Leics
Taunton	Somerset v Essex
Bury St Edmunds	Suffolk v Northants
Hove	Sussex v Berkshire
Edgbaston	Warwicks v Wilts
Headingley	Yorkshire v Scotland

Tourist Match

The Parks	Oxbridge v Australia (1 day)

JULY 1, SATURDAY

Britannic Assurance Championship

Derby	Derbyshire v Somerset
Gloucester	Glos v Notts
Southampton	Hants v Yorkshire
Hinckley	Leics v Warwicks
Lord's	Middlesex v Lancs
Northampton	Northants v Worcs
Horsham	Sussex v Essex

Tourist Match

Neath	*Glamorgan v Australia

JULY 2, SUNDAY

Refuge Assurance League

Derby	Derbyshire v Somerset
Gloucester	Glos v Notts
Southampton	Hampshire v Yorkshire
Leicester	Leics v Warwicks
Lord's	Middlesex v Lancs
Tring	Northants v Worcs
Horsham	Sussex v Essex

JULY 5, WEDNESDAY

Britannic Assurance Championship

Derby	Derbyshire v Essex
Gloucester	Glos v Sussex
Maidstone	Kent v Northants
Leicester	Leics v Lancs
Guildford	Surrey v Notts
Worcester	Worcs v Warwicks

Other Match

Lord's	Oxford Univ v Cambridge
	Univ (Varsity Match)

JULY 6, THURSDAY

Third Cornhill Test

Edgbaston	ENGLAND v AUSTRALIA

JULY 8, SATURDAY

Britannic Assurance Championship

Swansea	Glamorgan v Essex
Maidstone	Kent v Glos
Lord's	Middlesex v Derbyshire
Northampton	Northants v Hants
Trent Bridge	Notts v Warwicks
Guildford	Surrey v Somerset
Kidderminster	Worcs v Leics
Middlesbrough	Yorkshire v Sussex

Other Match

Dublin	*Ireland v Scotland (3 days)

JULY 9, SUNDAY

Refuge Assurance League

Neath	Glamorgan v Essex
Maidstone	Kent v Glos
Lord's	Middlesex v Derbyshire
Northampton	Northants v Hampshire
Trent Bridge	Notts v Warwicks
The Oval	Surrey v Somerset
Worcester	Worcs v Leics
Middlesbrough	Yorkshire v Sussex

JULY 12, WEDNESDAY
NatWest Bank Trophy (2nd round)
Cambs or Worcs v Derbys or Ireland
Durham or Middlesex v Herts or Notts
Glamorgan or Staffs v Cheshire or Hants
Kent or Dorset v Warwicks or Wilts
Northumberland or Surrey v Yorkshire or
Scotland
Oxfordshire or Glos v Cumberland or Lancs
Somerset or Essex v Suffolk or Northants
Sussex or Berkshire v Shropshire or Leics

JULY 15, SATURDAY
Benson & Hedges Cup
Lord's   Final

Tourist Match
Glasgow   Scotland v Australia (1 day)
  (Hamilton Cres)

JULY 16, SUNDAY
Refuge Assurance League
Bristol   Glos v Hampshire
Canterbury   Kent v Derbyshire
Old Trafford   Lancs v Northants
Leicester   Leics v Notts
Taunton   Somerset v Glamorgan
The Oval   Surrey v Sussex
Scarborough   Yorks v Worcs

JULY 17, MONDAY
Tourist Match
Trowbridge   Minor Counties v Australia
                 (1 day)

JULY 19, WEDNESDAY
Britannic Assurance Championship
Southend   Essex v Kent
Bristol   Glos v Glamorgan
Old Trafford   Lancashire v Worcs
Leicester   Leics v Northants
Trent Bridge   Notts v Somerset
Headingley   Yorkshire v Middlesex

Tourist Match
Southampton   Hampshire v Australia

JULY 22, SATURDAY
Britannic Assurance Championship
Derby   Derbyshire v Glamorgan
Southend   Essex v Yorkshire
Portsmouth   Hampshire v Lancs
Uxbridge   Middlesex v Kent
Northampton   Northants v Notts
Taunton   Somerset v Leics
Hove   Sussex v Worcs

Tourist Match
Bristol   *Glos v Australia

JULY 23, SUNDAY
Refuge Assurance League
Heanor   Derbyshire v Glamorgan
Southend   Essex v Yorkshire
Portsmouth   Hampshire v Lancs
Lord's   Middlesex v Kent
Finedon   Northants v Notts
Taunton   Somerset v Leics
Hove   Sussex v Worcs
Edgbaston   Warwicks v Surrey

JULY 26, WEDNESDAY
Britannic Assurance Championship
Cardiff   Glamorgan v Leics
Portsmouth   Hampshire v Glos
Uxbridge   Middlesex v Essex
Northampton   Northants v Derbyshire
Worksop
  (Central Ave)   Notts v Lancs
Hove   Sussex v Somerset
Edgbaston   Warwicks v Yorkshire
Worcester   Worcs v Surrey

JULY 27, THURSDAY
Fourth Cornhill Test
Old Trafford   ENGLAND v AUSTRALIA

JULY 29, SATURDAY
Britannic Assurance Championship
Derby   Derbyshire v Surrey
Cardiff   Glamorgan v Hampshire
Lord's   Middlesex v Leics
Trent Bridge   Notts v Essex
Edgbaston   Warwickshire v Glos
Worcester   Worcs v Kent

JULY 30, SUNDAY
Refuge Assurance League
Derby   Derbyshire v Surrey
Cardiff   Glamorgan v Hampshire
Lord's   Middlesex v Leicester
Northampton   Northants v Somerset
Trent Bridge   Notts v Essex
Edgbaston   Warwicks v Glos
Worcester   Worcester v Kent

AUGUST 2, WEDNESDAY
NatWest Bank Trophy
Quarter-finals

Tourist Match
Trent Bridge
  or The Oval   Notts or Surrey v Australia

AUGUST 3, THURSDAY
Other Match
Jesmond   England XI v Rest of the
                 World XI (1 day)

AUGUST 4, FRIDAY
Other Match
Jesmond   England XI v Rest of the
                 World XI (1 day)

AUGUST 5, SATURDAY

Britannic Assurance Championship

Derby	Derbyshire v Hampshire
Colchester	Essex v Worcs
Cheltenham	Glos v Lancs
Canterbury	Kent v Warwicks
Weston-super-Mare	Somerset v Middlesex
The Oval	Surrey v Glamorgan
Eastbourne	Sussex v Notts
Sheffield	Yorkshire v Northants

Tourist Match

Leicester	*Leics v Australia

AUGUST 6, SUNDAY

Refuge Assurance League

Derby	Derbyshire v Hampshire
Colchester	Essex v Worcs
Cheltenham	Glos v Lancs
Canterbury	Kent v Warwicks
Weston-super-Mare	Somerset v Middlesex
The Oval	Surrey v Glamorgan
Eastbourne	Sussex v Notts
Sheffield	Yorkshire v Northants

AUGUST 9, WEDNESDAY

Britannic Assurance Championship

Chesterfield	Derbyshire v Lancs
Colchester	Essex v Northants
Cheltenham	Glos v Middlesex
Bournemouth	Hampshire v Warwicks
Canterbury	Kent v Surrey
Weston-super-Mare	Somerset v Worcs
Eastbourne	Sussex v Leics

AUGUST 10, THURSDAY

Fifth Cornhill Test

Trent Bridge	ENGLAND v AUSTRALIA

AUGUST 12, SATURDAY

Britannic Assurance Championship

Swansea	Glamorgan v Sussex
Cheltenham	Glos v Derbyshire
Bournemouth	Hampshire v Worcs
Lytham	Lancs v Essex
Lord's	Middlesex v Northants
Edgbaston	Warwicks v Somerset
Scarborough	Yorkshire v Kent

AUGUST 13, SUNDAY

Refuge Assurance League

Swansea	Glamorgan v Sussex
Cheltenham	Glos v Derbyshire
Bournemouth	Hampshire v Worcs
Old Trafford	Lancs v Essex
Lord's	Middlesex v Northants
The Oval	Surrey v Notts
Edgbaston	Warwickshire v Somerset
Scarborough	Yorkshire v Kent

AUGUST 14, MONDAY

Bain Clarkson Trophy
First Semi-final (1 day)

AUGUST 15, TUESDAY

Bain Clarkson Trophy
Second Semi-final (1 day)

AUGUST 16, WEDNESDAY

NatWest Bank Trophy
Semi-finals

Tourist Match

Canterbury or Hove	Kent or Sussex v Australia

AUGUST 19, SATURDAY

Britannic Assurance Championship

Canterbury	Kent v Glamorgan
Old Trafford	Lancashire v Yorkshire
Leicester	Leics v Surrey
Northampton	Northants v Warwicks
Trent Bridge	Notts v Derbyshire
Taunton	Somerset v Hampshire
Hastings	Sussex v Middlesex

Tourist Match

Chelmsford	*Essex v Australia

AUGUST 20, SUNDAY

Refuge Assurance League

Moreton-in Marsh	Glos v Northants
Canterbury	Kent v Glamorgan
Old Trafford	Lancs v Yorkshire
Leicester	Leics v Surrey
Trent Bridge	Notts v Hampshire
Hastings	Sussex v Middlesex
Edgbaston	Warwicks v Derbyshire
Worcester	Worcs v Somerset

AUGUST 24, THURSDAY

Sixth Cornhill Test

The Oval	ENGLAND v AUSTRALIA

Britannic Assurance Championship (4 days)

Chesterfield	Derbyshire v Yorkshire
Cardiff	Glamorgan v Warwicks
Folkestone	Kent v Leics
Old Trafford	Lancs v Surrey
Northampton	Northants v Essex
Trent Bridge	Notts v Middlesex
Hove	Susex v Glos
Worcester	Worcs v Somerset

AUGUST 27, SUNDAY

Refuge Assurance League

Chesterfield	Derbyshire v Yorkshire
Aberystwyth	Glamorgan v Warwicks
Folkestone	Kent v Leics
Old Trafford	Lancs v Surrey
Northampton	Northants v Essex
Trent Bridge	Notts v Middlesex
Hove	Sussex v Glos

Britannic Assurance Championship (4 days)
Chelmsford   Essex v Surrey
Leicester   Leics v Derbyshire
Hove   Sussex v Hampshire
Worcester   Worcs v Glos
Headingley   Yorkshire v Warwicks

AUGUST 30, WEDNESDAY
Other Match
Scarborough   Michael Parkinson
                 International XI Match
                 (3 days)

SEPTEMBER 2, SATURDAY
NatWest Bank Trophy
Lord's   Final

Other Match
Scarborough   Michael Parkinson
                 International XI Match
                 (1 day)

SEPTEMBER 3, SUNDAY
Other Match
Scarborough   Four Counties Knock-out
                 Competition (3 days)

SEPTEMBER 4, MONDAY
Bain Clarkson Trophy
Final (1 day)

SEPTEMBER 6, WEDNESDAY
Refuge Assurance Cup
Semi-finals

SEPTEMBER 7, THURSDAY
The White Horse Yorkshire Ashes
Scarborough   Yorks v The Yorkshiremen
                                  (1 day)

SEPTEMBER 8, FRIDAY
Britannic Assurance Championship (4 days)
Derby   *Derbyshire v Notts
Bristol   *Glos v Somerset
Southampton   *Hampshire v Glamorgan
Leicester   *Leics v Essex
Lord's   *Middlesex v Sussex
The Oval   *Surrey v Kent
Edgbaston   *Warwickshire v Northants
Scarborough   *Yorkshire v Lancs

SEPTEMBER 13, WEDNESDAY
Britannic Assurance Championship (4 days)
Pontypridd   Glamorgan v Worcs
Bristol   Glos v Hampshire
Canterbury   Kent v Middlesex
Old Trafford   Lancs v Derbyshire
Trent Bridge   Notts v Leics
Taunton   Somerset v Warwickshire
The Oval   Surrey v Sussex

SEPTEMBER 17, SUNDAY
Refuge Assurance Cup
Egbaston   Final